Orestes and Electra

Myth and Dramatic Form

❖ ❖ ❖
❖

EDITED BY

William M. Force

INDIANA UNIVERSITY OF PENNSYLVANIA

Houghton Mifflin Company · *Boston*

NEW YORK · ATLANTA · GENEVA, ILL. · DALLAS · PALO ALTO

PREFACE

◇◇◇◇◇◇◇◇◇◇◇◇◇◇◇◇◇◇◇◇◇◇◇◇◇◇◇◇◇◇◇◇◇◇

THE STORY of Electra and Orestes has been told many times in the theatre, always from a different point of view. Contrasting as the shifting emphasis has been with regard both to plot and characterization, the tale has served well as a vehicle for the statement of theme, a confirmation of the principle that it is the function of drama to explicate life. This volume provides an opportunity for comparing the methods and insights five playwrights have brought to their dramatizations of an ancient and powerful myth.

The depiction of a family tainted by ancestral curse was a favored subject in Greek drama, one that found a rich vein of pathos in the threatened destruction of innocence. The agony of Electra and Orestes, not dissimilar to that experienced by the disenchanted Hamlet, finds an echo in the lives of all people who have been victimized by the corruptive power of evil.

The *Oresteia* of Aeschylus is the only extant Greek trilogy. It is in the second play, *The Libation Bearers*, that Orestes' return to Argos is shown, and it is in this play that Electra makes her sole appearance, dual factors that support the inclusion of only this segment of the trilogy in the present collection. Aeschylus' limited interest in Electra was shared neither by Sophocles nor Euripides, both of whom made Agamemnon's daughter the central figure of their plays.

Recent dramatists have freely adapted the myth to suit their purposes. Hugo von Hofmannsthal's *Electra* blazes with violence and sensuality, while Jean Giraudoux' play of the same name mingles theatricality, wit, and political metaphor. *The Flies* of Jean-Paul Sartre depicts the evolution of Orestes into an existentialistic hero, Eugene O'Neill's *Mourning Becomes Electra* combines an American setting with a Freudian point of view, and *The Prodigal* of Jack Richardson affirms the desire of an antiheroic Orestes to avoid involvement in an act of violence. Analytic comparison of the five plays in this volume will reveal thematic variations, structural contrasts, and diverse handling of character and dialogue, all of which should create for the reader a heightened awareness of the means by which a prescribed situation can be variously employed by a quintet of gifted writers.

The book consists of three parts: the first is a statement of the myth; the second, the plays with pertinent biographic notes about their authors and selective bibliographies; and the last, a series of essays intended to supplement the study of the plays as well as to afford a limited number of secondary sources for use in research papers. It is hoped the questions and suggested topics for papers will add to the student's comprehension of each play while simultaneously suggesting the line of development a paper might take.

Elsewhere in this book acknowledgment has been made for the use of copyrighted material. Here may I express my gratitude to my wife, Patricia, for her capable assistance with both typing and proofreading.

W.M.F.

CONTENTS

PART THREE · COMMENT

PART ONE

The Vengeance of Orestes

The Vengeance of Orestes

Robert Graves

ORESTES was reared by his loving grand-parents Tyndareus and Leda and, as a boy, accompanied Clytaemnestra and Iphigeneia to Aulis.[1] But some say that Clytaemnestra sent him to Phocis,
shortly before Agamemnon's return; and others that on the evening
of the murder, Orestes, then ten years of age, was rescued by his
noble-hearted nurse Arsinoë, or Laodameia, or Geilissa who, having
sent her own son to bed in the royal nursery, let Aegisthus kill him
in Orestes's place.[2] Others again say that his sister Electra, aided by
her father's ancient tutor, wrapped him in a robe embroidered with
wild beasts, which she herself had woven, and smuggled him out of
the city.[3]

b. After hiding for awhile among the shepherds of the river Tanus,
which divides Argolis from Laconia, the tutor made his way with
Orestes to the court of Strophius, a firm ally of the House of Atreus,
who ruled over Crisa, at the foot of Mount Parnassus.[4] This Strophius
had married Agamemnon's sister Astyochea, or Anaxibia, or Cyndra-
gora. At Crisa, Orestes found an adventurous playmate, namely Strophius's son Pylades, who was somewhat younger than himself, and
their friendship was destined to become proverbial.[5] From the old
tutor he learned with grief that Agamemnon's body had been flung
out of the house and hastily buried by Clytaemnestra, without either

Reprinted from *The Greek Myths* by Robert Graves by permission of
Collins-Knowlton-Wing, Inc., Messrs. A. P. Watt & Son, and Penguin
Books Ltd. Copyright © 1955 by International Authors, N.V.

[1] Euripides: *Orestes* 462 and *Iphigeneia in Aulis* 622.

[2] Aeschylus: *Agamemnon* 877 ff. and *Libation-bearers* 732; Euripides:
Electra 14 ff.; Pindar: *Pythian Odes* xi. 17, with scholiast.

[3] Apollodorus: *Epitome* vi. 24; Euripides: *loc. cit.* and 542 ff.; Aeschylus:
Libation-bearers 232.

[4] Euripides: *Electra* 409–12; Sophocles: *Electra* 11 ff.; Pindar: *Pythian
Odes* xi. 34–6.

[5] Hyginus: *Fabula* 117; Scholiast on Euripides's *Orestes* 33, 764, and 1235;
Euripides: *Iphigeneia Among the Taurians* 921; Apollodorus: *Epitome* vi.
24; Ovid: *Pontic Epistles* iii. 2. 95–8.

libations or myrtle-boughs; and that the people of Mycenae had been forbidden to attend the funeral.[6]

c. Aegisthus reigned at Mycenae for seven years, riding in Agamemnon's chariot, sitting on his throne, wielding his sceptre, wearing his robes, sleeping in his bed, and squandering his riches. Yet despite all these trappings of kingship, he was little more than a slave to Clytaemnestra, the true ruler of Mycenae.[7] When drunk, he would leap on Agamemnon's tomb and pelt the head-stone with rocks, crying: "Come, Orestes, come and defend your own!" The truth was, however, that he lived in abject fear of vengeance, even while surrounded by a trusty foreign bodyguard, never passed a single night in sound sleep, and had offered a handsome reward in gold for Orestes's assassination.[8]

d. Electra had been betrothed to her cousin Castor of Sparta, before his death and demi-deification. Though the leading princes of Greece now contended for her hand, Aegisthus feared that she might bear a son to avenge Agamemnon, and therefore announced that no suitor could be accepted. He would gladly have destroyed Electra, who showed him implacable hatred, lest she lay secretly with one of the Palace officers and bore him a bastard; but Clytaemnestra, feeling no qualms about her part in Agamemnon's murder, and scrupulous not to incur the displeasure of the gods, forbade him to do so. She allowed him, however, to marry Electra to a Mycenaean peasant who, being afraid of Orestes and also chaste by nature, never consummated their unequal union.[9]

e. Thus, neglected by Clytaemnestra, who had now borne Aegisthus three children, by name Erigone, Aletes, and the second Helen, Electra lived in disgraceful poverty, and was kept under constant close supervision. In the end it was decided that, unless she would accept her fate, as her sister Chrysothemis had done, and refrain from publicly calling Aegisthus and Clytaemnestra "murderous adulterers," she would be banished to some distant city and there confined in a dungeon where the light of the sun never penetrated. Yet Electra despised Chrysothemis for her subservience and disloyalty to their dead father, and secretly sent frequent reminders to Orestes of the vengeance required from him.[10]

[6] Euripides: *Electra* 289 and 323–5; Aeschylus: *Libation-bearers* 431.

[7] Homer: *Odyssey* iii. 305; Euripides: *Electra* 320 ff. and 931 ff.; Sophocles: *Electra* 267 ff. and 651.

[8] Euripides: *Electra* 33, 320 ff. and 617 ff.; Hyginus: *Fabula* 119.

[9] Euripides: *Electra* 19 ff., 253 ff., and 312 ff.

[10] Hyginus: *Fabula* 122; Ptolemy Hephaestionos: iv, quoted by Photius p. 479; Euripides: *Electra* 60–4; Aeschylus: *Libation-bearers* 130 ff.; Sophocles: *Electra* 341 ff., 379 ff. and 516 ff.

f. Orestes, now grown to manhood, visited the Delphic Oracle, to enquire whether or not he should destroy his father's murderers. Apollo's answer, authorized by Zeus, was that if he neglected to avenge Agamemnon he would become an outcast from society, debarred from entering any shrine or temple, and afflicted with a leprosy that ate into his flesh, making it sprout white mould.[11] He was recommended to pour libations beside Agamemnon's tomb, lay a ringlet of his hair upon it and, unaided by any company of spearmen, craftily exact the due punishment from the murderers. At the same time the Pythoness observed that the Erinnyes would not readily forgive a matricide, and therefore, on behalf of Apollo, she gave Orestes a bow of horn, with which to repel their attacks, should they become insupportable. After fulfilling his orders, he must come again to Delphi, where Apollo would protect him.[12]

g. In the eighth year — or, according to some, after a passage of twenty years — Orestes secretly returned to Mycenae, by way of Athens, determined to destroy both Aegisthus and his own mother.[13] One morning, with Pylades at his side, he visited Agamemnon's tomb and there, cutting off a lock of his hair, he invoked Infernal Hermes, patron of fatherhood. When a group of slave-women approached, dirty and dishevelled for the purposes of mourning, he took shelter in a near-by thicket to watch them. Now, on the previous night, Clytaemnestra had dreamed that she gave birth to a serpent, which she wrapped in swaddling clothes and suckled. Suddenly she screamed in her sleep, and alarmed the whole Palace by crying that the serpent had drawn blood from her breast, as well as milk. The opinion of the soothsayers whom she consulted was that she had incurred the anger of the dead; and these mourning slave-women consequently came on her behalf to pour libations upon Agamemnon's tomb, in the hope of appeasing his ghost. Electra, who was one of the party, poured the libations in her own name, not her mother's; offered prayers to Agamemnon for vengeance, instead of pardon; and bade Hermes summon Mother Earth and the gods of the Underworld to hear her plea. Noticing a ringlet of fair hair upon the tomb, she decided that it could belong only to Orestes: both because it closely resembled her own in colour and texture, and because no one else would have dared to make such an offering.[14]

[11] Apollodorus: *Epitome* vi. 24; Aeschylus: *Eumenides* 622 and *Libation-bearers* 269 ff.

[12] Sophocles: *Electra* 36–7 and 51–2; Euripides: *Orestes* 268–70; Aeschylus: *Libation-bearers* 1038.

[13] Homer: *Odyssey* iii. 306 ff.; *Hypothesis* of Sophocles's *Electra;* Apollodorus: *Epitome* vi. 25.

[14] Aeschylus: *Libation-bearers*.

h. Torn between hope and doubt, she was measuring her feet against Orestes' foot-prints in the clay beside the tomb, and finding a family resemblance, when he emerged from his hiding place, showed her that the ringlet was his own, and produced the robe in which he had escaped from Mycenae.

Electra welcomed him with delight, and together they invoked their ancestor, Father Zeus, whom they reminded that Agamemnon had always paid him great honour and that, were the House of Atreus to die out, no one would be left in Mycenae to offer him the customary hecatombs: for Aegisthus worshipped other deities.[15]

i. When the slave-women told Orestes of Clytaemnestra's dream, he recognized the serpent as himself, and declared that he would indeed play the cunning serpent and draw blood from her false body. Then he instructed Electra to enter the Palace and tell Clytaemnestra nothing about their meeting; he and Pylades would follow, after an interval, and beg hospitality at the gate, as strangers and suppliants, pretending to be Phocians and using the Parnassian dialect. If the porter refused them admittance, Aegisthus's inhospitality would outrage the city; if he granted it, they would not fail to take vengeance.

Presently Orestes knocked at the Palace gate, and asked for the master or mistress of the house. Clytaemnestra herself came out, but did not recognize Orestes. He pretended to be an Aeolian from Daulis, bearing sad news from one Strophius, whom he had met by chance on the road to Argos: namely, that her son Orestes was dead, and that his ashes were being kept in a brazen urn. Strophius wished to know whether he should send these back to Mycenae, or bury them at Crisa.[16]

j. Clytaemnestra at once welcomed Orestes inside and, concealing her joy from the servants, sent his old nurse, Geilissa, to fetch Aegisthus from a near-by temple. But Geilissa saw through Orestes's disguise and, altering the message, told Aegisthus to rejoice because he could now safely come alone and weaponless to greet the bearers of glad tidings: his enemy was dead.[17]

Unsuspectingly, Aegisthus entered the Palace where, to create a further distraction, Pylades had just arrived, carrying a brazen urn. He told Clytaemnestra that it held Orestes's ashes, which Strophius had now decided to send to Mycenae. This seeming confirmation of the first message put Aegisthus completely off his guard; thus Orestes had no difficulty in drawing his sword and cutting him down. Clytaemnestra then recognized her son, and tried to soften his heart

---

[15] Aeschylus: *ibid.*
[16] Aeschylus: *ibid.*
[17] Aeschylus: *ibid.*

by baring her breast, and appealing to his filial duty; Orestes, however, beheaded her with a single stroke of the same sword, and she fell beside the body of her paramour. Standing over the corpses, he addressed the Palace servants, holding aloft the still blood-stained net in which Agamemnon had died, eloquently exculpating himself for the murder of Clytaemnestra by this reminder of her treachery, and adding that Aegisthus had suffered the sentence prescribed by law for adulterers.[18]

k. Not content with killing Aegisthus and Clytaemnestra, Orestes next disposed of the second Helen, their daughter; and Pylades beat off the sons of Nauplius, who had come to Aegisthus's rescue.[19]

l. Some say, however, that these events took place in Argos, on the third day of Hera's Festival, when the virgins' procession was about to begin. Aegisthus had prepared a banquet for the Nymphs near the horse-meadows, before sacrificing a bull to Hera, and was gathering myrtle-boughs to wreathe his head. It is added that Electra, meeting Orestes by Agamemnon's tomb, would not believe at first that he was her long-lost brother, despite the similarity of their hair, and the robe he showed her. Finally, a scar on his forehead convinced her; because once, when they were children together, chasing a deer, he had slipped and fallen, cutting his head upon a sharp rock.

m. Obeying her whispered instructions, Orestes went at once to the altar where the bull had now been slaughtered and, as Aegisthus bent to inspect its entrails, struck off his head with the sacrificial axe. Meanwhile, Electra, to whom he presented the head, enticed Clytaemnestra from the palace by pretending that, ten days before, she had borne a son to her peasant husband; and when Clytaemnestra, anxious to inspect her first grand-child, visited the cottage, Orestes was waiting behind the door and killed her without mercy.[20]

n. Others, though agreeing that the murder took place at Argos, say that Clytaemnestra sent Chrysothemis to Agamemnon's tomb with the libations, having dreamed that Agamemnon, restored to life, snatched his sceptre from Aegisthus's hands and planted it so firmly in the ground that it budded and put forth branches, which overshadowed the entire land of Mycenae. According to this account, the news which deceived Aegisthus and Clytaemnestra was that Orestes had been accidentally killed while competing in the chariot race at the Pythian Games; and that Orestes showed Electra neither a ringlet nor an embroidered robe, not a scar, in proof of his identity, but

[18] Hyginus: *Fabula* 119; Aeschylus: *Eumenides* 592 and *Libation-bearers* 973 ff.
[19] Ptolemy Hephaestionos: iv, quoted by Photius p. 479; Pausanias: i. 22. 6.
[20] Euripides: *Electra.*

Agamemnon's own seal, which was carved from a piece of Pelops's ivory shoulder.[21]

o. Still others, denying that Orestes killed Clytaemnestra with his own hands, say that he committed her for trial by the judges, who condemned her to death, and that his one fault, if it may be called a fault, was that he did not intercede on her behalf.[22]

❖

1. This is a crucial myth with numerous variants. Olympianism had been formed as a religion of compromise between the pre-Hellenic matriarchal principle and the Hellenic patriarchal principle; the divine family consisting, at first, of six gods and six goddesses. An uneasy balance of power was kept until Athene was reborn from Zeus's head, and Dionysus, reborn from his thigh, took Hestia's seat at the divine Council (see 27. *k*); thereafter male preponderance in any divine debate was assured — a situation reflected on earth — and the goddesses' ancient prerogatives could now be successfully challenged.

2. Matrilinear inheritance was one of the axioms taken over from the pre-Hellenic religion. Since every king must necessarily be a foreigner, who ruled by virtue of his marriage to an heiress, royal princes learned to regard their mother as the main support of the kingdom, and matricide as an unthinkable crime. They were brought up on myths of the earlier religion, according to which the sacred king had always been betrayed by his goddess-wife, killed by his tanist, and avenged by his son; they knew that the son never punished his adulterous mother, who had acted with the full authority of the goddess whom she served.

3. The antiquity of the Orestes myth is evident from his friendship for Pylades, to whom he stands in exactly the same relation as Theseus to Peirithous. In the archaic version, he was doubtless a Phocian prince who ritually killed Aegisthus at the close of the eighth year of his reign, and became the new king by marriage to Chrysothemis, Clytaemnestra's daughter.

4. Other tell-tale traces of the archaic version persist in Aeschylus, Sophocles, and Euripides. Aegisthus is killed during the festival of the Death-goddess Hera, while cutting myrtle-boughs; and despatched, like the Minos bull, with a sacrificial axe. Geilissa's rescue of Orestes ("mountaineer") in a robe "embroidered with wild beasts," and the tutor's stay among the shepherds of Tanus, together recall the

---

[21] Sophocles: *Electra* 326 and 417 ff.; 47–50 and 1223, with scholiast.
[22] Servius on Virgil's *Aeneid* xi. 268.

familiar tale of a royal prince who is wrapped in a robe, left "on a mountain" to the mercy of wild beasts, and cared for by shepherds — the robe being eventually recognized, as in the Hippothous myth (see 49. *a*). Geilissa's substitution of her own son for the royal victim refers, perhaps, to a stage in religious history when the king's annual child-surrogate was no longer a member of the royal clan.

5. How far, then, can the main features of the story, as given by the Attic dramatists, be accepted? Though it is improbable that the Erinnyes have been wantonly introduced into the myth — which, like that of Alcmaeon and Eriphyle (see 107. *d*), seems to have been a moral warning against the least disobedience, injury, or insult that a son might offer his mother — yet it is equally improbable that Orestes killed Clytaemnestra. Had he done so, Homer would certainly have mentioned the fact, and refrained from calling him "god-like"; he records only that Orestes killed Aegisthus, whose funeral feast he celebrated jointly with that of his hateful mother (*Odyssey* iii. 306 ff.). The *Parian Chronicle*, similarly, makes no mention of matricide in Orestes's indictment. It is probable therefore that Servius has preserved the true account: how Orestes, having killed Aegisthus, merely handed over Clytaemnestra to popular justice — a course significantly recommended by Tyndareus in Euripides's *Orestes* (496 ff.). Yet to offend a mother by a refusal to champion her cause, however wickedly she had behaved, sufficed under the old dispensation to set the Erinnyes on his track.

6. It seems, then, that this myth, which was of wide currency, had placed the mother of a household in so strong a position, when any family dispute arose, that the priesthood of Apollo and of Zeus-born Athene (a traitress to the old religion) decided to suppress it. They did so by making Orestes not merely commit Clytaemnestra to trial, but kill her himself, and then secure an acquittal in the most venerable court of Greece: with Zeus's support, and the personal intervention of Apollo, who had similarly encouraged Alcmaeon to murder his treacherous mother Eriphyle. It was the priests' intention, once and for all, to invalidate the religious axiom that motherhood is more divine than fatherhood.

7. In the revised account, endogamy and patrilinear descent are taken for granted, and the Erinnyes are successfully defied. Electra, whose name, "amber," suggests the paternal cult of Hyperborean Apollo, is favourably contrasted with Chrysothemis, whose name is a reminder that the ancient concept of matriarchal law was still golden in most parts of Greece, and whose "subservience" to her mother had hitherto been regarded as pious and noble. Electra is "all for the father," like the Zeus-born Athene. Moreover, the Erinnyes

had always acted for the mother only; and Aeschylus is forcing language when he speaks of Erinnyes charged with avenging paternal blood (*Libation-bearers* 283–4). Apollo's threat of leprosy if Orestes did not kill his mother, was a most daring one: to inflict, or heal, leprosy had long been the sole prerogative of the White Goddess Leprea, or Alphito (*White Goddess,* Chapter 24). In the sequel, not all the Erinnyes accept Apollo's Delphic ruling, and Euripides appeases his female audience by allowing the Dioscuri to suggest that Apollo's injunctions had been most unwise (*Electra* 1246).

8. The wide variations in the recognition scene, and in the plot by which Orestes contrives to kill Aegisthus and Clytaemnestra, are of interest only as proving that the Classical dramatists were not bound by tradition. Theirs was a new version of an ancient myth; and both Sophocles and Euripides tried to improve on Aeschylus, who first formulated it, by making the action more plausible.

PART TWO ◇—◇—◇—◇—◇—◇—◇—◇—◇—◇—◇

Five Plays

AESCHYLUS

❖◇❖◇❖◇❖◇❖◇❖◇❖◇❖◇❖◇❖◇❖◇❖◇❖◇❖

CONCERNED primarily with the moral dilemma of its hero, *The Libation Bearers* raises questions regarding the nature of justice which are resolved in the third play of the trilogy, *The Furies*. *The Libation Bearers* avoids both an indulgence in melodrama and the subtleties of definitive characterization in its depiction of the homecoming of Orestes, his reunion with Electra, and the divine edict to avenge his father's murder. Tainted by bloodshed and polluted by evil that imprisons its victims in the grip of inherited vice, the world of the play throbs with tensions, hate, and intrigue. Vengeance is achieved, but the terrible act of matricide is committed at the cost of reason. Only at the end of his tribulations is Orestes purified; atonement has won acquittal; justice, the day.

The author of approximately ninety plays, of which only seven are extant, Aeschylus of Athens (525–456 B.C.) was the world's first known dramatist. It was he who added a second actor to the first of Thespis, the results of which were an increased complexity of the plot together with a diminution of the function of the chorus.

Aeschylus' view that life could be considered a conflict between principles is made explicit in *The Oresteia*, which examines the clash between allegiance to the vendetta as opposed to acceptance of arbitrated justice. Punishment for sin is inevitable in the world of Aeschylus; excessive pride invites painful retribution. Suffering begets wisdom, evil breeds evil, while vengeance must surrender to humanity, brutality to mercy. Fate is a potent force in the lives of men, but fate is not absolute; man must assume some degree of responsibility for his deeds.

In Aeschylus one discovers an affirmation of the greatness of the gods. They know best what is good for man, who is limited by the fact of being human and compelled to glean what knowledge he can from the basically tragic experience of being alive.

Aeschylus' plots are uncomplicated, their action inclining toward

13

the static. The characters experience little development; their tribulations are induced less by what they are than by the crimes which they commit. Yet there is grandeur in his plays, and style and poetry and an enormous awareness of the profundity of the moral questions that are basic to the meaning of experience.

It will be helpful to remember that Greek drama was originally presented in a vast amphitheatre seating an audience of thousands who came in quest of knowledge and a renewed awareness of their capacities and obligations as human beings. The main occasion for Greek drama was a festival held to honor the divine Dionysus. Approximately 20,000 Athenians would assemble periodically to witness a sacrifice upon his altar — the *thymele*. This was followed by a competition in which four plays — three tragedies and a comedy called a satyr play — were presented. The entire festival consumed five or six days, three of which were devoted to the contests.

The physical structure of the theatre was simple and functional. Nearly surrounding the circular *orchestra* where the chorus performed was the *theatron* composed of row upon row of stone seats divided by aisles into sloping wedges. At the far end of the amphitheatre rose the *skene* building, before which the actors appeared and within which they retired for costume changes. The façade of the *skene* was called the *proscenium*, helpfully suggesting on occasion a palace or a temple. At its center was an entrance beyond which lay the *eccyclema*, a platform which could be projected into view and upon which were mounted in tableaux scenes of carnage and terror, the execution of which it was considered an impropriety to depict in performance. Then there was the *periaktos*, a triangular prism mounted on a pivot which in revolution revealed on each panel the painted depiction of a scene. Probably the *periakti* were placed in or near the side entrances which flanked the center opening containing the *eccyclema*. And finally there was a rather intriguing device called the *deus ex machina* which consisted of a metal crane mounted atop the *skene;* it permitted the suspension of a basket in which a god-figure was placed, his presence a guarantee of a swift if somewhat contrived conclusion to the tragedy being performed. There is considerable debate on the question of a raised stage. If there was one, it may have been a slightly elevated structure running parallel to the *skene* and enclosed on either end by projecting wings called the *paraskenia*.

The Greek actor wore a mask, an oversized cork and linen visage which bore the molded features and salient expression of the represented character. The religious overtones of tragedy were indicated in the color, line, and decoration of the costume; in comedy the bizarre was stressed, with the symbolic phallus on the satyr's costume a visible reminder that Dionysus was the god of procreation.

Not a great deal is known about the style of acting, but a certain amount can be surmised. It is doubtful, for example, that a Greek audience would have tolerated anything but the best talent and the most accomplished technique. Movement in tragedy was probably dignified, though surely never dull. It is quite conceivable that it was conventional. Like the voice, it had to be projected, made larger than life to reach all spectators, and very possibly certain movement and selected gesture denoted specific meaning. Acting for comedy was no doubt a lively art akin, perhaps, to the gymnastic, farcical style of a burlesque comedian. Versatility was essential; the actor had to be able to portray a variety of roles, project metrical lines in a strong and resonant voice, sing and dance on occasion, and maintain total control of his body every second of performance. Acting was a demanding discipline; it is reassuring to know that the man who did it well occupied an honored place in Greek society, enjoying sundry social and political privileges, not the least of which was exemption from an intrusive period of military service.

In addition to the principal actors and the lesser players who supported them, there was the chorus, in tragedy numbering fifteen and in comedy, twenty-four. Integrally involved in the world of the play, the chorus might advise the principals, debate with one another, or address the audience. Their songs and dances blended into the action of the performance, resulting in a cohesive fusion of vocal and musical statement.

Structurally the tragedies followed prescribed form. The *prologue* was followed by the *parados*, which provided for the entrance of the chorus. *Episodes*, or scenes of dramatic action, alternated with the *stasima*, or choral odes, and the play closed with a final scene of action called the *exodos*.

The tragedies were unified with regard to action (there were never sub-plots) but not rigidly so with reference to time and place. Since subject matter was borrowed from myths long known to the populace, interest in the plays tended to focus on the treatment of the material, along with the religious and ethical overtones with which the play was imbued.

The greatness that was Greek lives on not only in the handful of extant plays that may be enjoyed in occasional revivals (only 57), but to a significant degree in its continuing influence upon contemporary drama. With regard to scope, concept, and on occasion, method, the modern playwright persists in assaulting the heights the great Attic dramatists so magnificently scaled.

Sources containing interesting and useful information about the Greek theatre include James Turney Allen, *Stage Antiquities of the Greeks and Romans and Their Influence* (New York, 1927); Margarete Bieber, *The History of the Greek and Roman Theatre* (Princeton, 1939); R. C. Flickinger, *The Greek Theatre and Its Drama* (Chicago, 1936); and A. E. Haigh and A. W. Pickard-Cambridge, *The Attic Theatre* (Oxford, 1907). An abundance of material concerning the period, its dramatists, and its plays can also be found in the extremely useful history by John Gassner, *Masters of the Drama* (New York, 1954).

Aeschylus is the subject of extended comment in the following works: Gilbert Murray, *Aeschylus, the Creator of Tragedy* (Oxford, 1940); J. T. Sheppard, *Aeschylus and Sophocles: Their Work and Influence* (New York, 1927); H. W. Smith, *Aeschylean Tragedy* (Berkeley, 1924); and G. D. Thomson, *Aeschylus and Athens: a Study of the Social Origins of Drama* (London, 1941). Helpful critical statements concerning Aeschylus as well as Sophocles and Euripides are included in the following: H. D. F. Kitto, *Greek Tragedy* (New York, 1950); D. W. Lucas, *The Greek Tragic Poets* (New York, 1959); John Jones, *On Aristotle and Greek Tragedy* (London, 1962), and Richmond Lattimore, *The Complete Greek Tragedies*, Vol. I (Chicago, 1953).

The Libation Bearers

Translated by Peter D. Arnott

❖ ❖ ❖

CHARACTERS

ORESTES, *son of the late king Agamemnon and Clytemnestra*
ELECTRA, *his sister*
CLYTEMNESTRA, *Queen of Argos*
AEGISTHUS, *Clytemnestra's lover, now King of Argos*
CILISSA, *Orestes' old nurse*
PYLADES, *friend of Orestes*
PORTER
SERVANT *of Aegisthus*
CHORUS *of slavewomen*

Scene: At first, by the grave of Agamemnon; later, before the door of the royal palace.

> (*The grave of* AGAMEMNON. ORESTES *kneels in prayer. His friend* PYLADES *stands silent at a distance.*)

ORESTES. Hermes, spirit of the underworld
And father's regent, lend to me
Your strength, and stand my champion, I pray,
For I have come home to my land again
And on this mounded tomb invoke my father
To listen and attend.

> (*Laying a lock of hair upon the grave.*)

From *The Libation Bearers and the Eumenides* by Aeschylus, edited and translated by Peter D. Arnott. Copyright © 1964 by Meredith Publishing Company. Reprinted by permission of Appleton-Century-Crofts.

1. *Hermes:* messenger-god, one of whose functions was to escort the spirits of the dead to the underworld. Thus he is frequently appealed to, both in this play and *The Eumenides,* as the intermediary between the living and the dead.

A lock of hair to Inachus, for manhood;
Its fellow here, as token for the dead;
For I was not at hand to mourn your passing,
My father, or salute your burial.   10

> (*The* CHORUS *of mourning women, with* ELECTRA *among them, appear in the distance. They carry urns with libations to pour over the grave.*)

But what is here now? What processional
Of women, in dignity of mourning black,
Is coming? What should I make this to mean?
A signal of new sorrow for the palace?
Or am I to suppose these women bring
Libations as late offerings to my father?
So it must be; for I think I see my sister
Electra among them, grief scored bold
Upon her face. Zeus, give me revenge
For my dead father; be my willing aid.   20
Pylades, let us give them room.
I must assure myself about this cry of women.

> (ORESTES *and* PYLADES *conceal themselves as the women approach the grave.*)

CHORUS. Forth from the palace gates, as I was bid,
With urns I come, with drumming hands,
Torn cheeks, the nails' fresh furrows
A talisman of red,
And in my heart old sorrow;
With rending of my robes, with fingers tearing
Wild at the linen on my breast
In grief of glad days gone.   30

For in the dead watch Fright with streaming hair
Shrilled from its cell, and to the dreaming house
Told things to come, a gust of rancor stirring
Fresh out of slumber,
Beating ironfisted on the doors
Of women. The seers swore by the gods their masters

---

7. *a lock of hair:* common votive offering, particularly in acts of mourning. *Inachus:* river-god of Argos.

31. *Fright with streaming hair:* personification of Clytemnestra's prophetic nightmare, recounted more explicitly in vv. 555 ff.

32. *Shrilled from its cell:* the language deliberately suggests the apparatus of Apollo's oracular shrine at Delphi.

That anger was pulsing in the grave
Against the murderers.

So in hollow office of appeasement,
Earth, O Earth, in mock of holy law,   40
She sends me forth. But there is fear
At such a word.
For who can ransom blood once spilled
On the ground? O joyless hearth,
O desolation of our house,
Sun hid his face, the pestilence
Of darkness fell thick on our palace
At the killing of our kings.

The splendor of our yesterdays, that stood
Triumphant, matchless and invincible   50
To thrill men's hearts with story, is departed
And terror comes.
Success is god, and greater than god
For mortal men. But Justice holds
Her balance attentive, coming swift
On some by day, for some waits ripening
Till evenfall, and those remaining
Are swallowed up in night.

Blood poured for mother earth to drink
Lies crusted, a living sore   60
To cry revenge. Destruction works
On the sinner, spiking him with plague
Till he is rotten through.

As once the chambers of virginity
Are forced, there is no remedy,
So all the waters of the world
Would seek to wash blood clean from guilty
Hands, and do their work in vain.

On me and on mine the gods imposed
The hard necessity of conquest   70
And from the dwellings of my fathers
Brought me here to be a slave.
So I can do no other but approve
My masters, right or wrong—my life

Is new come in their keeping,
And I must struggle to suppress
The heart's loathing.
But still there run behind the veil
Tears for the errant destiny of kings
And to the secret places of my heart   80
Comes the cold touch of horror.

(ELECTRA *takes her place at the graveside.*)

ELECTRA. You serving-maids, who set our house to rights,
   Since you have trod this path of prayer with me,
   Give me your counsel here. How should I speak
   As I pour these offerings on my father's grave?
   With what address, what sacramental words?
   That this is love's commission to her love,
   To husband from his wife — and this my mother?
   I would not dare. Then what accompaniment
   Should herald these libations underground?   90
   I know not. Or could I say this—
   That men believe that those who send such wreaths
   As these, deserve to be repaid in kind
   With presents worthy of their merits?
   Or should I pour into the thirsty earth
   Without a word, without a salutation,
   In manner as he died, and fling the urn away
   As one who would be rid of it forever,
   And go my way without a backward glance?
   This is the question, friends. Advise me.   100
   We share a roof, a common hate.
   So do not hide your counsels out of fear
   Of . . . anyone. The free man and the slave,
   Each has his destiny. So speak;
   Perhaps you know a better.

CHORUS. If you will have it so, I'll speak my mind
   Before your father's tomb, which is for me
   A sacred shrine —
ELECTRA.   Then as you reverence
   My father's grave, speak to me now.
CHORUS. Pour, and call blessings on men of goodwill —   110
ELECTRA. And where among my friends could I find any
   To bear that name?
CHORUS. Yourself; then anyone who hates Aegisthus.
ELECTRA. You, then, and me. Is that to be my prayer?

CHORUS. You know what I mean. But you must say it.
ELECTRA. Whom else shall I number in this company?
CHORUS. Remember Orestes, banished though he be.
ELECTRA. That was well spoken, my good instructor.
CHORUS. And for the ones who shed this blood, remember —
ELECTRA. What? I am strange to this, you must dictate to me.   120
CHORUS. To call someone against them, from this world
   Or from the other —
ELECTRA. To judge, or to revenge? Explain yourself.
CHORUS. In plain words, to take life for life.
ELECTRA. May I so pray, without offence to heaven?
CHORUS. Why not? To pay your enemy in kind?
ELECTRA. God of darkness, Hermes, potent messenger
   Of this world and the next, I summon you
   To help me now, and call
   The spirits of the underworld, that watch   130
   My father's house, to hear me as I pray,
   And summon Earth, that brings all things to life
   And takes her rearing to her womb again.
   As I pour out these vessels to the dead,
   I call upon my father. Pity me,
   And light Orestes' lamp within our house,
   For we are homeless now, our mother's chattels
   With which she purchased for herself a man,
   Aegisthus, who was partner in your murder.
   I am no better than a slave; Orestes   140
   Is banished from his rich inheritance,
   While they loll back in luxury, and reap
   The harvest of your labor. Thus I pray,
   My father, listen close. Let fortune bring
   Orestes home, and let me show myself
   More modest than my mother was, my hand
   More virtuous.
   These prayers for us. This for our enemies:
   Father, I charge you show us your avenger.
   Kill them who killed you. Render them this justice.   150
   And let me set against their curse
   My curse, to fall on them.
   Bring us blessings from the underworld;
   The gods be on our side, and Earth,
   And justice triumphant.
   Such is the litany to which I pour
   These offerings.

(*To the* CHORUS) And you, as the custom is,
Must crown the prayers with your lament, and sing
Your hymnal to the dead.
CHORUS. Let fall now for the fallen lord   160
A watering of tears
As pitchers are upturned
On this holy mound, a bastion
Against evil, and a curse that must be laid.
Hear me, majesty; lord, as you lie dim,
Give this your mind. What champion will rise
To be our palace's deliverance?
What warrior to wield the backbent
Bow of Scythia, or come
Firmhilted to the handfight?   170
ELECTRA. The earth has drunk. My father has his due.
                (*Seeing the lock of* ORESTES' *hair.*)
But here is something strange to tell,
Something for all of us.
CHORUS. Tell me what you mean.
Fear is stepping nimble in my heart.
ELECTRA. Look, on the tomb. A lock of hair.
CHORUS. Whose? Man's or woman's?
ELECTRA. Guess. Nobody could mistake it.
CHORUS. What is it? Your young years must teach my age.
ELECTRA. This curl could not have come from any head   180
But mine.
CHORUS. His nearest hate him, they would never
Cut hair in his mourning.
ELECTRA. But look at it — so very like —
CHORUS. Like whose hair? Tell me.
ELECTRA. My own. So like. Compare them.
CHORUS. Orestes? Has he come in secret
To make this offering?
ELECTRA.   Yes, he has hair
Like this.
CHORUS. He would not dare to come.
ELECTRA. He sent it, then; this shorn lock,   190
A lovegift to his father.
CHORUS. Then I have no less cause to weep
If he will never set foot in this land again.
ELECTRA. I too. The full tide of my anger now

---

169. *Bow of Scythia:* the Scythians were famous archers in antiquity.

Has come, it is a knife to rend my heart.
The dyke is down, the tears fall from my eyes
Unslaked, my grief is at the flood
To see this hair. Oh, how could I imagine
That this lock could have come from any other
In Argos? It was not the murderess   200
That cropped her hair, my mother — what a name
For her, that fiend who hates her children!
But how can I say straight and clear
This glory comes from him I love the best,
Orestes — oh, I am hope's fool!
If it had wit to speak, if it could tell me,
Then I should not be torn between two minds,
But know for sure if I should cast it out
For being fathered by a head I hate
Or if it is one blood with mine, my sorrow's partner   210
To grace this grave, and reverence my father.
But on the gods we call, who know
What tempests have beset our voyaging,
And if it is ordained we come safe home,
Great trunks from little seeds may grow.

                    (*Seeing footprints on the ground.*)

A second witness! Marks upon the ground
Like those my feet have made, the very same . . .
No, there's a double set of footprints here,
One his, and one somebody's that was with him. . . .
The heel, the tracing of the toes; these measurements   220
Exactly fit with mine — I cannot bear it!
This is too much to think of!

            (ORESTES *and* PYLADES *step from their hiding place.*)

ORESTES. You may inform the gods your prayers are answered.
    Now pray to be as lucky in the future.
ELECTRA. Why? What favor have I won from them?
ORESTES. You are in sight of what you prayed to see so long.
ELECTRA. The man I prayed for — what is he to you?
ORESTES. I know how you long to see Orestes.
ELECTRA. What makes you think my prayers are answered?
ORESTES. Here I am. Look no further. You will never find   230
    A closer friend.
ELECTRA. I do not know you. Are you playing tricks on me?
ORESTES. If so, I play a trick upon myself.
ELECTRA. Have you come here to laugh at my misfortunes?

ORESTES. If they are your misfortunes, they are mine.
ELECTRA. Let me pretend you are Orestes, then,
   And bid you —
ORESTES.   I am Orestes,
   And you do not know me when you see me.
   But when you saw this hair cut off in mourning,
   When you looked on the earth my feet had trod,   240
   Your mind flew on the instant to the thought
   That what you saw was me.
   Look, lay this lock of hair where it was cut;
   It is your brother's — see, it matches yours.

               (*Showing a child's garment.*)

   And look, the jerkin that you wove for me:
   The texture, this embroidery of beasts —

        (ELECTRA *is convinced, and weeps for joy.*)

   Control yourself, and do not let your joy
   Outweigh discretion. I am well acquainted
   With our dear friends, and how they hate us.
ELECTRA. Oh dearest treasure of our father's house,   250
   Its hope, its future seed; how we have wept for you.
   It shall be yours again. You have your father's strength
   Behind you. Face that I have longed to see;
   You have divided me, and made four loves from one.
   One for my father — that is your name now;
   One for my loving duty to my mother —
   Her share is yours; to her I give my hate;
   One for my sister's cruel sacrifice;
   One for the brother true that I have found you,
   The only one of all my family   260
   To give me dignity.
   So Might and Justice fight upon my side
   And Zeus Almighty, greatest of them all,
   To make a third.
ORESTES. Zeus, O Zeus, look down at what has passed here.
   Look at us both, the eagle's children,
   Parentless, their father strangled
   In the deadly embraces of a snake.
   Their father's dead, and they must starve,
   For they have not his art, to bring their catch   270
   Home to the lair, as he did. It is myself I mean

---

258. *my sister's cruel sacrifice:* Iphigeneia, sacrificed by Agamemnon to
win the gods' favor at the outset of the Trojan War.

And this girl, Electra. We stand here in your sight
Two children, fatherless, and both alike
Cast from our homes. Our father
Was lavish in his tithes to honor you.
Destroy his young, you will look hard to find
Another hand so generous to feast you.
If you suffer the eagle's progeny to die
Who will believe you when you manifest yourself
Hereafter? If this ministering branch   280
Is left to wither, when the day comes round
To serve the altar, it will not be there
To wait on you with sacrifice. Take heed:
You may uplift this house and make it great
Although it seems to lie in ruins now.

CHORUS. Children, saviors of your father's house
Be silent, or some tattletale will warn
Our overlords. I hope I live to see them
Dead, and burning in the spitting fire!

ORESTES. One thing will never fail, the potent oracle   290
Of Apollo. It was he who bade me walk
This perilled way, and in the secret hours
Whispered to me a litany of horrors
To turn my blood to ice, should I neglect
To hound my father's murderers and kill them
As they killed him, round on them, gore them,
Strip them of all they have. If I should fail,
He said my own self would be forfeit; I should suffer
Miseries uncounted . . . he made it plain
And told how, when the dead are angry,   300
Their rancor rises as a pestilence
Up through the ground, to ride upon our bodies,
Creeping, feeding; cancer sets its teeth
In flesh once fair, and leaves its mark upon
Our faces, scabbed with silver scales.
He spoke of other visitations too,
Of Furies forming in the father's blood.
Dead things work by dark. Then murdered men
Come crying to their kin "Revenge!" and terror stalks
By night, to haunt him. Wild hallucinations   310
Come vivid on his eyes, although he screw them
Tight shut in the dark, and drive him forth

291. *Apollo:* god of prophecy and Orestes' patron; see note on v. 31.

With barbs and scourges from the land that bred him.
For such an outcast there can be
No common bowl, no loving-cup,
No prayer at altars — there a sentry stands,
His father's ghost; no man will share a roof with him
Or take him in, till friendless and unmourned
He shrivels up and dies in misery.
Such was the oracle. Could I then deny it?   320
Even if I could, the deed must still be done,
For there are many calls on me, unanimous
To urge me on — the gods' commandment,
Grief for my father — there is weight in this —
The press of poverty, and my desire
That the marvel of the earth, my countrymen,
Whose glorious spirit subjugated Troy
Should not bow down before this pair of women —
For he is woman at heart; if I am one
He soon shall learn!   330

    (ORESTES, ELECTRA *and the* CHORUS *join in a lament over the
    tomb.*)

CHORUS. O you presiding Destinies
By the will of god make ending
In the turnabout of justice.
Let hate cry quittance to hate once spoken.
So Justice proclaims herself aloud, exacting
Atonement; blood for blood
And stroke for stroke, do and be done by;
Thus the lesson three ages old.

ORESTES. O terrible my father,
What word of mine, what act   340
Can blow fair to the far shore,
Where fast you lie, a light
The measure of your darkness?
And yet it has been called
A work of grace, to tell old glories
In mourning for the champions
Of the house of Atreus fallen.

CHORUS. Child, when a man dies flesh is frayed
And broken in the fire, but not his will.

347. *Atreus:* Agamemnon's father.

He shows his wrath though late.   350
For the dead man there is mourning,
For the guilty man a finding,
And the deathsong for a parent and a father
Is a call to judgement, ranging through
The universe disquieted
To hunt and find.

ELECTRA. Hear me in turn, my father,
My weeping and long sorrow.
Here two children at your graveside
Raise our chant for the departed.   360
Your tomb is haven
For outcasts, and for those
Who pray for aid. What here is good,
What refuge from calamity?
Can we try a fall with fate?

CHORUS. Even from such as these the god
At will can shape a gladder strain,
And from the lamentation at the graveside
A song of triumph may arise
Within the palace, to carry home   370
The well-beloved, the dear unknown.

ORESTES. If you had only died, my father,
At Troy, upon the field of honor,
And struck down by a foreign hand.
Then had you left your house
A legacy of glory, to your children
As they walked abroad, undying
Regard; then had you made
A heavy tomb upon a foreign shore
But for your family light burden.   380

CHORUS. Welcome then would he have gone
To those who loved him, to the nobled dead,
And in the nether world
Would have kept high state, in honor
Held and majesty, first minister
To the most mighty, to the kings of darkness.
For he was monarch on earth, and ruled
Those who command men's lives, who wield
The sceptre of dominion.

ELECTRA. No, that was not a place   390
  For you to die, my father,
  Under the battlements of Troy,
  And by Scamander's ford to find
  A plot of ground among the herd,
  The reaping of the spear. Far better
  That those who killed him should have died as he did,
  And in far countries strangers to our sorrow
  Had heard tell of the manner of their passing.

CHORUS. Child, you talk of riches passing mortal,
  Of miracles, felicity   400
  They only know who live beyond the wind.
  Dreams are free. But the double scourge
  Beats louder in the land; beneath
  The earth there is a mustering
  Of forces in our aid; our lords
  Have hands unclean, and the curse is on them;
  The children's day is coming.

ORESTES. There now is a word
  To rivet the ear. O Zeus,
  Zeus, send up from below   410
  The laggard punisher
  For men of wrath and guilty hand
  And let the score be settled for the parents.

CHORUS. May it be given me to raise
  A cheer at the slaying of the man,
  The woman's dying. Why should I hide
  The thought that deep within flies free?
  For in the voyage of the heart
  There is a freight of hatred, and the wind
  Of wrath blows shrill.   420

ELECTRA. Zeus two-fisted come
  To smite them, yes, to smash
  Heads; let there be a place
  For faith again; where there is wrong
  I say let right be done; O hear me
  Earth, and dignities of darkness.

393. *Scamander:* river of Troy.
401. *who live beyond the wind:* the legendary Hyperboreans, who lived
in the far north and were particular favorites of Apollo.

CHORUS. This is the law. Blood spilt upon the ground
  Cries out for more, the act
  Of desecration is a summons to the Fury
  Who for the dead once fallen heaps   430
  Havoc on havoc, new upon the old.

ORESTES. O potentates of darkness, see,
  See, curses that come mighty from the dead,
  The house of Atreus, all that is left of us,
  Helpless, driven from our rightful homes.
  Where is there aid, O Zeus?

CHORUS. And my heart too has quivered
  To hear your sorrow's utterance.
  At such a word came despair,
  A shadow on the heart. But when   440
  I see you standing strong, there comes
  Hope, and lightening of sorrow
  At this fair sign.

ELECTRA. What shall our tale be then? What other
  Than sorrows suffered for our parents' sake?
  Fawn away, there can be no assuaging.
  Anger ravens wolfish and implacable,
  Child of the mother.

CHORUS. As in Aria the women beat their breasts
  Then beat I mine, and in Cissian style   450
  Made show of mourning. There was a sight
  Of drumming fists, of blood-bruised flesh,
  A dance of hands, plucking
  Higher, lower, till my sorry head
  Rang with their hammering.

ELECTRA. O ruthless, O relentless, O my mother,
  Who in forced and meagre offices
  Thought fit to bury him, a king
  Far from his folk, without
  The rites of mourning,   460
  Without a tear, your husband.

449. *Aria, Cissian style:* regions in Asia Minor. The chorus liken their
reaction to Agamemnon's death to that of professional Asiatic mourners,
with the difference that their grief was sincere.

ORESTES. In such dishonor, say you?
  But she shall pay for slighting him,
  My father, by the help
  Of the immortals, by the help
  Of these my hands.
  So let me kill her, and then die.

CHORUS. This too you must know. His limbs were lopped
  And travestied, upon her word
  Who ordered this his grave,   470
  Intent to lay crushing grief
  On your young life.
  So was your father slighted.

ELECTRA. As you tell it, so he died. I was not by;
  I had no rights there, I was nothing,
  Only a cur that must be locked away
  Inside, for fear she'd bite. I hid
  The welling of my grief
  Though tears came readier than smiles that day.
  Hear this, and write it in your memory!   480

CHORUS. Yes, write, and let the tale bore deep
  Into your heart. But bide your time
  In patience still. So stands
  The story now. You yearn
  To know the end. Steadfast
  Comes fittest to the fight.

ORESTES. Pay heed, my father. Work beside your own.
ELECTRA. Your weeping daughter adds her voice to his.
CHORUS. And so cries all this company together.
  Obey, and come to light; make one   490
  Against your enemies.

ORESTES. Battle now match battle, right with right.
ELECTRA. O gods, bring justice and accomplishment.
CHORUS. Fear comes over me as I hear you pray.
  Long destiny has waited; now
  When summoned it may come.

  O curse inborn, sour song
  Of fate, the bloody chastisement.

O hard and heavy sorrows, grief
That has no easy end.   500

The cure is in the house, not brought
By other hands from distant places
But by its own, in agony and blood.
Thus we sing unto the dark ones.

But listen to our prayer, O blessed ones
Below, and send your willing aid
To these the children. Let them fight and conquer.

ORESTES. Father, who died out of the royal way,
   I pray you make me master in your house.
ELECTRA. I ask a like gift from your hands, my father: 510
   Aegisthus' death, a husband for my own. . . .
ORESTES. So when there is feasting here on earth
   May you come welcome. If not, in the banquet days
   When steaming meats are offered to the dead
   No portion shall be yours.
ELECTRA.   Let me but come
   Into my own, and on my bridal day
   I'll bring gifts from the mansions of my fathers
   To pour for you, and honor this tomb above all others.
ORESTES. Earth, loose my father. Let him see my fight.
ELECTRA. Queen Persephone, give us grace and strength.   520
ORESTES. Remember your laving and your death, my father —
ELECTRA. Remember the strange weaving that you wore —
ORESTES. Hobbled in fetters forged by no man's hand, my
   father —
ELECTRA. And wrapped about in shroud of foul devising —
ORESTES. Do these taunts sting you from your sleep, my father?
ELECTRA. And do you lift the head that we so love?
ORESTES. Send forth your chastisement to fight with those
   You love, or let us turn the hold on them
   If you would change defeat to victory.
ELECTRA. And father, hear this cry, my last: 530
   See these nestlings huddled on your tomb

520. *Persephone:* wife of the god Hades and Queen of the Underworld.
521. *your laving . . . strange weaving:* Clytemnestra murdered Agamemnon in his bath, having entangled him in his own robe. It is this robe that
Orestes displays to the chorus later in the play, vv. 1058 ff.

And pity them, the girlchild and the boy together.

ORESTES. And do not write an end to Pelops' line.

Through them you live, though you are in your grave.

ELECTRA. For when a man has died, his children keep

His fame alive; we are the corks upon the net

That hold the skein from sinking in the waters.

ORESTES. For you these tears, so give them heed.

Reward our speech, and save yourself.

CHORUS. The tomb lacks nothing of its honor now.   540

Long have you spoken, and the debt of tears

Is paid. But if your mind is firm to act

Go on, and make experiment of fate!

ORESTES. So be it. But there is a question still to ask

And to the point. Why did she send

These offerings? What persuaded her to make

These late amends for sorrow long past healing?

A miserable favor, lavished on

The dead, the mindless! What these gifts might mean

I could not start to guess. How small they weigh   550

Beside her sin! Spend blood, there needs no more,

And you may spend the world to pay for it

And lose your labor. Thus the proverb runs.

Speak, if you know. You'll find a ready ear.

CHORUS. I saw, and know, child. There was a dream,

A horror in the night; she woke in fear

And sent these offerings in mock of piety.

ORESTES. What did she dream? If you know, tell all.

CHORUS. She gave birth to a snake — this was her story.

ORESTES. And then? What was the sequel to this tale?   560

CHORUS. She wrapped it like a babe in cradle clothes.

ORESTES. What did it ask for food, this beast new-born?

CHORUS. In the dream, she gave it her own breast to suck.

ORESTES. How could she, and the nipple not be torn

By this foul thing?

CHORUS.   It sucked milk and clotted blood.

ORESTES. No riddle here. This vision means a man —

CHORUS. Then she awoke, and screamed in terror,

And in the dark house at the mistress' cry

The shuttered lamps began to blink their eyes;

And thinking to find surgery for pain   570

She sent at once these offerings to the dead.

ORESTES. I pray this earth, my father's sepulchre,

That this dream find accomplishment in me.

533. *Pelops:* remote ancestor of the house of Atreus.

Thus I interpret; it is of a piece:
The serpent came from that same place
That brought forth me; she wrapped it in the robes
That cradled me; its mouth spread on the breast
That suckled me, and with lifegiving milk
Drew clotted blood, and at this dreadful thing
My mother screamed in fear; then surely she   580
Is doomed to die, and by no gentle hand
For bringing such a fearful prodigy
Into the world, and I am made the snake
To kill her, as this dream foretells.

CHORUS. Then you are the interpreter I trust
And cry amen. Expound the rest
To your friends now, who is to work, who wait —

ORESTES. It can be quickly told. My sister must go home
And see that nothing of our plan leaks out,
So they who killed by treachery a man   590
Deserving of great honor, may be caught
By treachery, and in the selfsame net
May die; for thus Apollo prophesied,
The prophet-god who never yet has lied.
Accoutred like a traveller I'll come
Before the outer gates, with this man here
Whose name is Pylades, my friend, the bounden
Champion of me and mine. We'll both
Assume the accent of Parnassus, and talk
The way men do in Phocis. If nobody   600
Opens the gates for us and bids us welcome
Because the house is busy with its troubles,
We'll stay where we are, so anyone who passes
Will point and say "Is Aegisthus home?
Does he know they are here? Then why
Does he bar his doors to those who ask shelter?"
And if I gain admission at the gates
And find that man upon my father's throne
Or if he comes to look me up and down
And question me to my face, before he says   610
"Where is this stranger from?" I'll strike him dead,
And in the flashing of a sword he'll fall.
So the Fury, that has never yet been starved of slaughter,
Will drink pure blood, the third draught and the last.

600. *Phocis:* district on the northern shore of the Gulf of Corinth, containing Mount *Parnassus,* traditional home of the Muses, and Delphi, the shrine of Apollo.

(*To* ELECTRA.)

Your part to manage everything within
The house, so all may hang together,

(*To the* CHORUS.)

And yours, to keep a guard upon your tongue,
Speak when you should, be silent when you must.
And all the rest I summon this one here
To oversee, when I have made   620
All ready for the trial at arms.

> (*Exeunt* ORESTES *and* PYLADES *to disguise themselves,* ELECTRA
> *to the palace.*)

CHORUS. Great the progeny of nature, strange
And dreadful; in the cradle of the sea
Lurk monsters; in the hinterland
Of earth and heaven, fire
Has wings to fly; and birds
And creeping things can tell
The malice of the stormwinds.

  But who could put to words the vaunting
Pride of man, the overmastering   630
Selfwill of woman, bedfellow
Of sorrows for mankind?
For when her passion turns
From wedlock and home, no beast
Or man can rage as she.

Let him who has a mind to plumb the depths
Of things, learn how the sad Althaea once,
Armed with prescience of fire,
Devised death for her son, and burnt
The red brand that was of an age with him   640
Since he came forth crying from his mother's womb,
Whose span was his, to the appointed day.

619. *this one here:* without the stage gesture which would originally have
accompanied these words, it is impossible to say who is meant. It could be
Pylades, Agamemnon or Apollo.

637. The chorus offer examples from mythology of women who have been
carried away by their passions. *Althea* was the mother of Meleager. When
her son was born the Fates told her that he would die when a brand then
burning in the fire was consumed. She promptly extinguished the brand
and locked it away. When Meleager grew to manhood, he quarrelled with
his mother's brothers and killed them. In her grief and anger Althea re-
kindled the brand and Meleager died.

There is another written black in story,
Scylla, who dealt in death, and was seduced
By enemies to kill one of her nearest.
Tempted her bitch-heart was and won
By Minos' gift, the necklace wrought of gold,
To cut from Nisus as he heedless slept
The lock of lasting life; and from this world went he.

And now I have begun this bloody history   650
Should there not be a place
For the loveless wedlock that this house
Would fain see gone? You came
In guise of enemy upon
Your husband, working on him with
Your wiles, and sly as only woman may,
On your husband armored strong in might,
And over him you prized
A house whose hearth is barren of its fire,
The heart of the man-woman.   660

Of all the evils that the world can tell
Lemnos takes pride of place, a name
To fright the ear, a blasphemy,
And whatsoever dreadful thing
Shall pass, there will be one to christen it
"The crime of Lemnos." So angry were the gods
That from earth the race has gone dishonored.
For what is evil in heaven's sight
Is so for men. Does any of these tales
Not fit our case?   670

Now stands the sword at the lifebreath
To thrust sharp home, and at the hilt
Is Justice aiding; for it is not fit
That those who trod the majesty of Zeus
Underfoot, should not be trampled
Down in their turn.

644. *Scylla:* daughter of *Nisus*, king of Megara, often confused with the sea
monster of the same name. Her father's life depended on a lock of red hair
growing on his head. *Minos*, King of Crete, who was attacking Megara,
persuaded Scylla to sever it, thus killing Nisus and causing the surrender
of the city.
662. *Lemnos:* island off the coast of Asia Minor whose women, according
to tradition, had risen against their husbands and killed them.

Now the anvil of Justice stands foursquare
And Fate the swordsmith has the edge made keen.
For from the abyss of her mind the Fury,
Late come to honor, visits on the house   680
The child of blood shed in the former time
To make atonement.

> (*The palace.* ORESTES *and* PYLADES, *disguised as travellers, come
> to the door and knock.*)

ORESTES. Boy, do you hear? There's someone knocking!
  Is anyone there? Boy, I say! Who's at home?
  For the third time, somebody come to the door,
  If there is still shelter to be had here
  Now that Aegisthus is in charge.
PORTER (*Within*). All right, I hear you! Where are you from?
ORESTES. Go tell the masters of this house.
  They are the ones I seek. I bring strange news.   690
  And hurry; night's dark chariot comes
  Apace; this is the hour
  When merchants must drop anchor in a house
  That opens up its doors to travelling men.
  Send us someone in authority,
  The mistress, or her man, for preference.
  With women we must be polite, and talk
  Around the matter. Man to man speaks straight
  And to the point, without prevarication.

> (*The door opens. Enter* CLYTEMNESTRA.)

CLYTEMNESTRA. Travellers, you have only to state your needs.   700
  Such entertainment as this house can offer
  Is at your command — a warm bath, or a bed
  To magic weariness away, and honest
  Eyes to wait on you. But if
  You have more weighty business to discuss,
  That is the man's work, and we shall inform him so.
ORESTES. Daulis is my home. I am a traveller from Phocis.
  I was on my way with merchandise to Argos
  On business of my own. When I turned off here,
  A man I had met — we were strangers to each other —   710
  Asked my destination, and told me his.
  He was Strophius the Phocian — that came out
  In conversation — and he said to me

---

712. *Strophius:* friend to Argos, to whose hands the infant Orestes had
been entrusted.

"Since you must go to Argos anyway,
Think to look out the parents of Orestes
And tell them he is dead. Do not forget.
Whatever his family decides to do,
Whether to bring him back, or have him buried
Out of his land, to lie forever among strangers,
Bring word accordingly, when you come back again,   720
For we have done but this — shed proper tears
Above his ashes, and unfolded them
In the belly of a brazen urn." That was all he told me.
But whether I talk to those who have
Authority and interest in this business
I do not know. I think his father should be told.

CLYTEMNESTRA. Oh,
You tell of how the waters of our grief
Rise clear above our heads. O curse upon our house
That ever throws disaster in our way,
How little slips your eyes, with what sure aim   730
You send your shafts to strike down from afar
Even the things that carefully were set
Out of your path, to strip me desolate
Of those I love. So now it is Orestes,
He who was so well schooled to tread around
This slough of death. There was a hope
Of decency, of revel in our house;
By this we kept alive; now take that hope
And by its name write "Liar."

ORESTES. I would have rather introduced myself   740
To entertainment so munificent
By telling of more pleasant things; for none
Could be more anxious to oblige than travellers
Their hosts. But I should have looked upon myself
As breaking a sacred trust, if I neglected
To carry this matter through. I gave my promise
To Strophius, and am under obligation
To you now, as your guest.

CLYTEMNESTRA. This changes nothing. You will be received
According to your merits, and shall have   750
No less regard, while you are in our house.
If it had not been you who brought this message
It would have been another. It is now
The hour when footsore travellers should reap
The promise of their long day's march.

(To her servants.)

Take him inside, to the guestrooms where
We lodge the menfolk, his attendants too
And fellow travellers. See that they receive
The comforts proper to a house like ours.
You have your orders. You are answerable to me.   760
I shall go tell the master of the house
What I have heard, and with my friends about me
Take the measure of this new disaster.

    (CLYTEMNESTRA, ORESTES *and* PYLADES *go inside the palace.*)

CHORUS. Come friends and fellow servants all,
  Is it not time for us to show
  The power of our voices, and so aid
  Orestes? O sovereign Earth and sovereign
  Mound of the tomb, who lie upon
  The body of the sealord and our king,
  Now hear us, grant us aid.   770
  Now is the time ripe for Persuasion
  To marshal all her wiles
  And for the god of the dark journey, Hermes,
  And him that dwells in night, to stand
  Sentinel as the sword comes to the match.

    (*Enter* CILISSA.)

The harm must be afoot, the traveller is busy —
Here is Orestes' nurse in tears.
Where are you going from the gates, Cilissa,
With misery, the uninvited guest
Free ever of her company, to step beside you?   780
CILISSA. Our mistress sent me hurrying to find
Aegisthus for the travellers, so he
Could talk to them man to man, and learn
The ins and outs of what they have to tell him.
She had a wry face for her servants, but behind
Her eyes she hid a smile that things had worked
So well for her — but for this house
It's nothing short of tragedy — the tale
The travellers told, and that's plain enough.
And it will be good news to that one   790
When he hears it. Oh, the pity of it!
All the troubles that we had, and never
Two alike, here in the house of Atreus,

774. *him that dwells in night:* Agamemnon.

More than a body could stand; oh, how they vexed
This heart of mine! And yet I never
Had to endure anything like this.
The rest I got through when I set my mind to it.
Orestes, bless him, plagued the life out of me —
I had the rearing of him from his mother,
And all those times he got me up 800
By crying in the night — and what good did it ever
Do me? Babes are little animals,
They can't think for themselves, you have
To guess what they want, what else can you do?
The child in his cradle doesn't have the words
To tell us if he's hungry, if he's thirsty,
Or wants to wet; no arguing
With young insides. I needed second sight,
And I was often wrong, believe me, and had to be
His washerwoman too. Feed him, clean up after him, 810
It was all the same job, and I
Doubled these offices, ever since I took
Orestes from his father's hands; and now
He's dead, they say; so much the worse for me.
Well, I must go to find the man who ruined
This house, and he'll be glad enough to hear it.
CHORUS. Did she say he was to come in state?
CILISSA. Say that again, so I may catch your meaning.
CHORUS. With his bodyguard, or by himself?
CILISSA. She told him to bring his servants armed — 820
CHORUS. Then as you hate your master, do not tell him this.
Say he must come alone, so his informants
May talk without constraint. Bid him hurry
And be of good heart. It is the messenger
Who takes the crooked word and makes it straight.
CILISSA. But are you happy over what I told you?
CHORUS. And if Zeus means to send a wind
To blow away foul weather?
CILISSA.   How?
Orestes is dead; the house has lost its hope.
CHORUS. Not yet. He would be a poor diviner 830
Who traced things so.
CILISSA.   What do you mean?
Do you know something we have not been told?
CHORUS. Go with your message, do as you are bid.
The gods will take care of their own affairs.

CILISSA. I'll go, and do as you have told me;
  And heaven grant it turn out for the best!

                          (*Exit.*)

CHORUS. Grant this my prayer, O Zeus
  The godhead, father of Olympus,
  That those who long to see
  This mansion set to rights may have their hope   840
  Accomplished; what I have said
  Is nothing if not just, O Zeus;
  Do you enforce it.

    O Zeus, rank him who now
  Is in the house above his enemies.
  For if you raise him to eminence
  Two and threefold will he repay you,
  Zeus, and cheerfully.

    For be advised, this colt,
  The orphan of a man much loved,   850
  Is harnessed in the chariot
  Of suffering; and you must set a measure
  To the course, so we may never
  See him break step, but extend himself
  Full tilt across the ground.

    O Zeus, rank him who now
  Is in the house above his enemies.
  For if you raise him to eminence
  Two and threefold will he repay you,
  Zeus, and cheerfully.   860

    And you that haunt the inner sanctum of the house
  In pride of wealth, O gods
  That think as we do, hear us.
  Come, rid us of this bloody stain
  Of things done in olden time.
  Make manifest your justice, let
  Old murder breed in the house no more.

    And you who live
  At the mouthpiece of the world

_____

869. *the mouthpiece of the world:* the meaning of this whole passage is obscure; probably Apollo's shrine at Delphi is meant.

Grant to those who fell in glory
This kindness, that they may look up again
To the house of a hero, and that eyes of love
May see it as a beacon shining, free
From enshrouding shadows.

And let the son of Maia give us fitting aid
For he is mightiest
To give a deed fair passage
If so he will, for many a time
He deigns to make the dark word plain
Or wraps the eyes in shadows, speaking   880
Riddles that no clearer come by daylight.

And you who live
At the mouthpiece of the world
Grant to those who fell in glory
This kindness, that they may look up again
To the house of a hero, and that eyes of love
May see it as a beacon shining, free
From enshrouding shadows.

Then at last will the house be rid
Of double evil; with united voice   890
We shall speed the work, as women may,
Break out the mourning song, and sing
"The ship sails fair."
Mine, mine to reap the argosy, and wreck
Is far from my beloved.

When the time comes for doing, be
Stoutedhearted; when she calls
"My child," shout her down
With cry of "Father," and act
The sin that is grace, her murder.   900

And with Orestes' mind combine
The heart of Perseus; for your friends
On earth and under it, perform
This favor, though it sting you sore.

875. *the Son of Maia:* Hermes.
902. *Perseus:* mythical hero who killed the Gorgon, she-monster with hair
of snakes whose glance turned men to stone.

Let death and blood
Run wild within, and bring upon the man
Who killed, a death in punishment.

(*Enter* AEGISTHUS.)

AEGISTHUS. I do but as they bid me, and am come
In answer to the message. There are people
Lodging here, they say, who tell a tale   910
We never hoped to hear, the death
Of Orestes. This house has wounds still raw
From bloodshed long ago; now must it take
Another burden on itself, a thing
Of running blood? What can I make of this?
The living truth? The terrified imaginings
Of women make bubble-tales that burst
Upon the air. Can you say anything
Of this, to make me certain in my mind?
CHORUS. We heard the same. But go in to the travellers   920
And let them tell you. It is better always
To go to the source than learn secondhand.
AEGISTHUS. Yes, I should like to see this messenger
And ask if he was with him when he died
Or speaks the words of groping rumor only.
The mind must have an eye for trickery.

(*Exit.*)

CHORUS. Zeus, Zeus, what shall I say? And where begin
My prayer for the gods' aid?
How, before the ending, find
Words worthy of my will?   930
For now the bloody cutting-edge
Comes close, to rend a man.
Now in the house of Agamemnon
Will he bring ruin upon all
Or light the fire of liberty again
And in the kingdom of his father
Live rich, the honored son.
To such a wrestle must Orestes come
The challenger, by the gods' advisement
One against two; and may he throw them!   940

(*A cry within.*)

Ah, what is that?
What has happened in the house?
Let us stand aside till the work is finished

So there may come no blame on us all
In this foul business, for the fight
Is at an end.

(*Enter* SERVANT *from the palace.*)

SERVANT. Cry desolation, for our lord is dead,
And cry again, a triple cry of sorrow!
Aegisthus is gone. Come, no delay;
Open the portals of the women's chambers,   950
Slide back the bolts; we need young strength
To fight for us, a man, but not for him
Who is dead and gone; no purpose there.
Ahoy, ahoy!
I call on the deaf, on those who lie
In idle slumber and do nothing. Where
Is Clytemnestra, what does she do now?
Her head is on the block, and soon
Must fall, in measure as she did to others.

(*Enter* CLYTEMNESTRA.)

CLYTEMNESTRA. What is this? What means this shouting in the
    house?   960
SERVANT. Listen to me. The dead are killing the living.
CLYTEMNESTRA. You speak in riddles, but I read you well.
By sleight we killed, by sleight we are to die.
Come, hurry, bring an axe to kill a man.

(*Exit* SERVANT.)

Let us make certain, then. It must be he or I,
So far have I come now in this sad history.

(*Enter* ORESTES *with a drawn sword,* PYLADES *beside him.*)

ORESTES. You are the one I seek. His part is played.
CLYTEMNESTRA. Are you dead, my love? Is brave Aegisthus
    gone?
ORESTES. You love that man? Then in one tomb you shall
    Be buried, and be faithful after death.   970
CLYTEMNESTRA. Hold back, my son, have pity on this breast
    My child, where often slumbering
    You lay, and suckled milk to make you strong.
ORESTES. Pylades, what shall I do? How may I kill my mother?
PYLADES. What of the oracles still unfulfilled
    Apollo spoke at Delphi? Your sworn promise?
    Better the world should hate you than the gods.

ORESTES. Your world has won. You show the way that I must
    go.

(*To* CLYTEMNESTRA.)

Come in, for I would kill you on his body.
In life you thought him better than my father;   980
Then sleep with him in death, if such you love
And give to him whom you should love your hate.

CLYTEMNESTRA. You took my youth. May I not share your age?

ORESTES. You killed my father. Would you share my house?

CLYTEMNESTRA. The blame is Destiny's as well as mine.

ORESTES. Then it is Destiny who kills you now.

CLYTEMNESTRA. Have you no terror of a mother's curse?

ORESTES. You bore me and then cast me out to sorrow.

CLYTEMNESTRA. To live with friends. This was no casting out.

ORESTES. I was born of a free father and you sold me.   990

CLYTEMNESTRA. Then where is the price that I received for you?

ORESTES. I could not bring myself to tell you shame.

CLYTEMNESTRA. Tell all, but tell your father's follies too.

ORESTES. Blame not him. He toiled, you sat at home.

CLYTEMNESTRA. Women suffer when the man is gone, my child.

ORESTES. Man's labor feeds the women who sit idle.

CLYTEMNESTRA. My child, I think you mean to kill your mother.

ORESTES. I will not kill you. You will kill yourself.

CLYTEMNESTRA. Take care. Your mother's curse will hound you
    down.

ORESTES. My father's curse will find me if I fail.   1000

CLYTEMNESTRA. This is the serpent that I bore and fed.

ORESTES. Indeed the terror of your dreams spoke true.
    You sinned in killing. Now be sinned against.

(ORESTES *and* PYLADES *drive* CLYMNESTRA *into the house.*)

CHORUS. Even for these I can find tears, and for
    Their coupled death. But since Orestes has been bold
    To top this long and bloody history
    We find it better that the light within
    The house not be extinguished utterly.

    In time there came to the sons of Priam
    Justice heavy in punishment   1010
    And on the house of Agamemnon came
    The lions paired to battle two.
    Then pressed he to the uttermost, the exile
    To whom god had spoken, eager
    Under heaven's admonition.

Cry joy now for the mansions of our lords,
The end of pain, the end of rich things wasted
By two in infamy, the dark days gone.

He came; and his part was to deceive,
To scheme and conquer. In the fight   1020
His hand was guided by the very child
Of Zeus — we mortals know her name
As Justice, and we have good cause —
She who in a blast of hate
Comes on her foes destroying.

Cry joy now for the mansions of our lords,
The end of pain, the end of rich things wasted
By two in infamy, the dark days gone.

As Apollo spoke from his deep-riven
Cavern on Parnassus, so   1030
Has it passed; the innocent deceit
Comes home to fight harm grown old.
Divinity has ways to keep
From going down to evil; it is fit
That we should laud the powers that reign in heaven.

Now is there light to see, the bit
Is gone that held our house so hard.
So up, you halls, arise; for time
Too long have you lain fallen.

Not long, and Time that brings all   1040
To pass will enter in
Our gates, when the evil presence
Is cast from our hearth, and ceremonies
Have made all clean; then chance
Will come up ever fair for those
Who take their lodging here in aftertime.

Now is there light to see, the bit
Is gone that held our house so hard.
So up, you halls, arise; for time
Too long have you lain fallen.   1050

(*The doors open.* ORESTES *is seen standing sword in hand over
the bodies of* CLYTEMNESTRA *and* AEGISTHUS. *He holds the robe
in which* AGAMEMNON *was killed.*)

ORESTES. See here the double lordship of this land
  Who killed my father and laid waste my house.
  A while they sat upon their thrones in state,
  And they are lovers still, as you may judge
  By what befell; their oath has kept its promise.
  Together they swore to kill my wretched father
  And die together; they are not forsworn.

                    (*Displaying* AGAMEMNON'S *robe*.)

  See too, all you who look on this sad story,
  The trick they used to bind my wretched father,
  Chains for his hands, a halter for his feet.   1060
  Come, spread it out and make a circle round
  To show this net to catch a man.
  So may the father see — I mean not mine,
  But he who watches every living thing,
  The Sun — my mother's filthy handiwork.
  So at the judgement day, whenever it shall come,
  He may appear to testify
  That I had just cause to pursue the death
  Of this my mother. On Aegisthus' death
  I waste no words. It is written, adulterers   1070
  Shall be punished — but she who worked so vile a thing
  Against her man, whose children she conceived
  And bore beneath her cincture, sweet load once,
  Now this you see, a curse, a thing of hate —
  What do you think her now? A water-snake, a viper
  Who needs no fangs, whose very touch
  Will rot a man, so venomous
  Her mind, so quick to strike . . .
  And this, what shall I call it? Has it any name
  That one may say with decency? A snare   1080
  To catch an animal, a winding sheet,
  A tenting for the bath? A net, a skein
  We well could say, a robe to hobble feet —
  The sort of thing a cozener might use
  Who lived by catching travellers and robbing them
  Of money; such a trick as this
  Would win him many victims, and would keep
  His heart warm inside him. . . .
  May such a woman never come to share
  My home and bed; may heaven first destroy me,   1090
  Before I have begotten me a child.

CHORUS. Sing sorrow for things done:
  For you a hateful death, and for the one
  Who lives, the ripening of pain.

ORESTES. Did she do this or not? This mantle testifies
  That it was dyed red by Aegisthus' sword.
  Dip it and dip again, and still
  The stain of blood and its accomplice, Time,
  Have spoilt the work. Now I can praise him, now
  Make lamentation over him; and when   1100
  I speak to this, the robe that killed my father,
  I sorrow for the doing and the death,
  For all our race, the tainted prize
  Of this, my inconsiderable conquest.

CHORUS. No mortal man can live his life
  Through to the end untouched by suffering.
  There is trouble here, and more to come.

ORESTES. But hear me now; I cannot see the end;
  My chariot has run me from the course,
  My rebel senses lead me where they will,   1110
  While fear draws breath to sing within my heart
  And it must dance to his angry tune. While I
  Have wits about me still, I call upon my friends
  To hear. I killed my mother, but I say
  There was some right in this; my father's blood
  Had tainted her, she was a thing unclean
  In heaven's sight.
  And for the blandishments that made me bold
  To such a deed, I cite as culpable
  Apollo, seer of Delphi, who proclaimed in oracles   1120
  That I could do this thing and still
  Be innocent; but if I failed —
  What then would come on me I will not say.
  Draw bow at hazard, you would never
  Come within measure of my suffering.

          (He arrays himself as a suppliant.)

See me how I go forth, with wreath
Upon my head, with branch in hand,
To the centrestone of earth, Apollo's seat
And holy shrine, that famous place
Whose fire burns everlasting; I will go   1130
Out from my own, from blood that is my own;

1126. *wreath, branch:* customary emblems of the suppliant.

Apollo charged me that I should not turn
To any other sanctuary but his.
To all who live in Argos in the future time
I say remember how these evil things were done
And speak for me when Menelaus comes.
And I shall go on an outcast from my land
To walk among strangers, and leave behind
In life, in death, this memory of me.

CHORUS. What you did was well. Do not let foul speech   1140
Harness your mouth, or turn your tongue to evil.
For you brought liberty to all who live
In Argos, when you came upon
This pair of snakes and cut their heads off clean.

(ORESTES *points and cries out*.)

ORESTES. O servants of this house, they come
In shapes of Gorgons, clad in robes of black,
Their hair a nest of snakes; I cannot stay!

CHORUS. If any man has earned a father's love
You are the one; so what imaginings
Are these, that send you reeling? Stay,   1150
Behold, you have good cause.

ORESTES. I suffer, these are no imaginings
But real; the hounding of my mother's hate.

CHORUS. It is the blood still wet on your hands
That comes on you now to shake your senses.

ORESTES. O Lord Apollo, are they coming yet?
They weep, their eyes are running foul with blood.

CHORUS. There is one way to purify yourself. Apollo
Will lay his hands on you, and make you free
Of this affliction.   1160

ORESTES. You do not see them, but I see them.
I must go forth, I can stay here no longer.

(*Exit.*)

CHORUS. Good luck go with you, then, and may the god
Look kindly on you, and preserve you safe
In fortune.
Now for the third time

1136. *Menelaus:* Agamemnon's brother.
1146. *Gorgons:* Orestes sees the Furies advancing on him, still invisible to
the chorus. They were traditionally represented as women with hair of
snakes and carrying blazing torches—thus resembling the Gorgons, to whom
Orestes compares them. See note on v. 902.

Has storm come from the race, to blow
Upon the palace of our kings, and passed.
One was the child-feast,
The grief and desolation of Thyestes.   1170
Two was the death of kings, when the lord
Of the Achaean host was struck
Down in the bath.
Three was the coming of the savior
Or death — which shall I call it?
When will there be an ending, when
Will wrath be spent, and fate lulled to slumber?   1177

◇ ◇ ◇

STUDY AIDS

Prologue (lines 1–22)

1. Note how swiftly the play begins. In Orestes' opening lines, we
meet the protagonist, learn through exposition of the death of
Agamemnon, encounter the chorus of mourning women accompanied
by Electra, and hear Orestes swear vengeance for the murder of his
father. Aeschylus wastes no time before gaining our attention. How
does the use of a prologue such as this compare with other techniques
for beginning plays?

Parados (lines 23–81)

1. Note how the choral speech suggests that a pall of guilt and
fear hangs over the house of Agamemnon. Note that the chorus
attaches importance to dreams. Dreams were considered important
prophetic instruments by the Greeks. What is Aeschylus accomplish-
ing in these allusions?

2. The chorus tells us that dead men hold grudges. How does this
statement contribute to a note of foreshadowing and the beginning
of suspense?

3. Mood is created by reference to blood-soaked ground, a sunless
world in which men fear to walk. Why would such lines provide a
helpful aid to Greek audiences of the fifth century B.C.?

First Episode (lines 82–330)

1. Electra appears to be confused and hesitant concerning what to

---

1169. *the child-feast:* Atreus, Agamemnon's father, had killed his brother
Thyestes' children and served them up as a feast.
1172. *Achaean:* Greek.

say in honoring the memory of her father. She has not, she declares, the daring to misrepresent her mother's character. How does her state of confusion aid in establishing her character? Does it underline a pathetic quality about her?

2. Does Electra's reliance upon the chorus for advice serve to weaken her as a character? How does it serve to heighten the function of the chorus? What advice does the chorus offer Electra? How does it contribute to the theme of vengeance which is so important in the play? You will want to read the entire *Oresteia* trilogy to follow Aeschylus' thinking concerning this matter.

3. Electra prays to Hermes for pity for Orestes and herself. What is the effect of such a plea? Does the plight of Electra and Orestes suggest that the innocent must unfairly suffer for the wrongdoing of the guilty?

4. What does Electra's reference to Aegisthus and Clytemnestra tell us about these two? What is the effect upon us of Electra's plea for vengeance?

5. In his *Electra* play Euripides ridicules Aeschylus' recognition scene. Remember this when you read the later play. At present, do you find the scene unduly contrived or genuinely touching? Is coincidence over-employed through the use of both the lock of hair and the footprints? In view of the larger goals in which the playwright is interested, is the use of incredible coincidence a flaw?

6. Does Orestes' plea to Zeus add to the pathos with which we view his and Electra's situation?

7. Orestes declares he was urged by the oracle of Apollo to avenge his father's murder. Read *The Eumenides* again to discover where this advice leads. Can you cite other Greek plays in which oracles were heard? Why did the Greeks pay attention to oracles?

First Stasimon (*lines 331–426*)

1. Chanting at the grave of Agamemnon, the chorus, Orestes, and Electra dedicate themselves to an act of vengeance. Orestes' determination is fixed. What effect has the chanting and her participation in it had upon Electra? Is the change we perceive in her convincing? Has it been justified by the prayers and vows preceding it?

2. Does the first stasimon contribute anything to the play beyond revealing Electra's altered attitude and reaffirming Orestes' resolutions?

Second Episode (*lines 427–621*)

1. Clytemnestra's dream is horrible. For that very reason why is it appropriate? Is Orestes' interpretation of the dream convincing? How does he use the dream to justify his intended murder?

2. The second episode concludes on a note of tension. Why does Electra vanish at this point in the play?

Second Stasimon (lines 622–682)

1. What comment do these lines make on the existence of evil in the world? To what lengths may misguided passion drive a woman? How does the stasimon conclude on a positive note?

Third Episode (lines 683–836)

1. When Clytemnestra is told that Orestes is dead, she conceals her elation by pretended remorse. Does her self-control help explain how she could be an accomplice to the murder of her husband?

2. Nurses frequently appear in the classic drama, usually serving as confidantes to whom leading characters impart important information, which the audience is privileged to overhear. On other occasions, as in the case of Cilissa, the nurse gives the audience information about the world of the play and its people. Analyze Cilissa's lengthy speech with reference to what we learn about her position in the house of Atreus and particularly, at the moment, about the way she predicts Aegisthus will receive the news of Orestes' presumed death.

Third Stasimon (lines 837–907)

1. This stasimon reiterates the desire of the chorus to deny a shred of mercy to Clytemnestra and Aegisthus. Does the chorus's support of Orestes suggest a widespread acceptance of the law of retribution, of what the Bible called "an eye for an eye and a tooth for a tooth"?

Fourth Episode (lines 908–1003)

1. Aegisthus expresses the wish to interview the messenger concerning the report of Orestes' death. Does his request add a note of suspense to the scene?

2. The killing of Aegisthus off stage conforms to Greek custom in the handling of bloodshed in the theatre. Does loss or gain result from failing to show killings on stage? If you answer gain, you might try to explain Shakespeare's willingness to avoid such restraint.

3. What is the effect of Orestes' hesitating to kill his mother?

4. In begging Orestes to spare her life, Clytemnestra claims that when she slew her husband she was the victim of fate. How mitigating do you consider this excuse?

Fourth Stasimon (lines 1004–1050)

1. What prophecy does the chorus make in this passage?

Exodus (lines 1051–1177)

1. What is the effect of displaying the robe in which Agamemnon

was slaughtered? What impact is realized through displaying the bodies of Clytemnestra and Aegisthus?

2. What is the effect of having Orestes declare it was Apollo who compelled him to kill Clytemnestra and Aegisthus? Does his excessive rationalization effectively foreshadow the dissolution of his mind?

TOPICS FOR DISCUSSION

1. The ethical problem of vengeance: is the blood feud moral? Clearly this question is the central one in the play.

2. The perpetuation of evil: one crime begets another, inflicting suffering upon the guilty and innocent alike. This factor, like others explored in the play, has current applicability, especially as one ponders contemporary concepts of justice, judgment, and punishment, along with the effect of environment and circumstance upon character and human conduct.

3. The subordination of character to theme in *The Libation Bearers*.

4. The subordination of action to dialogue. *The Libation Bearers* is primarily designed to provoke thought. The play also provides an element of suspense, but it is a secondary element.

5. Aeschylus' understanding of the human psyche as revealed in the final moments of the play: the madness of Orestes.

6. The dilemma of Orestes: if he obeys the oracle of Apollo he becomes guilty of matricide; if he ignores the oracle, along with the counsel of his friend Pylades and his sister Electra, he sacrifices honor and must eventually forfeit his own life.

7. The construction of the play. Aeschylus handles his story in a direct, swift manner, never becoming unduly involved in plot. The theme is always foremost.

SOPHOCLES

<><><><><><><><><><><><><><><><><><><><><><><><><><><>

THE *Electra* of Sophocles (ca. 497–405 B.C.) is a study of the dissolution of normal familial relationships. In a world rent by corruption, the consequent suffering coarsens human conduct, and the heroine, Electra, grows resolute to a fault. Murder must be avenged and, as in *Antigone*, a determined girl resists the blandishments of a prudent sister and a chorus who fruitlessly urge moderation and caution. Suspense and irony heighten the effectiveness of the Sophoclean *Electra*; religious and ethical significance is of less consequence than dramatic impact. Essentially a tragedy of character, the play perceptively explores the psychology and personality of a victim of hate that has been generated by an act of murder.

Emphasis upon the character of Electra underlines Sophocles' conviction that human nature is the chief causative factor in human suffering. The most successful of the Greek dramatists, Sophocles introduced old myths into new plays, employing the stuff of legend to make clear his conviction that arrogance begets retribution, that pride indeed precedes a fall. Of his approximately 125 plays, only seven are extant, but these reveal his skill in the construction of a tightly-knit plot, the dramatic use of suspense and irony, and the careful delineation of character. The Sophoclean hero is one of enormous strength, a figure who drives relentlessly toward the achievement of a goal, only to be vanquished by the sin of hubris or defeated by an error of judgment. Inevitably he must recognize the limitations to which all men are subject, for in the final analysis only the gods are supreme. Suffering induces wisdom, tragedy invites humility.

Interspersed among the heroic protagonists are men and women of average capacities, prudent people who supply cautious words to the moderate voices of reason. Predictably, their counsel goes unheeded by those blinded by their own arrogance.

Aside from his achievements as a playwright, Sophocles introduced.

the third actor into performance, possibly invented scene painting, and established the number of the tragic chorus at fifteen.

Critical studies of Sophocles include the following: S. M. Adams, *Sophocles the Playwright* (Toronto, 1957); W. N. Bates, *Sophocles, Poet and Dramatist* (Philadelphia, 1961); C. M. Bowra, *Sophoclean Tragedy* (Oxford, 1944); and T. B. L. Webster, *An Introduction to Sophocles* (Oxford, 1936); Sir George Young, *The Dramas of Sophocles* (New York, 1920); Richmond Lattimore, *The Complete Greek Tragedies*, Vol. II (Chicago, 1953). *Sophocles* (New Jersey, 1966), edited by Thomas Woodard includes a number of essays of considerable interest, two of them dealing exclusively with the *Electra*. The volume also includes a selected bibliography.

Electra

Translated by Francis Fergusson

◇ ◇ ◇

CHARACTERS

> PAIDAGOGOS
> ORESTES
> ELECTRA
> CHRYSOTHEMIS
> CLYTEMNESTRA
> AEGISTHOS
> CHORUS *of Mycenaean Women*

Scene: Mycenae, before the palace of Agamemnon.

   (*Dawn.* ORESTES, *the* PAIDAGOGOS, *and* PYLADES *are discovered.*)

PAIDAGOGOS. Child of that chief who led the army once in Troy,
  Son of Agamemnon, here before you lies
  For you to see, what you have longed to see.
  It is the ancient and beloved Argos,
  Refuge of Inachos' tormented daughter,
  Apollo the Wolfgod's forum. On that side
  Hera's familiar altar, and just before you
  Golden Mycenae you may see, Orestes,
  And that same murderous House of Pelops, whence
  Your sister snatched you from your father's killers,   10
  And brought you to me to guard, till you reached the age
  When you could avenge that father's murder.

But now, Orestes, and you Pylades,
We must decide at once what's to be done.
The sunlight already bright about us
Has started the early voices of the birds,
And the dark sky of stars has faded.
Before someone emerges from the house,
Come, lay your plans; this is no time to pause,
For you are on the verge of deeds.   20

ORESTES. Old friend,
How plainly you show your loyalty to me!
Even in these perils
You urge us on, and lead the way yourself.
I shall explain the plan. Listen acutely
And make corrections if I miss the mark.
When I resorted to the Pythian seer
To learn how I might best avenge my father
Upon his killers, Apollo answered,
With neither shield nor army, secretly   30
Your own just hand shall deal them their due pay.
With this advice in mind, friend, slip into the house
When you can find an opportunity;
See what goes on, then come report to us.
They won't suspect you; with the changes of time
You'll pass unknown. Tell some such tale as this:
You are a Phocian sent by Phanteus,
For he you know is their greatest ally.
Tell them on oath that you come to report
Orestes' death in a fatal accident;   40
Thrown, say, from his speeding chariot
At the Pythian Games: have this your story.
We meanwhile shall adorn my father's tomb
With our shorn hair and our wine offerings,
As Apollo ordered. We shall return
With that funeral urn we hid in the thicket,
A proof for them of the sweet tale we bring.
That I am already dust and ashes!
What harm is there for me in my rumored death
When I am alive in deed and gaining fame?   50

But you fathergods, and gods of the country:
O House of my Fathers, on these new paths
Receive me kindly! At the god's urging,
With justice, I come to purify you.

May this land not reject me in dishonor,
But take me in, to make it flourish again.

We have said enough. You go at once, old friend,
And do as I explained. We shall depart,
Obeying Time, which rules all difficult deeds.

(*Wail inside the palace.*)

PAIDAGOGOS. I thought I heard a servant cry indoors.   60
ORESTES. The wretched Electra, can it be?
Shall we wait to hear what she is wailing?
PAIDAGOGOS. No. Not till we try to do as the god said,
And pour our lustral offerings to your father.
We must start with that, for that will give us
Control and victory in the present action.

(*Exeunt* ORESTES, PYLADES *and the* PAIDAGOGOS. *Enter* ELECTRA
from the palace.)

ELECTRA. O daylight,
O air, the sheath of earth,
How you have shaken with mourning,
And you have felt   70
The breast beaten for grief
At the hour of night's going.
Ah, it is with shame I lie
In that house, mourning all night
My father's wretched death.
No far-off wargod killed him,
My mother with her lover, with
Cruel Aegisthos, axe to oak,
Brought down his head.
In your house no wailing   80
But mine, Father,
For such perishing.

But I will not stop wailing
While I can see the stars glittering,
Or this day.
So a bird cries with her young lost,
And I scream at my father's doors.
O dark House, Persephone's,
O earthy Hermes, and you grave
Furies, you are aware   90
Of murders and adulteries.

Come! Help! Avenge
My father's murder!
Send me my brother!
I begin to sink
Under my trouble.

(*Enter the* CHORUS *of Mycenaean women. Here begins the
Kommos, or lament sung by actor and chorus.*)

CHORUS. Ah Electra, child. Child
Of godless mother. Will you
Still waste for Agamemnon, long since
Guile-snared by that mother, by her delivered   100
Into the hand of the killer? So may she be
To death delivered. This I dare to pray.

ELECTRA. Gentle women,
You come to comfort me.
This I know, but I can never,
But I will never
Stop mourning my father dead.
You, in your love,
Abandon me to grief,
Only this I crave.   11·

CHORUS. But you shall never bring him back with
Prayers and weeping from
The common marsh of death: but in that helpless grief
You waste away, your evils are
Unsolved in these tears.
Why then do you feed your misery?

ELECTRA. Those heads are weak that cannot hold
The death of parents.
But I have set my heart
With that bewildered bird who tells the god,   12·
Crying *Ityn, Ityn* all night. Ah Niobe,
Unfortunate you are, yet blessed
To weep in stone.

CHORUS. But you are not alone unlucky
Among mortals, child: your kin
Chrysothemis and
Iphianassa are so, and that one
Whose youth is hidden, whose sufferings covered, whom
The Mycenaean land is to receive,
When the god sends him, as   130
The King: Orestes.

ELECTRA. Him I expect without rest,

Being unwed and childless,
Having my grief, and a fruitlessly evil lot.
Whatever he hears he forgets, or else
Why should he not come as he says?
He longs to, but his longings fall short.
CHORUS. Take heart, child, take heart.
Still in the sky
Great Zeus sees everything, and rules. 140
Give over your anger to him,
Neither forgetting, nor hating too much.
Time is an easy god:
Here by the pasture,
Here by the beach of Krisa,
Agamemnon's child will not be iron forever;
No more will the god who rules by Acheron.
ELECTRA. But most of life has slipped by,
And will not come to me again.
As one whom no parents bore, 150
One whom no man cherishes,
As a stranger and a beggar in my father's house,
Meanly clothed:
So I wait here by the empty board.
CHORUS. With a terrible cry,
Agamemnon met
The murdering edge
In his own bed.
Figure of horror, the issue
Of pleasure and slyness, whether 160
Some god or a mortal the maker.
ELECTRA. That was my bitterest day: that night
The unspeakable supper was like death for me:
Feast when my father perished at the hands
That were to take my life away.
For them, O god, provide your punishments,
Never enjoyment of their work's fruits.
CHORUS. Stop. Stop speaking so.
Can you not think how you distract yourself,
Make yourself pitifully fail? 170
You increase your troubles when you breed
War in your gloomy soul;
There's no fighting the strong.
ELECTRA. I know I am horror-forced,
And anger will not let me go.

But I will not hold back
So long as I live.
Ah kindly women, from whom shall I hear ever
The good word in season?
Leave me, friends,   180
Call this trouble issueless.
So shall I hold my lamentations ceaselessly.
LEADER. I speak in kindness, as a faithful mother:
Do not feed your frenzy.
ELECTRA. But where is the end of this evil?
Where do they dare to forget the dead,
Among what peoples? There may I be
Unhonored. Or if I ever wed good fortune,
Nesting in peace, still may I never fold
The sharp wings of the wailing due my father.   190
If the dead are dust and nothing,
If they lie disregarded,
If they are never given
Their due for murder,
Then fear and piety are utterly gone
From among us mortals
LEADER. I came for your sake as well as mine, my child.
If my words are wrong, do as you wish,
I follow you still.
ELECTRA. My friends, I am ashamed, you think I mourn too much.   200
But bear with me, since I have no choice;
What alternative for one who sees the evil?
And I see it, night and day I see it,
Not diminishing, growing. My own mother
Hates me, I live with my father's killers
And obey them; from them I receive the means of life,
Or perish. And that life: do you suppose
It is sweet to me to have to see Aegisthos
In my father's seat, wearing my father's clothes,
Pouring libations at the hearth   210
Where he brought my father down? When I see
The final insolence accomplished: in my mother's bed
(If I must call her mother) my father's killer?
And she is so calloused, so hardened
With the disease itself, that she fears nothing.
Now she celebrates her work, remembers
The day of the month when with guile she killed him,
To offer the housegods sacrifice and dance.

But I, watching, keep under cover,
Bewail the bitter feast day of my father.   220
Yet I cannot wail as I would, for she
Attacks me: "Ungodly, ugly girl!
Are you the only one whose father died,
The only miserable mortal? May you sink to Hell,
And the gods of Hell not stop your wailing!"
So she screams till she hears that Orestes is coming.
Then she will shout in my ear, "Did you do this?
Is this your work, you who stole Orestes from me?
But you shall pay for everything!"
So she screams, and behind her, egging her on,   230
Her lover, that illustrious weakling,
That loud talker, that female fighter!
But I, waiting for Orestes to bring relief,
I begin to fail. He drains my hope,
My hope of hope, with his delaying.
Here is neither wisdom nor piety, my friends,
But evils, which force me to evil.

LEADER. Tell me, is Aegisthos near? Or has he left the house?
ELECTRA. He has left, of course. How should I be out,
If he were near?   240
LEADER. If he is away, then,
I may speak further with you?
ELECTRA. Yes, you may speak.
LEADER. Let me enquire about your brother.
Is he coming? Delaying? I must know.
ELECTRA. He says he is coming but does not come.
LEADER. A man with a great work likes to delay.
ELECTRA. When I saved him I did not delay.
LEADER. Take courage. He is the man to help those he loves.
ELECTRA. I trust him, or I should not still be alive.   250
LEADER. Hush for now, hush.
Chrysothemis is at the door, your own sister.
She is bringing offerings for the gods of the dead.

(*Enter* CHRYSOTHEMIS *with offerings. She comes from the palace.*)

CHRYSOTHEMIS. Sister, what are you proclaiming out here at the
door?
Won't you learn, after all this time,
Not to pamper a helpless anger?
And you must know that I too suffer

And that if I had the strength
I too should show them what I think of them.
But in foul weather I lower my sails,   260
I never threaten when I am helpless.
If you would only do the same! . . . Well,
What I say is immoral, of course,
And you are right. And yet, if I am to breathe freely,
I must listen to what they say.

ELECTRA. Horrible; the own child of such a father
And you forget him for that mother!
Your moralizing of course is from her,
None of it yours. Well, choose: either be foolish,
Or else be very prudent, and forget   270
Those who have been dear to you. Consider:
You say you'd show your hatred if you had the strength,
But you give me no help, though I am given
Completely to the cause of vengeance; you dissuade me even.
So we must be cowards too in our misery?
But tell me, what should I gain by silence?
Or I'll tell you. Have I life now? Little;
And yet enough, for I harrow them
To the honor of the dead, if the dead know honor;
While you are a hater in word only,   280
Living in deed with your father's killers.
I would not yield so —
If they offered me everything that you enjoy,
I would not so yield. For you,
Let the tables of life be richly spread.
Let them overflow. For my sole pasturage
I would be unoffending, I do not crave
Your honors — nor would you, if you were wise.
You might have been your father's: be your mother's:
Belong to her who everyone knows is evil,   290
The betrayer of your dying father and your own kin!

LEADER. By the fear of the gods, no anger!
If you will learn from her, and she from you,
You may still profit from these words.

CHRYSOTHEMIS. I am accustomed to what she says, my friends,
And I should never have approached her now,
Had I not heard of a greater misfortune coming
To end her mourning.

ELECTRA. What? Tell me of a greater
And I say no more.   300

CHRYSOTHEMIS. I'll tell you all I heard.
Unless you stop wailing, they will send you in
Where you cannot see the light of the sun:
Far away and under a low roof
You shall sing your sorrows. Think, therefore;
Do not blame me later, when you suffer,
But think in time.
ELECTRA. And this they really plan?
CHRYSOTHEMIS. At once; as soon as Aegisthos returns.
ELECTRA. Well then, let him come soon. 310
CHRYSOTHEMIS. What, are you mad?
ELECTRA. If that's what he intends, let him come soon!
CHRYSOTHEMIS. To bring you suffering? What are you think-
ing of?
ELECTRA. Of escaping you all.
CHRYSOTHEMIS. Your life here
Means nothing to you?
ELECTRA. How beautiful it is!
CHRYSOTHEMIS. It might have been if you had learned wisdom.
ELECTRA. Teach me no treachery to those I love.
CHRYSOTHEMIS. I don't. I teach you to yield to the strong. 320
ELECTRA. Go. Fawn. Fawn on the strong. I cannot.
CHRYSOTHEMIS. Still, it would be well not to fall through *folly*.
ELECTRA. I will fall — if I must, to honor my father.
CHRYSOTHEMIS. But you know that our father understands.
ELECTRA. That's what traitors say.
CHRYSOTHEMIS. Then you will not listen
To what *I* say?
ELECTRA. No. I have my wits still.
CHRYSOTHEMIS. Then I shall go about my own business.
ELECTRA. Where are you going? For whom are those offerings? 330
CHRYSOTHEMIS. My mother sent me with them to our father's
grave.
ELECTRA. What, to the grave of her mortal enemy?
CHRYSOTHEMIS. Of the man she slaughtered, as you like to say.
ELECTRA. From whom or what did that inspiration come?
CHRYSOTHEMIS. From something she saw in the night, I think.
ELECTRA. O fathergods! Come! Help!
CHRYSOTHEMIS. Do you take courage
From her fear?
ELECTRA. If you would tell me what she saw,
I should answer that. 340
CHRYSOTHEMIS. I know very little to tell.

ELECTRA. But tell me, tell! It is the little things
  By which we rise or fall.
CHRYSOTHEMIS. They say
  She saw our father with her in the light of day.
  On the hearth he was, planting his sceptre
  Which Aegisthos holds now. From that sceptre grew
  A swelling branch which brought at last
  The whole land of Mycenae under its shadow.
  This I heard   350
  From one who heard her tell her dream to the sun.
  It is all I know
  Except that it was in fear she sent me.
  Now, by the gods I beg you, listen! Don't fall through folly!
  It will be the worse for you if you push me away!
ELECTRA. Sister, let none of these things touch his tomb.
  It is against piety, against wisdom,
  To offer our father gifts from that woman.
  Give them to the wind, or bury them deep in the dust
  Where they can never reach our father's bed;   360
  When she is dead, there let her find them.
  Only a woman of brass, an iron woman,
  Would offer her murder victim gifts.
  Do you suppose the dead man would receive them gladly?
  From her who killed him in dishonor and cruelty,
  After mutilation washing the bloodstained head
  To cleanse herself of murder? No! Throw them away,
  And cut a lock of hair from your head and one from mine,
  And give him also this poor thing, all I have,
  This plain and unembroidered belt; then fall on your knees   370
  And pray that a helper may rise for us
  Out of the earth, against our enemies: pray
  That the young Orestes may come in his strength
  To trample them underfoot, so that with fuller hands than
    these
  We may make offering. I think, I think
  It was he who sent this dream, prophetic of evil.
  Therefore help yourself in this, my sister,
  And me, and him, the dearest mortal:
  Our father lying underground.
LEADER. This girl speaks wisely. You, my friend,   380
  If you are prudent, will do as she requests.
CHRYSOTHEMIS. I will. For it is right to join for action,
  Not wrangle back and forth. But in the name of the gods,

Let there be silence among you, friends,
While I make this effort! If my mother hears,
I shall have bitter things to endure.

(*Exit* CHRYSOTHEMIS.)

CHORUS. If I am not an utterly false diviner
Bereft of mind,
I am inspired
By Dike, bringing justice with power.   390
She is coming, my child, coming in no long time!
My courage
Rises, when
I hear this dream.
Your father, King of the Greeks, did not forget,
Nor did that double-edged bronze-headed axe
That struck him miserably down to shame.

Comes on many feet the many-handed
Bronze-shod Fury,
Terrible from ambush.   400
The godless conjunctions of that mating,
Murder-dabbled, have received no blessing.
Therefore never,
Never in vain
Has this sign come,
To the doers and their helpers! Portents for mortals
Are neither in terrible dreams nor in marvels,
If this night vision is not full of boded good.

Ah Pelops! Your ancient
Chariot racing   410
Has proved unrelenting
To this, our land.
Since Myrtilos was hurled
From his golden car
To an Ocean bed;
Uprooted cruelly, thrown:
Slain with treachery, slain:
Ever,
Ever with us at home
Suffering and shame.   420

(*Enter* CLYTEMNESTRA *from the palace. She is followed by a
servant girl bearing an offering of fruits.*)

CLYTEMNESTRA. I see you have twisted loose again.
Aegisthos is gone, who always keeps you in
Where you cannot revile your kin publicly.
With him away you do not fear me,
For you have often enough informed the city
That I was a tyrant, lost to all justice,
Outraging you and yours. But it is not I
Who am insolent, I only answer you.
Your father, only he, has been your pretext,
Because I killed him. I killed him: quite clearly   430
I say this, for I cannot deny it.
But Justice seized him also, not I alone;
And you would have helped too, had you been wise.
Because that man who you still cry for
Was the one Greek who could bear to sacrifice
Your sister. He had not suffered as I had;
He sowed her, and I bore her. So be it.
But tell me why, tell me for whom, he killed her?
For the Argives, you say? But for them
He had no right to offer up my child.   440
Or was it for his brother Menelaos
My child was slain, and I am not to claim justice?
Did he not himself have two children,
Who rather should have died, since for *their* parents' sake
That voyage was undertaken?
Or had the world of the dead a special craving
To feast, not on their child, but on mine only?
Or did your miserable father lack love
For my child, while tender to Menelaos'?
Choice of an evil and foolish father.   450
So I believe, and so, though you disagree, I say;
So the dead girl would say, if she were here.
I do not grieve for these things done;
Blame me for them, if you think me wrong
When you can hold your own judgment even.
ELECTRA. This time you will not say that it was I
Who started or probed you for these painful things.
But if you allow me, I shall speak the truth,
About the dead man and about my sister.
CLYTEMNESTRA. I do allow you. If you had always spoken so   460
I could have listened without pain.
ELECTRA. Then I shall speak. You say you killed my father:
What word more hideous than that avowal,

Wherever justice lay? But I shall show
That you killed against justice, in depraved obedience
To the man with whom you are united now.

For what offense did Artemis-who-hunts-to-hounds
Hold all the winds still, there in Aulis?
I'll tell you: my father once (or so I heard it),
Playing within the goddess' sacred grove,   470
Startled an antlered deer with dappled skin,
Boasted that he had killed it.
At that the maiden Artemis grew angry,
And held the Greeks back till my father paid,
With the sacrifice of his child, for her stag.
Such was the sacrifice: there was no other way
To loose the fleet, either toward home or Troy.
And so, against his will, constrained, with pain,
He gave her up; not for his brother's sake.

But say I'm wrong and you are right,   480
Say he offered her up for Menelaos' sake,
Must *you* then murder him? And by what law?
Take care, or in issuing this decree
You issue yourself remorse and punishment.
For if a killer merits death,
You must die next, to satisfy that justice.
Take care, you offer lies for pretexts.

And now if you will tell me besides
Why you accept the shameful fruits of your labors;
Sleep with the very murderer with whom   490
You brought my father down; bear children to him,
Reject your decent children decently born?
Must I approve? Or will you say
That all of this is vengeance for your daughter?
An ugly pretext: because of a daughter
To join with a mortal enemy in marriage!
But there is no convincing you, you only scream
That I am being insolent to my mother.
Tyrant I call you, no less than mother,
For under you and your lover   500
I live in misery, while your other child, Orestes,
Barely escaped you, and now wastes in exile.
You say I raised him up to plague you;

I did, I would, I will if I can, be sure of that;
And therefore if you wish, you may call me
Foul-mouthed and impious.
For I am close to you, close to your nature.
LEADER. I see she breathes anger, and whether she is just,
No more concerns her.
CLYTEMNESTRA. Then what attention should she receive,   510
Attacking her mother, old as she is!
Do you think she would wince from any horror?
ELECTRA. I have not lost all sense of shame,
Though you think so. I understand that I
Am lost, that I am beyond the pale.
But it is your heartlessness that forces me;
Crime is quickly learned from crime.
CLYTEMNESTRA. A monstrous nursling! She preaches on me
As her text; on what I do, on what I say!
ELECTRA. It is you who talk. It is your deeds that talk.   520
Even in my words it is your deeds that talk!
CLYTEMNESTRA. Artemis! Queen! Witness! When Aegisthos
comes
She shall diminish this impudence!
ELECTRA. Do you see?
Having given me leave to say what I would
She will not listen.
CLYTEMNESTRA. And so, though you have had your say,
You will keep me from sacrifice by screaming?
ELECTRA. Go. I invite you. Sacrifice.
Do not blame my tongue, for I say no more.   530
CLYTEMNESTRA (to servant with offering of fruits). Go, my girl,
and take these fruits as offerings
That I may raise a prayer up to the King
And cleanse me of the horrors I contain.

Protecting Phoebos, hear the hid thing I say.
I do not speak among friends,
And it would be wrong to open it to the light
While she is near, or with her murderous voice
She would sow through the city futile words.
Listen so, for so shall I pray.

The spectre that I saw last night, Apollo, King,   540
In that ambiguous dream:
If it is healthful, then fulfill it; if evil,

Let it turn back against my enemies.
Do not let plotters deprive me of my riches,
But let me live always as I am: in safety:
Having the House of Atreus and the sceptre:
Having the friends who now are near me, having
Those of my children who are not bitter toward me.
Apollo, King: listen graciously;
Grant to all mine all that I beg of you.   550
Also those other things behind my silence:
I know that you know them, being a god;
Being a child of Zeus you know everything.

(*Enter the* PAIDAGOGOS, *as a traveler.*)

PAIDAGOGOS. Kind women, may I learn
   Whether this is King Aegisthos' house?
LEADER. It is; you have guessed rightly.
PAIDAGOGOS. And am I right that this is the King's wife?
   She seems to be a queen.
LEADER. Yes. That is the Queen.
PAIDAGOGOS. My greetings, lady. I bring sweet news   560
   To you and to Aegisthos, from a friend.
CLYTEMNESTRA. I welcome your words, but must know first
   who sent you.
PAIDAGOGOS. Phanoteus of Phocis, on important matters.
CLYTEMNESTRA. What are they, stranger? Speak; for I am sure
   That coming from a friend they will be pleasant.
PAIDAGOGOS. Orestes is dead, to sum it up briefly.
ELECTRA. a-á a-á! This day I die.
CLYTEMNESTRA. What did you say? What did you say? Don't
   listen to her!
PAIDAGOGOS. Orestes is dead, I tell you again.
ELECTRA. a-á a-á! I have ceased to live.   570
CLYTEMNESTRA. You: about your business! And you, friend,
   Tell me the truth: how did he die?
PAIDAGOGOS. That's what I was sent for, I'll tell you everything.
   First of all, you must know he went
   To the great Greek festival, the Delphic Games.
   And there, to be brief where there is much to tell,
   I never knew such power or such a man.
   Of all the games the judges heralded
   He was acclaimed the victor,
   Orestes, the Illustrious,   580
   The son of Agamemnon-great-in-Troy.

Such his beginnings. But when a god lays snares
No man can get away, though he be strong.

And so, one day near sundown,
When the swift chariots gathered for a race,
He too drove in among the thronging wheels:
Ten chariots all together, one from Athens.
At first all went well, but at the seventh circling
The Athenian's hard-mouthed foals bolted: swinging round,
Crashed full into the Barcaean car;   590
And at that accident one after the other
Collided, smashed up together, heaped
The Krisan plain with wreckage of chariots.
But this the sly Athenian saw, made way
For the turbulent wave of racers down the center.
Orestes was last, holding his horses in,
Trusting to the finish.
But when he saw that one competitor ahead,
He screamed to pierce his horses' ears, gave chase;
And so they sped, the yokes just even,   600
First one, then the other winning by a head.

For the whole course so far unfortunate Orestes
Had driven safely, guided his team aright.
But now he loosed the left-hand rein too far,
Forgetting the goalpost, crashed.
The axle broke and he was thrown
Over the rail and twisted in the reins;
As he struck the ground his team bolted away.
And now the multitude who saw him thrown
Set up a wailing for that youth   610
Who did such deeds and met such end:
Thrown up, legs first, then dragged along the ground,
Till the other drivers brought his horses to a stop,
And freed the bleeding body which his friends
Could recognize no more.
The Phocians burnt it on a pyre,
And in a little urn their envoys bring
The giant corpse, now paltry dust,
To find a grave here in its native earth.

Such is my tale to you, even in words painful,   620
But for those who watched, for those who saw

As I saw, with my eyes, the greatest horror.
LEADER. a-á! a-á! It seems our master's tree
  Is withered to the root.
CLYTEMNESTRA. O Zeus, these tidings:
  Joyful, shall I call them,
  Or terrible but advantageous?
  It is my misery to save my life
  Through the sufferings of my own children.
PAIDAGOGOS. Why so disheartened at this news, lady?   630
CLYTEMNESTRA. A terrible thing, child bearing.
  Though a mother suffer hate, she cannot hate her child.
PAIDAGOGOS. Then it seems we came to you in vain.
CLYTEMNESTRA. Never in vain: How can you say *in vain*
  If you have brought trustworthy evidence
  Of his death? — who had his life from mine,
  His nourishment from my breasts, then fled?
  — Forgot me with this land he left; and ever since
  Though never seeing me, has named me
  His father's killer who must die in horror?   640
  Neither in the nighttime nor in the daytime
  Has sweet sleep covered me, but time in minutes has passed
    me
  As one on the verge of death.
  And now, on this very day, I lose my fear.
  Fear of him, and of her too; for she it was
  Living here with me, who was the wider wound,
  Draining my lifeblood;
  And now at last my days are to be free
  Both of her and of all her threats!
ELECTRA. Misery. Now, now may I mourn   650
  Your fate, Orestes, for now is added
  Your mother's scorn. Is it not well?
CLYTEMNESTRA. Not with you; but he is well as he is.
ELECTRA. Listen, fierce spirit, you the newly dead!
CLYTEMNESTRA. It listened. And decided well.
ELECTRA. Exult, for now you have reached your happiness.
CLYTEMNESTRA. You and Orestes shall not destroy it.
ELECTRA. No, it is we who are destroyed, not you.
CLYTEMNESTRA (*to the* PAIDAGOGOS). Your coming would have
  been a boon indeed
  If you had destroyed this screaming mouth.   660
PAIDAGOGOS. Then I may take my leave, if all is well.
CLYTEMNESTRA. Not at all, that would be quite unworthy

Both of me and of my friend who sent you:
Come in, come in; leave her outside to wail
Her evils and the evils of her friends.

(CLYTEMNESTRA *and the* PAIDAGOGOS *enter palace.*)

ELECTRA. Did you think that she was bitterly mourning
The wretched son who perished so?
No, she vanished with laughter. Misery.
Beloved Orestes, your death destroyed me.
I have lost all heart for my one hope,   670
That you would return alive someday
To avenge my father and me. Where must I go?
I am alone without you and my father.
I must go back, I must serve
My father's murderers, my sorest
Human affliction. Is it not well with me?
But never, in such time as may be left me,
Will I go in to them. Here by the gate
I will lay my loveless life to dry up.
If any in the house think me offensive   680
Let him put me to death: death would be grace,
But life is pain, I have no thirst for life.

CHORUS. Where are Zeus' lightnings, where is bright Helios
If they watch this and hide it away in silence?

ELECTRA. e e ai ai

CHORUS. Child, why do you weep?

ELECTRA. ai ai

CHORUS. Sh, not that great wail.

ELECTRA. You crush me.

CHORUS. How?   690

ELECTRA. On those who are surely going down
To the land of death, you place my hope, and so
Drain me the more.

CHORUS. I know that King Amphiareus went down
For a woman's golden chain, and now below the ground

ELECTRA. ai ai

CHORUS. He rules the dead.

ELECTRA. ai ai

CHORUS. Yes, cry, that murderess

ELECTRA. Was murdered   700

CHORUS. Yes.

ELECTRA. I know, I know; appeared an avenger
For that mourner, but I have none, the one
Whisked off, clean gone.

CHORUS. You have really found misery

ELECTRA. Misery most familiar,
  Accumulating year by year
  Stubbornly, on my life.

CHORUS. We have seen its tears

ELECTRA. Then do not turn me   710

CHORUS. Where?

ELECTRA. Where no hope is:
  Of my brother to help me.

CHORUS. His was the fate of all mortals.

ELECTRA. To fall among competing hooves?
  To fall, as that wretched one,
  Among the furrowing edges?

CHORUS. Unthinkable that horror.

ELECTRA. And he in exile lies

CHORUS. ai ai   720

ELECTRA. Without my burying hands,
  Without my tears.

(*Enter* CHRYSOTHEMIS.)

CHRYSOTHEMIS. My dearest, I am running to you with joy
  Because I have good news, and the cessation
  Of all your troubles and misfortunes!

ELECTRA. And how could you have found me any help
  For my misfortunes, when there is none to find?

CHRYSOTHEMIS. Orestes is with us, listen to me!
  Here in the flesh, just as you see me now!

ELECTRA. Poor girl, are you mad? Out of your sorrows   730
  And out of my sorrows, you are making jokes.

CHRYSOTHEMIS. No, by our father's hearth, in all soberness,
  I do assure you I know that he is here.

ELECTRA. Poor girl. And from whom can you have heard
  This tale of yours? Who is it you trust so?

CHRYSOTHEMIS. Myself I trust, and no one else,
  On the clearest evidence of my eyes.

ELECTRA. Poor girl. What evidence? What did you see
  To make you heat yourself in this crazy fire?

CHRYSOTHEMIS. Listen, by the gods, listen! And when you've
    heard   740
  What I still have to tell, decide if I am mad.

ELECTRA. Yes, speak, speak, if it pleases you to speak.

CHRYSOTHEMIS. I will, I'll tell you everything I saw.
  As I approached our father's sepulchre
  I saw that from the top of the barrow

Fresh streams of milk had flowed, and that a wreath
Of many kinds of flowers crowned the tomb.
I marveled as I looked, and I peered about
For fear someone might be approaching me.
But when I saw that everything was quiet,   750
I crept a little closer, and I saw,
Close to the tomb, a lock of new-cut hair.
As I looked, there came to me in my sadness
A familiar image; that sign I saw
Was from my best-loved Orestes!
I took it in my hands, I did not cry out,
But my eyes, for joy, filled at once with tears.
I knew at once, just as I know now,
That this shining thing could only be from him.
Who else but you or me could have placed it there?   760
It was not I who did it, that I know;
Nor you: how could you, if you cannot leave the house
Even to offer mourning to the gods?
Our mother certainly would never wish to,
And she could never do it and be unseen:
Orestes it is who made that offering.
Therefore take courage: even for you
The god will not decree the same fate forever.
That fate has been hard so far. But now, at last, the day
Gives promise of good things beginning!   770

ELECTRA. How I pity you for your fondness.

CHRYSOTHEMIS. Why? Is this not good news I bring you?

ELECTRA. You don't know where you are or what it is you
believe.

CHRYSOTHEMIS. Am I not to believe what I plainly see?

ELECTRA. He is dead, poor girl, and from him will come
Nothing to save you. Look no more to him.

CHRYSOTHEMIS. a-á a-á! From whom did you hear that?

ELECTRA. From one who was with him when he was destroyed.

CHRYSOTHEMIS. Where is the man? Oh, I am utterly lost.

ELECTRA. In the house gratifying our mother.   780

CHRYSOTHEMIS. a-á a-á! And from whom then can have come
All those death-offerings on my father's grave?

ELECTRA. I should think they must have come from one
Who wished to remember dead Orestes kindly.

CHRYSOTHEMIS. Oh, miserable fool. How joyfully
I ran with those bright tidings, and never knew

My own delusion! But here I find
The old evils still, and new ones too.
ELECTRA. Yes, that is so. If you take my advice
You'll lighten the burden of this suffering.   790
CHRYSOTHEMIS. I suppose I am to raise the dead again?
ELECTRA. That's not what I said, I'm not so crazed as that.
CHRYSOTHEMIS. What do you ask that I am able to do?
ELECTRA. To undertake to do what I advise.
CHRYSOTHEMIS. If it promises well, I shall not hold back.
ELECTRA. You know nothing is achieved without toil.
CHRYSOTHEMIS. I know. I am with you while my strength lasts.
ELECTRA. Then hear what I have decided to do.
Henceforth, you know, we have with us no friends;
Death has removed them, and we are left alone.   800
As long as I had reports of our brother
Alive and prospering, I still had hope
That he would come one day to avenge his father.
But now that he is gone I turn to you:
Aegisthos, our father's murderer,
You, with your sister, unflinchingly must slay.
So, I hide nothing from you.

How can you be so cold? What possible hope
Can you find to stare at? Your lot is wailing
For your father's vanishing wealth, and wailing   810
While you grow old unmarried and unloved.
You must not hope that you would ever marry,
That man Aegisthos is not so careless
As to permit children of ours to grow
For his own obvious destruction.
But if you follow the advice I give you,
You shall show your love for father and brother,
And so step forth as a free woman
Prepared for marriage; all men love the strong.
In the feasts and assemblies of the city   820
Everyone shall laud us for our male courage,
And that name shall not fail us, living or dead.

My sister, dearest, trust me, join your father,
Side with your brother, put an end to my sorrows
And to your own, in the certainty
That it is shameful for fine beings to live in shame.

LEADER. In these matters forethought is an ally
  Both for the speaker and the listener.
CHRYSOTHEMIS. Dear friends, if her forethought hadn't been per-
    verse,
  She would have kept the caution she discarded.   830

What were you thinking of, that you could be ready
For such madness, and ready to ask my help?
Don't you see? You are a woman, not a man;
You are not so strong as those inside the house.
They are growing larger day after day,
We are diminishing, we cannot thrive.
Who would expect to grapple such a man
And then escape unharmed from that folly?
Take care, ugly though our treatment is now,
We shall know worse if your words are overheard.   840
It would solve nothing for us, do us no good,
To win a good report by a shameful death.
Death itself is not hateful, but to need death,
And not be able to get it, is hateful.
I beseech you, before we are quite destroyed,
Before we are rooted out, restrain your anger.
All you have said I shall hold as though unsaid,
Coming to nothing. . . . And you, you be
Reasonable, even now;
Helpless as you are, yield to the strong.   850
LEADER. Listen, for us mortals there is no scheme
  To serve us better than foresight and wisdom.
ELECTRA. This of course is the expected answer;
  I knew you would reject what I told you.
  This work then must be done by me alone.
  I shall never refuse it as fruitless.
CHRYSOTHEMIS. a-á a-á!
  If only you had been of that same mind
  When our father died, you could have done all this!
ELECTRA. My mind was the same, my spirit weaker then.   860
CHRYSOTHEMIS. Try to keep your spirit always constant.
ELECTRA. This advice means that you will not help me.
CHRYSOTHEMIS. Your handiwork is likely to end badly.
ELECTRA. I envy you your wits, your cowardice I hate.
CHRYSOTHEMIS. I shall endure it also when you praise me.
ELECTRA. That you will never have to endure from me.
CHRYSOTHEMIS. The future shall decide that.

ELECTRA. Go: there is no help whatever in you.

CHRYSOTHEMIS. There is, but there is no teaching you.

ELECTRA. Then go to your mother and tell her everything. 870

CHRYSOTHEMIS. No, I don't hate you as much as that.

ELECTRA. But you plainly force me into dishonor.

CHRYSOTHEMIS. Dishonor, no; I am careful for you.

ELECTRA. Am I to accept your sense of what is right?

CHRYSOTHEMIS. When you are wise you shall guide us both.

ELECTRA. How hideous to speak so well, and wrongly.

CHRYSOTHEMIS. You describe your own malady exactly.

ELECTRA. Why? Don't I seem to you to speak with justice?

CHRYSOTHEMIS. There may be mischief even in justice.

ELECTRA. I cannot decide to live by that rule. 880

CHRYSOTHEMIS. But if you do what you intend, you'll see I'm
right.

ELECTRA. I will do it, and you shan't divert me.

CHRYSOTHEMIS. Is this your answer? You won't reconsider?

ELECTRA. No. Nothing is more hateful than bad advice.

CHRYSOTHEMIS. It is as though you did not hear what I say.

ELECTRA. These things have long been clear to me. Nothing has
changed.

CHRYSOTHEMIS. Then I shall go. You will never endure
The things I say, nor I the things you do.

ELECTRA. Yes, go in there; I shall never follow you,
Not though you come to me begging on your knees. 890
This hunt after vanities is mad.

CHRYSOTHEMIS. If you think you have all justice with you,
Continue to think so. When you fall on evil times
You will accept my words.

(CHRYSOTHEMIS *slowly enters the palace.*)

CHORUS. Why, when we see the wise and obedient birds
Heedful of those who dreamed them and brought them to
birth,
Can we not do as much?
Neither the thunder of God
Nor His laws in the stars
Shall be hid too long. 900
O subterranean voice, go, cry cruelly to Atreus' dead sons
mirthless news,

That their house is sick; their children, in the common strife,
Cannot agree, live out of love, two ways of life;

That alone Electra
Betrayed and shaken,
Like bird complaining,
Still wails her father.
Death she disregards, she is ready to face it
To snare those furies. What nature so splendid?

None but the lost   910
Accept imputed shame, or will to live
Without a name, my child.
Therefore you chose the common saeculum of grief,
And through that ugly dearth made your name safe:
Wise, and the best of daughters.

But I would have you live
Above your enemies' wealth, above their power
Higher than you now are lower.
I see that you labor on a road which is
Not easy, though fertile in the deepest verity,   920
Which you, in your great piety, bring forth.

> (*Enter* ORESTES, *as a weary traveler.* PYLADES *follows with the urn.*)

ORESTES. Tell me, ladies, have I been rightly guided,
    And have I nearly finished my journey?
LEADER. What were you seeking? What did you want?
ORESTES. I have been seeking a long time for Aegisthos' house.
LEADER. You have come to the right place; your guide was right.
ORESTES. Then will one of you tell those inside the house
    That our long-desired company is come?
LEADER. This girl, as the next of kin, must tell them.
ORESTES (*to* ELECTRA). Will you go then, and explain to them that   930
    Certain Phocians, whom Aegisthos expected —
ELECTRA. a-á a-á! Surely you do not bring
    Visible proof of the tale we heard?
ORESTES. I have not heard your tale. It was old Strophios
    Who sent me to bring you news of Orestes.
ELECTRA. What news, what news, friend? I am seized with dread.
ORESTES. We offer, as you see this narrow urn
    Containing the small vestiges of his death.
ELECTRA. a-á a-á! Surely my agony
    Lies visible and palpable before me!   940
ORESTES. If you are wailing for Orestes' death,
    Know that this vessel contains his ashes.

ELECTRA. Give me the vessel, friend, if it hides him,
  Give it to me to hold it in my hands,
  For I shall mourn myself and all my race,
  Mourning this dust.
ORESTES (*to* PYLADES). Bring it and give it to her, whoever she is,
  For she asks this with no evil intent,
  But as a friend or a blood relative.

          (PYLADES *gives* ELECTRA *the urn.*)

ELECTRA. O ashes of Orestes, best belovèd!   950
  I have you back now, with hope gone;
  I did not send you forth so.
  Ah, this is nothingness my hands lift up,
  And I sent you from your house all shining!
  I wish my life might have left me, before
  I sent you to a strange land, and with these hands
  Saved you from death; you would have died with him
  And lain in the one grave with your fathers.
  But now, away from home, in another country,
  Far from your sister, miserably you died;   960
  And I, with these hands of love, could neither
  Wash you nor dress you nor bear the wretched burden
  From the hungry fire.
  You were tended by the hands of strangers at the end,
  And now you come back to me in this little urn.

  Ah, the long joyful fruitless care I gave you!
  You were never your mother's, always mine,
  Of all in the house I alone was your nurse,
  I your sister, none had that name but me.
  Now with your death this is all wiped out   970
  In a single day, everything snatched away
  As though a storm had passed: our father gone,
  I dead in you, you vanished into death,
  The hateful laughing: remains for my pleasure
  That monstrous mother whom you so often told me
  That you would punish, when you came.
  But the bitter spirit, yours and mine,
  Has utterly bereaved us,
  Sent me, instead of the belovèd face,
  Dust and a vain shadow.   980

  a-á a-á! Pitiful body! a-á a-a!

You came a hard road, my love, it was my death;
A hard road, my love, my brother.
And now you must receive me under your roof,
Nothing to nothing. I with you down there
For the rest of time. Up here it was with us
Share and share alike; and now I crave to die,
And not to be excluded from your grave.
I do not think the dead have grief or mourning.

LEADER. Your father was mortal, Electra; think   990
  Orestes mortal. Do not wail too much,
  We all must suffer death.

ORESTES. a-á a-á! What to say? Among the helpless words,
  Which to choose? But I can no longer keep from words.

ELECTRA. Why do you suffer? Why do you cry out so?

ORESTES. Is it you who are Electra?

ELECTRA. Yes, it is I.

ORESTES. What a piteous change.

ELECTRA. Surely it is not I who afflict you so?

ORESTES. Oh ruined and dishonored being.   1000

ELECTRA. I am as you so cruelly say, my friend.

ORESTES. Oh loveless and bitter life!

ELECTRA. Why are you so hurt as you see me?

ORESTES. How little I knew my own misfortunes.

ELECTRA. Did something I said reveal them to you?

ORESTES. Seeing you so clearly in your suffering.

ELECTRA. Yet what you see is very little.

ORESTES. What more painful could there be?

ELECTRA. To share one's life with the killers —

ORESTES. Of whom? What evil do you mean?   1010

ELECTRA. Of my father, and to be forced to serve them —

ORESTES. Who forces you to that?

ELECTRA. My mother, she is called.

ORESTES. How? With violence? Does she persecute you?

ELECTRA. She persecutes me in every way.

ORESTES. And no one is helping you or holding her back?

ELECTRA. No. You have given me the dust of my one helper.

ORESTES. Poor creature. As I look my pity returns.

ELECTRA. You are the only one who has ever pitied me.

ORESTES. I am the only one with the same sorrow.   1020

ELECTRA. What! You can't be some kinsman of ours?

ORESTES. I should answer, if these women were on our side.

ELECTRA. They are on our side, take courage and speak.

ORESTES. Give back this jar and you shall learn everything.

ELECTRA. My friend, do not force me to that.

ORESTES. Do as I say and you shall not go wrong.

ELECTRA. Don't take away the dearest thing I have.

ORESTES. It is impossible.

ELECTRA. Ah Orestes, we are forlorn if I may not bury you! 1030

ORESTES. Be quiet, you have no right to sorrow.

ELECTRA. No right to sorrow for a dead brother?

ORESTES. It is wrong to speak of him so.

ELECTRA. Am I so dishonored by the dead?

ORESTES. No one dishonors you.

ELECTRA. Not though I hold here Orestes' body?

ORESTES. That is not his body, though meant to be taken for it.

ELECTRA. Then where is my wretched brother's grave?

ORESTES. There is none, the living have no grave.

ELECTRA. What do you say, boy?

ORESTES. Nothing that is not true. 1040

ELECTRA. He is alive?

ORESTES. If I am alive.

ELECTRA. Are you he?

ORESTES. Look at this ring of my father's and see if I speak the truth.

ELECTRA. O sacred day!

ORESTES. Sacred day I cry!

ELECTRA. O voice, do I hear you?

ORESTES. Ask nowhere else.

ELECTRA. Do I hold you in my arms?

ORESTES. As you shall henceforth. 1050

ELECTRA. O dearest friends, women of the city,
Look at this Orestes, who through trickery
Was dead, and now through trickery is saved!

LEADER. We see him, child, and in this blessèd issue
The tears of joy are rising in our eyes.

ELECTRA. O son,
Son of the most belovèd,
You came indeed;
You are found, you came, you see what you desired! 1060

ORESTES. I am here, but you must be silent.

ELECTRA. Why?

ORESTES. Be silent so that none within may hear us.

ELECTRA. No, by the eternal virgin Artemis,
I cannot think them worthy of my fear:
That excessive mass of womenfolk
Forever inside the house!

ORESTES. But think, in women also the wargod
Inhabits. You have experience of that.

ELECTRA. a-á a-á!
Clearly you remind me how insoluble,   1070
How unforgettable, is
This evil of ours.

ORESTES. I know, I know, but now that the chance invites us,
We must remember the work we have to do.

ELECTRA. O always,
Every moment I have, I would speak out,
And that is just,
For only now am I free to speak.

ORESTES. Yes, but you must preserve this freedom.

ELECTRA. How?   1080

ORESTES. Do not speak too long when we lack the time.

ELECTRA. But now that you've come,
Who would give up speech for silence?
Now that beyond thought
I see you, beyond hope?

ORESTES. You saw me when the god moved me to come.

ELECTRA. Now what you tell me is
More gracious still: if it was indeed a god
Who led you home, divine
I call your coming.   1090

ORESTES. I would not restrain your gratitude,
But I am afraid, your too great joy compels me.

ELECTRA. After so long, your belovèd coming!
But now that you have really appeared, do not —

ORESTES. Do not do what?

ELECTRA. Do not despoil me,
Do not deprive me of your face and presence.

ORESTES. If anyone tried I should be angry.

ELECTRA. You consent?

ORESTES. How could I not?   1100

ELECTRA. O my friends, hearing the unhoped for voice,
Neither withholding my passionate joys
Nor pouring them forth in cries
Stand I! . . . Now I have you, now you have come,
Shown me the belovèd face
Which even in evils I shall never lose!

ORESTES. Say nothing needless: do not tell me
How evil our mother is, nor how
Aegisthos in the house of our fathers

1110

Drains, exhausts and vainly scatters our substance;
The telling of it would destroy our chances.
But show me what is fitting at this moment;
Where and how, hidden or manifest,
We are to end our enemies' laughter.
And do not let our mother recognize
In your shining face, that we are in the house;
Falsely wail as though your fate were upon you.
When we shall have won, then we shall rejoice,
Then we shall laugh freely.

ELECTRA. What you wish, my brother, I wish also; 1120
All the pleasure I have I owe to you,
And I should not let you suffer a moment
To gain much for myself; that would never be
The way to serve the beneficent spirit.

You know how we stand, of course; you've heard
That Aegisthos is away from the house,
Our mother within. Do not be afraid
That she will see me smiling with pleasure,
My hatred of her is too old for that;
Besides, since seeing you I have been weeping 1130
For joy. How should I stop, since I have seen you come
Both in death and life? You have worked beyond hope,
So that if my father himself came to me alive
I should think it no marvel, but see and believe;
Therefore lead me as you will.
Alone, I should have done one of two things,
Saved myself in the right way, or found the right death.

ORESTES. Be still, I hear someone coming in the house.

(*Enter the* PAIDAGOGOS *from the palace.*)

ELECTRA. Go in, strangers;
You bring what none in the house will refuse, 1140
Even though receiving it may not be pleasant.

PAIDAGOGOS. You are mad!
Don't you care for life, or were you born witless?
Don't you know that you stand, not on the edge,
But in the midst of the most mortal dangers?
If I had not been waiting all this time
Here, by the door, to watch and to report,
Your plan would have been in the house before you!
This however my caution has prevented.

Now that you've finished all you had to say,   1150
All your insatiable shouting for joy,
Go in. Indecision is fatal;
It is essential to finish up.

ORESTES. What reception shall I meet when I go in?

PAIDAGOGOS. A good one. First of all, no one knows you.

ORESTES. You must have reported that I was dead.

PAIDAGOGOS. They speak of you as in the world below.

ORESTES. Are they glad? Or what do they say?

PAIDAGOGOS. I'll tell you at the proper time; meanwhile
Whatever they do, however bad, is good.   1160

ELECTRA. Orestes, tell me, who is this?

ORESTES. Don't you understand?

ELECTRA. No, and cannot guess.

ORESTES. Don't you know the man to whom you gave me once?

ELECTRA. What man? What do you mean?

ORESTES. The man who through your foresight took me to
   Phocis.

ELECTRA. Is this the one man I could find to trust
When our father was being murdered?

ORESTES. Yes. Ask no more.

ELECTRA. O sacred light! How did you come, the one rescuer   1170
Of Agamemnon's house? And was it really you
Who saved this man and me from many horrors?
O hands beloved! O feet come to serve!
How could you be with me so long and be unknown?
Destroy me with words, and keep your sweet work hidden?
Hail, Father! Father you are to me! Hail!
You must know that I have hated and loved you
Beyond all mankind, in this single day.

PAIDAGOGOS. Enough, I think. The tale of the time between,
In many revolving nights and days   1180
Shall make these things all clear to you, Electra.

Now, you two standing by: now is the time
To act; now Clytemnestra is alone,
None of her men are in the house; but think,
If you delay you will have to fight with them
And many more much cleverer than they.

ORESTES. Pylades, our work permits us no more words;
Let us go in at once, but first salute the gods
Who dwell here on the threshold of the house.

(ORESTES, *the* PAIDAGOGOS, *and* PYLADES *perform a brief ceremony
of purification and propitiation.*)

ELECTRA. O Lord Apollo, hear them graciously,   1190
And hear me too, who came to you so often
To offer you all I had with these hands.
For now, Apollo, Light God, Wolf God, with all I have
I pray, beseech and beg you, be propitious
To us and the things we intend to do;
Show forth the wages which the gods
Will pay to men for their ungodliness.

(*The men enter the palace, followed by* ELECTRA.)

CHORUS. Look, look where the wargod creeps,
Blood where he breathes and evil fighting.
And now within the house pursuing   1200
Crime, go the inescapable hounds;
Now it will not be long
Till my hovering dream come down.

And now led by the dead
The stealthy helper enters
His father's wealth, his old abode.
Bloodshed is newly whetted in his hand, and Hermes,
Hiding the snare in darkness,
Leads him to his prize without a pause.

(ELECTRA *enters from the palace.*)

ELECTRA. Beloved friends, at this very moment   1210
The men are at their work. Be silent.
CHORUS. What work, what are they doing?
ELECTRA. She wreathes the burial urn, the men stand close.
CHORUS. Why did you come out?
ELECTRA. For fear Aegisthos might come without our knowing.

(*Within the house.*)

CLYTEMNESTRA. ai ai,
O loveless rooms alive with death!
ELECTRA. A cry inside. Did you hear it, friends?
CHORUS. Heard it shivering. It was cruel to hear.
CLYTEMNESTRA. ai ai ai ai,   1220
Aegisthos, where are you, say?
ELECTRA. Listen, another wail.
CLYTEMNESTRA. Child, child, pity your mother!
ELECTRA. But you did not pity him, nor pity his father.

CHORUS. O city, O wretched tribe,
Your familiar horror is fading.
CLYTEMNESTRA. ai ai,
I am stricken!
ELECTRA. Strike, if you can, again.
CLYTEMNESTRA. ai ai. Again! Again!   1230
ELECTRA. The same for Aegisthos.
CHORUS. The prayers are answered, the earth-buried live,
The murderers' blood is seeping down
To the dead who have been thirsty long;

(The men enter from the palace.)

The men come forth, the purple hand
Drips with the struggle's sacrifice. I have no blame.
ELECTRA. Orestes, how did you fare?
ORESTES. Inside there,
Well, if Apollo guided us well.
ELECTRA. Is the woman dead?   1240
ORESTES. No longer fear
That your mother's will could humble you again.
CHORUS. Stop there, Aegisthos is in plain sight.
ELECTRA. Why don't you go back!
ORESTES. Where do you see him?
ELECTRA. Coming from the suburb, full of laughter.
CHORUS. Quick! Inside the house! Finish what's well begun!
ORESTES. Courage. We shall.
ELECTRA. Then go, go!
ORESTES. We are gone.   1250

(The men slip back into the palace.)

ELECTRA. What's here belongs to me.
CHORUS. Tell this man something pleasing in his ear
To rush him into the fatal struggle blind.

(Enter AEGISTHOS.*)*

AEGISTHOS. Does any of you know where the Phocians are
Who they say have brought us news
Of Orestes' death in a chariot wreck?
You. I mean you! Yes you, who were before
So insolent. It is for you, I think,
Who know the most about it, to inform me.
ELECTRA. I know, how could I not? Or else I were   1260
Careless of the fate of my dearest kin.
AEGISTHOS. Then where can the strangers be? Come, show me.
ELECTRA. Inside; for they have reached their dear hostess.

AEGISTHOS. Did they really report that he was dead?
ELECTRA. Yes, and not only in words, they showed us proof.
AEGISTHOS. Is it where I can see, to make certain?
ELECTRA. Yes, it is there. An unenviable sight.
AEGISTHOS. What you say pleases me more than usual.
ELECTRA. You shall be pleased, if your pleasure is there.
AEGISTHOS. Silence, I ask, and open out the doors.   1270
 Let all Mycenae and all Argos see,
 So that anyone who still vainly hoped
 For that man's return, may see the corpse
 And take the bit without constraint;
 Learn sense before he meets my punishment.
ELECTRA. This is accomplished in me. In this time
 I have learned this wisdom: yield to the strong.

  (*The doors of the palace open, revealing a veiled bier with
  the men grouped around it.* AEGISTHOS *approaches.*)

AEGISTHOS. O Zeus, without envy I see this fallen
 Figure: if this is impious I say nothing.

 Take the veil from the face. It is fitting   1280
 For the kindred and also for me to mourn.
ORESTES. Lift it yourself. It is for you, not me,
 To see what's lying there and kindly greet it.
AEGISTHOS. You are right. I will. And you go call me
 Clytemnestra, if she be in the house.
ORESTES. She is very close, don't look away.
AEGISTHOS. a-á a-á. What do I see?
ORESTES. Why are you afraid? Don't you know the face?
AEGISTHOS. Into whose terrible snares have I fallen!
ORESTES. Haven't you learned that the dead you spoke of are
 living?   1290
AEGISTHOS. a-á a-á. I see your meaning, you, you
 Are Orestes, you who are speaking to me!
ORESTES. You are a seer who has been deceived.
AEGISTHOS. I am lost! But let me say a word —
ELECTRA. Don't let him speak and extend his life with words.
 What good is a little time to a creature
 Who is fatally netted, and must die?
 Kill him as quickly as you can, and give him
 To the diggers of graves, to bury him
 Where we can never see him. That would be   1300
 The only expiation of the old wrongs.

Go in at once. The struggle is not in words,
But for your life.
AEGISTHOS. Why drive me in? If your work is comely,
Why in the dark? Why not out here?
ORESTES. Give me no orders. Go in where you killed my father.
It is there that you shall die.
AEGISTHOS. Must this house witness all Pelops' evils,
Now and to come!
ORESTES. Yours it must: that much I can foresee.   1310
AEGISTHOS. Your foresight did not include your father?
ORESTES. You have much to say, we are slow. Go on.
AEGISTHOS. You lead.
ORESTES. You must go first.
AEGISTHOS. So I won't escape?
ORESTES. No, so you may not die as you please.
I must make sure that death is bitter for you.
Justice should always be immediate;
If the law of death after such deeds
Were fixed, they would be few.   1320

(AEGISTHOS, ORESTES, PYLADES, PAIDAGOGOS *and* ELECTRA *disappear
into the palace. Then the doors open, showing the living and
the dead.*)

LEADER. O Atreus' suffering seed
To freedom barely emerged
Through this struggle realized.

❖ ❖ ❖

STUDY AIDS

Prologue (*lines 1–123*)

1. What initial function does the Paidagogos perform? Can you
name a celebrated modern play that employs a similar technique?

2. What effect is gained through having Orestes' childhood attendant initiate talk of avenging the murder of Agamemnon?

3. In *The Libation Bearers* Orestes does not delay reference to
Apollo's injunction to avenge his father's murder until late in the play.
What does Sophocles achieve by having Orestes refer to Apollo's
advice in his opening speech?

4. What impression do we gain of Electra from her first speech?

Parados (lines 124–199)

1. What advice does the chorus of women offer Electra? Is it good advice? How does it indicate the temper of the chorus? Is the counsel essentially feminine? What contrast is implied between the women of the chorus and Electra? Does this contrast heighten the dramatic impact of the scene?

2. Has Electra permitted her grief and loneliness to mar her life? Is her attitude characteristic of those who indulge in their grief?

3. What do the chorus' references to Zeus imply concerning Sophocles' view of the gods?

4. With reference to lines 168–173, what do you think of the chorus' analysis? Note how the contrast between these women and Electra is increasing.

First Episode (lines 200–386)

1. What is the purpose and the effect of Electra's long speech beginning with line 200?

2. The scene between Electra and Chrysothemis is reminiscent of a similar confrontation between Antigone and Ismene. How does the contrast between Electra and her sister heighten our awareness of Electra's strength ? Does her contemptuous treatment of Chrysothemis demean her or increase our respect for her firmness?

3. What effect does the threat have upon Electra? Does she seem to be a bit too assured, somewhat too smug in what is admittedly a stance of great courage? Is there an implied comment here about the effects of evil on human character?

4. What does the reference to Clytemnestra's dream reveal about the Greeks' understanding of conscience and the subconscious mind?

5. What effect have Electra's words had upon the chorus? And by implication, on us?

First Stasimon (lines 387–420)

1. What is the purpose of these lines?

Second Episode (lines 421–894)

1. Note how Clytemnestra reaches into the past to justify her actions. Does she make a convincing case in defense of her deed?

2. What impression does Clytemnestra make upon us at this moment of her first appearance?

3. How convincing is Electra's reply to her mother's defense? Note how Sophocles allows us to hear the viewpoints of both mother and daughter. You may feel at moments as though you were sitting on a jury, arbitrating the case.

4. Does Clytemnestra's comment about the relationship between

mother and child reveal an unsuspected strain of tenderness in her? Or is she speaking for effect before the Paidagogos?

5. How is a note of suspense generated in the scene between Electra and Chrysothemis?

6. Does Chrysothemis offer a convincing statement opposing Electra's plan? Electra refers to her sister's "cowardice." Is Chrysothemis cowardly or merely prudent? Which of the girls is the more credible?

Second Stasimon (*lines 895–921*)

1. What now is the attitude of the chorus toward Electra? Does it correspond to yours?

Third Episode (*lines 922–1197*)

1. What has Sophocles gained by delaying the meeting between Orestes and Electra until this point in the play? Note how Sophocles defers the moment of actual recognition. To what effect?

2. Has Sophocles succeeded in explaining Electra's great love for her brother?

3. What is the function of the Paidagogos in this scene?

Third Stasimon (*lines 1198–1209*)

1. What purpose is served in this brief scene?

Exodos (*lines 1210–1323*)

1. What note of irony is introduced in Aegisthos' dialogue with Orestes?

TOPICS FOR DISCUSSION

1. An analysis of Electra, the central character in the play. How complex a figure is she? To what degree does she develop or change during the course of the play? Does she enlist our sympathy? Has her hardness deprived her of her femininity?

2. The character and function of Chrysothemis. What attitude does she symbolize? Is she entitled to our respect and sympathy? How does her personality and attitude throw Electra's views into sharp relief?

3. How may the Orestes of Sophocles be contrasted with the Orestes of Aeschylus? The same question may be pertinently asked concerning the two Electras.

4. Compare the plots of Aeschylus and Sophocles, as well as the treatment of specific scenes. Analyze the means by which Sophocles develops suspense in his treatment. Note also his occasional use of irony.

5. Clytemnestra is what is called in the theatre a "strong" character. What qualities contribute to her commanding presence? Does her contemptuous treatment of Electra seem in any way justified? Is her explanation for killing Agamemnon at all plausible? Electra hates her mother because she killed her husband and married her lover. Why does Clytemnestra hate Electra?

6. Justice is the central issue in the play. Does the play appear to condone the act of matricide? Is Orestes' action justified?

EURIPIDES

THE Electra of Euripides (480–406 B.C.) is a melancholy heroine, a forlorn figure in whom the responses to rage, revulsion, and remorse come close to being neurotic. Euripides' depiction of both the girl and her brother as ordinary people whose emotions are frayed by the stress of circumstance renders them pitiful studies in confusion and despair. All this is a far cry from the way either Aeschylus or Sophocles treated the couple. The spectator might well conclude after viewing Euripides' *Electra* that with reference both to character and theme he came closer to the modern viewpoint than did either of his predecessors. Such a verdict would be amply supported by many of his other plays in which epic heroes are displaced by average men, traditional religion is questioned, war is condemned, and suffering is made a subject for compassion. Euripides was especially adroit at characterizing women, a skill to which the *Electra* aptly points. His work is at times melodramatic, at others sentimental, but the sum of its virtues far exceeds the total of its defects. Euripides is today esteemed as the most effective realist, the most trenchant social critic, and one of the most sensitive poets of the classic theatre. He was assuredly one of its three greatest playwrights.

The Electras of Aeschylus, Sophocles, and Euripides are the subjects of the second chapter of Sherman Plato Young, *The Woman of Greek Drama* (New York, 1953). Books which would be helpful in a study of Euripides include the following: R. B. Appleton, *Euripides, the Idealist* (London, 1927); W. N. Bates, *Euripides: A Student of Human Nature* (Philadelphia, 1930); G. M. A. Grube, *The Drama of Euripides* (London, 1941); Gilbert Murray, *Euripides and His Age* (New York, 1913); Gilbert Norwood, *Greek Tragedy* (London, 1928); Richmond Lattimore, *The Complete Greek Tragedies*, Vol. III–IV (Chicago, 1953); F. L. Lucas, *Euripides and His Influence* (New York, 1928).

Electra

Translated by Philip Vellacott

❖ ❖ ❖

CHARACTERS

A PEASANT *of Mycenae*
ELECTRA, *daughter of Agamemnon*
ORESTES, *son of Agamemnon*
PYLADES, *friend of Orestes*
CHORUS *of country women of Mycenae*
AN OLD MAN, *once a servant of Agamemnon*
A MESSENGER
CLYTEMNESTRA, *widow of Agamemnon*
THE DIOSCORI, *Castor and Polydeuces, sons of Zeus*

The scene is outside the PEASANT's *cottage. It is night, a little before sunrise.*

(*Enter the* PEASANT, *from the cottage.*)

PEASANT. Argos the ancient! River Inachus! It was here
That once King Agamemnon led his army forth
And with his thousand ships of war set sail for Troy;
And having killed Priam the king of Troy, and sacked
The noble city Dardanus founded, he returned
Home here to Argos, and on our temple walls hung high
His countless trophies taken from a barbarous race.
Abroad, he had good fortune; here in his own home
He died, by his wife Clytemnestra's treachery
And by Aegisthus' murderous hand, Thyestes' son.   10

So Agamemnon, parted from the ancient throne
Of Tantalus, is dead; Aegisthus is king now;

Electra by Euripides, translated by Philip Vellacott. Reprinted by permission of Penguin Books Ltd.

And Clytemnestra, Agamemnon's wife, is now
Aegisthus' wife. As for the children who were left
At home when the king went to Troy — the son, Orestes,
Aegisthus was resolved to kill; but an old slave
Who had once looked after the boy's father, took him off
To Phocis, and gave him to Strophius to bring up.
Electra stayed at home; when she was marriageable,
And nobles from all Hellas came to beg her hand,   20
Aegisthus, fearing, if her husband were a prince,
Her son would take revenge for Agamemnon's death,
Kept her at home, and would let no one marry her.

But this plan too seemed dangerous; she might bear a son
In secret to some man of noble blood. Therefore
Aegisthus planned to kill her. Clytemnestra then,
Cruel as she is, stopped him, and saved Electra's life.
She could claim reason for her husband's murder; but
She feared the hatred her child's death would bring on her.
Aegisthus then thought out another plan: he promised   30
To anyone who killed Orestes — now in exile —
A reward of gold; and gave Electra to be wife
To me. Well, I belong to a good family;
I've nothing to be ashamed of there — we're Mycenaeans,
And always have been; but we're poor; and when you're poor
Good breeding counts for nothing. So Aegisthus thought,
"Marry her to a nobody — I've nothing to fear."
A noble husband would go stirring up old blood
Which now lies quiet; Aegisthus then would have to pay
That debt he justly owes for Agamemnon's death.   40

Well, I'm her husband; but I swear by Aphrodite,
I've not come near her bed; she is a virgin still.
Her father was a king; I'm not her quality;
Therefore I'd be ashamed to take advantage of her.
I'm sorry for Orestes — he's my brother-in-law
In name! If only one day he'd come home again
To Argos, and see his sister married, and all well!

If any man thinks me a fool, for harbouring
A young girl in my house and never touching her,
He measures what's right by the wretched standard of   50
His own mind; he's a fool himself, I say, and worse.

(*Exit* PEASANT. *Enter* ELECTRA *from the cottage.*)

ELECTRA. O black night, you who nurse the golden stars! In you
   I go, bearing this jar poised on my head, to fetch
   Water from springs of rivers; not that any need
   Pushes me to this point, but so that I may show
   The gods the insolence of Aegisthus, and pour out
   My griefs under huge heaven to my father's spirit.
   My mother, Tyndareos' daughter, lost in wickedness,
   To show Aegisthus favour, drives me out of doors.
   And since she has borne Aegisthus other sons, she treats   60
   Me and Orestes both as bastards of her house.

                    (*The* PEASANT *returns.*)

PEASANT. Electra, why do you work so hard, all for my sake?
   You were brought up a princess; you're not made for toil.
   I've said this to you often — yet you will not rest.
ELECTRA. To me your kindness is the kindness of the gods;
   You take no advantage of my helpless misery.
   In this life it's a great thing to have found a friend
   To ease one's load of bitterness, as you do mine.
   I know you don't expect it; but it's right that I
   Should do my share, and work with all the strength I have   70
   To make life easier for you. You have enough
   Work on the farm; to keep things pleasant in the house
   Is my task. When a man comes home from the day's work
   He likes to find the house tidy and comfortable.
PEASANT. Go, then, if you wish; the well is not so far away.
   As soon as it grows light I'll take the oxen out
   And do some harrowing. Pious words and idle hands
   Bring in no breakfast.

           (*Exeunt* ELECTRA *and* PEASANT *severally. Enter* ORESTES *and*
           PYLADES.)

ORESTES. Pylades, you're the man I trust above all others.
   I've shared your home; you're a true friend — the only one   80
   Who has honoured me in spite of the condition to which
   Aegisthus has reduced me, murdering my father —
   He, and my fiendish-hearted mother. Now I have come,
   Sent by Apollo's oracle, to Argive soil,
   To shed the blood of those who shed my father's blood.
   No one knows I am here. Tonight I have visited
   My father's grave; I offered tears, and a shorn lock,
   And killed a lamb, and let its blood fall on the earth —
   All this unknown to those who tyrannize this land.

And now, instead of entering the city walls,   90
I have come here, near the border, with two ends in view:
First, to escape into some other country, if
A frontier guard should recognize me; secondly,
I am searching for my sister, who, so I am told,
Is married, and lives near. I must confer with her,
And get her help in executing our revenge.
I'll learn from her how matters stand inside the palace.

Look! The bright glance of dawn is rising. Let us leave
This place, and find some ploughman, or some slave-woman,
Whom we can ask whether my sister lives near by.   100

But wait — I see a slave-girl coming, carrying
A water-jar on her shorn head. Let us keep hidden.
We may get information from her, if she drops
Some word about those matters which have brought us here.

> (*They withdraw to one side. Enter* ELECTRA *carrying a jar of water.*)

ELECTRA.
Quicken your step; the hour grows late.
Walk weeping as you go,
Weeping, weeping.
Agamemnon was my father;
My mother was Clytemnestra,
The detested daughter of Tyndareos.   110
I am known to the people of Argos
As "poor Electra."
Oh! My misery is unbearable,
My life hateful.
And you, father — there you lie in the world of the dead,
Killed by your wife and her lover:
Agamemnon killed by Aegisthus!

Wake once more the same lament,
Revel in luxury of tears!

The hour is late; quicken your step,   120
Wailing loudly as you go,
Wailing, weeping as you go.
Brother, what fate is yours?
What city, what house holds you in bondage

Since you left your sister sad in her room at home,
To a future of bitterness and pain?

Come, my brother, save me from misery and weariness!
Zeus, O Zeus, hear me! Let Orestes,
Wherever he be, land on the shore of Argos
And punish the murderers of our father!   130

(*A slave appears from the cottage.*)

Take this jar from my head and set it down,
That I may weep for my father
And utter my night-long groanings loud in the morning air,
A cry of despair, a song of death.
Father, I call to you in the deep earth;
Hear the lamentation which fills all my days,
As nail tears cheek, and hand beats down
On head shorn in mourning for your death.

Weep, wail, beat the head!
As a swan, singing beside the broad river-reach,   140
Calls lovingly for her father
Lured to his death in a strangling snare,
So I, father, weep for your dreadful end.

How pitifully you lay in death,
After your last ritual cleansing!
Oh, father, father!
Cruel the axe's edge that cut your flesh,
Cruel the cunning that awaited you
When you finished your journey from Troy,
And your wife welcomed you home   150
Not with crown or garland
But with a two-edged sword,
To suffer the insults of Aegisthus;
And so won her treacherous lover.

(*Enter the* CHORUS.)

CHORUS. Electra, daughter of Agamemnon,
We have come to visit you in your country home.
A man from Mycenae, bred on mountain milk,
Has come to tell us that the people of Argos
Announce a festival for the day after tomorrow;
And all the unmarried girls are getting ready   160
To walk in procession to Hera's temple.

ELECTRA. Not fine dresses nor necklaces of gold,
    Dear friends, make my sad heart beat faster.
    I will not set the girls of Argos dancing,
    Nor will I twirl and stamp among them.
    My nights are drawn out with tears,
    My hopeless days are occupied with tears.
    Look at me — my hair uncared-for,
    My dress in tatters!
    Would not his daughter's appearance   170
    Bring shame to King Agamemnon,
    And make Troy blush to remember her conqueror?
CHORUS. Hera is great. Do come!
    Borrow from me a lovely gown, closely woven,
    And a gold necklace — I should be so pleased —
    To go with it. Do you expect
    Ever to overcome your enemies
    If you spend your time in weeping
    Instead of honouring the gods?
    Your day of happiness, my child, will come   180
    Not from sighs and groans
    But from pious prayers to the gods.
ELECTRA. Electra the wretched prays;
    Year after year her father's blood cries from the ground;
    But no god hears.
    Mourn for the king who died,
    Mourn for the prince who lives
    Exile and outcast in a foreign country,
    Serving another man's house for the sake of his roof —
    Son of so famous a father!   190
    While I, banished from my ancestral palace,
    Live in a labourer's cottage,
    Eating out my heart among these bleak crags;
    And my mother lies with a new husband
    In a bed stained with murder.
CHORUS. Your mother's sister Helen by her guilt has brought
    Grief without measure on Hellas and your family.

      (ORESTES *and* PYLADES *approach, accompanied by two Attend-*
      ants.)

ELECTRA. Look, friends! I see two men there! They were crouch-
    ing low
    And hiding; now they're coming out, towards the house.
    They're after no good; quick now, let's get out of their way.   200
    You go by the path, I'll hide indoors.

ORESTES.   Don't run away!
What are you afraid of? I won't do you any harm.

ELECTRA. Phoebus Apollo! Don't let them murder me, I — pray!

ORESTES. God grant I kill my enemies. You are no enemy.

ELECTRA. Go away, don't touch me! What right have you to take
my hand?

ORESTES. There's no one living whose hand I have more right to
take.

ELECTRA. Indeed? Then why lurk round my house with your
sword drawn?

ORESTES. Wait, now, and listen. You will soon agree with me.

ELECTRA. I'm waiting. You're the stronger; I am in your hands.

ORESTES. I bring news of your brother.

ELECTRA.   Oh! You are a friend!   210
Is he alive — or dead?

ORESTES.   Alive. So much is good.

ELECTRA. May happiness reward you for so dear a message.

ORESTES. May happiness indeed come to both you and me.

ELECTRA. Poor, exiled brother! In what land does he live now?

ORESTES. He goes from city to city, citizen of none.   •

ELECTRA. Is he in want of daily food?

ORESTES.   He is not in want;
But he is a refugee, and powerless.

ELECTRA.   What message
From him?

ORESTES.   To learn if you are alive; and then, what sort
Of life you have.

ELECTRA.   My face is withered, as you see.

ORESTES. Wasted with grief and suffering, as I weep to see.   220

ELECTRA. I've cut my hair off. Tell him of my Scythian scalp.

ORESTES. — To mark your grief for him, and for your father's
death.

ELECTRA. They are dearer to me than anything in my whole life.

ORESTES. Do you not think your brother loves you?

ELECTRA   He is not here;
He loves me from a distance.

ORESTES.   Tell me, Electra,
What makes you live so far from Argos?

ELECTRA.   I came here
When I was married. My marriage is a living death.

ORESTES. I grieve for Orestes. Is your husband a Mycenaean?

ELECTRA. Yes — one my father never hoped to give me to.

ORESTES. Who is he? Tell me, so that I can tell your brother.   230

ELECTRA. I live in this outlandish place. This is his house.

ORESTES. What, this? A ditcher, or a cowherd, might live here!

ELECTRA. He's poor, but generous-hearted; and he shows me reverence.

ORESTES (*indignant and resentful*). What sort of reverence does this husband have for you?

ELECTRA. He knows his place. He has never yet come near my bed.

ORESTES. Why? For religious reasons? Or perhaps he thinks You are not worthy of him

ELECTRA.   No; he thinks himself Unworthy, and does not wish to affront my ancestors.

ORESTES. He's pleased enough, no doubt, to have made such a marriage?

ELECTRA. He holds, the man who gave me to him had no such right.   240

ORESTES. I see; he fears Orestes may yet punish him.

ELECTRA. That too; but he's a man by nature virtuous.

ORESTES. He seems a truly generous man. We should reward him.

ELECTRA. We should indeed — if the exile ever returns home.

ORESTES. Your mother — was she content to see you married here?

ELECTRA. Friend, women's love is for their lovers, not their children.

ORESTES. What made Aegisthus put this outrage on you?

ELECTRA.   He hoped That, married to a clod, I should bear feeble sons.

ORESTES. Who would not burn to avenge you?

ELECTRA.   Yes, that was his thought. I trust he'll pay me for it one day.

ORESTES.   Does he know   250 You are still a virgin?

ELECTRA.   No, we keep him out of that.

ORESTES. These women can hear all we're saying — are they friends?

ELECTRA. Yes, to us both; they'll keep our counsel faithfully.

ORESTES. Suppose Orestes comes: how will he deal with this?

ELECTRA. You ask that? You insult him. Is the time not ripe?

ORESTES. But, once he came, how could he carry out this killing?

ELECTRA. Let him be resolute, as his father's murderers were.

ORESTES. Would you be resolute to help him kill your mother?

ELECTRA. I would — with the same axe by which my father died.

ORESTES. I'll tell him, then, that you are steadfast?

ELECTRA.   When I have shed   260
  Her blood to requite his, then I can die content.
ORESTES (*after a pause, realizing that she is twice as resolute as
    he*). I wish Orestes could be by, to hear you speak.
ELECTRA. Friend, if I saw him I should not recognize him.
ORESTES. No, naturally; you were both young when you were
    parted.
ELECTRA. Of all my friends there's only one who would know
    him now.
ORESTES. You mean the man who stole him away and saved his
    life?
ELECTRA. Yes, an old man who was my father's tutor once.
ORESTES. Now tell me: was your father given a proper grave?
ELECTRA. His body lies now where it fell, thrown out of doors.
ORESTES. No! How unspeakable! — Forgive me; but one feels   270
  The wound of such a wrong, though not involved oneself.
  For sympathy comes with perception: a brutal man
  Has none; while the perceptive pay a certain price
  For their too keen perception, in their own distress.

  Now tell me of your father's fate, and of your own —
  Unpleasant things to speak of, yet they must be told
  If I'm to take your brother back a full account.
CHORUS. I want to hear this too. Living so far from Argos,
  I don't know all that happened there; now I can learn.
ELECTRA. I'll tell you, since I must — I must, since you're a
    friend —   280
  About my father's wrongs and mine. Here are the words
  You've asked for: tell Orestes my disgrace and his;
  First, how I'm dressed; how I am stabled here; the filth
  That weighs me down, the squalid shack that has replaced
  My royal palace; how I must sit at the loom and weave
  Cloth for my own dress, or go naked; never a feast
  On holy days, never a dance; I cannot mix
  With wives, myself a virgin; as for Castor, who,
  Before he joined the gods, was courting me, his cousin,
  How can I think of him? Meanwhile my mother sits   290
  Lapped in the spoils of Troy, and Trojan waiting-maids
  My father captured and brought home, stand by her throne,
  Their Phrygian gowns buckled with golden clasps. And still
  The dark stain of my father's blood lies festering there;
  While he who killed him gets into my father's own
  Chariot, and rides forth and back, and swaggeringly

Grasps in his bloody hand the very sceptre which
My father carried when he led Hellas to war.
On Agamemnon's grave no wine was ever yet
Poured out, no wreath of myrtle laid; dishonoured, bare   300
Of pious adornment, there it lies. My mother's husband,
Royal Aegisthus, when he's drunk, so people say,
Jumps on the grave, or flings stones at my father's name
Inscribed there, and shouts words intended for us all,
Such as, "Where is your son Orestes? Should he not
Be here, to ensure proper protection for your tomb?"
The insult goes unanswered; Orestes is not here.

So, friend, I beg you, tell him everything I've said.
The message comes from many; I speak one for all —
My hands, my tongue, my anguished heart, my close-cropped
   head,   310
And, most of all, *his* father. Agamemnon brought
Death to the Phrygian nation: Orestes is still young,
And had a greater father — can't he kill one man?

CHORUS. Electra, look! I see your husband coming back;
   He has left his work, and is hurrying towards the house.

(*Enter the* PEASANT.)

PEASANT. Well! Who are these two strangers I see by the door?
   Now what should bring them to a country place like this?
   Is it me the gentlemen were wanting? — Now look, wife:
   It's not right to stand talking out here with young men.

ELECTRA. Dear husband, don't think any wrong of me. I'll tell
   you   320
   Just what has happened: these two men have brought me word
   Of Orestes. — Friends, forgive the way he spoke to you.

PEASANT. Well, what news have they brought? Is Orestes still
   alive?

ELECTRA. They say so, and I believe them.

PEASANT.   Does he bear in mind
   Your father's wrongs, and yours?

ELECTRA.   We can do no more than hope;
   A stateless man has few resources.

PEASANT.   What do they say
   Of him?

ELECTRA.   He sent them to spy out my desolate life.

PEASANT. Then some of it they've seen, the rest no doubt you've
   told them.

ELECTRA. They know; I've told them everything.

PEASANT.   Then why's the door
  Still shut? You ought to have asked them in. — Sirs, come
     inside   330
  For your good news, such entertainment as we have
  Is yours, and welcome. — Men, bring all their traps indoors.
  — Now don't say no; you're friends, and you've come from a
     friend.
  I've been a poor man all my life, but I'm not mean.
ORESTES. By the gods! Is this the man whose loyalty has made
  Your marriage no marriage, to save Orestes' honour?
ELECTRA. This is the man who is known as "poor Electra's hus-
     band."
ORESTES. Well!
  There's no clear sign to tell the quality of a man;
  Nature and place turn vice and virtue upside down.   340
  I've seen a noble father breed a worthless son,
  And good sons come of evil parents; a starved soul
  Housed in a rich man's palace, a great heart dressed in rags.
  By what sign, then, shall one tell good from bad? By wealth?
  Wealth's a false standard. By possessing nothing, then?
  No; poverty is a disease; and want itself
  Trains men in crime. Or must I look to see how men
  Behave in battle? When you're watching your enemy's spear
  You don't know who's brave, who's a coward. The best way
  Is to judge each man as you find him; there's no rule.   350

  This man is not a leading Argive citizen;
  He's not a well-known member of a famous house;
  He's one of the many; yet he's a true nobleman.
  Then, all you blunderers, full of empty theories,
  Why not give up your folly, and judge men's qualities
  By the company they keep and by the way they act?

  However, since a kind reception's due to both —
  To me in person, and in his absence to Orestes
  Whose messenger I am — come on, let us accept
  This house's hospitality. — Men, go inside.   360
  Give me a host who's poor but friendly, rather than
  A rich one. Yet, though I accept his invitation —
  Oh! how I wish your brother now, restored and royal,
  Were welcoming me into a rejoicing house!
  He may yet come. Human prognostications I've
  No use for; but Apollo's prophecies are sure.

(*Exeunt* ORESTES *and* PYLADES *with Attendants into the cottage.*)

CHORUS. Now more than ever, Electra, my heart warms with joy.
   Luck stirs at last, and may soon reach a happy end.
ELECTRA (*to her husband*). You fool, you know how bare your
      house is. These two guests
   Are far above your level. Why must you ask them in?   370
PEASANT. Why not? If they're as noble as they look, they'll be
   Equally at home in a cottage or anywhere else.
ELECTRA. Remember, you're "the poor." Still, since you've done
      it now,
   Go quickly and find my father's old servant, who, since
   They turned him out of Argos, tends a flock of sheep
   Close to the Spartan frontier, by the Tanaos;
   Tell him we have guests, and he must come and bring some-
      thing
   That I can cook and give them. He'll be pleased enough
   To know my brother, the child whom he once saved, still lives;
   He'll bless the gods. Well, we'd get nothing from my mother   380
   Out of my father's house. What's more, we'd suffer for it
   If she, the wretch, learnt that Orestes is alive.
PEASANT. Well, if you think it best, I'll go to the old man
   And take your message. You go in now straight away
   And get things ready. When a woman's put to it
   She can find odds and ends to make a meal look good.
   Well, surely there's at least enough left in the house
   To stuff their guts for one day? — When I find myself
   Frustrated in such matters, I think, "What a power
   There is in money! You can entertain a guest;   390
   Or, if you're ill, buy medicine and cure yourself."
   For the rest — well, each day's eating doesn't come to much.
   Rich bellies hold about the same amount as poor.

(*Exeunt* ELECTRA *and* PEASANT *severally.*)

CHORUS:
      Famous were the ships
      Which sailed long ago from Hellas to Troy,
      When the dancing of oars without number
      Joined in their journey the dancing sea-nymphs,
      Where, drawn by the music of flutes,
      Dolphins were leaping and rolling
      Beside the purple-painted prows,   400
      Bearing on his way the son of Thetis,
      The light-footed leaper Achilles,

Who went with Agamemnon's army
To the rocky Trojan coast and the Simois river.

Passing the headlands of Euboea
The Nereids came, carrying
Golden armour for a prince of fighters,
The labour of Hephaestus' forge,
To the slopes of Mount Pelion,
To the holy glens of precipitous Ossa,   410
The high haunts of mountain-nymphs,
Seeking Achilles the young runner,
Grandson of the salt sea,
Where for the sake of the sons of Atreus
The old Centaur was rearing him
As a light of hope for Hellas.

I heard a man from Troy describing,
As he stood in the harbour at Nauplia,
Your famous shield, son of Thetis,
Engraved all round with figures   420
Which terrified the Trojans:
On the outermost rim was Perseus
Hovering on winged sandals over the sea,
Holding the severed head of the dread Gorgon,
And with him Hermes, Zeus's messenger,
The son of Maia, god of country places.

In the centre of the shield blazed forth
The gleaming circle of the sun
Drawn by winged horses,
And the celestial dancing constellations,   430
The Pleiads and the Hyades,
Which Hector saw, and fled;
And on the helmet of beaten gold
Were Sphinxes, their claws clutching
The prey caught by their enchantments;
And on the rounded corselet
That lioness breathing fire,
Her clawed feet stretched in flight
At the sight of Pegasus the horse of Pyrene.

And on Achilles' deadly sword appeared   440
Four prancing horses harnessed together,

And the dust rose dark around their flanks.
Such were the warriors whose commander
Your adultery sent to his death,
Evil-hearted daughter of Tyndareos!
Therefore you too the heavenly gods will send to death;
The day will come when I shall see
The steel blade set to your throat
And your life pour forth in blood.

(*Enter an* OLD MAN *carrying various provisions.*)

OLD MAN. Where's my young mistress? Where's Electra, my
    princess,   450
Whose father Agamemnon I brought up? — Oh, dear!
This path up to her house is far too steep for me,
A wrinkled old man. Still, a friend's a friend; so I
Must drag myself up — bent back, wobbly knee, and all.

(ELECTRA *appears at the door.*)

Ah, there you are! My daughter! Look, I've brought you a
    lamb
Bred in my own flock; quite young — took it from the ewe
This morning; and some flowers; and cheese, straight from the
    press.
And here's a little of Dionysus' treasure — old,
Rich-scented; it's not much — but pour a cup of this
Into your weaker wine, to give it body. There!   460
Let someone take all this in to your guests. My eyes
Are full of tears, I must just wipe them on my old coat.
ELECTRA. Why do you weep, old man? It can't be *my* condition,
My grief that stirs your memory after all this time?
Or does the thought of Orestes' exile make you sad?
Or do you mourn my father, whom your care brought up —
Though you and those you love see no reward for it?
OLD MAN. No, no reward. But there's one thing I would not
    bear:
On my way here I passed his grave. I was alone.
I knelt down, and shed tears; and then I opened this   470
Wineskin I brought for your two guests, and poured some wine
There as an offering, and spread some myrtle-branches
Over the grave. And there, right on the altar, lay
A black-fleeced ewe just newly sacrificed — the blood
Still wet; and near it a lock of dark brown hair, cut off.
I wonder, now, who it could be? What man would dare
To visit that grave? Certainly no Argive would.

Perhaps — perhaps your brother came there secretly
And paid this reverence to his father's desolate tomb.
Go there yourself, and put that hair against your own;   480
See if their colour tallies. Children of one father
Often have many features that are similar.

ELECTRA. You should know better than to think that *my* brother,
My brave Orestes, would have come here secretly
Because he feared Aegisthus. Anyway, how could
The two locks correspond, the one a nobleman's,
Grown like an athlete's in the palaestra, mine a woman's,
Softened with combing? It's absurd. Besides, you'd find
Many with similar hair, who are not of the same blood.

OLD MAN. Then go and try the shoe-prints there with your own
   foot,   490
My child; see if the shape and size are like your own.

ELECTRA. Foot-prints? How could there be foot-prints on rocky
   ground?
And if there could, brother's and sister's feet would not
Be the same size; the weaker sex has smaller feet.

OLD MAN. That's true: if he *has* come, we can't be sure of it.
Yet, should you meet him face to face, would he not wear,
For recognition, the cloak, woven on your loom, in which
Long ago, to save his life, I smuggled him away?

ELECTRA. Surely you know that, when Orestes went away,
I was a child? Even if I had been weaving clothes,   500
Clothes don't grow larger on the body; he wouldn't now
Be wearing the same cloak he had in infancy.
No; either a stranger pitied the neglected grave
And laid a lock there; or some Argive dared to elude
The guards, and make dutiful offerings to the dead.

OLD MAN. But where are your two guests? I want to see them
   now
And question them about your brother.

ELECTRA.   Here they come.

   (ORESTES *and* PYLADES *come briskly out of the cottage.*)

OLD MAN (*aside*). They have nobility; but it may be counterfeit.
Many that are nobly born belie it. None the less —
   (*To* ORESTES *and* PYLADES) My courteous greeting to our guests.

ORESTES.   Greeting, old man.   510
   — Electra, whose friend is this antique relic here?

ELECTRA. This man, Sir, was my father's guardian when a child.

ORESTES. What? The same man who got your brother safely
   away?

ELECTRA. Yes; if Orestes lives, he owes his life to him.

ORESTES. Well . . . ?
  Why does he stare at me, like a man examining
  The head on a new silver coin? Perhaps he thinks
  I am like someone.

ELECTRA.   You are one of Orestes' friends;
  He is glad to see you.

ORESTES.   Yes, Orestes is my friend. —
  Why is he walking round me?

ELECTRA.   I am wondering too.   520

OLD MAN. My daughter, royal Electra! Pray to the great gods —

ELECTRA. What shall I pray for — of all things in heaven and
  earth?

OLD MAN. To grasp the precious treasure God reveals to you.

ELECTRA. Very well; I call upon the gods. — What do you mean?

OLD MAN. Look at this man, my child. There's no one you love
  more.

ELECTRA. I have been looking — to see if you have lost your wits.

OLD MAN. Lost my wits? When I see your brother before my
  eyes?

ELECTRA. My brother? No! I can't believe it.

OLD MAN.   You are looking
  At Agamemnon's son, Orestes.

ELECTRA.   Do you see
  Some token, to convince me?

OLD MAN.   This scar on his brow;   530
  He fell and cut it once at home, chasing a fawn
  With you.

ELECTRA. What's that? A scar? I see it, yes —

OLD MAN.   Then why
  Hesitate? He's your brother: take him in your arms!

ELECTRA. I will! Your tokens have convinced me. — O my
  brother!

              (*They embrace.*)

  I thought you'd never come. At last I hold you close.

ORESTES. At last you are in my arms.

ELECTRA.   I had despaired.

ORESTES.   I too.

ELECTRA. You really are Orestes?

ORESTES.   Yes; your one ally.
  And if I catch the prey I've come to hunt —

ELECTRA.   You will!
  I am certain. We can never again believe in gods   540

If wickedness is now to triumph over right.

CHORUS.
It has come, at last it has come!
The bright day has dawned;
Our deliverer stands before us,
A beacon of hope for Argos;
Who far from his father's house
Lived so many years a homeless exile.
God is with us, Electra;
God leads us in our turn to victory.
Lift your hands, lift your voice,   550
Pour your prayer to the gods
That with good success your brother
May enter the gates of Argos.

ORESTES. Enough, sister; this mutual meeting and embrace
Is a dear pleasure, which in time we will renew.
Now tell me, old man — your coming is a lucky chance —
I am here for vengeance on my father's murderer
And on my mother, his partner both in crime and lust:
What is my next step? Have I any friends in Argos?
Or am I bankrupt — as in fortune, so in all?   560
Whom shall I contact? Shall I go by night or day?
What way shall I set out to meet my enemies?

OLD MAN. My son, you are an exile: you have not one friend.
It's a rare piece of fortune if a man will share
Both good and bad with you. In your friends' eyes you are
Uprooted, finished; no one pins his hopes on you.
Listen: success lies in your luck and your strong arm,
If you're to get back Argos and your father's house.

ORESTES. Yes, that's my aim. What must I do to reach it?

OLD MAN.   Kill
Aegisthus and your mother.

ORESTES.   That's the glorious deed   570
I've come to attempt. But how achieve it?

OLD MAN.   It's no use
To think of getting inside the walls.

ORESTES.   Aegisthus has,
I take it, guards and sentries everywhere?

OLD MAN.   You're right.
He's afraid of you; he can't sleep.

ORESTES.   What do you suggest?

OLD MAN. Well, listen now; I've thought of something.

ORESTES.   May it be

A good proposal, and may I understand it right.

OLD MAN. On my way here I saw Aegisthus.

ORESTES.   Splendid: where?

OLD MAN. Not far off, in the pastures where his horses graze.

ORESTES. What was he doing? This may solve the insoluble.

OLD MAN. Preparing a banquet for the Nymphs — or so it
seemed.   580

ORESTES. As thanks for children, or vows for an expected birth?

OLD MAN. He had everything in hand to sacrifice a bull;
That's all I know.

ORESTES.   How many men were with him? Or
Had he just slaves?

OLD MAN.   Some of his household staff were there;
No Argives.

ORESTES.   Might there be some who would recognize me?

OLD MAN. They're slaves; they never saw you.

ORESTES.   Suppose I kill the man —
Would they be friendly?

OLD MAN.   Slaves will always serve success;
That's in your favour.

ORESTES.   How should I best get close to him?

OLD MAN. Go and stand where he'll see you at the sacrifice.

ORESTES. You mean, his land lies close along the road?

OLD MAN.   Why, yes;   590
He'll see you, and invite you in to share the feast.

ORESTES. By the gods' help, he'll find me an unwelcome guest.

OLD MAN. From then on you must make your plans as things turn
out.

ORESTES. You're right. Where is my mother?

OLD MAN.   She's in Argos still;
But she'll be with her husband for the festival.

ORESTES. Why did she not start out with him?

OLD MAN.   Why, she's afraid
Of harsh words from the people; so she stayed behind.

ORESTES. I well believe it; she knows what they think of her.

OLD MAN. That's so; she's hated by them as a woman accursed.

ORESTES. Well, then: am I to kill them both at the same time?   600

ELECTRA. The killing of my mother I shall claim myself.

ORESTES. Good; and in *my* part I'll take Fortune for my guide.

ELECTRA. And this old friend will help us in our separate tasks.

OLD MAN. I will. What plan have you for Clytemnestra's death?

ELECTRA. This: go and tell her I have borne a child — a son.

OLD MAN. Shall I say this was recent, or some time ago?

ELECTRA. Ten days ago, say; that gives time for purifying.

OLD MAN. And how is this to bring about your mother's death?

ELECTRA. When she is told of my confinement she will come.

OLD MAN. Will she? You think, daughter, she cares for you at all?   610

ELECTRA. Yes; she will come and weep over my son's low birth.

OLD MAN. Perhaps; but bring your argument back to the point.

ELECTRA. Once here, the rest is simple: she's as good as dead.

OLD MAN. But even suppose she comes here — comes right to your door — ?

ELECTRA. Surely from here it's just a short by-path to death?

OLD MAN. Let me once see this done, and I can die content.

ELECTRA. But first, now, you must show my brother where to go
  To find Aegisthus.

OLD MAN.   Yes, at the sacrifice.

ELECTRA.   — And then
  Go on to meet my mother and tell her what I said.

OLD MAN. Your very words — she'll think you're telling her your-self.   620

ELECTRA. Orestes, now to work. You draw first blood.

ORESTES.   I'm ready,
  Given a guide.

OLD MAN.   I'll take you there most willingly.

(They all raise their hands in prayer.)

ORESTES. Zeus! Conqueror of my father's enemies and mine!

ELECTRA. Have pity on us; for our state is pitiable.

OLD MAN. Have pity on them: they are yours by birth and blood.

ELECTRA. Hera, great Queen, to whom Mycenae's altars burn!

ORESTES. If these our prayers are just, O grant us victory.

OLD MAN. O grant them a just vengeance for their father's death.

(They kneel.)

ORESTES. My father, sent by foul crime to your home below!

ELECTRA. And Earth, great Sovereign, whom my beating hands
  invoke!   630

OLD MAN. Send now to these dear children strong defence and
  aid.

ORESTES. Bring the whole army of the dead to fight your cause.

ELECTRA. Bring all the brave who shared your victory over Troy.

OLD MAN. Bring all who hate impure hearts and polluted hands.

(A pause. ORESTES *and the* OLD MAN *rise.)*

ELECTRA. Father, so outraged by my mother! Do you hear?

OLD MAN. He has heard all, I am certain. — It is time to go.

(ELECTRA *rises.*)

ELECTRA. I give you then this token-word: "Aegisthus dies."
If in the struggle you are thrown and lose your life,
Be sure I shall not live: that moment is my death.
I'll drive a sword into my heart.

ORESTES.   I understand.   640

ELECTRA. Then take your courage in both hands.

(*Exeunt* ORESTES, PYLADES, OLD MAN, *and Attendants.*)

                                        Women! Your part
Will be, like beacons after battle, to raise the cry
For life or death. I'll be on watch; and my hand too
Will hold a sword. If I'm defeated, my enemies
Shall never glut their vengeance on my living flesh.

(*Exit* ELECTRA.)

CHORUS.

Long ago, in the mountains of Argos,
A soft young lamb under its ewe
(So say the grey-haired spinners of old tales)
Was found by Pan, prince of wild places,
Who breathes enchanting music on his tuned reeds;   650
And the lamb had a lovely fleece of pure gold.
And Pan, they say, brought it to Atreus king of Argos;
And there a herald stood on the marble steps, and cried,
"People of Mycenae, come all, come all!
Come and see this wonderful sight,
Our great king's treasure."
And the people came at once
And honoured the royal palace with dancing and singing.

And braziers of beaten gold were placed about;
And all over the city of Argos   660
Fire gleamed on the altars;
And the flute, servant of the Muses,
Sounded forth its sweet notes,
And lovely songs rose loud
In praise of the golden lamb.
Then Thyestes turned to treachery.
He lay secretly with Atreus' wife,
And persuaded her;
And he took the marvellous lamb to his own house.
Then going forth to the assembled people he proclaimed   670

That he held in his own house the horned marvel,
The lamb with the golden fleece.

Then, then it was that Zeus turned back
The glittering journeys of the stars
And the burning sun and the pale face of dawn;
And from that day on, the blaze of divine fire
Drives always towards the western sky;
And the wet clouds lie to the north,
And the parched plains of Ammon languish untouched by
     dew,
And Zeus withholds from them his sweet rain.   680

That is the story. But I can hardly believe
That the golden sun turned his face,
Changed his burning course,
To help a mortal's misfortune
And requite a human sin.
Nevertheless, frightening tales are useful:
They promote reverence for the gods.
O Clytemnestra, sister of two famous brothers!
Had you but remembered tales like these
As you raised your hand to kill your husband!   690

Ah!
Friends, what was that? Did I imagine it — a shout
Like subterranean thunder? Or did you hear it too?
The gale is up, I tell you, and brings news. — My lady!
Electra! Come out here!

                    (*Enter* ELECTRA.)

ELECTRA.   What is it? The fight is on —
Where do we stand?
CHORUS.   I heard a cry, like death. That's all.
ELECTRA. I heard a cry too; at some distance, but I heard.
CHORUS (*still listening*). The sound comes from far off, but un-
     mistakable.
ELECTRA. That was an Argive voice — a groan. Was it my
     brother?
CHORUS. I can't tell. There's a chorus now of mingled cries.   700
ELECTRA. That means the sword for me — now; I must lose no
     time.
CHORUS. No! Wait at least until you know the worst is true.
ELECTRA. I must not. We have lost. There would be news by
     now.

CHORUS. There will be. It's no easy matter to kill a king.

(*Enter a* MESSENGER.)

MESSENGER. Victory, women of Mycenae! Victory!
  To all friends I proclaim Orestes' victory!
  Aegisthus, Agamemnon's murderer, lies dead.
  Thanks be to all the gods!

ELECTRA.   Who are you? How do I know
  Your news is true?

MESSENGER.   You know me — I'm your brother's servant!

ELECTRA. Dear friend, forgive me. Terror made me blind; but
  now   710
  I recognize you well enough. Tell me again:
  The loathsome wretch who killed my father — is he dead?

MESSENGER. He's dead. Good news twice told is twice welcome
  to you.

ELECTRA. O gods, and Justice, who behold all things! At last
  You have come! — Friend, tell me point by point about this
  death.
  My brother killed Thyestes' son: how? I must know.

MESSENGER. After we left this cottage, we soon reached a road
  Wide enough for two wagons; and we followed this
  To where the great king of Mycenae was. He stood
  In a well-watered plot, cutting young myrtle-leaves   720
  To make a garland for his head. When he saw us
  He called out, "Greeting, strangers! Who are you? And
  where
  Do you come from? What's your country?" And Orestes said,
  "We are Thessalians, and we're going to the Alpheius
  To sacrifice to Olympian Zeus." When he heard that
  Aegisthus said, "Stay here today and be my guests.
  I'm killing a bull in honour of the Nymphs; and you
  Must share the banquet. Get up in good time tomorrow —
  You'll be there just as soon. Come on, into the house."
  And as he said this he was leading us by the hand —   730
  "I won't let you refuse," he cried. "Here, one of you,
  Bring water for these guests to wash; and let them stand
  Close to the altar, by the purifying bowl."

  Orestes answered, "We have purified ourselves
  Just now, in holy water from a running stream.
  So, King Aegisthus, if strangers may lawfully
  Join in the sacrifice with Argives, we will not
  Refuse your bidding; here we are." That settled that.

The slaves guarding the king laid by their spears; and all
At once were busy: some held baskets; others brought   740
The sacrificial bowl; others again lit fires
And put pots on to boil; and the whole house was full
Of noise and movement.

              Then your mother's lover took
Barley, and threw it on the altar, with these words:
"Nymphs of these rocks, I pray that many times both I
And my dear wife at home may offer sacrifice
With the same fortune we enjoy today; and may
Evil oppress my enemies" — by which he meant
You and Orestes. Then under his breath my master
Prayed contrary, to possess again his father's house.   750
Aegisthus from the basket took the straight-edged blade,
And cut from the beast's head one tuft; with his right hand
He placed this on the holy flame; then, as the slaves
Lifted the young bull shoulder-high, he cut its throat;
Then said to Orestes:

"I've heard it boasted that Thessalians are expert
At two things: cutting up a dead bull skilfully,
And breaking horses to the rein. Friend, here's the sword:
Show us now if that's true about Thessalians."

It was a well-made Dorian sword. He grasped it firm,   760
Threw off his buckled cloak, called Pylades to help,
Made all the slaves stand back; then took the bull-calf's leg,
And with one long sweep laid the pale flesh bare, and flayed
The carcase in less time than a fast runner takes
To run a mile; then opened up the guts. At once
Aegisthus took the augural parts and gazed at them.
The liver-lobe was missing; and the portal-vein
And gall-bladder portended evil visitations
To one that saw them. The king's face grew dark. Orestes
Asked him, "What has upset you?" "Friend, I'm much in
    fear,"   770
He said, "of treachery from abroad. Agamemnon's son,
Of all men living, is the most dangerous enemy
To me and to my royal house." Orestes said,
"What? You, king of a city, fear an exile's plots?
This Dorian knife's too small; bring me a Phthian sword;
I'll split the breast-bone, then we can fall to and feast."
They brought one, and he cut. Aegisthus took the parts

To separate them, bending over them. Orestes
Rose on his toes, and struck him on the joint of the neck,
Shattering his spine. His whole body from head to foot   780
Writhed, shuddered in death-agony. The king's guards ran
And seized their spears — a whole regiment against two.
They stood their ground and faced them boldly. Orestes cried,
"I am no enemy to Argos, not to you,
My comrades. This man was my father's murderer,
Whom I have punished — I am Orestes. You were once
My father's servants: will you take my life?" At this
They checked their spears; in a moment he was recognized
By an old man who had long served the royal house.
And there they were, cheering and shouting with delight,   790
And putting garlands on him. Now he's coming here,
Bringing no Gorgon's head to show you, but the head
Of your enemy, Aegisthus. His atrocious debt
Has fallen due; his life at last pays blood for blood.

CHORUS.
　　Oh, Electra! Set your feet dancing!
　　Dance like a light fawn
　　That springs in rapture heaven-high!
　　Orestes has achieved his task
　　And won a crown more glorious than the Olympic crown.
　　Come, match our dancing with your victory song.   800

ELECTRA. O holy light! O glorious chariot of the sun!
O earth! O night, that till this moment filled my eyes!
Now all is freedom, eyes may open unafraid:
Aegisthus lies dead, who destroyed my father's life.
Come, friends; such festive finery as I still possess
Stored in the house, I must bring out, to crown with joy
My brother's head, and celebrate his victory.

　　　　　　　(*Exit* ELECTRA *to the cottage.*)

CHORUS.
　　Go, then, bring the crown for his head;
　　We meanwhile will dance to delight the Muses.
　　Now our own true king,   810
　　Of the line that we loved in the old days,
　　Has destroyed the usurper
　　And holds his rightful rule in Argos.
　　Come, let heart and voice rise together.

　　(ELECTRA *returns carrying two crowns or wreaths, as* ORESTES
　　enters with PYLADES, *followed by others bearing the body of*
　　AEGISTHUS.)

ELECTRA. Welcome, brave conqueror! Welcome, Orestes,
    worthy son
  Of him who conquered Troy! Come, let me bind your hair
  With this triumphal crown. You have run your full course
  And come home bearing your just prize — your enemy
  Dead at your feet, who struck down your father and mine.
  — You too, receive from me this garland, Pylades,   820
  His brave comrade-in-arms, son of an honourable man.
  You have shared equally with him in this ordeal;
  I pray for both of you a long and happy life.
ORESTES. Name first the gods, Electra, as accomplishers
  Of this good fortune; give your second place of praise
  To me, who am the gods' and Fortune's instrument.
  I have in full truth killed Aegisthus. So that knowledge
  May be confirmed by visible truth, here is himself.

           (*He shows the head of* AEGISTHUS.)

  Do what you wish; throw out his carcase to the dogs,
  Impale him on a stake, to feed the birds of heaven.   830
  He's yours, Electra; once your master, now your slave.
ELECTRA. Shame makes me shrink from words which my will
    prompts me to.
ORESTES. What shame? There's nothing you need fear.
ELECTRA.   Shame makes me fear
  To insult the dead, lest sharp resentment point at me.
ORESTES. No one would blame you.
ELECTRA.   Our citizens are quick to blame
  And hard to please.
ORESTES.   Say what you wish, sister. The feud
  We had with this dead man was unconditional.
ELECTRA. Of all the harsh and bitter things I have to say,
  What shall come first, what last? and what shall come be-
    tween?
  For years I have never failed at sunrise to say over   840
  All that I longed to tell you to your face, if ever
  I left behind that terror-ridden past. And now
  I am free. I'll pay off now those evil words which I
  Wanted to say to you when you were still alive.

  You were the ruin of my life. I and my brother
  Did you no wrong; but you made us both fatherless.
  Adulterously you took my mother; then you killed
  Her husband, chief commander of the Greeks — though you
  Yourself never saw Troy. Then, you were such a fool

As to imagine, when you had shamed my father's bed,   850
That in my mother you would find a faithful wife.
When an adulterer corrupts his neighbour's wife,
And then is forced to marry her, let him be sure
Of this: he's to be pitied if he dreams that she,
Who cuckolded one husband, will not cuckold two.
It was a sorry life you lived, though unaware:
You knew your marriage was unholy; and she knew
Her husband was an enemy of the gods; so each,
Being evil, gained the other's evil destiny,
She yours, you hers. And no Argive called her your wife;   860
But always "Clytemnestra's husband" was your name.

Is it not shameful, when the wife, and not the husband,
Takes the first place at home? So too when boys are known
Not as their father's sons, but as their mother's — that
Is something which I hate. For when a man has married
A noble wife above his station, not a word
Is said about him; all the talk is of his wife.

What more than all deluded your dull mind was this:
You thought that having great wealth made you a great man.
But money keeps you company a little while;   870
What's firm and lasting is man's nature, not his wealth.
A noble nature is a lifelong friend, and lifts
Life's burdens; wealth makes unjust league with wickedness,
And, flowering a brief season, soon flies out of doors.

As for your way with women, since plain speech does not
Become a virgin, I'll pick words discreetly. You,
Equipped with both a royal palace and good looks,
Indulged. . . . Give me for husband not a girl-faced fop,
But a true man, whose sons devote themselves to arms.
The other sort shine at a dance, and nowhere else.   880

Then perish, ignorant how the ripe years have condemned
Your guilt! — Let no man, deep in wickedness like his,
Think, if at first his stride is strong, he can outstrip
Justice, till he has run his race and come safe home.
CHORUS. His crimes were fearful; and he has paid a fearful price
    To both of you. Justice is irresistible.
ELECTRA. Men, take his body in and put it out of sight.
    My mother must not see it before her throat is cut.

(ORESTES *sees* CLYTEMNESTRA *approaching some way off.*)

ORESTES. Wait. There are other things we must decide.

ELECTRA (*looking in the same direction*). What is it?   890
An armed force from Mycenae?

ORESTES.   No. It is my mother.

ELECTRA. Good: she is stepping straight into the trap. — Why,
look!
How fine she is — a carriage, slaves, and her best gown!

ORESTES. What shall we do, then? Are we going to kill our
mother?

ELECTRA. Have you grown soft, as soon as you set eyes on her?

ORESTES. She brought me up, she bore me! How can I take her
life?

ELECTRA. How? As she took our father Agamemnon's life.

ORESTES. Phoebus, your oracle is blind brutality!

ELECTRA. Whose eyes can hope to see, then, if Apollo's blind?

ORESTES. It is wrong to kill my mother! Yet you said I must.   900

ELECTRA. You avenge your father — what harm comes to you
from that?

ORESTES. Avenging him I am pure; but killing her, condemned.

ELECTRA. If you neglect to avenge him you defy the gods.

ORESTES. But if I kill my mother, shall I not be punished?

ELECTRA. *He* will pursue you, if you let his vengeance go.

ORESTES. Some fiend disguised as god commanded me.

ELECTRA.   A fiend —
Throned on the holy tripod? Most improbable.

ORESTES. I can't believe that what the god told me is right.

ELECTRA. You're not to lose your nerve and play the coward
now.
You're going to use the same deception that *she* used   910
When with Aegisthus' help she struck her husband down.

ORESTES. I'll go in. Every step is dreadful; and the deed
Before me, still more dreadful. Yet, if Heaven so wills,
Let it be done. Heaven cannot help my agony.

(*Exeunt* ORESTES *and* PYLADES *into the house.*)

(*Enter* CLYTEMNESTRA *attended by female slaves.*)

CHORUS.
Daughter of Tyndareos,
Queen of the land of Argos,
Sister of the two noble sons of Zeus
Who live among stars in the fiery heaven
And are honoured on stormy seas

As saviours of men's lives: 920
Greeting, Lady.
For your great wealth and prosperity
We worship you as one of the blessed gods.
We have waited long for this happy day;
Much will be put right by your coming.
Welcome, Queen.

CLYTEMNESTRA. Get out of the carriage, Trojan slaves. Now
    take my hand
And help me to the ground. — The spoils of Troy adorn
Our holy temples; these, the choicest of Troy's women,
Are mine — small compensation for the child I lost;   930
Still, they look lovely in my place.

ELECTRA.   Why should not I
Be given this privilege, to hold your royal hand?
I am a slave too, banished from my father's house
To misery.

CLYTEMNESTRA. I have my slaves here; pray don't trouble.

ELECTRA. You took me prisoner by the sword, uprooted me.
Was I not, like them, captured in a conquered palace?
Like them, am I not fatherless?

CLYTEMNESTRA.   Your father, child,
Brought all this on you by his wicked treachery
To one he should have loved. Listen: I know my tongue   940
Is sometimes bitter; that's because I'm spoken of
As a bad woman. I agree, one should not speak
Bitterly. But when people judge someone, they ought
To learn the facts, and then hate, if they've reason to.
And if they find no reason, then they should not hate.

When I married your father, I did not expect
To die, or see my children killed. He took my child
To Aulis, where the fleet lay bound; lured her from home
With lies about Achilles; held her high above
The altar; then her father cut her soft white throat —   950
My Iphigenia. If he had done it to avert
The capture of his city, or to exalt his house;
Or if, to save his other children, he had taken
One life for many, he could be forgiven. But no:
Helen was a whore, her husband didn't know how to handle
A randy wife; and *that* was Agamemnon's reason
For murdering my daughter. All the same, for that —
Wicked as it was — I would not have turned savage, or

Have killed my husband. But he must bring home with him
The mad prophetess; foist on me a second wife,   960
A fellow-lodger — two kept women in one house.

Well, women are frail, I grant you. But when, knowing this,
A husband looks elsewhere, and slights his lawful wife,
She'll copy him, and find herself another friend.
And then the glare of public censure lights on *us;*
The husbands are to blame — but they're not criticized.
Suppose Menelaus had been abducted secretly,
Would I have had to kill Orestes, to get back
My sister's husband Menelaus? Would your father
Have stood for that? No: he'd have killed me if I'd touched   970
His son; he killed my daughter — why should he not die?
I killed him. I took the only way open to me —
Turned for help to his enemies. Well, what could I do?
None of your father's friends would have helped me murder
   him.

So, if you're anxious to refute me, do it now;
Speak freely; prove your father's death not justified.
CHORUS. Your words are just; yet in your "justice" there remains
   Something repellent. A wife ought in all things to accept
   Her husband's judgement, if she is wise. Those who will not
   Admit this, fall outside my scope of argument.   980
ELECTRA. Mother, remember what you said just now. You
   promised
   That I might state my opinion freely without fear.
CLYTEMNESTRA. I said so, daughter; and I meant it.
ELECTRA.   Do you mean
   You'll listen first, and get your own back afterwards?
CLYTEMNESTRA. No, no; you're free to say what your heart wants
   to say.
ELECTRA. I'll say it, then. This is where I'll begin. I wish,
   Mother, your heart were purer. You and Helen both
   Were rightly praised for beauty; but unhappily
   In heart too you are sisters, both lascivious.
   Castor must blush for you. They talk of Helen's "rape" —   990
   She embraced her own corruption! You destroyed the life
   Of the most noble man in Hellas — your pretext,
   That you avenged your daughter with your husband's blood.
   There may be some believe you; but I know you well.

Before your daughter's sacrifice was decided on,
When Agamemnon still was scarcely out of sight,
You were before your mirror, smoothing out your hair.
A wife who in her husband's absence will take pains
To enhance her beauty, may be written off as bad.
She has no need to show a pretty face outdoors 1000
Unless she's seeking what she should not. You alone
Of all Greek women — as I know — if ever Troy
Gained some success, were happy; if Troy lost a battle
Your eyes were clouded. Why? Because you didn't want
Agamemnon to come back from Troy. And yet you had
Every inducement to be faithful. Agamemnon
Was not inferior to Aegisthus in descent;
A man whom Hellas chose for her Commander-in-chief.
Further, when Helen your sister so disgraced herself,
You had a chance to make your name; for wickedness 1010
Acts as a foil to virtue and makes it noticeable.

This next: if, as you say, my father killed your daughter,
What injury have I and my brother done to you?
Why, after you had killed your husband, did you not
Make over to us our father's house? Instead you took
As dowry to your lover what was not your own,
And bought yourself a husband. Aegisthus does not
Suffer exile in payment for Orestes' wrongs,
Nor death for mine, though he inflicts a living death
On me, far crueller than my sister's. And if death 1020
In justice demands death, why, then, I and your son
Orestes must kill you to avenge our father's death;
For if the one revenge is just, so is the other.
CLYTEMNESTRA. My child, your nature has always been to love
  your father.
It is natural; some children love their fathers best,
And some their mothers. I'll forgive you. I do not,
In fact, exult unduly over what I did.
With what insensate fury I drove myself to take
My grand revenge! How bitterly I regret it now!
ELECTRA. It's too late for regret; you can't undo what's done. 1030
  Well, though my father's dead, your son Orestes lives,
  Exiled from Argos. Why do you not bring him home?
CLYTEMNESTRA. Because I'm terrified; not for him, but for myself.
  They say he is full of anger for his father's death.
ELECTRA. Why do you let Aegisthus still persecute *me?*

CLYTEMNESTRA. You know his temper. Yours too is implacable.

ELECTRA. I have good reason; but I'll put my anger aside.

CLYTEMNESTRA. Do; and you'll find he will stop persecuting you.

ELECTRA. He lives in my house; and that makes him arrogant.

CLYTEMNESTRA. There you go, kindling the old quarrel once
    again.   1040

ELECTRA. I'll keep quiet. I'm afraid of him — so much afraid.

CLYTEMNESTRA. Let's change the subject. Child, why did you
    send for me?

ELECTRA. You were told of my confinement, were you not?

CLYTEMNESTRA.   I was.
But why are you in this state — so dirty, so ill-dressed?
The birth's well over now.

ELECTRA.   Will you do this for me? —
Offer the customary tenth-day sacrifice
For a son. I've never had a child before, so I'm
No expert in these matters.

CLYTEMNESTRA.   It is usually done
By the woman who delivered you.

ELECTRA.   I was alone.
I delivered myself.

CLYTEMNESTRA.   What? Is this house so far   1050
From any neighbour?

ELECTRA.   We are poor; we don't have friends.

CLYTEMNESTRA. Well, as a favour, I'll go in, and pay the gods
The proper dues for your son. And then I must be off
To where my husband's sacrificing to the Nymphs
Out in the pasture. (*To her servants*) — You, there! take
    the carriage away
And feed the horses. Give me as much time as I need
To make this offering to the gods; then come for me.
(*To* ELECTRA) I have my husband too to think of.

ELECTRA.   Please come in
To our poor house. Take care this smoky wall does not
Dirty your dress. Now you shall offer to the gods   1060
The sacrifice that is due.

           (CLYTEMNESTRA *goes in.*)
                     All is prepared. The sword
Of sacrifice which felled the bull, by whose side you
Shall fall, is sharpened for you. In the house of Death
You shall be still his bride whose bed you shared in life.
This "favour" is all I grant you. In return I take
Justice, your life in payment for my father's life.

(ELECTRA *goes in.*)

CHORUS.

Now retribution follows sin;
Through the fated house a new wind blows.
Long ago my beloved lord and king
Fell dead by the water of purification;   1070
And through the rooms, round the stone cornice,
Rang out his death-cry,
"O wicked, wretched wife, why will you murder me,
Returned after ten harvests
Home to my own country?"

Now like a returning tide
Justice arraigns the reckless adulteress
Who, when her husband after many years
Came home to his heaven-high Cyclopean fortress,
Grasped the whetted axe,   1080
With her own hand struck and felled him.
Pity the victim of her vengeance,
Whatever raging wrongs possessed her.
Like a lioness from the mountains
Roaming through meadows and orchards,
She carried out her purpose.

CLYTEMNESTRA (*within*). My children, for the gods' sake, don't
kill your mother!

CHORUS. Do you hear that shriek in the house?

CLYTEMNESTRA. Help! Oh, oh!

CHORUS 1.
She calls for pity, and I pity her,   1090
Done to death by her own children.

CHORUS 2.
Soon or late, Heaven dispenses justice.
Poor, desperate queen, your suffering was bitter;
But your revenge on your husband was unholy.

CHORUS. They are coming, clothed in fresh streams of their
mother's blood —
Trophy of triumph over that beseeching cry.
There is no other house, nor ever was, whose fate
More rends the heart, than the great house of Tantalus.

(*Enter* ORESTES *and* ELECTRA, *both overcome with horror. Attendants bring the body of* CLYTEMNESTRA.)

ORESTES.
O Earth!

O Zeus, whose eye sees everything men do: 1100
Look at this!
This bloody, abominable sight!
Two bodies lying together on the ground —
And my hand struck them down,
To avenge wrong done to me!
Where can I find tears enough?

ELECTRA.

Tears, my brother — let tears be endless.
I am guilty.
I was burning with desperate rage against her;
Yet she was my mother, I her daughter.   1110

CHORUS 1.

How terrible was your fate,
Mother of curses!
Now with doubled anguish
The curses you bore have turned upon you.

CHORUS 2.

Yet, since you killed their father,
Their revenge is just.

ORESTES.

O Phoebus, in the command of your oracle
Justice was hidden from me;
But in its fulfilment
You have made torment clear.   1120
You have bestowed on me, for my obedience,
A murderer's destiny, far from Hellas.
To what city shall I go?
Will any friend, will any man who fears God,
Dare to look in my face —
A son who has killed his mother?

ELECTRA.

Oh, what shall I do?
Where shall I go?
What happy company will welcome me
To a dance or a wedding?   1130
What man will accept me as his wife?

CHORUS.

Your mind has returned to itself,
And blows now with the wind of truth.
Now your thoughts are holy;
But then they defied the gods.
Dear Electra, you did a dreadful wrong to your brother,

Forcing him against his will.

ORESTES.

Did you see how, in her agony,
She opened her gown, thrust forth her breast,
And showed it to me as I struck? 1140
Her body that gave me birth
Sprawled there on the ground.
I had her by the hair . . .

CHORUS.

I know what torture you went through;
I heard her shriek — your own mother.

ELECTRA.

Yes; as she uttered that shriek
She was putting her hand on my face;
"My child, I implore you," she said.
Then she hung around my neck
So that the sword fell out of my hand. 1150

CHORUS.

Wretched, miserable woman! How could you bear
To see with your own eyes
Your mother gasping out her life?

ORESTES.

I held my cloak over my eyes,
While with my sword I performed sacrifice,
Driving the blade into my mother's throat.

ELECTRA.

And I urged you on,
And held the sword, my hand beside yours.

CHORUS.

Could any act be more dreadful?

ORESTES.

Come, help me to cover her limbs with her dress; 1160
And close her wounds.
— You were mother to your murderers.

ELECTRA.

As we wrap this cloak round you
We love you, though we hated you.

CHORUS.

This the appointed end of great sorrows.

(*The* DIOSCORI *appear above the house.*)

Look there! Shining above the house — who are they?
Immortal spirits, or gods from heaven?

They cannot be mortals; why have they come,
Visible to our human eyes?

CASTOR. Listen, son of Agamemnon! We are the sons of Zeus,   1170
Your mother's brothers; I Castor, this Polydeuces.
Now, having calmed the dangerous tossing of the sea,
We have come in haste to Argos. We were witnesses;
We saw you shed our sister's, and your mother's blood.
Her fate was just; but your act is not justified.
Phoebus, yes, Phoebus — but he is my lord, so I
Am silent. He is wise; but his command to you
Was not wise. What is already done we must accept;
The future Fate and Zeus have thus ordained for you.

First, give Electra to Pylades, to have for wife,   1180
Next, you must go from Argos; it is impossible
That you should set foot in the city, a matricide.
Moreover, those dread Fates, the dog-faced Goddesses,
Shall send you mad and drive you wandering through the
    world
Till you reach Athens. There in Athene's temple cling
Fast to her holy image. She will keep at bay
Their snake-tormented fury. When Athene holds
Over your head the circle of her Gorgon-shield,
They cannot touch you. There is a place in Athens called
The Hill of Ares, where the gods once sat to cast   1190
Their votes in the first murder-trial, when Ares, filled
With savage indignation for his daughter's rape,
Killed Halirrhothius, son of the Sea-god; a court
Where ever since, for mortal men, Justice sits firm,
Inviolable; and there you too must stand your trial
For this bloodshed. The votes being equal shall acquit you;
For Loxias, who commanded you to kill your mother,
Shall take the guilt upon himself. And this shall stand
As precedent for murder-trials in time to come,
That the accused, when votes are equal, wins his case.   1200

The dread Goddesses, struck with grief at your acquittal,
Shall enter a deep chasm under that same hill,
Where men shall honour their abode with pious awe.
Then, you must go to Arcadia, to the river Alpheius,
And there close to the precinct of Lycean Zeus,
Settle in a city which shall take its name from you.
Such is your destiny. The dead Aegisthus here

Men of Argos shall bury in a tomb of earth.
As for your mother, Helen her sister and Menelaus
Shall bury her. They have just now reached Nauplia, 1210
So many years since Troy was taken. Helen, in fact,
Never saw Troy; she has just come from Proteus' palace
In Egypt. Zeus sent off to Troy a phantom Helen
To stir up strife and slaughter in the human race.

Let Pylades, his virgin wife beside him, leave
This country for his home in Phocis. Let him take
With him the peasant who is your brother-in-law in name,
And make him a rich man. Orestes, you must cross
The neck of the Corinthian Isthmus, and press on
To Athens, Cecrops' city, and her god-favoured Rock. 1220
When you have fulfilled the appointed period of blood-guilt,
You shall be quit of trouble, and find happiness.

CHORUS.
    Sons of Zeus, is it lawful for us
    To speak and address you?

CASTOR.
    It is; you are not polluted with this murder.

CHORUS.
    Then why did you, being gods,
    And brothers of this murdered woman,
    Not shield her from the pursuing vengeance?

CASTOR.
    The pattern of Necessity
    Led where it had to lead, 1230
    Helped by the unwise utterance of Apollo.

ORESTES.
    Sons of Tyndareos, may I too speak?

CASTOR.
    You may; for I lay your guilt on Apollo's shoulder.

ELECTRA.
    Then what of me? No Apollo,
    No oracle named *me*
    As my mother's destined murderer.

CASTOR.
    You shared the deed, as you share the destiny.
    One fateful curse inherited from your fathers
    Ravaged you both.

ORESTES.
    Dear sister, after so many years 1240
    I have seen you again;

And now the love that I need from you
Is taken away.
I lose you, and you lose me.

CASTOR.

She has a husband and a home;
Her fate does not call for pity,
Except that she must leave Argos.

ELECTRA.

What grief is greater than to leave behind
The frontier of your home-land?

ORESTES.

But I must leave my home   1250
To answer for my mother's blood
Before the judgement of foreigners.

CASTOR.

Have courage: it is the holy city of Pallas
You are going to; so endure with patience.

ELECTRA.

Dearest brother, embrace me;
Let me hold you close.
The curse of our mother's blood
Drives us from our home,
You one way, me another.

ORESTES.

Fold your arms closely round me.   1260
Think that I am dead,
And you mourn over my grave.

CASTOR.

Words so charged with sorrow
Appal the heart even of gods.
For I too, and the greater gods of heaven,
Feel pity for the suffering of mankind.

ORESTES.

I shall never see you again.

ELECTRA.

Never shall I be within sight of you.

ORESTES.

These words are the last I shall speak to you.

ELECTRA.

Farewell, city of Argos.   1270
Farewell, women of my country.

ORESTES.

Most faithful sister, are you going now?

ELECTRA.

I go, my eyes hot with tears.

ORESTES.

Pylades, take Electra for your wife;
And blessing go with you.

CASTOR (*to* ORESTES).

Thoughts of marriage will be their comfort.
But you must set out for Athens
To escape these avenging hounds.
Step by fearful step they pursue you;
Their skin is black,   1280
Snakes twine round their arms;
They bring with them fierce pains for retribution.

> (*Exeunt* ORESTES *one way,* ELECTRA *and* PYLADES *another.*)

But I and my brother speed westward, to ensure
A safe voyage for the ships now sailing to Sicily.
Striding through the wide plain of heaven
We bring help — not to blasphemers,
But to those whose life has cherished
Goodness before god and man;
These we deliver from their troubles,
And bring them success.   1290

Therefore let none plot wickedness,
Nor sail in the same ship with perjured men.
I, a god, give this warning to mortals.

> (*Exeunt* DIOSCORI.)

CHORUS.

Farewell, sons of Zeus!

To be able to *fare well,*
To avoid the frustration of misfortune:
That, in this world, is happiness.   1297

◇ ◇ ◇

STUDY AIDS

Prologue (*lines 1–154*)

1. The appearance of the Mycenaean farmer and the expository
statements he makes indicate from the start that this treatment of

the story is going to have a different tone and quality from either of the two preceding plays. How, specifically, is this statement borne out in the scene? How does our initial impression of Electra further reinforce it?

2. What is the underlining mood of the exchange of dialogue between Electra and her farmer-husband? Does Electra's professed interest in domesticity seem somewhat surprising in the context of the legend?

Parados (lines 155–197)

1. What is the purpose of having Electra refer to her unkempt hair and her tattered dress?

First Episode (lines 198–366)

1. This scene includes the second reference to Electra's unconsumated marriage; what is the purpose of making this point so explicit?

2. Orestes says to Electra: "I wish Orestes could be by, to hear you speak." To which Electra replies, "Friend, if I saw him I should not recognize him." What is the effect of such a line?

3. Again in this scene Electra goes to some length to describe her doleful plight. Does she enlist our pity or try our patience?

4. Especially with reference to lines 329–334, what picture of the Peasant is achieving additional focus?

5. Note the Peasant's speech beginning with line 329. Does it seem appropriate to have a character of such folksy, homespun quality in a play of this sort?

6. What is the intent of Orestes' long speech beginning with line 338? Does a speech such as this add to or detract from the drama and movement of the scene in which it occurs? Does it add to the play as a whole? To whom is it really addressed?

First Stasimon (lines 367–449)

1. Aside from recalling Achilles' and Agamemnon's participation in the Trojan War, what else is said in this passage?

Second Episode (lines 450–541)

1. In his handling of the recognition scene Euripides clearly scoffs at the way Aeschylus and Sophocles handled the evidence by which Electra recognized her brother. How convincing do you find Euripides' treatment? Does his repudiation of the clues his predecessors employed merely prolong the scene or does it humanize Electra, making her more perceptive than the previous heroines?

2. Analyze the part each of the three participants — Electra, Orestes, and the Old Man — play in this scene.

3. On the basis of the evidence thus far presented, who is the stronger character, Electra or Orestes? What weakness, if any, does each possess? Why does Orestes delay revealing himself to his sister? Would Electra be denied a source of self-indulgent pity once she was compelled to recognize Orestes? Why was she so slow in acknowledging the scar as a positive mark of identification; it had been visible from the start of the scene.

Second Stasimon (lines 542–695)

1. "Nevertheless, frightening tales are useful: They promote reverence for the gods." How do these lines apply to many of the plays of the Greek dramatists?

Third Episode (lines 695–1066)

1. When Electra is told Aegisthus has been slain by Orestes she enthusiastically exclaims, "Friend, tell me point by point about this death." The request, of course, is the cue for the audience to be told of the slaying; does it also indicate something about the nature of Electra?

2. What is the effect of hearing Aegisthus described as both hospitable and civil? Is the manner in which Orestes delivered the death blow one to excite our admiration? Does it seem compatible with the impression we have formed of Orestes?

3. What is the purpose and the effect of displaying the corpse of Aegisthus on stage? Of Electra's speech addressed to the body?

4. Now that Orestes has killed Aegisthus, he demurs at the thought of killing his mother. Why? Does his hesitation add to his credibility as a character? How does it affect Electra?

5. Does Clytemnestra's explanation of why she killed Agamemnon seem reasonable and plausible? Does it seem to indicate an understanding of feminine thinking on the part of Euripides?

6. How does this scene compare in intensity with the similar one in the *Electra* of Sophocles? What is accomplished by the presence of a courteous, contained Clytemnestra?

Third Stasimon (lines 1067–1098)

1. Vengeance is about to be realized, Clytemnestra to be brought to justice. Does the prophecy arouse eager expectation or revulsion at the thought of a second horrible killing?

Exodos (lines 1099–1297)

1. Following the murder of their mother, Orestes and Electra are overcome with remorse. Is this the reaction we might have anticipated, considering what we know of these two? Explain.

2. The appearance of the Dioscuri is clearly a *deus ex machina* ending to the play. Do you find it aesthetically satisfying?

3. What does the Dioscuri's condemnation of Apollo imply about the judgment of Apollo?

4. What are the conclusions of the play concerning the blood-feud and matricide?

TOPICS FOR DISCUSSION

1. The *Electra* of Euripides is a psychological drama, a realistic treatment of the troubled Electra and an examination of the circumstances that led her to murder. After the deed we observe the psychological consequences of her act. Similarly we perceive in Orestes the figure of a tormented individual who is loathe to perform an act to which he is driven, the commission of which fills him with remorse. In other words, the epic hero has lost his stature through having been reduced in character to a very average being. At the same time humble people have been elevated through possession of superior traits and exemplary behavior. There are other ways in which the characters, especially Electra, differ from their counterparts in the plays of Aeschylus and Sophocles. What are they?

2. Comment upon the plot structure in Euripides' play. What use does he make of suspense? Does his play possess the quality of irony?

3. Is the quality of pathos present in the play? Sentimentality?

4. What evidence does the play contain to suggest that Euripides was skeptical concerning the infallibility of the gods?

5. Did you note anything about the stasimon which was peculiar to Euripides? The use of chorus?

6. To what effect does Euripides employ a messenger in the play?

7. The Clytemnestra of Euripides is almost totally different from her fiery counterpart in the other two plays. How does the way which Euripides depicts her affect our reaction to the description of her death?

JEAN GIRAUDOUX

THE PLAYS of Jean Giraudoux (1882–1944) are the-
atrical, witty, and literate — the works of a stylist who became the
leading French playwright in the period separating the two World
Wars. Adept in the fields both of tragedy and comedy — as well as in
the middle ground lying between them — Giraudoux attacked such
human failings as greed, selfishness, and that particular kind of
foolishness which leads men to the cataclysm called war. The
Electra is generally considered a reflection of his concern with the
tensions and contempt that had long marred relations between Germany and France; the play warns of the excesses to which an
individual — or a nation — may be driven by an untempered desire
for vengeance. The conscience which is impervious to compromise
becomes a forbidding element in the world of men impelled by a
destructive urge to settle a troublesome score. *Electra* invites attention
to such matters as the use of expediency, the nature of justice, and the
pitfalls encountered in making a moral choice. The qualities of love
and joy, the Beggar reminds us, are always preferable to those of
bitterness and hate. It is a declaration which brands Electra guilty
of immoderation in her quest for retribution.

Giraudoux' *Electra* is a subtle play, sophisticated in its diction
and enriched with a complex view. It is a play that makes a return
to the House of Atreus a journey worth taking, even if the house of
myth is no longer the home of classic drama.

Giraudoux was born in the little town of Bellac, a provincial setting
from which he was destined to wander into the world of affairs —
that of statesmen, writers, and the military; but for all that he knew
of worldly glamour, he never forgot the simplicity of Bellac, some
aspect of which is present in all his plays. He remained essentially
a provincial, although a learned one, for Giraudoux' education was
impressively extensive. An early interest in German literature took
him to Munich, from which he later went on to Harvard, where he

spent a year. He returned to France during the war, serving as a
military instructor, and then at the age of 27, he enlisted in the French
foreign service, eventually becoming Minister of Propaganda in the
ill-fated cabinet of Edouard Daladier. It was a post he held until the
German occupation.

Throughout his career as a diplomat, Giraudoux found the time
to write novels, essays, and plays. As a citizen of the world he wrote
of the world, his concern for man and the riddle of life bounded only
by the universe itself.

Two books which treat of Giraudoux and his work should prove
useful to the student desiring to know more about this dramatist:
Laurent LeSage, *Jean Giraudoux: His Life and Works* (Pennsylvania,
1959); and Donald P. Inskip, *Jean Giraudoux: The Making of a
Dramatist* (London, 1958). The entire Summer, 1958, issue of *The
Tulane Drama Review* is devoted to Giraudoux. John Gassner ex-
panded his essay which appeared in this issue (and which appears in
this volume) into "The Electras of Giraudoux and O'Neill" which
is published in his book, *The Theatre in Our Times* (New York,
1954).

Electra

English Version by Winifred Smith

❖ ❖ ❖

CHARACTERS

ORESTES

THE EUMENIDES, *first as three little girls, later as fifteen-year-olds*

GARDENER

PRESIDENT OF THE COUNCIL

AGATHA, *his young wife*

AEGISTHUS

BEGGAR

CLYTEMNESTRA

ELECTRA

YOUNG MAN

CAPTAIN

NARSES' WIFE

GUESTS, SERVANTS, MAIDS, SOLDIERS

ACT ONE · SCENE ONE

(A stranger, ORESTES, enters, escorted by three little girls, just as, from the opposite side, the GARDENER comes in dressed for a festival, and accompanied by guests from the village.)

FIRST LITTLE GIRL. How fine the gardener looks!

SECOND LITTLE GIRL. Of course! It's his wedding day.

THIRD LITTLE GIRL. Here it is, sir, your Agamemnon's palace!

STRANGER. What a strange façade! Is it straight?

FIRST LITTLE GIRL. No. There's no right side to it. You think you see it, but that's a mirage. Like the gardener you see coming, who wants to speak to you. He's not coming. He won't be able to say a word.

Electra by Jean Giraudoux. Reprinted by permission of Ninon Tallon Karlweis. Caution: Professionals and amateurs are hereby warned that *Electra*, being fully protected by copyright, is subject to a royalty. Inquiries should be addressed to Ninon Tallon Karlweis, 250 East 65th Street, New York, N.Y. 10021.

SECOND LITTLE GIRL. Oh he'll bray — or meow —

GARDENER. The façade is perfectly straight, stranger. Don't listen to these liars. You are confused because the right side is built of stones from Gaul and sweats at certain seasons; that the people say the palace is weeping. The left side is built of marble from Argos, which — no one knows why — will suddenly be flooded with sunshine, even at night. Then they say the palace laughs. Right now the palace is laughing and crying at the same time.

FIRST LITTLE GIRL. So it's sure not to be mistaken.

SECOND LITTLE GIRL. It's really a widow's palace.

FIRST LITTLE GIRL. Or of childhood memories.

STRANGER. I can't remember seeing such a sensitive building anywhere.

GARDENER. Have you already visited the palace?

FIRST LITTLE GIRL. As a baby.

SECOND LITTLE GIRL. Twenty years ago.

THIRD LITTLE GIRL. He couldn't walk yet.

GARDENER. But he must remember if he saw it.

STRANGER. All I can remember of Agamemnon's palace is a mosaic. They set me down on a square of tigers when I was naughty and on a hexagon of flowers when I was good — and I remember creeping from one to the other across some birds.

FIRST LITTLE GIRL. And over a beetle.

STRANGER. How do you know that, child?

GARDENER. And did your family live in Argos?

STRANGER. And I remember many, many bare feet. Not a face, faces were way up in the sky, but lots of bare feet. I tried to touch the gold rings under the edges of the skirts; some ankles were joined by chains, slaves' ankles. I remember two little feet, very white ones, the barest, the whitest. Their steps were always even, timid, measured by an invisible chain. I imagine they were Electra's. I must have kissed them, mustn't I? A baby kisses everything it touches.

SECOND LITTLE GIRL. Anyway that would have been the only kiss Electra ever had.

GARDENER. It surely would!

FIRST LITTLE GIRL. Jealous, gardener?

STRANGER. Electra still lives in the palace?

SECOND LITTLE GIRL. Still. But not much longer.

STRANGER. Is that her window, the one with jasmine?

GARDENER. No. That's the room where Atreus, the first king of Argos, killed his brother's sons.

FIRST LITTLE GIRL. The dinner when he served up their hearts took place in the room next it. I'd love to know how they tasted.

THIRD LITTLE GIRL. Did he cut them up or cook them whole?

SECOND LITTLE GIRL. And Cassandra was strangled in the sentry box.

THIRD LITTLE GIRL. They caught her in a net and stabbed her. She yelled like a crazy woman, through her veil. I'd love to have seen it.

FIRST LITTLE GIRL. That all happened in the laughing wing, as you see.

STRANGER. The one with roses?

GARDENER. Stranger, don't try to connect the windows with flowers. I'm the palace gardener. I plant them at random. They're just flowers.

SECOND LITTLE GIRL. Not at all. There are flowers and flowers. Phlox doesn't suit Thyestes.

THIRD LITTLE GIRL. Nor mignonette Cassandra.

GARDENER. Oh, be quiet! The window with the roses, stranger, is the one of the rooms where our king, Agamemnon, coming back from the war, slipped into the pool, fell on his sword and killed himself.

FIRST LITTLE GIRL. He took his bath after his death. About two minutes after. That's the difference.

GARDENER. That's Electra's window.

STRANGER. Why is it so high up, almost on the roof?

GARDENER. So she can see her father's tomb.

STRANGER. Why is she there?

GARDENER. Because it's Orestes' old room, her brother's. Her mother sent him out of the country when he was two and he's not been heard of since.

SECOND LITTLE GIRL. Listen, sisters, listen! They're talking about Orestes!

GARDENER. Will you clear out! Leave us! You're just like flies.

FIRST LITTLE GIRL. We certainly won't leave. We're with this stranger.

GARDENER. Do you know these girls?

STRANGER. I met them at the door. They followed me in.

SECOND LITTLE GIRL. We followed him because we like him.

THIRD LITTLE GIRL. Because he's a lot better looking than you are, gardener.

FIRST LITTLE GIRL. No caterpillars in his beard.

SECOND LITTLE GIRL. Nor June bugs in his nose.

THIRD LITTLE GIRL. If flowers are to smell sweet, the gardener has to smell bad.

STRANGER. Be polite, children, and tell us what you do all the time.

FIRST LITTLE GIRL. What we do is, we're not polite.

SECOND LITTLE GIRL. We lie, we slander, we insult.

FIRST LITTLE GIRL. But specially, we recite.

STRANGER. And what do you recite?

FIRST LITTLE GIRL. We never know ahead of time — we invent as we go along. But we're very, very good.

SECOND LITTLE GIRL. The king of Mycenae, whose sister-in-law we insulted, said we were very, very good.

THIRD LITTLE GIRL. We say all the bad things we can think up.

GARDENER. Don't listen to them, stranger. No one knows who they are. They've been wandering about the town for two days without friends or family. If we ask who they are, they pretend they're the little Eumenides. And the horrible thing is that they grow and get fat as you look at them. Yesterday they were years younger than today. Come here, you!

SECOND LITTLE GIRL. Is he rude, for a bridegroom!

GARDENER. Look at her! See how her eyelashes grow. Look at her bosom. I understand such things, I've seen mushrooms grow. They grow fast, like an orange.

SECOND LITTLE GIRL. Poisonous things always win out.

THIRD LITTLE GIRL (*to the* FIRST LITTLE GIRL). Really? You're growing a bosom?

FIRST LITTLE GIRL. Are we going to recite or not?

STRANGER. Let them recite, gardener.

FIRST LITTLE GIRL. Let's recite Clytemnestra, Electra's mother — You agree? Clytemnestra?

SECOND LITTLE GIRL. We agree.

FIRST LITTLE GIRL. Queen Clytemnestra has a bad color. She uses rouge.

SECOND LITTLE GIRL. Her color is bad because she sleeps badly.

THIRD LITTLE GIRL. She sleeps badly because she's afraid.

FIRST LITTLE GIRL. What is Queen Clytemnestra afraid of?

SECOND LITTLE GIRL. Of everything.

FIRST LITTLE GIRL. What's everything?

SECOND LITTLE GIRL. Silence. Silences.

THIRD LITTLE GIRL. Noise. Noises.

FIRST LITTLE GIRL. The idea that midnight is near. That the spider on its thread is about to pass from the time of day when it brings good luck to the time when it brings bad luck.

SECOND LITTLE GIRL. Of everything red, because blood is red.

FIRST LITTLE GIRL. Queen Clytemnestra has a bad color. She puts on blood.

GARDENER. What a silly story!

SECOND LITTLE GIRL. Good, isn't it?

FIRST LITTLE GIRL. See how the end goes back to the beginning — couldn't be more poetic!

STRANGER. Very interesting.

FIRST LITTLE GIRL. As you're interested in Electra we can recite about her. You agree, sisters? We can recite what she was like at our age.

SECOND LITTLE GIRL. We certainly do agree!

THIRD LITTLE GIRL. Even before we were born, before yesterday, we agreed.

FIRST LITTLE GIRL. Electra amuses herself by making Orestes fall out of his mother's arms.

SECOND LITTLE GIRL. Electra waxes the steps of the throne so her uncle Aegisthus, will measure his length on the marble.

THIRD LITTLE GIRL. Electra is preparing to spit in the face of her little brother, Orestes, if he ever returns.

FIRST LITTLE GIRL. Of course, *that* isn't true, but it'd be a good story.

SECOND LITTLE GIRL. For nineteen years she's prepared poisonous spittle in her mouth.

THIRD LITTLE GIRL. She's thinking of your slugs, gardener, to make her mouth water more.

GARDENER. Now stop, you dirty little vipers!

SECOND LITTLE GIRL. Oh, ha, ha, the bridegroom gets mad!

STRANGER. He's right. Get out!

GARDENER. And don't come back!

FIRST LITTLE GIRL. We'll come back tomorrow.

GARDENER. Just try to! The palace is forbidden to girls of your age.

FIRST LITTLE GIRL. Tomorrow we'll be grown up.

SECOND LITTLE GIRL. Tomorrow will be the day after Electra's marriage to the gardener. We'll be grown up.

STRANGER. What are they saying?

FIRST LITTLE GIRL. You've not defended us, stranger. You'll be sorry for that.

GARDENER. Horrible little beasts! You'd think they were three little Fates. Dreadful to be a child Fate!

SECOND LITTLE GIRL. Fate shows you her tail, gardener. Watch out if it grows.

FIRST LITTLE GIRL. Come, sisters. Let's leave them both in front of their tainted wall.

(*The little* EUMENIDES *go out, the* GUESTS *shrinking away from them in terror.*)

SCENE TWO

(*The* STRANGER. *The* GARDENER. *The* PRESIDENT OF THE COUNCIL *and his young wife,* AGATHA THEOCATHOCLES. *Villagers.*)

STRANGER. What did these girls say? That you are marrying Electra, gardener?

GARDENER. She'll be my wife an hour from now.

AGATHA. He'll *not* marry her. We've come to prevent that.

PRESIDENT. I'm your distant cousin, gardener, and the Vice-President of the Council; so I've a double right to advise you. Run away to your radishes and squashes. Don't marry Electra.

GARDENER. Aegisthus orders me to.

STRANGER. Am I crazy? If Agamemnon were alive, Electra's wedding would be a festival for all Greece — and Aegisthus gives her to a gardener, whose family, even, objects! Don't tell me Electra is ugly or hunch-backed!

GARDENER. Electra is the most beautiful girl in Argos.

AGATHA. Oh, she's not too bad looking.

PRESIDENT. And she's perfectly straight. Like all flowers that grow in the shade.

STRANGER. Is she backward? Feeble-minded?

PRESIDENT. She's intelligence personified.

AGATHA. An especially good memory. Not always for the same thing, though. I don't have a good memory. Except for your birthday, darling, *that* I never forget.

STRANGER. What can she have done, or said, to be treated this way?

PRESIDENT. She does nothing, says nothing. But she's always *here*.

AGATHA. She's here now.

STRANGER. She has a right to be. It's her father's palace. It's not her fault he's dead.

GARDENER. I'd never have dreamed of marrying Electra, but as Aegisthus orders me to, I don't see why I'd be afraid.

PRESIDENT. You have every reason to be afraid. She's the kind of woman that makes trouble.

AGATHA. And you're not the only one! Our family has everything to fear.

GARDENER. I don't understand you.

PRESIDENT. You will understand. Life can be pleasant, can't it!

AGATHA. Very pleasant! Immensely so!

PRESIDENT. Don't interrupt me, darling, especially just to repeat what I say. It *can* be very pleasant. Everything has a way of settling itself in life — spiritual suffering can be cured more quickly than cancer, and mourning than a sty. Take any group of human beings at random, each will have the same percentage of crime, lies, vice and adultery.

AGATHA. That's a horrid word, adultery, darling.

PRESIDENT. Don't interrupt me, especially to contradict! How does it happen that in one group life slips by softly, conventionally, the dead are forgotten, the living get on well together, while in another there's hell to pay? It's simply that in the latter there's a woman who makes trouble.

STRANGER. That means there's a conscience in the second group.

AGATHA. I can't help thinking of your word, adultery — such a horrid word!

PRESIDENT. Be quiet, Agatha. A conscience, you say! If criminals don't forget their sins, if the conquered don't forget their defeats, if there are curses, quarrels, hatreds, the fault is not with humanity's conscience, which always tends toward compromise and forgetfulness, it lies with ten or fifteen women who make trouble.

STRANGER. I agree with you. Those ten or fifteen women save the world from egoism.

PRESIDENT. They save it from happiness! I know Electra. Let's agree that she is what you say — justice, generosity, duty. But it's by justice, generosity, duty, and not by egoism and easy going ways, that the state, individuals, and the best families are ruined.

AGATHA. Absolutely! But why, darling? You've told me, but I forget.

PRESIDENT. Because those three virtues have in common the one element fatal to humanity — implacability. Happiness is never the lot of implacable people. A happy family makes a surrender. A happy epoch demands unanimous capitulation.

STRANGER. You surrendered at the first call?

PRESIDENT. Alas, no! Some one else got in first. So I'm only the vice-president.

GARDENER. Against what is Electra implacable? She goes every night to her father's tomb, is that all?

PRESIDENT. I know. I've followed her. Along the same road which my duty made me take one night, pursuing our most dangerous murderer, along the same river I followed and saw the greatest innocent in Greece. A horrible walk, behind the two of them. They stopped at the same places, at the yew, at the corner of the bridge, at the thousand year old milestone, all made the same signs to innocence and to crime. But because the murderer was there, the night was bright, peaceful, clear. He was the kernel taken out of the fruit, which, in a tart, might have broken your tooth. Electra's presence, on the contrary, confused light and darkness, even spoiled the full moon. Have you seen a fisherman, who before going out to fish, arranges his bait? All the way along the river, that was she. Every evening she spreads her net for everything that without her would have abandoned this pleasant, agreeable earth — remorse, confessions, old blood stains, rust, bones of murdered men, a mass of accusations. In a short time everything will be ready for the fisherman to pass by.

STRANGER. He always comes, sooner or later.

PRESIDENT. That's not so.

AGATHA (*much taken by the* STRANGER). A mistake!

PRESIDENT. This child herself sees the leak in your argument. A triple layer of earth daily piles up over our sins, our failures, our crimes, and stifles their worst effects! Forgetfulness, death, human justice. It is madness to remember those things. A horrible country, one where because of an avenger of wrongs, ghosts walk, dead men, half asleep — where no allowance is ever made for human weakness, or perjury, where a ghost and an avenger constantly threaten. When guilty men's sleep continues to be more troubled after legal prosecution than the sleep of an innocent, society is terribly disturbed. When I look at Electra, I'm troubled by the sins I committed in my cradle.

AGATHA. And I by my future sins. I'll never commit them, darling. You know that. Especially that adultery, which you will talk about. But those other sins already bother me.

GARDENER. I'm rather of Electra's opinion. I don't much care for wicked people. I love truth.

PRESIDENT. Do you know what truth is for our family that you proclaim it so openly? A quiet, well-thought-of family, rising fast. You'll not deny my assertion that you are the least important member of it. But I know by experience that it's not safe to venture on thin ice. It won't be ten days, if you marry Electra, before the discovery — I'm just inventing this — that our old aunt, when a young girl, strangled her baby so her husband wouldn't find out about it, and in order to quiet suspicion, stopped hushing up the various aspersions on her grandfather's virtue. My little Agatha, in spite of being gaiety itself, can't sleep because of all this. You are the only one who doesn't see Aegisthus' trick. He wants to pass on to the Theocathocles family everything that might some day throw a sinister light on the Atrides.[1]

STRANGER. And what have the Atrides to fear?

PRESIDENT. Nothing. Nothing that I know of, it's like every happy family or couple, every satisfied person. Yet it does have to fear the most dangerous enemy in the world, who would eat it through to the bone, Electra's ally, uncompromising justice.

GARDENER. Electra loves my garden. If she's a little nervous, the flowers will do her good.

AGATHA. But she'll not do the flowers good.

PRESIDENT. Certainly. You'll get to knew your fuchsias and geraniums. You'll see that they're not just pretty symbols. They'll show their

[1] Agamemnon and Menelaus, sons of Atreus.

knavery and their ingratitude. Electra in the garden is justice and memory among the flowers — that means hatred.

GARDENER. Electra is devout. All the dead are for her.

PRESIDENT. The dead! The murdered, half melted into the murderers, the shades of the robbed mingled with those of the thieves, rival families scattered among each other, and saying, "Oh, Heavens! here's Electra! And we were so peaceful."

AGATHA. Here comes Electra!

GARDENER. No, not yet. It's Aegisthus. Leave us, stranger, Aegisthus doesn't like strange faces.

PRESIDENT. You, too, Agatha. He's rather too fond of well-known women's faces.

AGATHA (*with marked interest in the stranger's good looks*). Shall I show you the way, handsome stranger?

(AEGISTHUS *enters, to the hurrahs of the* GUESTS, *as* SERVANTS *set up his throne, and place a stool beside a pillar.*)

SCENE THREE

(AEGISTHUS. *The* PRESIDENT. *The* GARDENER. SERVANT.)

AEGISTHUS. Why the stool? What's the stool for?

SERVANT. For the beggar, my lord.

AEGISTHUS. What beggar?

SERVANT. The god, if you prefer. This beggar has been wandering through the city for several days. We've never seen a beggar who's so much a beggar, so it's thought he must be a god. We let him go wherever he likes. He's prowling around the palace now.

AEGISTHUS. Changing wheat to gold? Seducing the maids?

SERVANT. He does no harm.

AEGISTHUS. A queer god! The priests haven't found out yet whether he's a rascal or Jupiter?

SERVANT. The priests don't want to be asked.

AEGISTHUS. Friends, shall we leave the stool here?

PRESIDENT. I think it will be better to honor a beggar than to insult a god.

AEGISTHUS. Leave the stool there. But if he comes, warn us. We'd like to be just a group of human beings for a few minutes. And don't be rude to him. Perhaps he is delegated by the gods to attend Electra's marriage. The gods invite themselves to this marriage, which the President considers an insult to his family.

PRESIDENT. My lord . . .

AEGISTHUS. Don't protest. I heard everything. The acoustics in this palace are extraordinary. The architect apparently wanted to listen to the council's discussions of his salary and bonus, he built it full of echoing passages.

PRESIDENT. My lord . . .

AEGISTHUS. Be quiet. I know everything you're about to say on the subject of your fine honest family, your worthy sister-in-law, the baby-killer, your uncle, the satirist and our nephew, the slanderer.

PRESIDENT. My lord . . .

AEGISTHUS. An officer, in a battle, to whom the King's standard is given to turn the enemy's fire on him, carries it with more enthusiasm. You're losing your time. The gardener will marry Electra.

SERVANT. Here is the beggar, my lord.

AEGISTHUS. Detain him a moment. Offer him a drink. Wine is appropriate for a beggar or a god.

SERVANT. God or beggar, he's drunk already.

AEGISTHUS. Then let him come in. He'll not understand us, though we must speak of the gods. It might even be amusing to talk about them before him. Your notion of Electra, President, is true enough, but it's peculiar, definitely middle-class. As I'm the Regent, allow me to give you more elevated philosophical ideas. You believe in the gods, President? .

PRESIDENT. Do you, my lord?

AEGISTHUS. My dear President, I've often asked myself if I believe in the gods. Asked myself because it's the only problem a statesman must decide for himself. I do believe in the gods. Or rather, I believe I believe in the gods. But I believe in them, not as great caretakers and great watchmen, but as great abstractions. Between space and time, always oscillating between gravitation and emptiness, there are the great indifferences. Those are the gods. I imagine them, not constantly concerned with that moving mould on the earth which is humanity, but as having reached the stage of serenity and universality. That is blessedness, the same thing as unconsciousness. They are unconscious at the top of the ladder of being, as the atom is at the bottom. The difference is that theirs is the unconsciousness of lightning, omniscient, thousand-faceted, so that in their normal state, like diamonds, powerless and deaf, they only *react* to light, to omens, without understanding them.

BEGGAR (*at last seated, feels he must applaud*). Well said! Bravo!

AEGISTHUS. Thanks. On the other hand, President, it's undeniable that sometimes there seem to be interruptions in human life so opportune and extensive that it's possible to believe in an extraordinary superhuman interest or justice. Such events have something superhuman or divine about them, in that they are like coarse work, not at all well designed. The plague breaks out in a town which has sinned by impiety or folly, but it also ravages the neighboring city, a particularly holy one. War breaks out when a nation becomes degenerate and vile, but it destroys all the just, the brave, and preserves the cowards. Or, whose ever the fault, or by whom committed, it's the same family that pays, innocent or guilty. I know a mother of seven children, who always spanked the same child — she was a divine mother. This fits our idea of the gods, that they are blind boxers, always satisfied by finding the same cheeks to slap, the same bottoms to spank. We might even be surprised if we understood the confusion that comes from a sudden waking to beatitude, that their blows weren't given more at random; that the wife of a good man, and not a perjurer's, is brained by a shutter in a wind storm; that accidents strike down pilgrims and not troops. Always humanity suffers . . . I'm speaking generally. We see crows or deer struck down by an inexplicable epidemic — perhaps the blow intended for mankind went astray, either up or down. However it be, it's certain that the chief duty of a statesman is to watch fiercely that the gods are not shaken out of their lethargy, and to limit the harm they do to such reactions as sleepers snoring, or to thunder.

BEGGAR. Bravo! That's very clear! I understand it very well!

AEGISTHUS. Charmed, I'm sure!

BEGGAR. It's truth itself. For example, look at the people walking along the roads. Sometimes every hundred feet you'll see a dead hedgehog. They go over the roads at night by tens, male and female, and get crushed. You'll say they're fools, that they could find their mates on their side of the road. I can't explain it, but love, for hedgehogs, begins by crossing a road. What the devil was I trying to say? I've lost the thread . . . Go on, it'll come back to me.

AEGISTHUS. Indeed! What is he trying to say!

PRESIDENT. Shall we talk about Electra, my lord?

AEGISTHUS. What do you think we've been talking about? Our charming little Agatha? We were talking only about Electra, President, and about the need I feel to get her out of the royal family. Why, since I've been Regent, while other cities are devoured by dissension, other citizens by moral crises, are we alone satisfied with other people and with ourselves? Why are we so rich? Why in Argos alone are raw materials so dear and retail prices so low? Why, when we're exporting more cows, does butter go down in price? Why do storms pass by our vineyards, heresies our temples, animal diseases our barns? Because, in this city, I wage merciless war against all who signal to the gods.

PRESIDENT. What do you mean, signal to the gods?

BEGGAR. There! I've found it!

AEGISTHUS. Found what?

BEGGAR. My story, the thread of my story. I was speaking of the death of hedgehogs.

AEGISTHUS. One moment, please. We're speaking of the gods.

BEGGAR. To be sure! Gods come first, hedgehogs second. But I wonder if I'll remember.

AEGISTHUS. There are no two ways of signaling, President: it's done by separating one's self from the crowd, climbing a hill and waving a lantern or a flag. The earth is betrayed, as is a besieged city, by signals. The philosopher signals from his roof, the poet or a desperate man signals from his balcony or his swimming pool. If for ten years the gods have not meddled with our lives, it's because I've kept the heights empty and the fairgrounds full. I've ordered dreamers, painters, and chemists to marry; and because, in order to avoid racial trouble between our citizens — something that can't help marking human beings as different in the eyes of the gods — I've always given great importance to misdemeanors and paid slight attention to crimes. Nothing keeps the gods so quiet as an equal value set on murder and on stealing bread. I must say the courts have supported me splendidly. Whenever I've been forced to be severe, they've overlooked it. None of my decisions has been so obvious as to allow the gods to avenge it. No exile. I kill. An exile tends to climb up a steep road, just like a ladybird. I never execute in public. Our poor neighboring cities betray themselves by erecting their gallows on the top of a hill; I crucify at the bottom of a valley. Now I've said everything about Electra.

GARDENER. What have you said?

AEGISTHUS. That there's just one person in Argos now to give a signal to the gods, and that's Electra. What's the matter?

(BEGGAR *moves about among the* GUESTS.)

BEGGAR. Nothing's the matter. But I'd better tell you my story now. In five minutes, at the rate you're talking, it won't make sense. It's just to support what you say. Among those crushed hedgehogs you'll see dozens who seem to have died a hedgehog's death. Their muzzles flattened by horses' hoofs, their spines broken under wheels, they're just smashed hedgehogs, nothing more. Smashed because of the original sin of hedgehogs — which is crossing the main or side road on the pretext that the snail or partridge egg on the far side tastes better but actually to make hedgehog love. That's their affair. No one stops them. Suddenly you see a little young one, not flattened like the others, not so dirty, his little paw stretched out, his lips closed, very dignified, and you feel that he's not died a hedgehog's death, but was struck down for someone else, for you. His cold little eye is your eye. His spikes, your beard. His blood, your blood. I always pick up those little ones, they're the youngest, the tenderest to eat. A year goes by, a hedgehog no longer sacrifices himself for mankind. You see I understand. The gods were mistaken, they wanted to strike a perjurer, a thief, and they kill a hedgehog. A young one.

AEGISTHUS. Very well understood.

BEGGAR. And what's true of hedgehogs holds for other species.

PRESIDENT. Of course! Of course!

BEGGAR. Why, of course? That's all wrong. Take the martin. Even though you're a President of the Council, you'll never pretend to have seen birds dying for you?

AEGISTHUS. Will you let us go on talking about Electra!

BEGGAR. Talk! Talk! But I must add, when you see dead men, many seem to have died for bulls or pigs or turtles, not many for mankind. A man who seems to have died for man, he's hard to find, or even for himself. Are we going to see her?

AEGISTHUS. See whom?

BEGGAR. Electra. I'd like to see her before she's killed.

AEGISTHUS. Electra killed? Who says Electra's to be killed?

BEGGAR. You.

PRESIDENT. There's been no thought of killing Electra.

BEGGAR. I have one gift. I don't understand words — I've had no education — but I do understand people. You want to kill Electra.

PRESIDENT. You don't understand at all, stranger. This man is Aegisthus, Agamemnon's cousin, and Electra's his darling niece.

BEGGAR. Are there two Electras? The one he was talking about who ruins everything, and the other one, his darling niece?

PRESIDENT. No! There's only one.

BEGGAR. Then he wants to kill her. No doubt of it. He wants to kill his darling niece.

PRESIDENT. I repeat, you don't understand in the least.

BEGGAR. Oh, I move about a lot. I knew a family, name of Narses. She was better than he. She was sick, her breathing bad. But a great deal better than he. No comparison.

GARDENER. He's drunk, a beggar, you know.

PRESIDENT. He's raving. He's a god.

BEGGAR. No. I started to tell you they had a wolf cub. It was their darling little pet. But one day around noon, wolf cubs, you know, grow up. They couldn't foretell the day. Two minutes before noon they were petting her, one minute after twelve she jumped at their throats. I didn't mind about him!

AEGISTHUS. Well?

BEGGAR. Well, I was just passing by. And I killed the wolf. She was beginning to eat Narses' cheeks, she liked them. Narses' wife got away, not too badly hurt. Thanks! You'll see her. She's coming for me pretty soon.

AEGISTHUS. What's the connection . . . ?

BEGGAR. Oh, don't expect to see an Amazon queen. Varicose veins age a person.

PRESIDENT. He asked, what's the connection?

BEGGAR. The connection? It's because I think this man, as he's head of the state, must be more intelligent than Narses. No one could imagine such stupidity as Narses'. I never could teach him to smoke a cigar except by the lighted end. And what about knots? It's terribly important to know how to make knots. If you make a curly-cue where you ought to have a knot, and vice versa, you're lost. You lose your money, you catch cold, you choke, your boat veers away or collides, you can't pull off your shoes. I mean if you want to pull them off. And the laces? You know Narses was a poacher.

PRESIDENT. We've asked you, what is the connection?

BEGGAR. Here's the connection. If this man distrusts his niece, if he knows that one of these days she'll give a signal, as he said, she'll begin to bite, to turn the city upside down, push up the price of butter, start a war, et cetera, he can't hesitate. He ought to kill her dead before she reveals herself. When will she reveal herself?

PRESIDENT. What do you mean?

BEGGAR. What day, at what time will she reveal herself? When will she turn into a wolf? When will she become Electra?

PRESIDENT. But nothing tells us she'll turn into a wolf.

BEGGAR (*pointing to* AEGISTHUS). Yes. He thinks so. He says so.

GARDENER. Electra is the gentlest of women.

BEGGAR. Narses' wolf cub was the gentlest of wolves.

PRESIDENT. Your expression "reveals herself" doesn't make sense.

BEGGAR. My expression doesn't make sense? You know nothing about life. The 29th of May, when you see the hills astir with thousands of little red, yellow, and green balls flying, squawling, quarreling over every little bit of thistle fluff, never making a mistake nor going after dandelion down, aren't the butterflies revealing themselves? And June 14th when you see on the river bank two reeds move without wind or wave till June 15th, and, too, without bubbles made by carp, isn't the pike revealing himself? And judges like you, the first time they condemn to death, when the condemned man appears, distraught, don't they reveal themselves by the taste of blood on their lips? Everything in nature reveals itself. Even the king. And the question today, if you'll believe me, is whether the king will reveal himself as Aegisthus before Electra reveals herself as Electra. So he has to know the day when it will happen to the girl, so he can kill her on the eve, down in a valley, as he said, down in a little valley, the handiest and least visible, in her bath.

PRESIDENT. Isn't he awful?

AEGISTHUS. You're forgetting the wedding, beggar.

BEGGAR. True. I am forgetting the wedding. But a wedding, if you want to kill someone, isn't as sure as death. Especially as a girl like her, sensitive, rather retarded et cetera, will reveal herself the moment a man takes her in his arms for the first time. You're marrying her?

AEGISTHUS. At once. Right here.

BEGGAR. Not to the king of a neighboring city, I hope?

AEGISTHUS. Not on your life! To this gardener.

PRESIDENT. To this gardener.

BEGGAR. She'll take him? I'd not reveal myself in the arms of a gardener. But everyone to his taste. I revealed myself in Corfu, at the fountain near the bakery, under the plane trees. You should have seen me that day! In each tray of the scales I weighed a hand of the baker's wife. They never weighed the same. I evened them up in the right tray with flour, in the left with oatmeal . . . Where does the gardener live?

GARDENER. Outside the walls.

BEGGAR. In a village?

GARDENER. No. My house stands alone.

BEGGAR (*to* AEGISTHUS). Bravo! I catch your idea. Not bad! It's quite easy to kill a gardener's wife. Much easier than a princess in a palace.

GARDENER. Whoever you are, I beg you . . .

BEGGAR. You'll not deny that it's easier to bury someone in compost than in marble?

GARDENER. What are you imagining? For one thing she'll not be a minute out of my sight.

BEGGAR. You'll bend down to plant a pear tree. Transplant it again because you hit a hard clod. Death has passed by.

PRESIDENT. Stranger, I fear you don't know where you are. You're in Agamemnon's palace, in his family.

BEGGAR. I see what I see, I see this man is afraid, he lives with fear, fear of Electra.

AEGISTHUS. My dear guest, let's not misunderstand each other. I'll not deny I'm anxious about Electra. I know misfortunes and troubles will come to the family of the Atrides the day she reveals herself, as you say. And to us all, for every citizen is affected by what happens to the royal family. That's why I'm handing her over to a lowly family, unseen by the gods, where her eyes and gestures will not inflame, where the harm will be only local and in the middle class, the Theocathocles family.

BEGGAR. A good idea, a good idea! But the family ought to be especially lowly.

AEGISTHUS. It is, and I'll see that it stays so. I'll see that no Theocathocles distinguishes himself by talent or courage. As for boldness and genius, I'm not afraid they'll make their mark.

BEGGAR. Take care! This little Agatha is not exactly ugly. Beauty too can give a signal.

PRESIDENT. I beg you to leave Agatha out of our argument.

BEGGAR. Of course it's possible to rub her face with vitriol.

PRESIDENT. My lord!

AEGISTHUS. The case has been argued.

PRESIDENT. But I'm thinking of fate, Aegisthus! It's not a disease. You think it's infectious?

BEGGAR. Yes. Like hunger among the poor.

PRESIDENT. I can hardly believe that fate will be content with one obscure little clan instead of the royal family, or that it will become the fate of the Theocathocles instead of the Atrides.

BEGGAR. Don't worry. A royal cancer spreads to the middle classes.

AEGISTHUS. President, if you don't want Electra's entrance into your family to mark the disgrace of its members, don't add a word. In a third-class zone the most implacable fate will do only third-class harm. I personally am distressed, because of my great esteem for the Theocathocles family, but the dynasty, the state, and the city can no longer take risks.

BEGGAR. And perhaps she can be killed a little anyway, if an occasion arises.

AEGISTHUS. I have spoken. You may fetch Clytemnestra and Electra. They're waiting.

BEGGAR. It's not too soon. Without blaming you, I must say our talk lacks women.

AEGISTHUS. You'll have two, and talkers!

BEGGAR. And they'll argue with you a little, I hope?

AEGISTHUS. You like arguing women?

BEGGAR. Adore them. This afternoon I was in a house where a dispute was going on. Not a very high-toned discussion. Not compared to here. Not a plot of royal assassins as here. They were arguing whether they ought to serve guests chickens with or without livers. And the neck, of course. The women were furious. Had to be separated. Now I think of it, it was a fierce dispute. Blood flowed.

SCENE FOUR

(The same. CLYTEMNESTRA. ELECTRA. MAIDS.*)*

PRESIDENT. Here they both are.

CLYTEMNESTRA. Both! That's a manner of speaking. Electra is never more absent than when she's present.

ELECTRA. No. Today I'm here.

AEGISTHUS. Then let's make the most of it. You know why your mother has brought you here?

ELECTRA. It's her habit. She's already led a daughter to sacrifice.

CLYTEMNESTRA. There's Electra to the life! Never a word that's not treason or insinuation.

ELECTRA. Excuse me, mother. The allusion is quite apropos in the family of the Atrides.

BEGGAR. What does she mean? Is she angry with her mother?

GARDENER. It would be the first time anyone has seen Electra angry.

BEGGAR. All the more interesting!

AEGISTHUS. Electra, your mother has told you of our decision. We've been anxious about you for a long time. I hardly think you realize that you're like a sleepwalker in broad daylight. In the palace and the city people speak of you only in whispers, they're so afraid you'd wake and fall if they raised their voices.

BEGGAR *(shouting).* Electra!

AEGISTHUS. What's the matter with him?

BEGGAR. Oh, I'm sorry, it's just a joke. Excuse it. But you were scared, not she. Electra's no sleepwalker.

AEGISTHUS. Please —

BEGGAR. At least the experiment has been made. You were the one who flinched. What would you have done if I'd shouted, "Aegisthus"?

PRESIDENT. Let our Regent speak.

BEGGAR. I'll shout "Aegisthus" pretty soon, when nobody expects it.

AEGISTHUS. You must get well, Electra, no matter what it costs.

ELECTRA. To cure me, that's easy. Give life to a dead man.

AEGISTHUS. You're not the only one who grieves for your father. But he'd not ask you to make your mourning an offense to the living. We wrong the dead to attach them to our lives, for that deprives them of the freedom of death, if they know it.

ELECTRA. He's free. That's why he comes.

AEGISTHUS. Do you really think he's pleased to see you weep for him, not like a daughter but like a wife?

ELECTRA. I am my father's widow, for lack of another.

CLYTEMNESTRA. Electra!

AEGISTHUS. Widow or not, today we'll celebrate your marriage.

ELECTRA. Yes, I know your plot.

CLYTEMNESTRA. What plot? Is it a plot to marry a twenty-one year old daughter? At your age I had the two of you in my arms, you and Orestes.

ELECTRA. You carried us badly. You let Orestes fall on the marble floor.

CLYTEMNESTRA. What could I do? You pushed him.

ELECTRA. That's a lie. I never pushed him.

CLYTEMNESTRA. What do you know about it? You were only fifteen months old.

ELECTRA. I did *not* push Orestes! I remember it, far back in my memory. Oh, Orestes, wherever you are, hear me! I did not push you.

AEGISTHUS. That's enough, Electra.

BEGGAR. This time they're really at it! It'd be funny if the little girl revealed herself right in front of us.

ELECTRA. She lies. Orestes, she lies!

AEGISTHUS. Please, Electra!

CLYTEMNESTRA. She did push him. Obviously at her age she didn't know what she was doing. But she did push him.

ELECTRA. With all my strength I tried to hold him: by his little blue tunic, by his arm, by the end of his fingers, by his shadow. I sobbed when I saw him on the floor, with the red mark on his forehead.

CLYTEMNESTRA. You shouted with laughter. The tunic, by the way, was mauve.

ELECTRA. It was blue. I know Orestes' tunic. When it was drying you couldn't see it against the sky.

AEGISTHUS. Can *I* get a word in? Haven't you had time these twenty years to settle this debate?

ELECTRA. For twenty years I've waited for this chance. Now I have it.

CLYTEMNESTRA. Why can't she understand that she might be wrong, even honestly?

BEGGAR. They're both honest. That's the truth.

PRESIDENT. Princess, I beg of you! Of what interest is this question today?

CLYTEMNESTRA. Of none, I grant you.

ELECTRA. What interest? If I had pushed Orestes I'd rather die, I'd kill myself. My life would have no meaning.

AEGISTHUS. Must I force you to keep quiet? Are you as mad as she, queen?

CLYTEMNESTRA. Electra, listen. Let's not quarrel. This is exactly what happened: he was on my right arm.

ELECTRA. On your left!

AEGISTHUS. Have you finished, Clytemnestra, or haven't you?

CLYTEMNESTRA. We've finished. But a right arm is a right arm, a mauve tunic is mauve, not blue.

ELECTRA. It was blue. As blue as Orestes' forehead was red.

CLYTEMNESTRA. That is true. Very red. You touched the wound with your finger and danced around the little prone body. You laughed as you tasted the blood.

ELECTRA. I? I wanted to bruise my head on the step that hurt him. I trembled for a week.

AEGISTHUS. Silence!

ELECTRA. I'm still trembling.

BEGGAR. Narses' wife tied hers with an elastic rope that had some play. Often it was askew, but he didn't fall.

AEGISTHUS. Enough. We'll soon see how Electra will carry hers. For you agree, don't you? You accept this marriage?

ELECTRA. I agree.

AEGISTHUS. I must admit not many suitors throng around you.

BEGGAR. They say . . .

AEGISTHUS. What do they say?

BEGGAR. They say you've threatened to kill the princes who might marry Electra. That's what they say in the city.

ELECTRA. Good! I don't want any prince.

CLYTEMNESTRA. You'd rather have a gardener?

ELECTRA. I know you two have decided to marry me to my father's gardener. I accept.

CLYTEMNESTRA. You shall not marry a gardener.

AEGISTHUS. Queen, we settled that. Our word is given.

CLYTEMNESTRA. I take mine back. It was a wicked word. If Electra is ill we'll care for her. I'll not give my daughter to a gardener.

ELECTRA. Too late, mother. You have given me.

CLYTEMNESTRA. Gardener, you dare to aspire to Electra?

GARDENER. I'm unworthy, queen, but Aegisthus commands me.

AEGISTHUS. I do command you. Here are the rings. Take your wife.

CLYTEMNESTRA. If you persist, gardener, it's at the risk of your life.

BEGGAR. Then don't persist. I'd rather see soldiers die than gardeners.

CLYTEMNESTRA. What's that man saying? Marry Electra, gardener, and you die.

BEGGAR. It's your business. But go into the garden a year after the death of the gardener. You'll see something. You'll see what's happened to the endive, widowed by its gardener. It's not like kings' widows.

CLYTEMNESTRA. That garden won't suffer. Come, Electra.

GARDENER. Queen, you can deny me Electra, but it's not nice to say bad things about a garden you don't know.

CLYTEMNESTRA. I know it — empty land, with scattered plantings.

GARDENER. Empty? The best tended garden in Argos.

PRESIDENT. If he begins to talk about his garden we'll never finish.

AEGISTHUS. Spare us your descriptions!

GARDENER. The queen provoked me, and I answer. My garden is my dowry and my honor.

AEGISTHUS. Never mind! Enough of quarrels.

GARDENER. Empty, indeed! It covers ten acres of hilly land, and six of valley. No, no, you'll not silence me! Not a sterile inch, is there, Electra? On the terraces I have garlic and tomatoes, on the slopes grape vines and peach trees. On the level land vegetables, strawberries, and raspberries. A fig tree at the bottom of each slope against the wall, which warms the figs.

AEGISTHUS. Fine! Let your figs get warm and take your wife.

CLYTEMNESTRA. You dare talk of your garden! I've seen it from the road. It's all dry, a bald skull. You shall not have Electra.

GARDENER. All dry! A brook flows between the box and the plane trees, never dry in hottest weather; I've dug two little trenches from it — one turned on the meadow, the other cut in the rock. Try to find skulls like that! And scattered plantings! In spring it's full of narcissus and jonquils. I've never seen Electra really smile, but in my garden, I saw something on her face almost like a smile.

CLYTEMNESTRA. See if she's smiling now!

GARDENER. I call that Electra's smile.

CLYTEMNESTRA. Smiling at your dirty hands, your black nails . . .

ELECTRA. Dear gardener . . .

GARDENER. My black nails? Look, see if my nails are black! Don't believe it, Electra. You're unlucky today, queen, I spent this morning whitewashing my house, so there's not a sign of mice there, and my nails came out, not black, as you say, but mooned with white.

AEGISTHUS. That's enough, gardener.

GARDENER. I know, I know it's enough. And my dirty hands! Look! Look at these dirty hands! Hands that I washed after taking down the dried mushrooms and onions, so nothing would trouble Electra's nights. I'll sleep in the outhouse, Electra; there I'll keep guard so that nothing disturbs your sleep, whether an owl, or the open floodgate, or a fox, hunting the hedge, with a chicken in his mouth. I've said my say.

ELECTRA. Thanks, gardener.

CLYTEMNESTRA. And that's how Electra will live, Clytemnestra's daughter, watching her husband going around his border, two pails in his hands. . . .

AEGISTHUS. There she can weep for her dead to her heart's content. Get ready your wreaths of everlasting tomorrow.

GARDENER. And there she'll escape from anxiety, torture, and perhaps tragedy. I don't understand people, queen, but I do know the seasons. It's time, full time, to transplant misfortune from our city. The Atrides won't be grafted on our poor family, but on the seasons, the fields, the winds. I think they'll lose nothing by that.

BEGGAR. Be persuaded, queen. Don't you see that Aegisthus hates Electra so much he'll be driven to kill her, giving her to the earth by a kind of play on words: he gives her to a garden. She gains by that, she gains life. (AEGISTHUS *rises*.) What? Was I wrong to say that?

AEGISTHUS (*to* ELECTRA *and the* GARDENER). Come here, both of you.

CLYTEMNESTRA. Electra, I beg you!

ELECTRA. You're the one who wanted it, mother.

CLYTEMNESTRA. I no longer want it. You see I don't want it now.

ELECTRA. Why don't you want it? Are you afraid? Too late!

CLYTEMNESTRA. How can I make you remember who I am and who you are?

ELECTRA. You'll have to tell me I didn't push Orestes.

CLYTEMNESTRA. Stupid girl!

AEGISTHUS. Are they beginning again?

BEGGAR. Yes, yes, let them begin again.

CLYTEMNESTRA. And unjust! And stubborn! I let Orestes fall! I who never break anything! Never let fall a glass or a ring! I'm so steady that birds light on my arms. It's possible to fly away from me but not to fall. That's just what I said when he lost his balance, "Why, why did an ill fate bring his sister so near him?"

AEGISTHUS. They're crazy!

ELECTRA. And I said to myself, as soon as I saw him slipping, "If she's a true mother she'll stoop to soften his fall, or she'll bend to make a slope and catch him on her thigh or her knees. We'll see if they'll catch him, the noble knees and thighs of my mother. I'm not sure. I'll see."

CLYTEMNESTRA. Be quiet!

ELECTRA. "Or she'll bend backward, so little Orestes will slip off her like a child from a tree where he's picked off a nest, or she'll fall so *he* won't, or so he'll fall on her. She knows all the ways a mother uses to catch her son, she still knows them. She can still be a curve, a shell, a motherly slope, a cradle." But she stood fixed, straight, and he fell right down from the full height of his mother.

AEGISTHUS. The case is heard. Clytemnestra, we'll leave.

CLYTEMNESTRA. Just let her remember what she saw when she was fifteen months old and what she didn't see. That's the point.

AEGISTHUS. Who but you believes her or listens to her?

ELECTRA. There are a thousand ways of preventing a fall, and she did nothing.

CLYTEMNESTRA. The slightest movement, and *you* would have fallen.

ELECTRA. Just as I said. You calculated. You figured it all out. You were a nurse, not a mother.

CLYTEMNESTRA. My little Electra . . .

ELECTRA. I'm not your little Electra, your motherly feeling is tickled awake by your rubbing your two children against you. But it's too late.

CLYTEMNESTRA. Please — !

ELECTRA. There you are! Open your arms, see what you've done. Look, everybody. That's just what you did.

CLYTEMNESTRA. Let's go, Aegisthus.

(*She leaves.*)

BEGGAR. I believe the mother is frightened.

AEGISTHUS (*to the* BEGGAR). What's that you say?

BEGGAR. I? I say nothing. I never say anything. When I'm hungry I talk, everyone hears me. Today I've drunk a little something.

SCENE FIVE

(ELECTRA. BEGGAR. GARDENER. STRANGER. AGATHA.)

AGATHA. This is the right time, Aegisthus isn't here. Get out, gardener.

GARDENER. What do you mean?

AGATHA. Get out, fast. This man will take your place.

GARDENER. My place with Electra?

STRANGER. Yes, I'll marry her.

ELECTRA. Let go my hand.

STRANGER. Never.

AGATHA. Just look at him, Electra. Before you turn your back on a man, at least look at him. I'm sure you'll lose nothing by that.

ELECTRA. Gardener, help!

STRANGER. I owe you nothing, gardener. But look me in the eye. You understand species and kinds. Look at me and see the kind I am. So! Look, with your poor peasant eyes, with the gaze of humble folk, a blear-eyed mixture of devotion and fear, the sterile look of the poor, unchanged by sunshine or misfortune, see if I can give way to you. Fine! Now give me your ring. Thanks!

ELECTRA. Agatha, cousin! Help me! I swear I'll not tell about your rendezvous, your quarrels, I'll tell nothing.

AGATHA (*leading off the* GARDENER). Come, the Theocathocles are saved. Let the Atrides work it out.

BEGGAR. She runs away — like a wood-louse, hiding under a stone to escape from the sun.

SCENE SIX

(ELECTRA. STRANGER. BEGGAR.)

STRANGER. Struggle no more.

ELECTRA. I'll struggle till I die.

STRANGER. You think so? In a minute you'll take me in your arms.

ELECTRA. No insults!

STRANGER. In a minute you'll embrace me.

ELECTRA. Shame on you for profiting from two infamies!

STRANGER. See how I trust you. I let you go.

ELECTRA. Farewell forever!

STRANGER. No! I'll say one word to you and you'll come back to me, tenderly.

ELECTRA. What lie is this?

STRANGER. One word, and you'll be sobbing in my arms. One word, my name.

ELECTRA. There's only one name in the world that could draw me to anyone.

STRANGER. That's the one.

ELECTRA. Are you Orestes?

ORESTES. Ungrateful sister, only recognizing me by my name!

(CLYTEMNESTRA *appears.*)

SCENE SEVEN

(CLYTEMNESTRA. ELECTRA. ORESTES. BEGGAR.)

CLYTEMNESTRA. Electra!

ELECTRA. Mother?

CLYTEMNESTRA. Come back to your place in the palace. Leave the gardener. Come!

ELECTRA. The gardener has left, mother.

CLYTEMNESTRA. Where is he?

ELECTRA. He's given me to this man.

CLYTEMNESTRA. What man?

ELECTRA. This man. He's my husband now.

CLYTEMNESTRA. This is no time for jokes. Come!

ELECTRA. How can I come? He's holding my hand.

CLYTEMNESTRA. Hurry!

ELECTRA. You know, mother, those clogs they put on the legs of foals to prevent their running away? This man has put them on my ankles.

CLYTEMNESTRA. This time I command you. You must be in your room by tonight. Come!

ELECTRA. What? Leave my husband the night of my wedding?

CLYTEMNESTRA. What are you doing? Who are you?

ELECTRA. He'll not answer you. This evening my husband's mouth belongs to me, and all the words he speaks.

CLYTEMNESTRA. Where do you come from? Who is your father?

ELECTRA. A misalliance maybe. But not such a bad one.

CLYTEMNESTRA. Why do you look at me like that? Why the challenge in your eyes? Who was your mother?

ELECTRA. He never saw her.

CLYTEMNESTRA. She's dead?

ELECTRA. Perhaps what you see in his eyes is that he never saw his mother. Handsome, isn't he?

CLYTEMNESTRA. Yes. He looks like you.

ELECTRA. If our first married hours make us look alike, that's a good omen, isn't it, mother?

CLYTEMNESTRA. Who are you?

ELECTRA. What does it matter to you? Never was a man less yours.

CLYTEMNESTRA. Whatever or whoever you are, stranger, don't give in to her caprice. We'll see tomorrow if you're worthy of Electra. I'll win over Aegisthus. But I've never known a less propitious night. Leave this man, Electra.

ELECTRA. Too late! His arms hold me.

CLYTEMNESTRA. You can break iron if you want to.

ELECTRA. Iron, yes, *this* iron, no!

CLYTEMNESTRA. What has he said against your mother that you accept him this way?

ELECTRA. We've had no time yet to speak of my mother or his. Go, we'll begin!

ORESTES. Electra!

ELECTRA. That's all he can say. If I take my hand from his mouth, he just says my name without stopping. You can't get anything else out of him. Oh, husband, now that your mouth is free, kiss me!

CLYTEMNESTRA. Shame! So this madness is Electra's secret!

ELECTRA. Kiss me, before my mother.

CLYTEMNESTRA. Farewell! But I didn't think you were a girl to give yourself to the first passer-by.

ELECTRA. Nor I. But I didn't know what the first kiss was like.

SCENE EIGHT

(ELECTRA. ORESTES. BEGGAR.)

ORESTES. Why do you hate our mother so, Electra?

ELECTRA. Don't speak of her, above all not of her! Let's imagine for a minute that we were born without a mother. Don't talk.

ORESTES. I have everything to tell you.

ELECTRA. You tell me everything just by being here. Be quiet. Close your eyes. Your words and your look touch me too poignantly, they wound me. I often wished that I'd find you in your sleep, if I ever found you. Now I can't bear to have all at once to look, the voice, the life of Orestes. I ought to have stumbled on your image, dead at first, then coming alive little by little. But my brother was born like the sun, a golden animal at his rising. Either I'm blind or I find my brother by groping — oh, the joy of being blind for a sister who finds her brother. For twenty years my hands have fumbled over mean or indifferent things, and now they touch — a brother — a brother in whom everything is true. Some dubious or some false bits might have been in this head, this body, but by a wonderful chance, everything in Orestes is brotherly, everything is Orestes.

ORESTES. You smother me.

ELECTRA. I don't smother you. I don't kill you. I caress you. I'm calling you to life. From this brotherly shape which my dazzled eyes have scarcely seen I'm making my brother in all his features. See, how I've made my brother's hand, with its straight thumb. See how I've made my brother's chest, which I'm animating so it swells and breathes, giving life to my brother. See how I make this ear, little, curled, transparent like a bat's wing. One last touch and the ear is finished. I make the two alike. Quite a success, these ears! And now I'll make my brother's mouth, gentle and dry, and fasten it on his face. Take your life from me, Orestes, not from our mother.

ORESTES. Why do you hate her? Listen . . .

ELECTRA. What's the matter with you? Are you pushing me away? That's the ingratitude of sons. They're hardly finished before they get away and escape.

ORESTES. Someone is watching us from the staircase.

ELECTRA. It's she, certainly she. From jealousy or fear. It's our mother.

BEGGAR. Yes, yes, it's she.

ELECTRA. She suspects we're here, creating ourselves, freeing ourselves from her. She thinks that my caresses will cover you, wash you clear of her, make you an orphan. Oh, brother, who else could do me such a service!

ORESTES. How can you speak so of her who bore you? Though she was harsh to me, I'm less hard on her.

ELECTRA. That's just what I can't stand about her, that she bore me. That's my shame. I feel that I came into life in a dubious way, that her motherhood is only a plot to bind us together. I love everything that comes from my father. I love the way he put off his fine wedding garment and lay down to beget me, from his thought and from his body. I love his eyes, and his surprise the day I was born; I came from him far more than from my mother's pains. I was born from his nights of deep sleep, his nine months' emaciation, the comfort he found with other women while my mother was carrying me, his fatherly smile when I was born. I hate everything about my birth that comes from my mother.

ORESTES. Why do you detest women so?

ELECTRA. I don't detest women, I detest my mother. And I don't detest men, I detest Aegisthus.

ORESTES. Why do you hate him?

ELECTRA. I don't know yet. I only know it's the same hatred. That's why it's so hard to bear, that's why I'm suffocating. Many times I've tried to find out why I hate both of them with a special hatred. Two little hatreds could be borne — like sorrows — one balances the other. I tried to think I hated my mother because she let you fall when you were a baby, and Aegisthus because he stole your throne. But it's not true. I really pitied this great queen, who ruled the world, yet suddenly, frightened and humble, let her child fall, like a feeble grandmother. I pitied Aegisthus, that cruel tyrant, whose fate is to die miserably from your blows. All the reasons I had for hating them made me think them human, pitiable, but no sooner had my hatred washed them clean and re-clothed them and I found myself gentle, obedient before them, than a yet heavier wave, charged with a yet more virulent hatred, flowed over them. I hate them with a hatred that is not really me.

ORESTES. I'm here. It will vanish.

ELECTRA. You believe that? I used to think your return would free me of this hatred. I thought my illness was because you were far away. I prepared for your return by becoming all tenderness, tenderness for everyone, for them too. I was wrong. My pain tonight is caused by your being here and all the hatred in me laughs and welcomes you, it is my love for you. It caresses you as a dog does the hand that frees him. I know that you have given me the sight, the smell of hatred. The first scent, and now I follow the trail. Who's there? Is it she?

BEGGAR. No, me. You're forgetting the time. She's gone up. She's undressing.

ELECTRA. She's undressing. Before her mirror, looking long at herself, our mother, Clytemnestra, undresses. Our mother, whom I love for her beauty and pity because she's aging, whose voice and looks I admire, our mother, whom I hate.

ORESTES. Electra, sister darling, please calm yourself.

ELECTRA. Then I'm to follow the trail?

ORESTES. Calm yourself.

ELECTRA. I? I'm perfectly calm. I'm all sweetness. Sweet to my mother, very sweet. It's this hatred for her that swells up and kills me.

ORESTES. Now it's your turn not to talk. We'll think about that hatred tomorrow. This evening let me taste for an hour at least, the sweetness of the life I've never known and now return to.

ELECTRA. An hour. All right, one hour.

ORESTES. The palace is so beautiful beneath the moon. My palace. All the power of our family is emanating from it. My power. In your arms let me imagine all the happiness these walls might have held for calmer, more reasonable people. Oh, Electra, how many of our family's names were originally sweet and tender, and should have been happy names!

ELECTRA. Yes, I know. Medea, Phaedra.

ORESTES. Even those, why not?

ELECTRA. Electra. Orestes.

ORESTES. Isn't there still time? I've come to save them.

ELECTRA. Silence! She's there.

ORESTES. Who?

ELECTRA. She with the happy name: Clytemnestra.

SCENE NINE

(ELECTRA. ORESTES. CLYTEMNESTRA. *Then* AEGISTHUS.)

CLYTEMNESTRA. Electra?

ELECTRA. Mother?

CLYTEMNESTRA. Who is this man?

ELECTRA. Guess.

CLYTEMNESTRA. Let me see his face.

ELECTRA. If you can't see it at a distance you'd see him less well near to.

CLYTEMNESTRA. Electra, let's stop fighting. If you really want to marry this man, I'll agree. Why do you smile? Wasn't it I who wanted you to marry?

ELECTRA. Not at all. You wanted me to be a woman.

CLYTEMNESTRA. What's the difference?

ELECTRA. You wanted me in your camp. You didn't want the face of your worst enemy constantly before you.

CLYTEMNESTRA. You mean my daughter's?

ELECTRA. Chastity, rather!

ORESTES. Electra . . . !

ELECTRA. Let me alone, let me alone. I've found the trail.

CLYTEMNESTRA. Chastity! This girl who's devoured by desire talks about chastity! This girl at two years old couldn't see a boy without blushing. It was because you wanted to embrace Orestes, if you want to know, that you pulled him out of my arms.

ELECTRA. Then I was right. I'm proud of it. It was worth while.

(*Trumpets. Shouts. Faces in the windows.* AEGISTHUS *leans down from a balcony.*)

AEGISTHUS. Are you there, queen?

BEGGAR. Yes, she's here.

AEGISTHUS. Great news, queen. Orestes is not dead. He's escaped. He's coming toward Argos.

CLYTEMNESTRA. Orestes!

AEGISTHUS. I'm sending my bodyguard to meet him. I've posted my most faithful men around the walls. You say nothing?

CLYTEMNESTRA. Orestes is coming back?

AEGISTHUS. Coming back to seize his father's throne, to prevent my being regent, and you being queen. His emissaries are preparing a revolt. But don't worry. I'll keep order. Who's down there with you?

CLYTEMNESTRA. Electra.

AEGISTHUS. And her gardener?

BEGGAR. And her gardener.

AEGISTHUS. I hope you're not still trying to separate them? You see how well founded my fears were! You agree now?

CLYTEMNESTRA. No. I'm not trying any more.

AEGISTHUS. Don't let them leave the palace. Them especially. I've ordered the gates closed till the soldiers return. You hear me, gardener?

ELECTRA. We'll not leave.

AEGISTHUS. Queen, come upstairs. Go back to your room. It's late and the Council is to meet at dawn. I wish you a goodnight.

ELECTRA. Thanks, Aegisthus.

AEGISTHUS. I was speaking to the queen, Electra. This is no time for irony. Come, queen.

CLYTEMNESTRA. Good-bye, Electra.

ELECTRA. Good-bye, mother.

(CLYTEMNESTRA *goes, then turns back.*)

CLYTEMNESTRA. Good-bye, my daughter's husband.

BEGGAR. What you see in families! You see everything!

ELECTRA. Who spoke?

BEGGAR. No one! No one spoke. You think someone would speak at a time like this?

SCENE TEN

(ELECTRA. ORESTES. BEGGAR.)

ORESTES. Tell me, Electra! Tell me!

ELECTRA. Tell you what?

ORESTES. Your hatred. The reason for your hatred. You know it now, when you were talking to Clytemnestra a moment ago you almost fainted in my arms. It might have been from joy — or horror.

ELECTRA. It was both joy *and* horror. Are you strong or weak, Orestes?

ORESTES. Tell me your secret and I'll find out.

ELECTRA. I don't know my secret yet. I hold only one end of the thread. Don't worry. Everything will follow. Take care! Here she is.

(CLYTEMNESTRA *appears at the back of the stage.*)

SCENE ELEVEN

(ELECTRA. CLYTEMNESTRA. ORESTES. BEGGAR.)

CLYTEMNESTRA. So it's you, Orestes?

ORESTES. Yes, mother, it's I.

CLYTEMNESTRA. Is it sweet to see a mother when you're twenty?

ORESTES. A mother who sent you away? Sad and sweet.

CLYTEMNESTRA. You look at her from far away.

ORESTES. She's just as I imagined her.

CLYTEMNESTRA. My son. Handsome. Regal. And yet I draw near.

ORESTES. Not I. At a distance she's a magnificent mother.

CLYTEMNESTRA. Who tells you that near to her magnificence remains?

ORESTES. Or her motherliness? That's why I don't move.

CLYTEMNESTRA. The mirage of a mother is enough for you?

ORESTES. I've had so much less until today. At least I can tell the mirage what I'd never tell my real mother.

CLYTEMNESTRA. If the mirage deserves it, that's all right. What will you tell her?

ORESTES. Everything I never tell you. Everything that would be a lie if said to you.

CLYTEMNESTRA. That you love her?

ORESTES. Yes.

CLYTEMNESTRA. That you respect her?

ORESTES. Yes.

CLYTEMNESTRA. That you admire her?

ORESTES. That the mother and the mirage can share.

CLYTEMNESTRA. It's the opposite for me. I don't love the mirage of my son. But when my son is actually before me, speaking, breathing, I lose my strength.

ORESTES. Think of hurting him, you'll recover it.

CLYTEMNESTRA. Why are you so hard? You don't look cruel. Your voice is gentle.

ORESTES. Yes, I'm exactly like the son I might have been. You too, of course. You look so like a wonderful mother. If I weren't your son, I'd be deceived.

ELECTRA. Why are you both talking? Where does this horrible maternal coquetry get you, mother? At midnight the little window which allows a mother and son to see each other as they are not opens for a minute. Shut it, the minute has passed.

CLYTEMNESTRA. Why so quickly? How do you know one minute of maternal love is enough for Orestes?

ELECTRA. Everything tells me you have no right to more than a minute of your son's love in your whole life. You've had it. And that's the end. What a comedy you're playing! Go!

CLYTEMNESTRA. Very well. Good-bye.

FIRST LITTLE GIRL (*appearing from behind the columns*). Good-bye, truth of my son!

ORESTES. Good-bye.

SECOND LITTLE GIRL. Good-bye, mirage of my mother!

ELECTRA. You might say *au revoir*. You'll meet again.

SCENE TWELVE

(ELECTRA *and* ORESTES *asleep. The little* EUMENIDES. BEGGAR. *The* EUMENIDES *now seem to be about twelve or thirteen years old.*)

FIRST GIRL. They're asleep. It's our turn to play Clytemnestra and ORESTES. But not the way they played. Let's play it truly.

BEGGAR (*to himself, though out loud*). The story of push or not push
— I'd like to know . . .

SECOND GIRL. You there, let us play. We're playing.

(*The three little* EUMENIDES *take the positions of the actors in
the preceding scene and play it as a parody. Masks could be
used.*)

FIRST GIRL. So it's you, Orestes?

SECOND GIRL. Yes, it's me, mother.

FIRST GIRL. You've come to kill me and Aegisthus?

SECOND GIRL. News to me!

FIRST GIRL. Not to your sister. You've done some killing, little Orestes?

SECOND GIRL. The things one kills when one is good! A doe. And to
be a little kind, I killed her fawn too, so it wouldn't be an orphan.
But to kill my mother, never! That would be — parricide.

FIRST GIRL. Was that the sword you did your killing with?

SECOND GIRL. Yes. It will cut iron. See, it went through the fawn so
fast he felt nothing.

FIRST GIRL. I'm not suggesting anything. I don't want to influence
you. But if a sword like that were to kill your sister, we'd all be at
peace!

SECOND GIRL. You want me to kill my sister?

FIRST GIRL. Never! That would be — fratricide. If the sword were
to kill her by itself, that would be ideal. Let it come out of its scab-
bard, like this, and kill her by itself. I'd just quietly marry Aegisthus. We'd call you home, Aegisthus is getting old. You'd succeed
him very soon. You'd be King Orestes.

SECOND GIRL. A sword doesn't kill by itself. It needs an assassin.

FIRST GIRL. Certainly! I should know! But I'm talking about the
times when swords will kill by themselves. People who avenge
wrongs are the curse of the world. And they get no better as they
get older, I beg you to believe that. As criminals improve with age,
good people always become criminals. Surely this is a fine moment
for a sword to think for itself, move of itself, and kill by itself.
They'd marry you to Alcmena's second daughter, the laughing one,
with the fine teeth — you'd be Orestes, the married man.

SECOND GIRL. I don't want to kill my sister, I love her, nor my mother,
I detest her.

FIRST GIRL. I know, I know. In a word you're weak and you have
principles.

THIRD GIRL. Why are you two talking? Because the moon is rising,
the nightingale singing here in the middle of this night of hatred
and threats; take your hand off the hilt of your sword, Orestes, and
see if it will have the intelligence to act by itself.

FIRST GIRL. That's right. Take it off . . . It's moving, friends, it's moving!

SECOND GIRL. It really is! It's a thinking sword. It thinks so hard it's half out!

ORESTES (*asleep*). Electra!

BEGGAR. Off with you, screech owls! You're waking them.

ELECTRA (*asleep*). Orestes!

SCENE THIRTEEN

(ELECTRA. ORESTES. BEGGAR.)

BEGGAR. I'd love to get straight that story of pushed or not pushed. For whether it's true or false, it would show whether Electra is truthful or lying and whether she lies knowingly or whether her memory plays her false. I don't believe she pushed him. Look at her: two inches above ground she's holding her sleeping brother as tight as if they were over an abyss. He's dreaming that he's falling, evidently, but that's not her fault. Now the queen looks like those bakers' wives who never stoop, even to pick up their money, or like those bitches who smother their prettiest pup while they sleep. Afterward they lick it as the queen licked Orestes, but no one ever made a child with saliva. I can see the story as if I'd been there. It's understandable, if you imagine the queen had put on a diamond pin and a white cat had passed by. She's holding Electra on her right arm, for the girl was getting heavy, and the baby on the left, a bit away from her so he'll not scratch himself on the brooch or drive it into him. It's a queen's pin, not a nurse's. And the child sees the white cat, a magnificent creature — a white life, white hair — his eyes follow it, he rocks himself, and she's an egotistical woman. Anyway, seeing the child capsizing, in order to hold him she need only free her arm of little Electra, throw little Electra off on the marble floor, get rid of little Electra. Let little Electra break her neck so the son of the king of kings be unhurt! But she's an egotist. For her a woman is as good as a man, she's a woman; the womb as good as the phallus, and she's a womb; she wouldn't dream for a second of destroying her daughter to save her son, so she keeps Electra. Now look at Electra. She's revealed herself in her brother's arms, and she's right. She couldn't wish for a better moment. Fraternity is the mark of human beings. Beasts know only love . . . cats, parrots, et cetera, they only recognize fraternity by the hair. To find brothers they have to love men, to turn to men. . . . What does the duckling do when he gets away from the other ducks and, with his tender little eye shining on his slanting duck's cheek, he looks at us humans, eating and playing games, because he knows men and women are his brothers? I've taken little ducks in my hands, and could have wrung their necks, because they came to me so fraternally, trying to understand what I was doing. I, their brother, cutting my bread and cheese and adding an onion. Brother of ducks, that's our real title, for when they raise the little heads they've plunged into the water and look at a man, they're all neatness, intelligence and tenderness — not eatable except for their brains. I could teach those little duck heads to weep! . . . So Electra didn't push Orestes! That makes everything she says legitimate, everything she undertakes irrefutable. She's unadulterated truth, a lamp without a wack. So if she kills, as looks likely, all happiness and peace around her, it's because she's right. It's as if the soul of a girl, in bright sunlight, felt a moment of anguish, as if she sniffed escaping gas in the midst of splendid festivals, and had to go after it, for the young girl is the guardian of truth; she has to go after it whether or not the world bursts and cracks down to to its foundations, whether innocents die the death of innocents to let the guilty live their guilty lives. Look at those two innocents! What will be the fruit of their marriage? To bring to life, for the world and for ages to come, a crime already forgotten, the punishment of which will be a worse crime? How right they are to sleep away this hour that is still theirs! Leave them. I'm going for a walk. If I stayed, I'd wake them. I always sneeze three times when the moon is full, and, right now, to sneeze would be taking a frightful risk. But all you who remain here, be quiet, now. This is Electra's first rest, and the last rest of Orestes.

CURTAIN

Interlude: The Gardener's Lament

I'm not in the play any more. That's why I'm free to come and tell you what the play can't tell you. In stories like this the people won't stop killing and biting each other in order to tell you that the one aim of life is to love. It would be awkward to see the parricide stop, with upraised dagger, and make a speech praising love. That would seem artificial. A lot of people wouldn't believe him. But I really don't see what else I can do here in this loneliness and desolation. And I speak impartially. I'll never marry anyone but Electra, and I'll never have her. I was made to live with a woman day and night, but I'll always live alone. I was meant to give myself fully, and yet I have to keep myself to myself. This is

my wedding night that I'm living through, all alone — but thank
you for being here — and the orangeade I'd prepared for Electra
I had to drink up myself; there's not a drop left, and this was a long
wedding night. Now who will doubt my word? The trouble is
that I always say the opposite of what I mean, and that would be
miserable today when my heart is so heavy and my mouth so bitter
— oranges are really bitter — and if I forgot for an instant that I
must speak to you of joy. Yes, love and joy. I come to tell you
they're preferable to bitterness and hate. That's a motto to carve
on a porch, or to put on a handkerchief, or better, in dwarf bego-
nias in a clump. Of course, life is a failure, yet it's very, very good.
Of course nothing ever goes right, never is well planned, yet you
must confess, sometimes everything comes out splendidly, is splendidly planned. . . . Not for me . . . or perhaps just for me. . . .
If I can judge from my wish to love everything and everyone,
which is the result of the greatest misfortune in my life! What
will happen to people who've had less bad luck? How much love
must men feel who marry wives they don't love, what joy must
those feel who leave a wife they adore, after having had her in their
home one hour? And people whose children are ugly? Of course,
tonight in my garden, I wasn't very happy. As a little festival it
didn't come off. I pretended sometimes that Electra was near
me, I talked to her and said: "Come in, Electra! Are you
cold, Electra?" But no one was deceived, not even the dog,
not to say myself. The dog thought: "He promised us a bride,
and he only gives us a word. My master has married a word;
he put on his white garment, the one my paws soil, which
keeps me from caressing him, just to marry a word! He gives
his orangeade to a word. He scolds me for barking at shadows,
real shadows which aren't alive, yet he tries to embrace a word."
And I didn't lie down: to sleep with a word was impossible. I can
speak with a word, that's all! But if you were sitting like me in
this garden, where everything is confused at night, where the moon
is shining on the sundial, and the blind owl tries to drink the
cement walk instead of the brook, you'd understand what I've understood: the truth! You'd understand that the day your parents
died, that day your parents were born; the day you were ruined,
that day you were rich; when your child was ungrateful, he was
gratitude itself; when you were abandoned, the whole world was
coming to you in rapture and tenderness. That was what happened to me in this empty, silent suburb. All these stony trees,
these immovable hills, rushed toward me. This all applies to our
play. To be sure, we can't say Electra is all love for Clytemnestra.
But note the difference: she tries to find a mother and would see

one in the first comer. She was marrying me because I was the only man who could be a kind of mother to her, though I'm not *really* the only one. There are men who'd be glad to carry a child nine months, if they had to, just to have daughters. All men, actually. Nine months are rather long, but . . . a week, or a day . . . any man would be proud. Perhaps to find a mother in *her* mother she'd have to cut her breast open, though with royalty that's rather theoretical. Among kings there are experiences 'never found among humble folk, pure hatred, for instance, and pure wrath. Always purity. That's tragedy, with its incests and parricides: purity, meaning — innocence. I don't know if you're like me, but to me, in tragedy, Pharaoh's daughter killing herself means hope, the treasonous Marshall means faith, the Duke-Assassin speaks of tenderness. Cruelty is a deed of love — excuse me, I mean: tragedy is a deed of love. That's why I'm sure this morning, that if I asked, Heaven would approve me, would give a sign that a miracle is near, which would show you that joy and love are written in heaven, and that they echo my motto, though I'm abandoned and alone. If you wish, I'll ask. I'm as sure as I'm here that a voice from on high would answer me, that loud speakers and amplifiers and God's thunder are all prepared by God himself to shout, if I ask: "love and joy." But I'd rather you didn't ask. First it would be indecent. It's not the gardener's role to demand of God a storm, even a storm of tenderness. Moreover it would be useless. We know so well that at this moment, and yesterday and tomorrow and always, they're all up there, as many as there are, or perhaps only one, or even if that one is absent, they're all ready to shout: love and joy. It's much better for a man to take the gods at their word — this is euphemism — without forcing them to underline it, or to be held by it, or to create among themselves obligations of creditor and debtor. I'm always convinced by silences. Yes, I've begged them, haven't I? not to shout love and joy. But let them shout it if they really want to. Yet I'd rather conjure them, I conjure you, God, as a proof of your affections, of your voice and all your shouting, to keep silent, silent for one second. . . . That's much more convincing. . . . Listen! . . . Thanks!

ACT TWO • SCENE ONE

(The same setting, shortly before dawn. ELECTRA, *seated, holding* ORESTES, *asleep.* BEGGAR. *A cock. Sound of a trumpet in the distance.)*

BEGGAR. It won't be long now, eh, Electra?

ELECTRA. No. It's not far away.

BEGGAR. I said "it," I meant the day.

ELECTRA. I meant the light.

BEGGAR. It's not enough for you that liars' faces are shining in the sun? That adulterers and murderers move about freely? That's what the day brings — not too bad.

ELECTRA. No. But I want their faces to look blank at noon, and their hands red. That's what light brings out. I want their eyes to be rotten, their mouths diseased.

BEGGAR. As you say, one can't ask too much!

ELECTRA. There's the cock . . . shall I wake him?

BEGGAR. Wake him if you wish, but if I were you, I'd give him another five minutes.

ELECTRA. Five minutes of nothingness! A poor gift!

BEGGAR. You never know. I believe there's an insect that lives only five minutes. In five minutes he's young, adult, noisy; he runs through childhood and adolescence, to the time of lame knees and cataract, and legitimate and morganatic unions. While I'm speaking he must be having measles and growing to puberty.

ELECTRA. Let's wait till he dies. That's all I'll agree to.

BEGGAR. Our brother sleeps well.

ELECTRA. He went to sleep right away. He escaped from me. He slipped into sleep as though that were his real life.

BEGGAR. He's smiling. It *is* his real life.

ELECTRA. Tell me anything you like, beggar, except that Orestes' real life is a smile.

BEGGAR. Loud laughter, love, fine clothes, happiness. I guessed that as soon as I saw him. Orestes would be gay as a lark, if life were good to him.

ELECTRA. He has bad luck.

BEGGAR. Yes, he's not very lucky. All the more reason for not hurrying him.

ELECTRA. Good! As he was made to laugh, to dress well, as he's a lark, I'll give Orestes five minutes, for he'll wake to a lifetime of horror.

BEGGAR. In your place, since you can choose, I'd see to it that this morning light and truth depart at the same time. That doesn't mean much, but it would be a young girl's role and would please me. Man's truth is part of his habits, it leaves him somehow, whether at nine o'clock in the morning when workers strike, or at six in the evening, when women confess, et cetera; these are always bad things, always unclear. Now I'm used to animals. They know when to leave. A rabbit's first jump in the heather, the very second the sun rises, the plover's first flight, the young bear's first run from his rock, these, I can tell you, go toward the truth. If they don't get there, that's because they don't have to. A mere nothing distracts them, a gudgeon, a bee. Do as they do, Electra, go toward the dawn.

ELECTRA. A fine kingdom where gudgeons and bees are liars! But your animals are moving already!

BEGGAR. No. Those are the night creatures turning in. Owls. Rats. The night's truth turning in. Hush! Listen to the last two, the nightingales, of course the nightingales' truth.

SCENE TWO

(The same. AGATHA. *A* YOUNG MAN.*)*

AGATHA. Darling, you do understand, don't you?

YOUNG MAN. Yes, I have an answer for everything.

AGATHA. If he sees you on the stairs?

YOUNG MAN. I have come to see the doctor on the top floor.

AGATHA. You forget already! He's a veterinary. Buy a dog. . . . If he finds me in your arms?

YOUNG MAN. I've picked you up in the street, you've sprained your ankle.

AGATHA. If it's in our kitchen?

YOUNG MAN. I'll pretend to be drunk — I don't know where I am. I'll break the glasses.

AGATHA. One will be enough, darling, a small one, the large ones are crystal. If it's in our room and we're dressed?

YOUNG MAN. I'm looking for him, to talk politics. I had to go there to find him.

AGATHA. If it's in our room and we're undressed?

YOUNG MAN. I entered unexpectedly, you're resisting me, you are perfidy itself, you treat as a thief a man who's pursued you six months. . . . You're a tart!

AGATHA. Darling!

YOUNG MAN. A real tart!

AGATHA. I understand. It's almost day, my love, and I've hardly had you for an hour, and how many more times do you think he'll believe I walk in my sleep, and that it's less dangerous to let me stroll in the grove than on the roof? Oh, my love, can you think of any pretext for letting me have you in *our* bed at night, me between you two, so it would seem quite natural to him?

YOUNG MAN. Think! You'll invent something.

AGATHA. A pretext for letting you two talk about your elections and the races over the body of your Agatha, so he'd not suspect anything. That's what we need — that's all.

YOUNG MAN. All!

AGATHA. Oh dear! Why is he so vain? Why is his sleep so light? Why does he adore me?

YOUNG MAN. The eternal litany! Why did you marry him? Why did you love him?

AGATHA. I? Liar! I never loved anyone but you!

YOUNG MAN. I? Remember in whose arms I found you day before yesterday!

AGATHA. That was only because I'd sprained my ankle. The man you mention was picking me up.

YOUNG MAN. First I've *heard* of any sprain.

AGATHA. You! You understand nothing. You don't realize that accident gave me an idea for us to use.

YOUNG MAN. When I meet him on the stairs he has no dogs, I can tell you, and no cats.

AGATHA. He rides horseback. You can't take a horse to the doctor upstairs.

YOUNG MAN. And he's always leaving your room.

AGATHA. Why do you force me to betray a state secret? He comes to consult my husband. They're afraid of a plot in the city. Please don't tell anyone, that would mean his dismissal. You'd bring me to the stake.

YOUNG MAN. One evening he was hurrying, his scarf not fastened, his tunic half unbuttoned. . . .

AGATHA. Of course, that was the day he tried to kiss me. I fixed him!

YOUNG MAN. You didn't let him kiss you, and he so powerful? I was waiting downstairs. He stayed two hours. . . .

AGATHA. He did stay two hours, but I didn't let him kiss me.

YOUNG MAN. Then he kissed you without your leave. Confess, Agatha, or I'll go away.

AGATHA. Force me to confess! That's a fine reward for my frankness. Yes, he did kiss me . . . once . . . on my forehead.

YOUNG MAN. And that seems dreadful to you?

AGATHA. Dreadful? Frightful!

YOUNG MAN. And you don't suffer for it?

AGATHA. Not at all! . . . Ah, do I suffer? It's killing me, killing me! Kiss me, darling. Now you know everything, and I'm glad of it. Aren't you happy everything is cleared up between us?

YOUNG MAN. Yes. Anything is better than a lie.

AGATHA. What a nice way you have of saying you prefer me to everything else, darling!

SCENE THREE

(ELECTRA. ORESTES. BEGGAR. *Then the* EUMENIDES. *They are taller than before, and seem fifteen years old.*)

BEGGAR. A dawn song, at the dawn of such a day! It's always like this.

ELECTRA. The insect is dead, beggar?

BEGGAR. Dispersed in the universe. His great-grandchildren are now fighting gout.

ELECTRA. Orestes!

BEGGAR. You see he's no longer asleep. His eyes are open.

ELECTRA. Where are you, Orestes? What are you thinking about?

FIRST FURY. Orestes, there's just time. Don't listen to your sister.

SECOND FURY. Don't listen to her. We have learned what life holds for you, it's wonderful!

THIRD FURY. Just by chance. As we grew up during the night.

SECOND FURY. We're not saying anything about love to you, does that seem strange?

FIRST FURY. She's going to spoil everything with her poison.

THIRD FURY. Her poison of *truth*, the only one that has no antidote.

FIRST FURY. You're right. We know what you're thinking. Royalty is magnificent, Orestes: young girls in the royal parks, feeding bread to the swans, King Orestes' miniature hanging on their blouses — they kiss it secretly; soldiers going to war, the women on the roofs, the sky like a veil over them, a white horse prancing to music; the return from war, the king's face looking like the face of a god, just because he's chilly or hungry or a little frightened, or pitying his people. If the truth is going to spoil all that, let it perish!

SECOND FURY. You're right. And love is magnificent. Orestes! Lovers, it seems, will never part. They're never separated but they rush back to each other, to clasp hands. Or if they go away, they find each other face to face again immediately. The earth is round for the sake of lovers. Everywhere I run into him I love, though he's not yet alive. All this Electra wants to take from you, and from us too, with her Truth. We want to love. Flee Electra!

ELECTRA. Orestes!

ORESTES. I'm awake, sister.

ELECTRA. Wake from your awakening. Don't listen to these girls.

ORESTES. Are you sure they aren't right? Are you sure that it's not the worst kind of arrogance for a human being to try to retrace his steps? Why not take the first road and go forward, at random?

Trust yourself to me. At this moment I can see so clearly the track
of the game called happiness.

ELECTRA. Alas! That's not what we're hunting today.

ORESTES. The only thing that's important is not to leave each other.
Let's go to Thessaly. You'll see my house, covered with roses and
jasmin.

ELECTRA. Darling Orestes, you've saved me from the gardener not just
to give me to flowers!

ORESTES. Be persuaded! Let's slip out of the trap which will soon
catch us! Let's rejoice that we woke up before it did! Come!

FIRST FURY. It's awake! Look at its eyes!

THIRD FURY. You're right. The spring is wonderful, Orestes. When
you can see over the hedges only the moving backs of the beasts
grazing in the new grass, and the donkey's head looking at you
over them. That donkey's head would look funny if you murdered
your uncle. Pretty funny, a donkey looking at you when your
hands are red with your uncle's blood —

ORESTES. What's she saying?

THIRD FURY. Talk on about the spring! The buttery mould that floats
on the watercress in the brooks — you'll see what a comfort that
will be for a man who kills his mother. Spread your butter that
day with a knife, even if it's not the knife that killed your mother,
and you'll see!

ORESTES. Help. Electra!

ELECTRA. So! You're like all men, Orestes! The least little flattery
relaxes them, the slightest breath captivates them. Help you? I
know what you'd like me to say.

ORESTES. Then tell me.

ELECTRA. That on the whole human beings are good, that life, too,
after all, is good.

ORESTES. Isn't that true?

ELECTRA. That it's not a bad fate to be young, handsome, and a
prince, to have a young sister who's a princess. That it's enough to
leave men alone in their mean, vain business — not lancing human
ulcers, but living for the beauty of the earth.

ORESTES. Isn't that what you're telling me?

ELECTRA. No! I'm telling you our mother has a lover.

ORESTES. You lie! That's impossible.

FIRST FURY. She's a widow. She has the right.

ELECTRA. I'm telling you our father was murdered.

ORESTES. Agamemnon! Murdered!

ELECTRA. Stabbed, by assassins.

SECOND FURY. Seven years ago. It's ancient history.

ORESTES. You knew that and let me sleep all night!

ELECTRA. I didn't know it. It's the night's gift to me. These truths were tossed to me by the night. Now I know how prophetesses work. They hold their brother close to their heart through one night.

ORESTES. Our father killed! Who told you?

ELECTRA. He himself.

ORESTES. He spoke to you before he died?

ELECTRA. Dead, he spoke to me. The very days of his death, but it's taken seven years for his word to reach me.

ORESTES. He appeared to you?

ELECTRA. No. His corpse appeared to me last night, looking like him the day he was murdered, but illuminated; I just had to read. There was a fold of his garment which said, I'm not a fold of death but of murder. And on his shoe there was a buckle which repeated, I'm not an accidental buckle but a criminal buckle. And on his eyelid there was a wrinkle which said, I didn't see death, I saw regicides.

ORESTES. And about our mother, who told you that?

ELECTRA. She herself, herself again.

ORESTES. She confessed?

ELECTRA. No. I saw her dead. Her body betrayed her. There's no possible doubt. Her eyebrow was the eyebrow of a dead woman who'd had a lover.

ORESTES. Who is this lover? Who is this murderer?

ELECTRA. I've waked you so you can find out. Let's hope they're both the same, then you'll have to strike just one blow.

ORESTES. Girls, I think you'll have to clear out. My sister presents me as I wake with a harlot queen and a murdered king . . . my parents.

FIRST FURY. That's not too bad. Add nothing more.

ELECTRA. Forgive me, Orestes.

SECOND FURY. Now she's excusing herself.

THIRD FURY. I'm killing you, but excuse it, please.

BEGGAR. She's wrong to excuse herself. This is the kind of awakening we generally reserve for our wives and sisters. They seem to be made for that.

ELECTRA. They are made just for that. Wives, sisters-in-law, mothers-in-law, they're the ones to shake up the men who, barely awake, see nothing but purple and gold, till the women give them, with their coffee and hot water, a hatred of injustice and a scorn for small joys.

ORESTES. Forgive me, Electra!

SECOND FURY. It's his turn to beg pardon. Aren't they polite in this family!

FIRST FURY. They take off their heads and bow to each other.

ELECTRA. And they watch for their waking. For men put on the armor of happiness if they sleep no more than five minutes: and with it satisfaction, indifference, generosity, appetite. And a spot of sunlight reconciles them to all blood spots. And a bird song to all lies. But the women are there, all of them, worn by insomnia, with jealousy, envy, love, memory and truth. Are you awake, Orestes?

FIRST FURY. And we'll be as old as he in an hour! Let's hope heaven makes us different!

ORESTES. I believe I'm waking up.

BEGGAR. Here comes our mother, children.

ORESTES. Where's my sword?

ELECTRA. Bravo! That's what I call a good awakening. Take up your sword. Take up your hatred. Take up your strength.

SCENE FOUR

(*The same.* CLYTEMNESTRA.)

CLYTEMNESTRA. Their mother appears. And they turn into statues.

ELECTRA. Orphans, rather.

CLYTEMNESTRA. I'm not going to listen to an insolent daughter any longer.

ELECTRA. Listen to your son.

ORESTES. Who is it, mother? Confess.

CLYTEMNESTRA. What kind of children are you, turning our meeting into a melodrama? Leave me, or I'll call.

ELECTRA. Whom will you call? Him?

ORESTES. You struggle too much, mother.

BEGGAR. Be careful, Orestes. An innocent creature struggles as much as a guilty.

CLYTEMNESTRA. Creature? What kind of creature am I for my children? Speak, Orestes, speak!

ORESTES. I don't dare.

CLYTEMNESTRA. Electra, then. She'll dare.

ELECTRA. Who is it, mother?

CLYTEMNESTRA. Of whom, of what are you speaking?

ORESTES. Mother, it is true you have . . . ?

ELECTRA. Don't specify, Orestes. Just ask who it is. There's a name somewhere in her. However you ask your question, the name will come out.

ORESTES. Mother, is it true you have a lover?

CLYTEMNESTRA. That's your question too, Electra?

ELECTRA. It might be put that way.

CLYTEMNESTRA. My son and daughter ask if I have a lover?

ELECTRA. Your husband can't ask it now.

CLYTEMNESTRA. The gods would blush to hear you.

ELECTRA. That would surprise me. They've not been doing much blushing lately.

CLYTEMNESTRA. I have no lover. But watch your step. All the evil in the world is caused by the so-called pure people trying to dig up secrets and bring them to light.

ELECTRA. Rottenness is born of sunshine, I grant that.

CLYTEMNESTRA. I have no lover, I couldn't have a lover if I wanted one. But take care. Curious people have had no luck in our family: they tracked down a theft and found a sacrilege; they carried on a love affair and ran into an incest. You'll not find out I have a lover, because I haven't, but you'll stumble on a stone which will be fatal to your sisters and yourselves.

ELECTRA. Who is your lover?

ORESTES. Electra, at least listen to her.

CLYTEMNESTRA. I have no lover. But who would call it a crime if I had?

ORESTES. Oh, mother, you're a queen.

CLYTEMNESTRA. The world is not old and day is just dawning. But it would take us at least till twilight to recite the list of queens who've had lovers.

ORESTES. Mother, please! Fight on this way. Convince us. If this struggle restores a queen to us, it's blessed, everything is restored.

ELECTRA. Don't you see you're giving her weapons, Orestes?

CLYTEMNESTRA. That's enough. Orestes, leave me alone with Electra, will you?

ORESTES. Must I, sister?

ELECTRA. Yes. Yes. Wait there, under the arch. And run back to me as soon as I call, Orestes. Run as fast as you can. It will mean I know all.

SCENE FIVE

(CLYTEMNESTRA. ELECTRA. *The* BEGGAR.)

CLYTEMNESTRA. Help me, Electra!

ELECTRA. Help you to what? To tell the truth or to lie?

CLYTEMNESTRA. Protect me.

ELECTRA. It's the first time you stoop to your daughter, mother. You must be afraid.

CLYTEMNESTRA. I'm afraid of Orestes.

ELECTRA. You lie. You're not the least afraid of Orestes. You see what he is: passionate, changeable, weak — still dreaming of an idyl in the Atrides' family. It's I you're afraid of, it's for me you're playing this game, the meaning of which still escapes me. You have a lover, haven't you? Who is he?

CLYTEMNESTRA. He knows nothing. And he's not in question.

ELECTRA. He doesn't know he's your lover?

CLYTEMNESTRA. Stop acting like a judge, Electra. Stop this pursuit. After all, you're my daughter.

ELECTRA. After all! Exactly after all! That's why I'm questioning you.

CLYTEMNESTRA. Then stop being my daughter. Stop hating me. Just be what I look for in you — a woman. Take up my cause, it's yours. Defend yourself by defending me.

ELECTRA. I'm not a member of the Women's Association, and someone other than you would have to recruit me.

CLYTEMNESTRA. You're wrong. If you betray your equal in body, in misfortune, you're the first one Orestes will loathe. Scandal always strikes back at the people who start it. What good does it do you to bespatter all women by bespattering me? In Orestes' eyes you'll sully all the qualities you get from me.

ELECTRA. I'm not like you in anything. I never look in my mirror except to be certain of that piece of luck. All the shiny marble, all the fountains of the palace have cried out to me, your own face cries it: Electra's nose is not the least like Clytemnestra's nose. My forehead is my own. My mouth's my own. And I have no lover.

CLYTEMNESTRA. Listen! I have no lover. I'm in love.

ELECTRA. Don't try that trick. You throw love at me the way drivers pursued by wolves throw them a dog. Dog meat is not my food.

CLYTEMNESTRA. We're women, Electra. We have a right to love.

ELECTRA. There are many rights in the sisterhood of women. I know. If you pay the entrance fee, which is steep, which means admission only for weak, lying, base women, you have a right to be weak, lying, and base. Unfortunately women are strong, loyal, and noble, so you're wrong. You had the right to love my father only. Did you? On your wedding night, did you love him?

CLYTEMNESTRA. What are you driving at? Do you want me to say that your birth owes nothing to love, that you were conceived in indifference? Be satisfied. Not everyone can be like your Aunt Leda, and lay eggs. You never spoke in me. We were indifferent to each other from the first. You didn't even cause me pain at your birth. You were small and withdrawn, your lips tight. When you were a year old, your lips were sealed, so "mother" wouldn't be your first word. Neither of us cried that day. We've never wept together.

ELECTRA. Weeping parties don't interest me.

CLYTEMNESTRA. You'll weep soon, perhaps over me.

ELECTRA. Eyes can weep by themselves. That's what they're there for.

CLYTEMNESTRA. Yes, even yours, which look like two stones. Some day tears will drown them.

ELECTRA. I hope that day comes! But why are you trying to hold me by cold words instead of by love?

CLYTEMNESTRA. So you'll understand I have a right to love. So you'll know that my whole life has been as hard as my daughter from her very first day. Since my marriage I've never been alone, never at peace. I never went to the forest except for festivals. No rest, even for my body which was covered every day by golden robes and at night by a king. Always mistrust, even of things, animals, plants. I often said to myself, as I looked at cross, silent lindens, smelling like a wet nurse: "They're like Electra's head, the day she was born." No queen has ever suffered so deeply the fate of queens, a husband's absence, a son's suspicions, a daughter's hatred. What had I left?

ELECTRA. What the others had left: waiting.

CLYTEMNESTRA. Waiting, for what? Waiting is horrible.

ELECTRA. For her who has caught you today, perhaps.

CLYTEMNESTRA. Can you tell me what you're waiting for?

ELECTRA. I no longer wait. For ten years I've waited — for my father. Waiting is the only happiness in the world.

CLYTEMNESTRA. A virgin's happiness, a solitary happiness.

ELECTRA. You think so? Except for you and the men, everything in the palace awaited my father with me, everything was party to my waiting. It began in the morning with my early walk under the lindens which hate you, which waited for my father with an eagerness they tried in vain to repress; they were sorry to live by the year and not by the decade, ashamed every spring that they couldn't hold back their flowers and perfume, that they grew weak with me over his absence. It went on till noon when I went to the brook that was the luckiest of us all, for it awaited my father as it ran to the river that ran to the sea. And in the evening, when I wasn't strong enough to wait near his dogs and his horses, poor short-lived beasts, that couldn't wait for centuries, I took refuge with the columns and the statues. I modeled myself on them. I waited in the moonlight for hours, motionless like them, without thought, lifeless. I awaited him with a stony heart — marble, alabaster, onyx — though it was beating, shattering my breast. Where would I be if there weren't still hours to wait, to wait for the past, wait for him still!

CLYTEMNESTRA. I'm not waiting. I love.

ELECTRA. Everything goes well with you now?

CLYTEMNESTRA. Very well.

ELECTRA. Flowers obey you? Birds talk to you?

CLYTEMNESTRA. Yes, your lindens signal to me.

ELECTRA. Quite likely. You've robbed me of everything in life.

CLYTEMNESTRA. Fall in love. We'll share.

ELECTRA. Share love with you?! Are you offering to share your lover with me? Who is he?

CLYTEMNESTRA. Electra, have pity! I'll tell you his name, though it will make you blush. But wait a few days. What good will a scandal do you? Think of your brother. Can you imagine the Argives letting Orestes succeed an unworthy mother?

ELECTRA. An unworthy mother? What are you getting at with this confession? What time do you want to gain? What trap are you setting for me? What brood are you hoping to save, limping off like a partridge, toward love and unworthiness?

CLYTEMNESTRA. Spare me public disgrace! Why do you force me to confess I love someone below me in rank?

ELECTRA. Some little nameless lieutenant?

CLYTEMNESTRA. Yes.

ELECTRA. You're lying. If your lover were some little nameless in-glorious officer, or a bathhouse attendant, or a groom, you'd love him. But you're not in love, you've never loved. Who is it? Why do you refuse to name him, as you'd refuse a key? What piece of furniture are you afraid of opening with that name?

CLYTEMNESTRA. Something of my own, my love.

ELECTRA. Tell me the name of your lover, and I'll tell you if you love. And we'll keep it to ourselves forever.

CLYTEMNESTRA. Never!

ELECTRA. You see! It's not your lover but your secret that you're hiding from me. You're afraid his name would give me the one proof I'm lacking in my pursuit.

CLYTEMNESTRA. What proof? You're mad.

ELECTRA. The proof of the crime. Everything tells me, mother, that you committed it. But what I don't yet see, what you must tell me, is why you committed it. I've tried all the keys, as you say. Not one opens it — yet. Not love. You love nothing. Not ambition. You scoff at queenship. Not anger. You're deliberate, calculating. But our lover's name would clear up everything, tell us everything, wouldn't it? Who do you love? Who is he?

SCENE SIX

(*The same.* AGATHA, *pursued by the* PRESIDENT.)

PRESIDENT. Who is he? Who do you love?

AGATHA. I hate you.

PRESIDENT. Who is it?

AGATHA. I tell you that's enough. Enough lies. Electra's right. I'm on her side. Thanks, Electra, you give me life.

PRESIDENT. What is this song?

AGATHA. Wives' song. You'll soon know it.

PRESIDENT. So, she's going to sing!

AGATHA. Yes, we're all here, with our unsatisfactory husbands or our widowhood. And we all kill ourselves, trying to make life and death pleasant. And if they eat cooked lettuce they have to have salt and a smile with it. And if they smoke we have to light their horrid cigars with the flame of our hearts.

PRESIDENT. Who are you talking about? I never ate cooked lettuce.

AGATHA. Sorrel, if you prefer.

PRESIDENT. Your lover doesn't eat sorrel or smoke cigars?

AGATHA. The sorrel my lover eats turns into ambrosia, and I lick up what's left. And everything soiled by my husband's touch is puri-fied by his hands or lips. I myself! God knows!

ELECTRA. I've found out, mother, I've found out!

PRESIDENT. Collect yourself, Agatha.

AGATHA. Precisely. I've done just that. Twenty-four hours a day we kill ourselves to please someone whose displeasure is our only joy, for a husband whose absence is our only delight, for the vanity of the only man who humiliates us daily by showing us his toes and his shirt tails. And he has the gall to reproach us for stealing from him one hour a week of this hell! But, sure enough, he's right. When this wonderful hour comes, we don't greet it with a dead hand!

PRESIDENT. Electra, this is your work. This very morning she kissed me!

AGATHA. I'm pretty and he's ugly. I'm young and he's old. I'm bright and he's stupid. I have a soul and he hasn't. Yet he has everything. At least he has me. And I have nothing, though I have him! Until this morning, I gave everything and had to seem grateful. Why? I black his shoes. Why? I brush off his dandruff. Why? I make his coffee. Why? The truth might be that I'm poisoning him, rubbing his collar with pitch and ashes. Of course you can understand about the shoes. I spit on them. I spit on you. But it's all over, finished. Welcome, truth! Electra has given me her courage. I'm through. I'd as soon die.

BEGGAR. Don't these wives sing well!

PRESIDENT. Who is it?

ELECTRA. Listen, mother! Listen to yourself. It's you talking.

AGATHA. Who is it? All husbands think it's just one person.

PRESIDENT. Lovers? You have lovers?

AGATHA. They think we deceive them only with lovers. Of course we have lovers, too. But we deceive you with everything. When I wake and my hand slips along the wooden bedstead, that's my first adultery. Let's use your word for once, adultery. How often, when I'm wakeful, I've caressed that wood — olive wood, so soft! What a pretty name! I start when I hear an olive tree mentioned in the street — I hear my lover's name! And my second adultery is when I open my eyes and see daylight through the blinds. And my third, when my foot touches the bathwater and when I jump in. I betray you with my fingers, with my eyes, with the soles of my feet. When I look at you, I deceive you. When I listen to you and pretend to admire you in court, I'm deceiving you. Kill the olive trees, the pigeons, the five-year-old children, boys and girls, and water and earth and fire! Kill this beggar. You're betrayed by all of them.

BEGGAR. Thanks!

PRESIDENT. And yesterday this woman was still pouring my tea! And finding it too cool, having the water boiled again! You're all pleased, aren't you? This little scandal within a great one can't displease you!

BEGGAR. No. It's like the squirrel in a big wheel. It gives the right rhythm.

PRESIDENT. And this scene before the queen herself. You'll pardon it?

ELECTRA. The queen envies Agatha. The queen would give her life to have the chance Agatha has today. Who is it, mother?

BEGGAR. Sure! Don't let anything distract you, president. It's almost a minute since you asked her who it is.

PRESIDENT. Who is it?

AGATHA. I've told you. Everybody. Everything.

PRESIDENT. It's enough to drive me to suicide, to make me bash my head against the wall.

AGATHA. Don't stop on my account. The Mycenean wall is solid.

PRESIDENT. Is he young? Or old?

AGATHA. A lover's age — between sixteen and eighty.

PRESIDENT. And she thinks she's disgracing me by insulting me! Your insults only hurt yourself, abandoned woman!

AGATHA. I know, I know. Outrage is called majesty. In the streets the most respectable people slip on dung.

PRESIDENT. At last you'll find out who I am! Whoever your lovers are, I'll kill the first one I find here.

AGATHA. The first one you find here? You choose the place badly.

PRESIDENT. I'll make him kneel down and kiss the marble.

AGATHA. You'll see how he'll kiss the marble when he comes into this court in a minute and sits on the throne.

PRESIDENT. Wretch, what are you saying?

AGATHA. I'm saying that at present I have two lovers, and one is Aegisthus.

CLYTEMNESTRA. Liar!

AGATHA. What! She too!

ELECTRA. You too, mother?

BEGGAR. That's funny. I'd have thought, if Aegisthus had a liking, it was for Electra.

PAGE (*announcing*). Aegisthus!

ELECTRA. At last!

THE FURIES. Aegisthus!

> (AEGISTHUS *comes in. Much more majestic and calm than in the first act. Far above him, a bird hovers in the air.*)

SCENE SEVEN

(*The same.* AEGISTHUS. *A* CAPTAIN. SOLDIERS.)

AEGISTHUS. Electra is here. . . . Thanks, Electra! I'll stop here, Captain. Headquarters are here.

CLYTEMNESTRA. I, too, am here.

AEGISTHUS. I'm glad. Welcome, queen!

PRESIDENT. I too, Aegisthus!

AEGISTHUS. Good, president. I need your help.

PRESIDENT. And now he insults us!

AEGISTHUS. What's the matter with you all, that you stare at me so?

BEGGAR. What's the matter is that the queen is waiting for a perjurer, Electra for an infidel, Agatha for a faithless lover. He's more humble, he's waiting for the man who seduced his wife. They're all waiting for you, but it's not you that's come!

AEGISTHUS. They have no luck, have they, beggar?

BEGGAR. No, they have no luck. Waiting for a rascal, they see a king enter! I don't care about the others, but for our little Electra, the situation is complicated.

AEGISTHUS. You think so? I think not.

BEGGAR. I knew it would happen. I told you so yesterday. I knew the king would reveal himself in you. He has your strength and your years. He finds the right moment. Electra is near. That might have involved a bloody act. But you've revealed yourself. Fine for Greece! But not so gay for the family.

CLYTEMNESTRA. What do these riddles mean? What are you talking about?

BEGGAR. Lucky for us, too! Since there has to be *some* kind of meeting, better let Electra meet nobility than wickedness. How did you get this way, Aegisthus?

AEGISTHUS (*looking at* ELECTRA). Electra is here! I knew I'd find her looking toward me, her statuesque head, her eyes which see only when the lids are closed, deaf to human speech.

CLYTEMNESTRA. Listen to me, Aegisthus!

PRESIDENT. How well you choose your lovers, Agatha! What impudence!

CAPTAIN. Aegisthus, there's no time!

AEGISTHUS. Your ears are ornaments, aren't they, Electra? Mere ornaments. . . . The gods said, we gave her hands so she'd not touch, eyes so she'd be seen, we can't let her head be without ears! People would soon discover that she hears only us. . . . Tell me, what would we hear if we placed our ears near hers? What roaring! And where from?

CLYTEMNESTRA. Are you mad? Take care! Electra's ears do hear you.

PRESIDENT. They blush for it.

AEGISTHUS. They hear me. I'm sure of that. Since what happened to me just now in the outskirts of Argos, my words come from beyond myself. And I know she sees me too, she's the only one who does see me. The only one to guess what I've become since that moment.

CLYTEMNESTRA. You're talking to your worst enemy, Aegisthus!

AEGISTHUS. She knows why I galloped toward the city from the mountains. Electra, you'd have thought my horse understood. He was beautiful, that light chestnut, charging toward Electra, followed by the thunder of the squadron, in which the knowledge of rushing toward Electra grew less, from the white stallions of the trumpeters to the piebald mares of the rear guard. Don't be surprised if my horse sticks his head between the pillars, neighing to you. He knew that I was strangling, with your name in my mouth like a golden stopper. I had to shout your name, and to you — shall I shout it, Electra?

CLYTEMNESTRA. Stop this outrageous behavior, Aegisthus.

CAPTAIN. Aegisthus! The city is in danger!

AEGISTHUS. True! Pardon me! Where are they now, Captain?

CAPTAIN. You can see their lances coming over the hills. I've never seen a harvest grow so fast. Nor so thick. There are thousands of them.

AEGISTHUS. The cavalry's no use against them?

CAPTAIN. Repulsed, prisoners taken.

CLYTEMNESTRA. What's happening, Aegisthus?

CAPTAIN. The Corinthians are surrounding us, no declaration of war, no reason for it. Their regiments entered our territory last night. The suburbs are on fire already.

AEGISTHUS. What do the prisoners say?

CAPTAIN. Their orders are to leave no stone standing in Argos.

CLYTEMNESTRA. Show yourself, Aegisthus, and they'll flee!

AEGISTHUS. I fear, queen, that wouldn't be enough.

CAPTAIN. They have friends in the city. The reserves of pitch have been stolen, so the middle-class quarters can be burned. Gangs of beggars are gathering around the markets ready to start pillaging.

CLYTEMNESTRA. If the guard is loyal, what is there to fear?

CAPTAIN. The guard is ready to fight. But they're muttering. You know, they've never willingly obeyed a woman. The city's the same way. They both demand a king, a man.

AEGISTHUS. They're right. They shall have one.

PRESIDENT. Whoever wants to be king of Argos, Aegisthus, must first kill Clytemnestra.

BEGGAR. Or simply marry her.

PRESIDENT. Never!

AEGISTHUS. Why, never? The queen can't deny that's the only way to save Argos. I don't doubt she'll consent. Captain, tell the guard the wedding has this moment taken place. Keep me informed of events. I'll wait here for your bulletins. And do you, president, go meet the rioters and tell them this news most enthusiastically.

PRESIDENT. Never! I must first speak to you, man to man, no matter what happens.

AEGISTHUS. No matter if Argos falls, if war comes? You're outrageous.

PRESIDENT. My honor, the honor of all Greek judges, is at stake.

BEGGAR. If Greek justice lies in Agatha's lap, that's just what it deserves. Don't hinder us at such a time. Look at Agatha, see if she cares for the honor of Greek judges, with her nose in the air.

PRESIDENT. Her nose in the air! Agatha is your nose in the air?

AGATHA. My nose *is* in the air. I'm looking at that bird hovering over Aegisthus.

PRESIDENT. Lower it!

AEGISTHUS. Queen, I'm waiting for your reply.

CLYTEMNESTRA. A bird? What is that bird? Get from under that bird, Aegisthus.

AEGISTHUS. Why? He's not left me since sunrise. He must have his reasons. My horse noticed him first. He kicked without any provocation. I looked all around and then up there. He was kicking at that bird, and plunging and rearing. It's exactly above me, isn't it, beggar?

BEGGAR. Exactly above. If you were a thousand feet tall, your head would be there.

AEGISTHUS. Like a mark on a page, isn't it? A black mark.

BEGGAR. Yes, at the moment you're the most marked man in Greece. We'll have to find out whether the mark is over the word "human" or the word "mortal."

CLYTEMNESTRA. I don't like this hovering bird. What is it? A kite or an eagle?

BEGGAR. He's too high up. I might recognize him by his shadow, but so high up we can't see it, it's lost.

CAPTAIN (*returning*). The guards are delighted, Aegisthus. They're joyfully getting ready to fight. They're waiting for you to appear on the balcony with the queen, so they can cheer you.

AEGISTHUS. My oath, and I'll go.

PRESIDENT. Electra, help me! Why should this rake teach us courage?

BEGGAR. Why? Listen! . . .

AEGISTHUS. Oh, Heavenly Powers, since I must pray to you on the eve of battle, I thank you for the gift of this hill which overlooks Argos the moment the fog evaporates. I dismounted, weary from the night patrol, I leant against the battlement, and suddenly I saw Argos as I had never before seen it — new, rebuilt by me; you have given it to me. You've given it all to me, its towers, its bridges, the smoke from its farm machines, the flying pigeons, its first movements, the grinding of its locks, its first cry. Everything in your gift has equal value, Electra, the sunrise over Argos, the last lantern in the city, the temple, the ruins, the lake, the tanneries. And the gift is forever! This morning I was given my city for eternity, as a mother her child, and in agony I asked myself if the gift were not even greater, if you hadn't given me far more than Argos. In the morning God never counts his gifts: he might even have given me the whole world. That would have been dreadful.

I should have felt a despair like that of a man who expects a diamond on his birthday and is given the sun. Electra, you see my anxiety! I anxiously stretched my foot and my thoughts beyond Argos. What joy! I had not been given the Orient, its plagues, earthquakes, famines: I realized that with a smile. My thirst was not like that of men who quench it in the great, warm rivers flowing through the desert, but, I discovered, I could quench it at an icy spring. And nothing in Africa is mine! Negresses can pound millet at the doors of their huts, the jaguar drive his claws into the crocodile's flank, not a drop of their soup or their blood is mine. I'm as happy over the gifts not given me as over the gift of Argos. In a fit of generosity the gods have not given me Athens or Olympia or Mycenae. What joy! They have given me the Argive cattle markets, not the treasures of Corinth, the short noses of the Argive girls, not the nose of Athena; the wrinkled prune of Argos, not the golden fig of Thebes! That's what they gave me this morning; me, the wastrel, the parasite, the knave, a country where I feel myself pure, strong, perfect; a fatherland; a country where, instead of being a slave, I am king, where I swear to live and die — you hear me, judge — a country I swear to save.

PRESIDENT. I rely on you only, Electra!

ELECTRA. Rely on me. No one should save his fatherland with impure hands.

BEGGAR. A coronation purifies everything.

ELECTRA. Who crowned you? Who witnessed your coronation?

BEGGAR. Can't you guess? Just what he begged of you. For the first time he sees you in your truth and power. The thought has suddenly dawned on him that Electra is included in this gift of Argos.

AEGISTHUS. Everything on my way consecrated me, Electra. As I galloped I heard the trees, the children, the streams shout to me: I was king. But the holy oil was lacking. I was a coward yesterday. A rabbit, whose trembling ears showed over a furrow, gave me courage. I was a hypocrite. A fox crossed the road, his eyes crafty, and I became frank. And a couple of magpies gave me independence, an ant hill, generosity. And if I hurried back to you, Electra, it was because you are the only creature who can give me her very being.

ELECTRA. And that is — ?

AEGISTHUS. I think it is rather like duty.

ELECTRA. My duty is certainly the mortal enemy of yours. You shall not marry Clytemnestra.

PRESIDENT. You shall not marry her.

CLYTEMNESTRA. And why shan't we marry? Why should we sacrifice

our lives to ungrateful children? Yes, I love Aegisthus. For ten
years I've loved Aegisthus. For ten years I've postponed this marriage for your sake, Electra, and in memory of your father. Now
you force us to it. Thanks! But not under that bird. That bird
annoys me. As soón as the bird flies away. I consent.

AEGISTHUS. Don't worry, Queen. I'm not marrying you in order to
create new lies. I don't know if I still love you, and the whole city
doubts that you ever loved me. For ten years our liaison has
dragged along between indifference and neglect. But marriage is
the only way to cast a little truth over our past lies, and it will
safeguard Argos. It must take place, this very hour.

ELECTRA. I don't believe it will take place.

PRESIDENT. Bravo!

AEGISTHUS. Will you be quiet? Who are you in Argos? A deceived
husband or the chief justice?

PRESIDENT. Both, of course.

AEGISTHUS. Then choose. I have no choice. Choose between duty and
prison. Time is short.

PRESIDENT. You took Agatha from me.

AEGISTHUS. I'm not the one who took Agatha.

PRESIDENT. Weren't you given all the deceived husbands in Argos this
morning?

BEGGAR. Yes. But he's not the man who deceived them.

PRESIDENT. I understand. The new king forgets the outrages he committed as regent.

BEGGAR. Agatha looks like a rose. Outrages make her rosy?

AEGISTHUS. A king begs you to pardon today the insult a rake inflicted on you yesterday. That must satisfy you. Listen to my orders. Go quickly to your courtroom, try the rebels, and be severe
with them.

AGATHA. Be severe. I have a little lover among them.

PRESIDENT. Will you stop looking at that bird? You irritate me.

AGATHA. I'm sorry. It's the only thing in the world that interests me.

PRESIDENT. Idiot! What will you do when it goes away?

AGATHA. That's what I'm wondering.

AEGISTHUS. Are you disobeying me, president? Don't you hear those
shouts?

PRESIDENT. I'll not go. I'll help Electra prevent your marriage.

ELECTRA. I don't need your help, president. Your role ended when
Agatha gave me the key to everything. Thanks, Agatha!

CLYTEMNESTRA. What key?

AEGISTHUS. Come, queen.

CLYTEMNESTRA. What key did she give you? What new quarrel are you trying to start?

ELECTRA. You hated my father! Oh, everything is clear in the light of Agatha's lamp.

CLYTEMNESTRA. There she goes again! Protect me, Aegisthus!

ELECTRA. How you envied Agatha just now! What joy to shout out your hatred to the husband you hate! That joy was not allowed you, mother. Never in your life will you have it. Till the day of his death he believed you admired and adored him. At banquets and festivals I've often seen your face harden, your lips move soundlessly, because you wanted to cry out you hated him. You wanted passers-by, guests, the servant pouring wine, the detective guarding the silver, to hear you, didn't you? Poor mother, you could never go to the country alone to cry out to the bushes! All the bushes say you adored him!

CLYTEMNESTRA. Listen, Electra!

ELECTRA. That's right, mother, cry it out to me! Though he's not here, I'm his substitute. Cry to me! That will do you as much good as to say it to him. You're not going to die without letting him know you hated him.

CLYTEMNESTRA. Come, Aegisthus! Never mind the bird!

ELECTRA. If you take one step, mother, I'll call.

AEGISTHUS. Whom will you call, Electra? Is there anyone in the world who can take from us the right to save our city?

ELECTRA. Save our city from hypocrisy, from corruption? There are thousands. The purest, the handsomest, the youngest is here, in this courtyard. If Clytemnestra takes a step, I'll call.

CLYTEMNESTRA. Come, Aegisthus!

ELECTRA. Orestes! Orestes!

(*The* EUMENIDES *appear and bar the way.*)

FIRST FURY. Poor girl! You're too naive! Do you think we'll let Orestes run around sword in hand? Accidents happen too quickly in this palace. We've gagged him and chained him up.

ELECTRA. That's not true! Orestes! Orestes!

SECOND FURY. You, too, it will happen to you.

AEGISTHUS. Electra, dear Electra, listen to me. I want to persuade you.

CLYTEMNESTRA. You're losing precious time, Aegisthus.

AEGISTHUS. I'm coming! Electra, I know you're the only one who understands what I am today. Help me! Let me tell you why you must help me!

CLYTEMNESTRA. What is this craze to explain, to argue? Are we roosters in this courtyard or human beings. Do we have to go on

explaining till our eyes are gouged out? Must the three of us be
carried off by force, to separate us?

PRESIDENT. I think that's the only way, queen.

CAPTAIN. I beseech you, Aegisthus! Hurry!

BEGGAR. Don't you understand? Aegisthus must settle once and for
all the business about Agamemnon — Clytemnestra — Electra. Then
he'll come.

CAPTAIN. In five minutes it will be too late.

BEGGAR. We'll all do our bit. It will be settled in five minutes.

AEGISTHUS. Take this man away.

> (*Guards take out the* PRESIDENT. *All the spectators leave. Silence.*)

AEGISTHUS. Now, Electra, what do you want?

SCENE EIGHT

(ELECTRA. CLYTEMNESTRA. AEGISTHUS. BEGGAR.)

ELECTRA. She's not late, Aegisthus. She just won't come.

AEGISTHUS. Of whom are you speaking?

ELECTRA. Of her you're waiting for. The messenger of the gods. If
divine justice absolves Aegisthus because he loves his city, and is
marrying Clytemnestra because he despises lies and wants to save
the middle class and the rich, this is the moment for her to appear
before the two of you, bearing her diplomas and her laurels. But
she'll not come.

AEGISTHUS. You know she has come. This morning's sunbeam on my
head was she.

ELECTRA. That was a morning beam. Every scurvy child thinks he's
a king when a morning sunbeam touches him.

AEGISTHUS. Do you doubt my sincerity?

ELECTRA. I don't doubt it. I recognize in it the hypocrisy and malice
of the gods. They change a parasite into a just man, an adulterer
into a husband, a usurper into a king. They thought my task not
painful enough, so they made a figure of honor out of you, whom I
despise! But there's one chance they can't carry through! They
can't transform a criminal into an innocent man. They bow to me
there.

ELECTRA. You have an inkling. Listen to the small voice beneath your
heroic soul. You'll understand.

AEGISTHUS. Who can explain what you're talking about?

CLYTEMNESTRA. Of whom *can* she talk? What has she always talked
about her whole life long? Of a father she never knew.

ELECTRA. I? I never knew my father?

CLYTEMNESTRA. You touched a corpse, ice that had been your father. But not your father.

AEGISTHUS. Please, Clytemnestra! How can you quarrel at such a moment!

CLYTEMNESTRA. Everyone must have a turn in this debate. It's my turn now.

ELECTRA. For once you're right. We've come to the heart of the matter. If I'd not touched my living father, from whom would I have drawn my strength, my truth?

CLYTEMNESTRA. Precisely. But now you're talking wildly. I wonder if you ever kissed him. I took care he didn't lick my children.

ELECTRA. I never kissed my father?

CLYTEMNESTRA. Your father's dead body, perhaps, not your father.

AEGISTHUS. I beg you . . . !

ELECTRA. Ah, now I see why you're so firm as you face me. You thought me unarmed, you thought I'd never touched my father. What a mistake!

CLYTEMNESTRA. You're lying.

ELECTRA. The day my father came home you two waited for him a minute too long on the palace stairs, didn't you?

CLYTEMNESTRA. How do you know? You weren't there!

ELECTRA. I was holding him back. I was in his arms.

AEGISTHUS. Now listen, Electra . . .

ELECTRA. I'd waited in the crowd, mother. I rushed toward him. His escorts were frightened, they feared an attempt on his life. But he recognized me, smiled at me. He understood Electra's attempt, and brave father, went to meet it. And I touched him.

CLYTEMNESTRA. You may have touched his leg armor, his horse, leather and hair!

ELECTRA. He got down, mother. I touched his hands with these fingers, his lips with these lips. I touched a skin you'd never touched, purified from you by ten years of absence.

AEGISTHUS. That's enough. She believes you!

ELECTRA. My cheek on his, I felt my father's warmth. Sometimes in summer the whole world is just as warm as my father. I faint from it. And I did hug him in these arms. I thought I was taking the measure of my love — it was also that of my vengeance. He freed himself, mounted his horse, more agile, more resplendent than before. Electra's attempt on his life was over. He was more alive, more golden, because of it. And I ran to the palace to see him again, but I was really running not toward him, but toward you, his murderers.

AEGISTHUS. Pull yourself together, Electra!

ELECTRA. Perhaps I am out of breath. I've reached my goal.

CLYTEMNESTRA. Rid us of this girl, Aegisthus. Give her back to the gardener. Or turn her over to her brother.

AEGISTHUS. Stop, Electra! Why, at the very moment that I see you, that I love you, when I'm at the point of understanding you — your scorn for abuses, your courage, your disinterestedness — why do you persist in fighting?

ELECTRA. I have only this moment.

AEGISTHUS. Don't you know Argos is in danger?

ELECTRA. We don't see the same dangers.

AEGISTHUS. Don't you know that if I marry Clytemnestra, the city will quiet down, the Atrides will be saved? If not, riots, conflagrations?

ELECTRA. Perhaps.

AEGISTHUS. Don't you know that I alone can defend the city against the Corinthians who are already at the gates? If not, pillage, massacre?

ELECTRA. Yes. You'd be victor.

AEGISTHUS. Yet you are obstinate! You ruin my work. And you sacrifice your family and your country to a dream!

ELECTRA. You're mocking me, Aegisthus! You pretend to know me yet you think I'm the kind to whom you can say, "If you lie and let other people lie, you'll have a prosperous country. If you hide your crimes, your country will be victorious." What is this poor country that you're all of a sudden placing between us and truth?

AEGISTHUS. Your country — Argos.

ELECTRA. You're wrong, Aegisthus. This morning, at the very hour you were given Argos, I also received a gift. I expected it, it had been promised me, but I still didn't know just what it would be. I had already been given a thousand gifts, which seemed incomplete. I couldn't see their appropriateness, but last night, near Orestes as he slept, I saw they were all one and the same gift. I'd been given the back of a truck driver, the smile of a laundress suddenly stopped in her work, watching the river. I'd been given a fat, naked little child, running across the street as his mother and the neighbors shouted to him. I'd been given the cry of a caged bird set free, and that of a mason I one day saw fall from a scaffold, his legs sprawling. I was given the water plant, resisting the current, fighting and dying; the sick young man, coughing, smiling and coughing; and my maid's red cheeks, puffed up each winter morning as she blows on the ashes of the fire. I too thought I was given Argos, everything in Argos that is modest, tender, beautiful and wretched, but just now I found out that it's not so. I knew I'd been given all the servants' cheeks as they blow on wood or coal, all the laundresses' eyes, whether round or almond-shaped, all the falling masons, all the water plants which seem lost and grow again in streams or the sea. But Argos is only a speck in this universe, my country only a village in that country. All the light and the cries in sad faces, all the wrinkles and shadows on joyful faces, all the desires and despair on indifferent faces — these are my new country. And this morning, at dawn, when you were given Argos and its narrow borders, I also saw it as tremendous, and I heard its name, which is not to be spoken, but which is both tenderness and justice.

CLYTEMNESTRA. So that's Electra's motto! Tenderness! That's enough. Let's go.

AEGISTHUS. And you dare call this justice, that makes you burn your city, damn your family, you dare call this the justice of the gods?

ELECTRA. Far from it! In this country of mine, concern for justice is not the gods' business. The gods are only artists. A beautiful light from a conflagration, beautiful grass on a battlefield, such is their justice. A magnificent repentance for a crime is the gods' verdict on your case. I don't accept it.

AEGISTHUS. Electra's justice consists in reexamining every sin, making every act irreparable?

ELECTRA. Oh, no! Some years, frost is justice for the trees, other times it's injustice. There are criminals we love, murderers we embrace. But when the crime is an assault on human dignity, infects a nation, corrupts its loyalty, then — no pardon is possible.

AEGISTHUS. Have you any idea what a nation is, Electra?

ELECTRA. When you see a huge face fill the horizon and you look straight at it with pure, brave eyes, that's a nation.

AEGISTHUS. You talk like a young girl, not like a king. There's also a huge body to rule and to nourish.

ELECTRA. I speak like a woman. There's a bright look to sift, to gild. And the only gold is truth. Those great eyes of truth, they're so beautiful, when you think of the real nations of the world.

AEGISTHUS. There are truths that can kill nations, Electra.

ELECTRA. Sometimes the eyes of a dead nation shine forever. Pray Heaven that will be the fate of Argos! But since my father's death, since our people's happiness came to be founded on injustice and crime, since everyone has become a cowardly accomplice in murder and lies, the city can prosper, sing, dance, conquer, heaven may shine on it, but it will be only a cellar where eyes are useless. Infants suck the breast without seeing it.

AEGISTHUS. A scandal can only destroy it.

ELECTRA. Possibly. But I can no longer endure the dim, lustreless look in its eyes.

AEGISTHUS. That will cost thousands of glazed, dead eyes.

ELECTRA. That's the price. It's not too high.

AEGISTHUS. I must have this day. Give it to me. Your truth, if there is such a thing, will find a way to be revealed at a time more suitable for it.

ELECTRA. The revolt shows this day is made for it.

AEGISTHUS. I beseech you! Wait till tomorrow.

ELECTRA. No. This is the day for it. I've seen too many truths fade away because they were a day too late. I know young girls who waited one second before saying no to an ugly, vile thing, and could then say nothing but yes, yes. The beautiful and cruel thing about truth is that she is eternal, but is also like a flash of lightning.

AEGISTHUS. I must save the city and Greece.

ELECTRA. That's a small duty. I'm saving their soul. — You did kill him, didn't you?

CLYTEMNESTRA. How dare you say that, daughter? Everyone knows your father slipped on the tiles.

ELECTRA. Everyone knows it because you said so.

CLYTEMNESTRA. Crazy girl, he slipped and fell.

ELECTRA. He did not slip. For one obvious reason. Because my father never slipped.

CLYTEMNESTRA. How do you know?

ELECTRA. For eight years I've been asking the grooms, the maids, his escort in rain and hail. He *never* slipped.

CLYTEMNESTRA. The war came after.

ELECTRA. I've asked his fellow soldiers. He crossed Scamander without slipping. He took the battlements by assault without slipping. He never slipped, in water or in blood.

CLYTEMNESTRA. He was in haste that day. You had made him late.

ELECTRA. I'm the guilty one, am I? That's Clytemnestra's kind of truth. Your opinion, too, Aegisthus? Electra murdered Agamemnon?

CLYTEMNESTRA. The maids had soaped the tiles too well. I know. I almost slipped myself.

ELECTRA. Ah, you were in the bathroom, too, mother? Who held you up?

CLYTEMNESTRA. What's wrong in my being there?

ELECTRA. With Aegisthus, of course?

CLYTEMNESTRA. With Aegisthus. And we weren't alone. Leo, my counsellor, was there, wasn't he, Aegisthus?

ELECTRA. Leo, who died the next day?

CLYTEMNESTRA. Did he die the next day?

ELECTRA. Yes. Leo slipped, too. He lay down on his bed and in the morning was found dead. He found a way to slip into death — sleeping, not slipping! You had him killed, didn't you?

CLYTEMNESTRA. Aegisthus, defend me. I call on you for help.

ELECTRA. He can do nothing for you. You've come to the place where you must defend yourself.

CLYTEMNESTRA. Oh, God! Have I come to this? A mother! A queen!

ELECTRA. Where is "this"? Tell us where you've come.

CLYTEMNESTRA. Brought there by this heartless, joyless daughter! Happily, my little Chrysothemis loves flowers.

ELECTRA. Don't I love flowers?

CLYTEMNESTRA. To come to this! Through this idiotic journey called life, to come to this! I, who as a girl loved quiet, tending my pets, laughing at meal time, sewing! . . . I was so gentle, Aegisthus, I swear I was the gentlest. . . . There are still old men in my birthplace who call gentleness Clytemnestra.

ELECTRA. If they die today, they needn't change their symbol. If they die this morning!

CLYTEMNESTRA. To come to this! What injustice! Aegisthus, I spent my days in the meadows behind the palace. There were so many flowers I didn't have to stoop to pick them, I sat down. My dogs lay at my feet, the one who barked when Agamemnon came to take me away. I teased him with flowers and he ate them to please me. If I only had him! Anywhere else, if my husband had been a Persian, or an Egyptian, by now I'd be good, careless, gay! When I was young I had a voice, I trained birds! I might have been an Egyptian queen, singing gaily; I'd have had an Egyptian aviary! And we've come to this! What has this family, what have these walls done to us?

ELECTRA. Murderers! . . . These are wicked walls.

MESSENGER. My lord, they've forced an entrance. The postern gate gave way.

ELECTRA. All right. Let the walls crumble.

AEGISTHUS. Electra, heed my final word. I forgive everything — your foolish fancies, your insults. But can't you see your country is dying?

ELECTRA. And I don't love flowers! Do you imagine flowers for a father's grave are picked sitting down?

CLYTEMNESTRA. Well, let this father return! Let him stop being dead! What nonsense, this absence, this silence! Let him come back, in his pomp, his vanity, his beard! That beard must have grown in the grave — a good thing, too!

ELECTRA. What are you saying?

AEGISTHUS. Electra, I promise that tomorrow, as soon as Argos is saved, the guilty, if there are any, shall disappear, for good and all. But don't be stubborn. You're gentle, Electra, in your heart you're gentle. Listen! The city will perish.

ELECTRA. Let it! I can already feel my love for a burnt and conquered Argos! No! My mother has begun to insult my father, let her finish!

CLYTEMNESTRA. Why are you talking about the guilty! What do you mean, Aegisthus?

ELECTRA. He's just told me in a word all that you deny!

CLYTEMNESTRA. And what do I deny?

ELECTRA. He's told me that you let Orestes fall, that I love flowers, and that my father didn't slip.

CLYTEMNESTRA. He did slip. I swear he slipped. If there's a truth in the world, let lightning from heaven show it to us. You'll see it revealed in all its brilliance.

AEGISTHUS. Electra, you're in my power. Your brother too. I can kill you. Yesterday I should have killed you. Instead of that I promise, as soon as the enemy is repulsed, to step down from the throne and place Orestes on it.

ELECTRA. That's no longer the question, Aegisthus. If the gods for once change their methods, if they make you wise and just in order to ruin you, that's their affair. The question now is, will she dare tell us why she hated my father!

CLYTEMNESTRA. Oh, you want to know that?

ELECTRA. But you'll not dare tell.

AEGISTHUS. Electra, tomorrow, before the altar where we celebrate our victory the guilty man shall stand, for there is only one guilty man, in a parricide's coat. He'll confess his crime publicly and determine his punishment himself. First let me save the city.

ELECTRA. You've "saved" yourselves today, Aegisthus, and in my presence. That's enough. Now I want her to finish!

CLYTEMNESTRA. So, you want me to finish!

ELECTRA. I dare you to!

MESSENGER. They're entering the courtyards, Aegisthus!

AEGISTHUS. Come, queen!

CLYTEMNESTRA. Yes, I hated him. Yes, you shall know what this fine father was like. Yes, after twenty years I'll have the joy that Agatha had today. A woman might belong to anyone, but there was just one man in the world to whom I couldn't belong. That man was

the king of kings, father of fathers! I hated him from the first day
he came to wrench me from my home, with his curly beard and
the hand with the little finger always sticking up. He raised it
when he drank, when he drove, when he held his sceptre . . . and
when he held me close I felt on my back only four fingers. It drove
me wild, and the morning he sacrificed your sister, Iphigenia —
horrible — I saw the little fingers of both his hands sticking out,
dark against the sun — king of kings! What nonsense! He was
pompous, indecisive, stupid. He was the fop of fops, the most
credulous creature. The king of kings was never anything more
than that little finger and the beard that nothing could soften. The
bathwater I soaked his head in didn't soften it, nor did the nights
of false love when I pulled and tangled it, nor the storm at Delphi
which turned the dancers' hair into manes; it came out in gold
ringlets from water, bed, and rain. He would beckon me with his
little finger and I would go smiling. . . . Why? He would tell
me to kiss his mouth in that fleece and I would run to kiss it. . . .
Why? And when I woke and was unfaithful to him, like Agatha,
with the wooden bedstead — a royal bed — and he bade me talk to
him, though I knew he was vain, empty, tiresome, I told him he
was modest, strange, even splendid. . . . Why? And if he persisted,
stammering, pathetic, I swore to him he was a god. King of kings!
The only excuse for that title is that it justifies a hatred of hatreds.
Do you know what I did, Electra, the day of his departure, when
his ship was still in sight? I sacrificed the curliest ram I could find
and toward midnight I stole into the throne room quite alone, and
took the sceptre in my hands! Now you know everything. You
wanted a hymn to truth, and here's a beautiful one.

ELECTRA. Oh, father, forgive!

AEGISTHUS. Come, queen.

CLYTEMNESTRA. Take this girl first and chain her up.

ELECTRA. Father, will you ever forgive me for listening to her?
Aegisthus, should she not die?

AEGISTHUS. Farewell, Electra.

ELECTRA. Kill her, Aegisthus. And I'll forgive you.

CLYTEMNESTRA. Don't let her go free, Aegisthus. They'll stab you in
the back.

AEGISTHUS. We'll see about that. Leave Electra alone. . . . Unbind
Orestes.

(AEGISTHUS *and* CLYTEMNESTRA *go out.*)

ELECTRA. The bird is coming down, beggar, the bird is coming down.
BEGGAR. Look, it's a vulture!

.

SCENE NINE

(ELECTRA. NARSES' WIFE. BEGGAR. *Then* ORESTES.)

BEGGAR. You here, Narses' wife?

NARSES' WIFE. All of us beggars, the lame, the halt and the blind, have come to save Electra and her brother.

BEGGAR. Justice, eh?

NARSES' WIFE. There they are, untying Orestes.

(*A crowd of* BEGGARS *enter, a few at a time.*)

BEGGAR. This is how they did the killing, listen, woman. This is the way it all happened, I never invent anything. It was the queen who had the steps soaped that go down to the bath; the two of them did it. While all the housewives in Argos scrubbed their thresholds, the queen and her lover soaped the doorsill to his death. Think how clean their hands were when they greeted Agamemnon at his entrance! And your father slipped, Electra, as he reached out his arms to her. You were right except on this one point. He slipped on the steps, and the noise of his fall, because of his golden cuirass and helmet, was that of a king falling. And she threw herself on him, he thought, to raise him up, but she held him down. He didn't understand why his darling wife was holding him down, he wondered if it was a love transport, but then why did Aegisthus stay? Young Aegisthus was awkward and indiscreet. (We'll consider his promotion.) The ruler of the world, the conqueror of Troy, who had just reviewed the army and navy parade, must have been humiliated, to fall like that, on his back and in his noisy armor, even if his beard was untouched, in the presence of his loving wife and the young ensign. All the more annoyed because this might be a bad omen. The fall might mean he'd die in a year, or in five years. And he was surprised that his beloved wife caught his wrists and threw herself on him to hold him down, as the fisherwomen do with big stranded turtles on the shore. She was wrong, and not so beautiful, her face flushed, her neck wrinkled. Not like young Aegisthus, who was trying to extricate his sword for fear he'd hurt himself, apparently, he looked handsomer every minute. What was strange, though, was that the two of them were silent. He said, "Dear wife, how strong you are!" "Young man," he said, "Pull out the sword — by its handle!" But they said nothing, the queen and the squire had become mutes in the last ten years, and no one had told him. They were as mute as travellers hurrying to pack a trunk when time is short. They had to do something quickly, before any-one else came in. What was it? Suddenly Aegisthus kicked his helmet as a dying man kicks his dog, and the truth was plain. And he cried, "Wife, let me go. Wife, what are you doing?" She took care not to answer, she couldn't say aloud, "I'm killing you, murdering you!" But she said to herself, "I'm killing you because there's not one gray hair on your beard, because it's the only way to murder that little finger."

She undid the laces of his cuirass with her teeth, and the gold turned to scarlet, and Aegisthus — beautiful with the beauty of Achilles killing Hector, of Ulysses killing Dolon — approached, with drawn sword. Then the king of kings kicked Clytemnestra's back, and she shook all over, her silent hand shook, and he shouted so loud Aegisthus had to roar with laughter to cover the noise. Then he drove in the sword. And the king of kings was no longer the mass of bronze and iron he'd thought himself, he was just soft flesh, as easy to pierce as a lamb, and the sword cut so deep it split the marble. The murderers were wrong to hurt the marble, for it revenged itself. I found out about the crime from that split tile.

So he stopped struggling, let himself go, between the woman, who became uglier every moment, and the man, who was handsomer and handsomer. One good thing about death is that you can trust yourself to her, death is your only friend in an ambush, she has a familiar look, he saw that and called on his children, first the boy, Orestes, then the girl, Electra, to thank them for avenging him in future, lending their hands of death. Clytemnestra, foam on her lips, did not let go of him, and Agamemnon as willing to die but not to have this woman spit in his face, on his beard. She didn't spit because she was walking around the corpse, trying not to get blood on her sandals; her red dress looked to the dying man like the sun. Then the shadow fell, because each of them took an arm and turned him over on the floor. On his right hand four fingers were already stiff. Then, as Aegisthus had pulled out the sword without thinking, they turned him over again and put it gently, deliberately, back in the wound. Aegisthus was grateful to the dead man for having let himself be killed so very easily. Dozens of kings of kings could be killed like that, if murder was so easy.

But Clytemnestra's hatred of the man who'd struggled so fiercely, so stupidly, grew as she foresaw how every night she would dream of this murder. That's just what happened. It's seven years since she killed, she's killed him three thousand times.

(ORESTES *has come in during this speech.*)

NARSES' WIFE. Here's the young man! Isn't he handsome?

BEGGAR. As beautiful as Aegisthus when young.

ORESTES. Where are they, Electra?

ELECTRA. Dear Orestes!

NARSES' WIFE. In the southern courtyard.

ORESTES. I'll see you soon, Electra, and we'll never part.

ELECTRA. Go, my lover.

ORESTES. Don't stop, beggar. Go on, tell him about the death of
Clytemnestra and Aegisthus.

(He goes out, sword in hand.)

NARSES' WIFE. Tell us, beggar.

BEGGAR. In two minutes. Give him time to get there.

ELECTRA. He has his sword?

NARSES' WIFE. Yes, daughter.

BEGGAR. Are you crazy? Calling the princess your daughter!

NARSES' WIFE. I call her daughter, I don't say she's my daughter. I've
often seen her father, though. Heavens, what a fine man!

ELECTRA. He had a beard, hadn't he?

NARSES' WIFE. Not a beard, a sun. A wavy, curly sun, a sun just rising
from the sea. He stroked it with his hand. The most beautiful
hand in the world.

ELECTRA. Call me your daughter, Narses' wife! I am your daughter.
. . . I heard a cry!

NARSES' WIFE. No, my daughter.

ELECTRA. You're sure he had his sword? He didn't go to them without a sword?

NARSES' WIFE. You saw him going. He had a thousand swords. Be
calm, be calm!

ELECTRA. What a long minute, mother, you waited at the edge of the
bath!

NARSES' WIFE. Why don't you tell us? Everything will be over before we know it.

BEGGAR. One minute! He's looking for them. Now! He's found them.

NARSES' WIFE. Oh, I can wait. Little Electra is soft to touch. I had
only boys, gangsters. Mothers who only have girls are happy.

ELECTRA. Yes . . . happy. . . . This time I do hear a cry!

NARSES' WIFE. Yes, my daughter.

BEGGAR. So, here's the end. Narses' wife and the beggars untied
Orestes. He rushed across the courtyard. He didn't touch or embrace Electra. He was wrong, for he'll never touch her again. He
found the murderers on the marble balcony, calming the rioters.
As Aegisthus leaned down to tell the leaders that everything was
going well, he heard behind him the cry of a wounded beast. But
it wasn't a beast crying, it was Clytemnestra. She was bleeding. Her
son had stabbed her. He struck at the couple blindly, his eyes
closed. A mother, though, even when unworthy, is sensitive and

human. She didn't call on Electra or Orestes but on her youngest
daughter, Chrysothemis, so Orestes thought he had killed another,
and an innocent, mother. She clung to Aegisthus' arm; she was right,
that gave her a last chance to stand up. But she prevented Aegisthus
from drawing his sword. He shook her, to free his arm. She was
too heavy to serve as a shield. And that bird was beating his head
with its wings and attacking him with its beak, so he struggled.
Just with his unarmed left arm, the dead queen, loaded with
necklace and pendants, on his right arm. He was in despair over
dying like a criminal, when he had become pure and holy; to be
fighting because of a crime which was no longer his; to find himself, though loyal and innocent, infamous before this parricide. He
struggled with one hand, which the sword was cutting little by little,
but the lacing of his cuirass caught on a brooch of Clytemnestra's,
and it opened. Then he resisted no longer; he only shook his right
arm to rid himself of the queen, not only to fight but to die alone,
to lie far from Clytemnestra in death. He didn't succeed. Forever
Clytemnestra and Aegisthus will be coupled. He died, calling a
name I'll not repeat.

AEGISTHUS (*voice off-stage*). Electra!

BEGGAR. I talked too fast. He caught up with me.

SCENE TEN

(ELECTRA. BEGGAR. NARSES' WIFE. *The* EUMENIDES, *who are of
exactly the same height and figure as* ELECTRA.)

SERVANT. Flee, everybody, the palace is on fire!

FIRST FURY. That's what Electra wanted. Three things: daylight, truth
— and this fire!

SECOND FURY. Satisfied, Electra? The city's dying.

ELECTRA. I'm satisfied. I know now that it will be born again.

THIRD FURY. And the people killing each other in the streets, will they
be born again? The Corinthians have started the attack, and it's a
massacre.

FIRST FURY. Your pride has brought you to this, Electra. You have
nothing left, nothing.

ELECTRA. I have my conscience, I have Orestes, I have justice, I have
everything.

SECOND FURY. Your conscience! Will you listen to your conscience in
the early mornings to come? For seven years you've not slept
because of a crime that others committed. Now you're the guilty
one.

ELECTRA. I have Orestes, I have justice, I have everything.

THIRD FURY. Orestes! You'll never see Orestes again. We're leaving *you* — to pursue *him*. We've taken on your age and your shape — to pursue him. Good-bye! We'll not leave him until he's been driven to madness or suicide, cursing his sister.

ELECTRA. I have justice. I have everything.

NARSES' WIFE. What are they saying? They're back. What have we come to, my poor Electra, what have we come to?

ELECTRA. What have we come to?

NARSES' WIFE. Yes, tell me. I'm not very quick to understand. I know something's happened but I don't know just what. How can you explain it, when a day begins like today, and everything's ruined and pillaged — though we're still breathing, we've lost everything, the city's burning, innocent people are killing each other, the guilty are dying, too — and the sun still rises?

ELECTRA. Ask the beggar. He knows.

BEGGAR. It all has a beautiful name, Narses' wife, it is called the dawn.

❖ ❖ ❖

STUDY AIDS

Act I, Scene 1

1. The gardener describes Agamemnon's palace as a building capable of responding to mood; Orestes, in fact, refers to it as "a sensitive building." How do these references to the palace help to establish a distinctive and richly theatrical approach to Giraudoux' treatment of the Electra-Orestes legend?

2. It is interesting to discover that in the opening scene Giraudoux employs three little girls as the Eumenides. What effect is realized in the childish yet gruesome exchange of lines concerning the Atreus' dinner and Cassandra's death? What characteristics do the little Eumenides possess?

3. What do you make of the gardener's account of Agamemnon's death?

4. With their childish prattle the little girls fulfill what traditional and useful function of the chorus? What are the ways in which these children set the stage for what is to follow?

Act I, Scene 2

1. What is implied concerning Electra, Aegisthus, and the gardener through the announcement that Electra will marry the gardener?

2. Summarize the President's views on life. What does he mean in saying that conscience "always tends toward compromise and forgetfulness" and that "happiness is never the lot of implacable people"?

3. What picture does the President give us of the character of Electra? Why does he declare that her ally is uncompromising justice? What are the implications for Aegisthus and Clytemnestra, if this is true? Of what abstractive agent does Electra seem to be assuming certain characteristics? What impression have you thus far of the President? Of his wife? Of the gardener?

Act I, Scene 3

1. What is the significance of Aegisthus' declaration that belief or disbelief in gods is the only problem a statesman must decide for himself? What is his concept of the gods? Compare Aegisthus' views with those of the ancient Greeks. Of what philosophic-literary movement are they characteristic?

2. What method has Aegisthus employed in keeping order in Argos? Why has he been successful? What is the threat posed by Electra?

3. What ideas does the beggar contribute to the discussion of why hedgehogs — and men — die? What is the function of the Beggar? Whom does he represent?

4. Why does Aegisthus so enthusiastically support the marriage of Electra and the gardener?

5. This is a play of ideas, filled with the kind of talk so admired by French playgoers. Is there a gathering note of suspense in the talk? Do you miss the presence of overt action?

Act I, Scene 4

1. What do we learn about the thoughts and attitudes of Clytemnestra in this scene? What are the origins of her quarrel with Electra? Why does she not want Electra to marry the gardener?

2. What does the scene add to our understanding of Electra? What is the significance of the quarrel between Clytemnestra and Electra concerning the color of Orestes' tunic?

3. How is the gardener shaping up as a character? What is the significance of his statement: "I believe the mother is frightened."

Act I, Scene 5

1. What motivation would Agatha have for participating as she does in this brief scene?

Act I, Scenes 6–7

1. The recognition scene has some very distinctive qualities. What are they? How does the treatment of this scene fit into the way in which the play has been handled thus far?

Act I, Scene 8

1. How would you analyze the hatred Electra feels toward her mother? Toward Aegisthus? Comment upon the affection in which she held her father.

2. What is the relationship between Orestes and Electra now? Which is the stronger?

Act I, Scenes 9–11

1. How do these scenes further illuminate the relationships among Clytemnestra, Orestes, and Electra?

Act I, Scene 12

1. What is the purpose of the parody in this scene?

2. The three little girls are growing up. What is the purpose of having them advance in years as they do? How does their function alter as the play progresses?

Act I, Scene 13

1. What is Giraudoux' purpose in introducing a lengthy speech such as this, uttered by a secondary character and addressed directly to the audience? Do the beggar's words concerning Electra add to our understanding of her? He concludes, "So if she kills, as looks likely, all happiness and peace around her, it's because she's right." Do you agree?

Interlude

1. Again, the device of addressing one's thoughts directly to the audience. What is the purpose of "The Gardener's Lament?"

2. What does the gardener assert is the one aim of life? Is the inclusion of such a thought somewhat ironic in a play dealing with murder and hate?

3. Notice the linking of such contradictory statements as "of course life is a failure, yet it's very, very good." Several of these paradoxes are included in the lament. To what effect?

4. What experiences does the gardener say kings have which are denied to humble men? What are the implications of this statement with regard to the meaning of tragedy?

5. What are the gardener's conclusions about the way in which God reveals himself to man?

Act II, Scene 1

1. What relationship between Orestes and Electra is emphasized in this brief scene?

2. Make a mental note of the beggar's injunction to "go toward the dawn." You will find him again alluding to the dawn in the final speech of the play.

Act II, Scene 2

1. What is the purpose of this scene which, with its wit and sophisticated humor, may seem at first to be borrowed from another play?

Act II, Scene 3

1. Why do the Eumenides urge Orestes not to listen to Electra?

2. What does the third fury, as she is now called, mean when she says that truth is the only poison that has no antidote?

3. Finally, after seven years the truth has been revealed to Electra, who has hated her mother without knowing why. Why do you think Giraudoux has delayed her knowledge of how Agamemnon met his death? How convincing is Electra's explanation of her vision?

Act II, Scene 4

1. "All the evil in the world," says Clytemnestra, "is caused by the so-called pure people trying to dig up secrets and bring them to life." What is your response to this statement and to the fact that it is Clytemnestra who makes it?

Act II, Scene 5

1. Does the insistence with which Electra attacks her mother increase or lessen our regard for her?

2. Does Clytemnestra's behavior in this scene have a claim on our sympathy? How do you respond to the character of Clytemnestra through this scene in the play?

Act II, Scene 6

1. Comment upon the role of Agatha in the play. How does her behavior correspond to that of Clytemnestra?

Act II, Scene 7

1. What function of the traditional Greek chorus is the beggar increasingly fulfilling in this and the preceding scene?

2. What complications does this scene add to the play?

3. Do you have an inkling of the kind of symbolic bird that hovers above Aegisthus?

4. How does this scene contribute to your understanding of the character of Aegisthus?

Act II, Scene 8

1. What does this scene contribute to the meaning of the play? Summarize the viewpoints and the arguments of Electra and Aegisthus. In this scene lies the central thesis of the play.

Act II, Scenes 9–10

1. The play concludes with a long and graphic description of the death of Agamemnon. What is the significance of Clytemnestra's

saying, "I'm killing you because . . . it's the only way to murder
that little finger."

2. What victory has Electra gained through Orestes' slaying of
Clytemnestra and Aegisthus. She exclaims, "I have justice, I have
everything." Yet the price of her triumph is high; the city has been
destroyed. How, then, can the beggar declare the carnage has "a
beautiful name . . . it is called the dawn"? Comment on the significance of this last line.

❖ ❖ ❖

TOPICS FOR DISCUSSION

1. Duality in Giraudoux' *Electra*. The play develops two themes:
the vengeance of Electra and the conflict that arises when achievement of vengeance conflicts with compassion for state. Inskip suggests that Electra's dilemma is similar to Hamlet's with reference to
achieving vengeance, but that upon Electra's decision rest additional
implications. What are they?

2. Electra as the embodiment of justice and fate. Is Electra an im-
moderate heroine, driven by her desire for vengeance? Does she
symbolize the law of the personal vendetta? LeSage declares in
Jean Giraudoux: His Life and Works that the French dramatist knew
that failure to yield in the face of expediency can spell disaster, and
that in the world of politics and statecraft, the Aegisthuses are right,
the Electras wrong. What are your views? It must be recalled that
at the time of *Electra*'s composition (1937) France was faced with the
alternatives of negotiating a peace or fighting a war. At the same
time, we must remember Electra's declaration: "But when the crime
is an assault on human dignity, infects a nation, corrupts its loyalty,
then — no pardon is possible."

3. The metaphysical implications of Giraudoux' *Electra*. The concepts of justice and fate, politics and government, expediency and
morality.

4. The element of theatricality in Giraudoux' *Electra*. The techniques, devices, and style found in the play.

5. The element of characterization in the play. An analysis of
familial relationships, especially of the bonds between Electra and
Orestes. The characters of Clytemnestra and Aegisthus. The secondary characters.

JACK RICHARDSON

❖❖❖❖❖❖❖❖❖❖❖❖❖❖❖❖❖❖❖❖❖❖❖❖❖❖❖❖❖❖❖❖❖❖

CHARACTERIZED by a vigorous style, provocative thought, and a thoroughly modern protagonist, *The Prodigal* is an absorbing treatment of the legend of Orestes. Unimpressed with what he considers his father's heroic posturing in the cause of a useless war, and contemptuous of Aegisthus' efforts to avoid civil unrest as well as political discord, Richardson's Orestes wants nothing so much as the luxury of detachment and the balm of a tranquil life. The price of foregoing commitments, however, is high, and Orestes becomes a tragic hero in spite of his desires rather than because of his beliefs. The public, it is explained, prefers that its heroes wade in blood rather than live in peace.

The Prodigal won both the Vernon Rice and the *Village Voice Obie* awards for the season of 1960. It is one of three plays Mr. Richardson has had produced in New York, the other two being *Gallows Humor* in 1961 and *Lorenzo* in 1963.

Born in 1935 and raised in Bristol, Virginia, Richardson attended Columbia University where he served as an instructor of Philosophy from 1956 to 1958. Upon receiving a Fulbright Fellowship, he took a special postgraduate course at the University of Munich. When he returned from Germany after a year and a half, he began writing pieces for *Esquire*. In 1963–64 he received Guggenheim and Brandeis University fellowships for creative writing. To date Mr. Richardson has not been the subject of a major critical study, hence the absence of bibliography at this time.

The Prodigal

❖ ❖ ❖

<h2 style="text-align:center">CHARACTERS</h2>

ORESTES

AGAMEMNON

ELECTRA

AEGISTHUS

CLYTEMNESTRA

PYLADES

CASSANDRA

PENELOPE

PRAXITHIA

SOLDIERS

PRIESTS

ACT I • SCENE 1

At rise of curtain, PENELOPE, *governess in* AGAMEMNON's *household, is combing* ELECTRA's *hair. She is in her middle fifties, strong in appearance, voice, and manner. She attends to her job with brusque thoroughness.*

ELECTRA, *at this point a pretty girl of fifteen, fidgets while her morning coiffure is taking place. Both* PENELOPE *and* ELECTRA *face the audience.*

PENELOPE. Can't you sit still for a moment? How can I put your hair in order when you move about so?

ELECTRA. I am looking for something, Penelope. Something more important than the set of my hair.

PENELOPE. If you were a woman, I'd hold you mad for saying that.

ELECTRA. Then you think women should be children. No, Penelope,

The Prodigal: A Play by Jack Richardson. Copyright © by Jack C. Richardson. Reprinted in its entirety by permission of E. P. Dutton & Co., Inc.

I had a dream last night — a marvelous dream, and to bring that vision to life I would shave my head of every curl you're fussing over now.

PENELOPE (*giving* ELECTRA'S *hair an extra-firm brush*). And what was this marvelous dream for which you'd sacrifice so much?

ELECTRA. Oh, Penelope, it would take poets far better than Aegisthus and all his silly priests to put my dream into words. It was so grand, so beautifully clear, so . . .

PENELOPE (*smiling at her exuberance*). Heavens, were you visited by Apollo?

ELECTRA. Greater than that. I saw my father's fleet return. They sailed into this very harbor.

PENELOPE. That was, indeed, a wonderful vision.

ELECTRA (*rising from the stool*). I was standing right here in the palace court, looking out over the waters, when suddenly I saw specks bobbing on those indifferent waves. Tiny points which, surrounded by the limitless sky, seemed insignificant and totally unworthy of being the first sign of my father's return. Only slowly then did the specks grow in size until the color of the sails could be seen — colors of many shades adding living brightness to the natural and single tones about them. Then closer until the golden shields along the ships' bows reflected the sun into my pained eyes; then the songs of rowers overpowering the waters breaking about the rocks, and, finally, the sight of our soldiers pressing eagerly against the sides of the boats to catch the first glimpse of their homes. And among them, Penelope, the greatest warrior of them all — our king, my father, Agamemnon, stood, calm and proud, while his fleet covered the bay and ocean behind him. Was not that a dream to wish true, Penelope?

PENELOPE. It was! By the gods it was!

ELECTRA (*returning to stool*). But now, Penelope, when I look at the horizon there is nothing but water, lowly fishing boats defiling the royal bay, and gulls that mock me with their obscene cries. Oh, I was so certain that today would see my father's return. After ten years of war with the Trojans, will it take him another ten to sail home?

PENELOPE. Many miles lie between us and Troy, and sailors have reported unusually poor winds. The journey home may be slow and difficult, but I'm sure your father will return soon. And when he does, the old ways will come with him. We will have men to rule again, instead of the hysterical, verse-spouting priests Aegisthus has turned the elders of Argos into.

ELECTRA. Oh, I pray you are right. When I see Aegisthus and my

mother make a mockery of everything Agamemnon spent his life
to build, I would see them both cringe beneath his sword.
PENELOPE. Hush, child. You must not say such things.

> (PYLADES *and* ORESTES *enter.* ORESTES *is in his early twenties
> with a physical being closer to the Greek mind than to Greek
> art.* PYLADES, *more robust, is the same age.*)

Your father will return, I promise you that. Aegisthus' face will
pale as it did when news of our victory at Troy first came. Agamemnon will return, and . . .
ORESTES. Lull us to sleep with tales of heroes, all of whom, fortunately
for the teller, are dead. (*He walks to* ELECTRA *and kisses her brow.*)
Good morning, little sister.
PENELOPE. Well, our noble prince is up and about early today. Usually
it takes him longer to dust away last night's pleasures from his
brain.
PYLADES. Now don't be bitter, Penelope. I'm sure if we peeked into
your past you'd be caught with your robes askew a few times.
Don't be angry because the seasons have changed.
PENELOPE (*stiffly*). I enjoyed the pleasures of a woman. But, believe
me, with better men than you, Pylades.
PYLADES (*feigning an injured tone*). Penelope, you mean you don't
find the men of Argos virile and attractive?
PENELOPE. The *men* of Argos left with Agamemnon. What we have
now are old men moving their toothless mouths in incessant prayer
or boys, like you two, who sleep away the sun's hours like sluggish
slaves.
PYLADES. Madam, you are speaking to your prince.
PENELOPE. One is proved a prince by his deeds.
ORESTES. And you find mine lacking in royal qualities?
ELECTRA. Please, no quarrels this morning. I am too excited, too
happy. I dreamt last night, Orestes . . .
ORESTES. I'm sure you did, Electra. But don't stop Penelope from
speaking her mind. There's no better way to begin the day than
with honest, objective, and well-meant faultfinding by old friends.
PENELOPE. Then I will say that I find it peculiar that a prince should
be indifferent to the reputation of his country; that he should allow
jests and insults about his father and himself to pass unnoticed and
unavenged; that he should be totally uncaring about the noble
traditions and laws his father shed blood to establish; that he should
turn to useless frolics when his palace is overrun with the oh-so-
sensitive misfits of all Greece and Africa; that he should allow a
weak charlatan (here I will not mince words and name Aegisthus)

to usurp his power and degrade his mother — yes, all this I find strange in a prince.

ORESTES. Well, Penelope, you must have had that prepared for some time. What could I possibly reply to such an impressive list of charges?

ELECTRA. Deny them, Orestes. Tell her you wait only for our father's return before driving Aegisthus from Argos.

PENELOPE. He waits for nothing but the chance to make poor jokes at the expense of better men.

PYLADES. Here, say what you will about the prince's character, but don't dare call his sense of humor poor.

PENELOPE. He may prove amusing to slave girls when speaking of the only thing they understand, but I find it offensive when the subject is . . .

ORESTES. My father, the great Agamemnon, king of kings, master of the seas and brother to the gods. Someone so powerful should be able to stand a jest now and then.

PENELOPE. Had you known your father you would not say such things.

(*The following is spoken with the exasperation of one who is forced to deal with an irrefutable absurdity; that is, trying with difficulty to remain amused.*)

ORESTES. Had I known my father? But who knows my father better than I? True, he left when I was a boy and has been gone for some ten years, but this has only served to make him more familiar to me. For when he set off to mutilate Trojans he left his legend behind, and how is a man known but through his legend? Can laughter, can intimacy, can touch tell more about a man, especially a king, than the personal myth he bequeaths to us in death or absence? For example, when the war was still going badly for us at Troy, I was brought stories of my father's past epic accomplishments. I was told how he, acting under the indubitable and humane principle that the seas should be free and orderly, took it upon himself to clear the Mediterranean of pirates, and how nearly a thousand of our citizens sank, as immortal heroes, of course, to its bottom putting this principle into effect. Was it not also related to me, in great detail by yourself, Penelope, how, when he heard a small island, I forget the name, was being ruled by a petty tyrant with unsavory whims, he set off to bring them a more liberal and morally antiseptic government? I won't bother you with what principles he used there — they seemed rather muddled when I heard them the first time — but you must know their worth since

a good five thousand lives were paid for them. Then, when the war
turned in our favor, the pleasant story was brought to me of how
my sister, Iphigenia, was sacrificed by her father so that his men,
inspired by such a sacrifice, would fight better for the principle
which had set them off again, sword in hand. This time it had to do
with a national insult and Helen's chastity. Helen's chastity! A
contradiction in terms. But the score is still not in on the numbers
who died substantiating that poor judgment of character. Not
know my father? Why, I even have a copybook filled with the
trenchant sayings he uttered while cracking Trojan heads. Not
know my father? All I need is the binder to wrap around his
principles and he is a closed, memorized, and understood book.
No, Penelope, I know my father only too well.

PENELOPE (*to* ELECTRA). And what do you think of your noble br
after that speech?

ELECTRA. The same blood swells his veins as mine. He talks a gr
deal but means little of what he says. I could not love the man
who spoke of my father in such a way, but I do love my brother.

PYLADES. Irrefutable logic.

PENELOPE. I wish I could believe that. (*To* ORESTES.) Agamemnon
was always ready to make the same sacrifices as the rest of his men.
One may doubt his reasons but never his courage.

ORESTES. Oh, I have heard how he gave a captured concubine to
Achilles so he could lead another attack on Troy. My poor father
passed several celibate nights, so they say, demonstrating his courage
in this immolation. What won't he do for the quote higher
principle?

PENELOPE. And, my prince, do you find the degradation caused by
Aegisthus and his hysterical priests a better substitute?

ORESTES. It does not interest me.

PYLADES. Oh, come now, Orestes, the temple virgins don't interest
you?

ORESTES. That's true. Dedicated virgins are much more appealing
than dedicated generals.

PENELOPE. Orestes, if your father . . .

ORESTES. Oh, enough about my father. If you add to the legend it
will smother me. Don't you know any happier stories?

PENELOPE. There is only one story I would call such, and that will
occur when, as in your sister's dream, Agamemnon's fleet appears
in this harbor.

ORESTES. Why are you so certain the fleet will appear at this entrance
to Argos?

ELECTRA. There are only two harbors, Orestes, and the other is used for fishing boats. That's not a suitable place for a royal fleet to appear.

ORESTES. Oh, my little sister, how poorly you know our father! From his legend I can safely deduce that he will enter the one where the fishing boats are anchored. This way he will prove that though he is a victorious general, he is still a friend of the common folk. It is a gesture his legend couldn't afford to waste.

PYLADES (*sniffing the air*). That smell. That frightful aroma. They are at it again. Every morning they pollute the air with those fumes.

PENELOPE. The sacrifice?

PYLADES. What else but a holy ritual could produce such an ungodly smell? Are they roasting goats in Zeus's name?

PENELOPE. Oxen in Athena's.

PYLADES. Well, I wish the wind would carry the odor to Olympus. The gods must be less sensitive to unpleasant smells than we mortals.

ELECTRA. The odor doesn't sicken me as much as the other things that go on at these rituals.

PENELOPE. Oh, yes, the drops of blood, dances by the priests, and Aegisthus declaiming his boring poems to the gods. It is beyond belief. To see the old men of Argos, men who once held manly honor worthy of the sword's defense, slithering about the ground in tears, hacking defenseless beasts to bits; to see this being done while Aegisthus mumbles his clumsy iambs and our queen sits at his feet in adoration; to see this makes me wish I were no woman, but a man whose blade could clear the mist that hangs over Argos and admit the sun's freshness again.

ELECTRA. My father is that man. Is that not so, brother? Tell us now what you really feel.

ORESTES. Why won't you believe what I've told you? Oh, if you only remembered Agamemnon as he was and not as the stories make him.

ELECTRA. I remember when I played he stood so his shadow would cool me from the sun.

ORESTES. He threw his shadow over everything.

ELECTRA. He brushed the flies from my face when I was falling asleep.

ORESTES. He enjoyed feeding them to his pet lizards, Electra.

ELECTRA. Don't tease me any longer, Orestes. Not about our father.

(*Chanting voices are heard approaching.*)

ORESTES. You must grow up. I'm teasing you to grow a little faster than most, that's all.

PYLADES. Isn't that lovely harmony a sign that Aegisthus is approaching with his following?

ELECTRA. I don't want to see him now.

PENELOPE. Come, we'll continue arranging your hair inside. I have
no use for such things either.

ORESTES. You should be amused, Penelope.

PENELOPE. I pity one who finds all things amusing, Prince.

ORESTES. And I one who finds nothing so.

ELECTRA. We both need our father's return to become what we were
meant to be. All before that is just play-acting, I know. Come,
Penelope, I don't want to be seen.

> (*Exit* ELECTRA *and* PENELOPE. ORESTES *and* PYLADES *move to rear
> of the court as* AEGISTHUS *and priests file in.* AEGISTHUS *is in his
> late forties. He is dressed in garments of many colors, and his
> manner is a mixture of effeminacy and strength. In the three
> priests with him there is no such balance: the former quality
> reigns unchallenged.*)

PRIESTS. Mighty are the gods who hold men in the greatness of their
hands; who let men drink from the flowing rivers of their palms;
eat the flesh of their fingers; breathe the perfume of their breaths;
and die between the crushing bones of their fists. Mighty are the
gods who . . .

AEGISTHUS. Enough, priests. I feel the gods are satisfied with today's
worship.

FIRST PRIEST. But we would give them more.

SECOND PRIEST. You have said, Aegisthus, that there should be no end
to worship.

THIRD PRIEST. Oh, let us continue. The gods hear us, I am sure of it.

AEGISTHUS. Go on if you like, but take your prayers into the temple
or your chambers. I call an end to the day's official worship.

FIRST PRIEST. May we make those we meet pray with us?

AEGISTHUS. Do what you like so that it may find divine approval.

FIRST PRIEST. We will use your new ode as our prayer.

THIRD PRIEST. But you are so poor at poetry and always muddle the
rhymes.

FIRST PRIEST. Fool! The gods are not interested in our ability to
match sounds. Anyway, the new ode has no rhymes, it is in *sincere*,
free verse.

SECOND PRIEST. Forgive me, but you are mistaken. The verse was not
free but had a rigid metric. (*Stamping his foot.*) It was: tum deede
tum deede . . .

AEGISTHUS. Enough of this! You are priests, not critics. Attend to
your worship. And one of you inform the queen that I wish to see
her.

FIRST PRIEST. I will go to the queen myself. Come, you two, and I
will teach you poetics on the way.

(PRIESTS *exit.*)

AEGISTHUS. At last peace. (*He walks to front of stage and peers out.*) A clear day. One can see miles out to sea. It should not be long. (*He notices* ORESTES *and* PYLADES.) Well, about so soon today, Orestes?

ORESTES. So everyone seems to think. I feel like the guest who arrives too early for the banquet.

AEGISTHUS. I did not notice you, but perhaps your early appearance means you attended our morning ritual?

ORESTES. No, I do as little commerce with the gods as possible these days.

AEGISTHUS. You consider it a question of trade?

ORESTES. Whatever the question is, for me it's much too complex. I ask nothing of the gods, if there are such things, but to be left alone.

AEGISTHUS. You speak thus because you enjoy the life of a young prince. You know neither age nor misfortune.

PYLADES. I feel with Orestes that it is better to ignore the gods altogether than to make them listen to free verse, no matter how tediously sincere.

AEGISTHUS. That is not for their benefit, as you know very well.

ORESTES. Oh, we know your theory of poetics: To show man the limits of mind. . . .

PYLADES (*stamping his foot*). Tum deede tum deede tum . . .

ORESTES (*picking up* PYLADES' *rhythm in his voice*). And his holy need of the poet.

PYLADES. . . . Deede tum deede tum deede tum. Perfect. It doesn't say much, but it has six solid feet. It should exactly suit your purpose, Aegisthus.

AEGISTHUS. A very shallow performance, but one should expect nothing better from either of you.

ORESTES. If only no one would.

AEGISTHUS. Not everyone knows you as well as I. Some refuse to believe their eyes and take you as you are. But then, again, I may be mistaken. To spend one's days in trivia and nonsense could mask other plans.

ORESTES. Other plans, Aegisthus?

AEGISTHUS. I will tell you, but in private if you don't mind.

ORESTES. Pylades is not easily shocked. I would like him to stay.

AEGISTHUS. What I have to say concerns you as a prince. It is, shall we say, an official matter.

PYLADES. Go ahead, have your talk. I'll wait for you on the beach, Orestes.

ORESTES. I'll join you in a few minutes and we'll play at being honorable men and set all the female slaves we find there free.

PYLADES. Set them free?

ORESTES. Yes, and after they've suitably rewarded us, we can lock them up again.

PYLADES. Marvelous! But how shall we answer them if they ask us what we are playing?

ORESTES. We'll call the game "history."

(PYLADES *exits.*)

AEGISTHUS. Your choice of friends is unfortunate.

ORESTES. Pylades' views mirror my own. For that reason I love him as much as I do myself.

AEGISTHUS. And is this the limit of your affection?

ORESTES. Are you inquiring into my personal life, Aegisthus?

AEGISTHUS. I am inquiring into your real nature, Prince. Things will soon be happening in Argos that will make it necessary for me to know the secret dreams of all its citizens.

ORESTES. Mine are quite harmless, I assure you.

AEGISTHUS. And yet you stand aside and mock all I do. Why?

ORESTES. Really, Aegisthus, you should know better. I have nothing against collective misery being turned to someone's advantage and called religion, but don't ask me to be enthusiastic about it.

AEGISTHUS. You think you stand above such things?

ORESTES. Above, below, or to the side, what difference? I feel uncomfortable when included in world schemes.

AEGISTHUS. You wish your freedom to be unique and question everything?

ORESTES. I wish my freedom to be indolent, unobtrusive, and uninvolved.

AEGISTHUS. The only one of your kind? The solitary quester!

ORESTES. If you mean I'm looking for something better than the present, yes. But after all I am young, Aegisthus. I should have that right.

AEGISTHUS. I'm tired of youth as an excuse.

ORESTES. As an excuse for what?

AEGISTHUS. As an excuse for being a danger to everything I have attempted to build in Argos. You, the young, discontent quester! You end by stirring up mischief for everyone else.

ORESTES. And how should I do that?

AEGISTHUS. I will be frank with you, Orestes. It is no longer a time for playing. Do you remember the condition of things in Argos before I began my reforms?

ORESTES. I was young then, Aegisthus.

AEGISTHUS. Then let me refresh your memory. The war had produced a mixed generation of frightened outcasts who had nothing to help them but your father's outmoded standards of importance. They were weak, and Agamemnon's model of man made them ashamed of their weakness.

ORESTES. Yes, yes. My father's principles are not filled with pity. I won't argue that.

AEGISTHUS. Well, then, remember that into this miserable situation I came and denounced this self-styled human perfection. With my poetry I removed the word "importance" from the people's vocabulary merely by singing the absurdity, and hence equality, of all life centered about man. I told the consumptive shepherd, in simple, masculine rhymes, of course, that the martialing of sheep was as useful as the martialing of men and empires. I sang the praises of the immediate and trivial; the next rug to be woven, the next net of fish, the coming harvest, the birth of cross-eyed children. With my poetry I leveled all, and for those whose temperaments were not suited to lyrical medium I brought a religion which confirmed my more melodic truths.

ORESTES. My father also recognized the need for gods. He went to the temple twice a year, and, if someone close to him died, there were, of course, added visits.

AEGISTHUS. Oh, yes, but my gods were not the friendly pranksters of Agamemnon's time whom you honored as you would entertaining dinner guests. No, my gods were angry, proud, and contemptuous of our vain little activities. They were always ready to answer well-meant questions with an inscrutable blow of anger, and this is what our people wanted, Orestes. Borders were established past which no man could go, and this divine blockade, added to the liquidation of importance from human affairs, created happiness and peace here for the first time in centuries. For what could one man desire from another since it was now clear that the gods had first choice on all that was worth having? What standards, what truth could he strive for, since it was now clear that such pompous dung was merely the leftover droppings of the gods?

ORESTES. Your choice of metaphor leaves something to be desired, Aegisthus. But why are you telling me all this? You speak of your past as if you were applying for employment.

AEGISTHUS. It is that you dared to call yourself a quester. Someone who will humorously question the fisherman seeing the design of life in a newly caught flounder, someone who will slyly ask the prostrate priest if his gods ever answer prayers, someone who points out the difference between the poetic symbol and the philosopher's truth, someone who will tell the almost honest politician that his proposal for underground sanitation won't alter man's miserable knowledge of himself in the least. For, if you were this one, Orestes, I would order your death in an hour. Yes, and though terrified by violence, I would use the dagger myself.

ORESTES. It was you who used the word "quester," Aegisthus, not I. I have no intention of causing even a small disturbance.

AEGISTHUS. That's not good enough, Orestes. Your refusal to side with your mother and me is disturbance. And now, especially now, it is dangerous.

ORESTES. How so, Aegisthus? Everyone knows I'm harmless.

AEGISTHUS. Everyone knows you're Agamemnon's son.

ORESTES. Now what has he to do with it?

AEGISTHUS. I have just received a report that his ships will appear on the horizon any minute. Soon he will be back in Argos and I must challenge him openly. I can put up with no spies.

ORESTES (*for a moment stunned*). My father bores me as much as you do, Aegisthus. If you two want to battle over this worthless city you can do so without any interference from me.

AEGISTHUS. I will have to make certain of that, Orestes.

(CLYTEMNESTRA *enters. She is near forty, beautiful, and completely the woman.*)

Ah, good morning, my queen.

ORESTES. If you have nothing further to say to me, Aegisthus, I'll join Pylades and the slaves.

CLYTEMNESTRA. Will you run away from me, Orestes?

ORESTES. Run away? I thought, under the circumstances, I was being discreet. You two, being such public figures, must wish to enjoy your moments of privacy without me.

AEGISTHUS. That will be enough. I warn you, Orestes, you will make things difficult only for yourself.

CLYTEMNESTRA. If you understood your mother, Orestes, you would not say such things.

ORESTES. You're quite right in challenging my powers of understanding. I will say nothing more.

AEGISTHUS. Then I would appreciate your giving your mother and me the privacy you insinuate we need so badly.

ORESTES. No, I hurt her with my attempt at discretion and she insulted my intellect. I think mother and son are through with their daily chat.

CLYTEMNESTRA. It could be different, Orestes. It was once.

ORESTES. But I was a child then, Mother. Not responsible for my actions.

CLYTEMNESTRA. A beautiful child, a sweet child. You understood love far better in those days.

ORESTES. That's true. Though my world was smaller, there seemed to be more room in it.

CLYTEMNESTRA (*putting her hands on* ORESTES' *shoulders*). It could be so again.

AEGISTHUS. These reminiscences are quaint, but I repeat I have something important to discuss with you alone, Clytemnestra.

ORESTES (*removing his mother's hands*). Yes, you have business with your . . . your priest, and I am no longer a child. Enjoy each other.

(*Exit* ORESTES.)

AEGISTHUS. Your son becomes more and more offensive to me.

CLYTEMNESTRA. He is so young, Aegisthus. Too young to be judged.

AEGISTHUS. Again youth as a defense. Were he still at your breast and behaving this way I would find it intolerable. But I will know how to treat Orestes when and if he forces me.

CLYTEMNESTRA. It is not my son whom you should fear, but the other — his father, Agamemnon.

AEGISTHUS. What? What have you heard?

CLYTEMNESTRA. Electra's laugh in the middle of the night as she cried his name in her sleep. Oh, it was not the laugh of a child beguiled with happy dreams, but that of a victorious woman. There is only one event that could bring such a sound from her: the sight of Agamemnon standing here again in the palace.

AEGISTHUS. And so a child dreams of an errant father. Should this be upsetting?

CLYTEMNESTRA. You should not take Agamemnon lightly. When he returns . . .

AEGISTHUS. Dear Clytemnestra, I take nothing lightly. Most people consider poets weaklings at best, cowards at worst, and they are not far wrong. But against your husband I feel invincible. If he returns at all, it will be as the leader of weary, forgotten soldiers with whom I have already negotiated in secret and found quite ready to rid themselves of Agamemnon and his costly inspirations. No, my darling queen, should your husband find his way back to Argos I will see to it that he does nothing more dangerous than a little hunting and an occasional piece of grand rhetoric addressed to the few toothless septuagenarians who might find him still tolerable.

CLYTEMNESTRA. You would still do well to fear him, Aegisthus. Fear breeds caution.

AEGISTHUS. Then I shall fear him — for many reasons, one of which concerns you.

CLYTEMNESTRA (*relaxing somewhat*). Me?

AEGISTHUS (*forcing a jealous tone*). That he might recall to you an older but fresher love.

CLYTEMNESTRA (*now enjoying a thoroughly female role*). A god must be perplexing our minds today, for there seems to be so little understanding among us.

AEGISTHUS. Is it thick-witted to think that a woman's first love will always be the most memorable?

CLYTEMNESTRA (*coquettishly*). A woman has only one love, Aegisthus.

AEGISTHUS. I hope you mean at a time.

CLYTEMNESTRA. No, it has nothing to do with time or number. Our love is a born talent, and is present before we, by practicing upon men, begin to expand and polish it into an art.

AEGISTHUS. Oh, that's very appealing. And what am I then, a five-finger exercise?

CLYTEMNESTRA. No, Agamemnon with his simple rhythms and lack of harmony was better suited to the beginner's ability. I experimented with him as an uncomplicated basis and discovered where my love needed more refinement and work. I learned its style and the technique which best adorned it. In short, with Agamemnon's simplicity, I practiced for all your difficult subtleties, and when you arrived I was prepared, or, better, my love was prepared to demonstrate its genius.

AEGISTHUS. And did you find me, as a composition I mean, worth all these preparations?

CLYTEMNESTRA (*putting her arms about* AEGISTHUS). Oh, you made my love's genius strain a bit, but, on the whole, you were worth every minute spent with Agamemnon.

AEGISTHUS. I am touched. (*He kisses* CLYTEMNESTRA *gently.*)

CLYTEMNESTRA (*holds* AEGISTHUS *tightly for a moment and then, as if shocked, pushes back from him*). You do breathe the same way!

AEGISTHUS. The same way?

CLYTEMNESTRA. Oh, why must I think of him now? It's so foolish, I know it is, but when I held you and felt your back slowly expanding and coming to rest I couldn't help but remember how similar it was with Agamemnon.

AEGISTHUS (*smiling*). I wish I could breathe differently then, but I'm afraid habit prevents it.

CLYTEMNESTRA. Oh, if it were only that, I would laugh, too. But it's just one of many signs I've noticed for several days.

AEGISTHUS. Signs? What type of signs?

CLYTEMNESTRA. It's as if he were making dramatic preparations for his return by setting a well-planned scene in my memory. It's been over five years since I've given him any thought at all, but now I can't turn about without something leaping at me and forcing my thoughts to admit him as if he never for a moment left them. I pass by a pear tree which I've looked at without harm a thousand times, but now I suddenly remember how he once climbed it to bring me the fruit from the highest branches. And the pool in front of the palace, for years it has meant nothing to me but an annoying lure for night-flying insects, but this morning I recalled how Agamemnon used to enjoy throwing pebbles at its oversized fish and how he excused his cruelty by making learned comments on the geometric ripples formed by the striking stones. And then last night Electra's laugh. Oh, Aegisthus, I'm sure all these are signs that he's coming and wants to make a well-timed entrance.

AEGISTHUS. Surely you don't think Agamemnon's behind those bits of memory?

CLYTEMNESTRA. What difference does that make? Whether he writes the drama or simply plays in it, he will still return and enjoy his great moment.

AEGISTHUS (*now somewhat impatient*). For the last time I repeat: Agamemnon will cause no disturbance here. To the citizens of Argos he has already become a parable used to tame unruly children. Every mother considers him a stumbling, meddlesome old man, continually getting himself into predicaments where he needs their sons' and husbands' lives to get him out. Even Orestes feels the same way. Now how could such a negative moral lesson affect a land which has, because of my work, become the direct opposite of Agamemnon's dream?

CLYTEMNESTRA. I still fear his return. The one moment he will have.

AEGISTHUS. The moment you speak of, if, as you say, it is a great one, it will also be, I promise you, short. But enough of dreams, memories, and speculations. What I wished to tell you from the beginning is that your errant husband is less than twenty miles from Argos now.

CLYTEMNESTRA. What are you saying, Aegisthus?

AEGISTHUS. Simply that the boats I posted to watch for Agamemnon's sails have returned with the information that sometime today he should be with us again. You and Orestes are the only ones I've told this to. Your son seemed indifferent, for the wrong reasons, I imagine, and you look as if I'd mentioned death instead of a home-coming husband.

CLYTEMNESTRA. You let me say all that I have said knowing this would be?

AEGISTHUS. I hoped I could diminish the importance of such a moment before I spoke.

(*Excited voices are heard offstage.*)

CLYTEMNESTRA. Oh, I am afraid.

AEGISTHUS. There is no reason to be, Clytemnestra. I have prepared Agamemnon's reception carefully.

(*The voices grow in volume.*)

Now what is going on?

CLYTEMNESTRA (*moving away from the voices*). The sounds frighten me, Aegisthus.

(*The* PRIESTS *re-enter.*)

AEGISTHUS (*to* PRIESTS). Be still. What mad behavior is that? Did I not send you off to pray? Or do you consider this cackling a proper way to address the heavens?

(*Through the following scene* CLYTEMNESTRA *stares blankly above her as if she has seen a fascinating object in the sky.*)

FIRST PRIEST. We were at our prayers and had collected a good audience, too; then right in the middle of a tightly rhymed stanza of yours whisperings began.

SECOND PRIEST. Rudeness! But what can one expect from the untutored ears of this city?

THIRD PRIEST. We ordered silence, but they would not listen. Then at that part of your poem where the words become rough and repetitive, to signify, as I have always said, the emotional tension of the subject, which is, is it not, resignation . . .

SECOND PRIEST. You are brilliant at misinterpreting the obvious. Resignation! If your loins weren't as dry as they are you'd know that what Aegisthus speaks of is love.

FIRST PRIEST. Love? Love? Is your mind ever on what you can no longer perform?

AEGISTHUS. Stop! Stop this nonsense, or by the gods I'll have new priests within the hour to replace and mourn the untimely death of you three hens. Now what happened at the temple?

THIRD PRIEST. After we cried for silence, as if on signal, everyone left the temple.

FIRST PRIEST. They seemed most excited, but for the life of us we could not find out the reason for such behavior.

(*A trumpet sounds and excited voices are heard offstage.*)

AEGISTHUS. He has been seen!

CLYTEMNESTRA. So he has come. The moment was too fine, too ripe for him to miss. He arrived as I and my lover spoke of him.

FIRST PRIEST. What is this, Aegisthus? Why has the trumpet sounded? And see, all those people running toward the fishing harbor?

AEGISTHUS. Our king is returning, my friends. Agamemnon's fleet has been sighted.

CLYTEMNESTRA. There are no clouds in the sky. A common sight, but it was Agamemnon who loved, above all else, a cloudless heaven.

AEGISTHUS (*to* CLYTEMNESTRA). Remember what I told you. He is impotent now. He can and will do nothing to harm us. I can promise you that.

CLYTEMNESTRA. I am trembling, Aegisthus.

AEGISTHUS (*putting his arm about* CLYTEMNESTRA, *begins to lead her offstage*). All will be well. I am ready for Agamemnon's rage. (*Notices* PRIESTS.) What? Are you still here? Did you not understand that Agamemnon is approaching? Get busy and prepare a sacrifice thanking the gods for his safe return.

FIRST PRIEST. Thank the gods for Agamemnon's return?

AEGISTHUS. Must I repeat my instruction?

SECOND PRIEST. We will attribute his victory to a happy evening Zeus spent with an Athenian shepherd.

AEGISTHUS. You understand my wishes perfectly.

(*Again the trumpet sounds and the* PRIESTS *exit.* ORESTES *and* PYLADES *enter.*)

ORESTES. Is it true, Aegisthus?

(AEGISTHUS *and* CLYTEMNESTRA *are almost offstage now.*)

Aegisthus, is it really my father?

AEGISTHUS (*just as he and* CLYTEMNESTRA *exit*). Yes, Orestes, it seems Agamemnon, king and father, is returning to us.

(*He exits with* CLYTEMNESTRA.)

PYLADES. Come, then, Orestes. We must not miss your fishing-bay prophecy come true.

ORESTES. You go, Pylades. I will follow in a minute.

(ELECTRA *and* PENELOPE *enter.*)

ELECTRA (*runs into* ORESTES' *arms*). Is he really coming? Has our father really been sighted?

PENELOPE. You must be calm. Your father will expect to see a princess and just look at your hair. It's impossible.

PYLADES. Your enjoyment will have to be mixed with the odor of fish. Agamemnon's entering the less noble harbor.

PENELOPE. What difference where he enters?

ELECTRA. He is coming! My dream, Penelope. My dream.

PENELOPE. Such dreams must come to be.

PYLADES. Come on, Orestes, don't brood. This should be great fun.

ORESTES (*after a pause*). You're right. There is no reason to postpone the long-waited meeting of father and son.

ELECTRA. Oh, what is he like, Orestes? I have heard and dreamt so much, but you remember him.

ORESTES (*smiling*). I know no more than you, Electra. We both have a legend, and now we must undergo the often painful experience of seeing it turned into a man.

CURTAIN

SCENE 2

A large chamber inside the palace a few hours later. AEGISTHUS, AGAMEMNON, *and* CASSANDRA *enter. A* SOLDIER, *who is with them, sits on a stool in corner of stage. At center stage there is a large chair suitable for a throne.*

AGAMEMNON *is between forty and fifty, still strongly built and not at all the idealistic buffoon* ORESTES *has described. However, there is fatigue etched into his body and he supports himself with a staff.* CASSANDRA, *well on in years, is small, round, and comical-looking, but her manner is forceful. She carries an incompleted wicker basket on which she works during the following scene.*

AEGISTHUS. I must apologize for not having the palace suitably decorated for your arrival, but you appeared so suddenly.

AGAMEMNON. Who wishes such ornaments? It's my family I wish to see, not royal carpets.

AEGISTHUS. They would have met you at the beach, but the crowd being what it was, I thought it best that the reunion take place here.

AGAMEMNON. That suits me perfectly, Aegisthus. I played in this room as a child, was married here, and, whenever possible, conducted the affairs of state from that chair.

AEGISTHUS. Then I shall summon them.

AGAMEMNON. Will you come back with them? Yours is the only face already familiar, and I confess I'm nervous over this meeting.

AEGISTHUS. No, I think it best that this be a family affair. My presence might be embarrassing to some.

(AEGISTHUS *exits.*)

CASSANDRA (*walking to the throne and sitting down*). I must sit down. The odor of that herring boat you put me in was upsetting. Really uncivilized treatment of a prisoner of war!

AGAMEMNON. As a prophetess you should have warned me that the wind would fail us a mile from Argos.

CASSANDRA. I am a slave, but I'll not stoop to forecasting the weather for you.

AGAMEMNON. Forget our misadventure with the winds. We are home, and my family will be here in seconds.

CASSANDRA. It will be a happy moment for you.

AGAMEMNON. Happy? I'm terrified, Cassandra. Will I even recognize them after ten years? Will I know my son as a man, and Electra who could barely speak when I left, will she be anything but frightened of me?

CASSANDRA. They will know you, Agamemnon, better than you think possible.

AGAMEMNON. And Clytemnestra? What a bridge of time and change must I cross before we speak again as husband and wife.

CASSANDRA (*beginning work on the wicker basket*). Your family have very good memories, Agamemnon. They'll help you go back ten years.

AGAMEMNON. I pray so. I want them now more than peace itself. I want them about me in the evenings. I would advise Orestes on women, scold Electra when she loves, or thinks she loves, some young boy I don't approve of, and, with my wife, I would argue about petty household things and sue for forgiveness of my temper at night.

CASSANDRA. And if you had all this, Agamemnon, how long would you enjoy it before starting off on another soldier's campaign?

AGAMEMNON. I would never leave Argos again, Cassandra. My work as king is done. I've brought all I can to my time, and now I would rest.

CASSANDRA. Can the conqueror of Troy rest?

AGAMEMNON. He can, Cassandra. You shall see. But now, say again how my family will appear to me. It's so hard to hold their image in my mind: like puffs of smoke they change form each second. So, once more, tell me how I shall see them.

CASSANDRA. Orestes will be to you as a god, and you will find Clytemnestra a greater woman than you left her.

(CLYTEMNESTRA, ELECTRA, PENELOPE, *and* ORESTES *enter.* ORESTES *is dressed in a suit of armor far too large for him. For several seconds they stare at each other in silence, then* AGAMEMNON *begins to walk slowly toward them.*)

CLYTEMNESTRA. Welcome home, Agamemnon.

(AGAMEMNON *holds out his arms tentatively toward* CLYTEMNESTRA, *but as he walks to her,* ELECTRA *rushes between them.*)

ELECTRA. Oh, Father, it's true! I'm holding you; touching you with my hands. It is no dream.

AGAMEMNON. Oh, I am an old man, upset by spectres and fears that don't exist. I thought we would not know each other; but there is no doubt you are Agamemnon's daughter. Little Electra! Now almost a woman, a beautiful woman. Oh, I am thankful for this.

ELECTRA. How I've waited for this moment. If you knew how long it has been for me.

AGAMEMNON. I was missed, then?

PENELOPE. She could not shut her eyes without seeing you.

ELECTRA. The very night before your ships were sighted I dreamt of your return. All were cries of triumph, proud processions, and the name "Agamemnon" was a fair greeting which citizens exchanged in passing and children wore in mock battles for your amusement. Banners hung from porches and old women knelt to kiss your hand as you walked slowly through the streets of Argos. Through all this, Father, I stood at your side, feeling . . .

CLYTEMNESTRA. It was a commendable dream, Electra, but such details are now unnecessary.

AGAMEMNON (*to* CLYTEMNESTRA). The child is perfect. You have watched over her well.

CLYTEMNESTRA. Penelope was her nurse.

AGAMEMNON. Then accept as your reward a father's gratitude.

PENELOPE. I could wish no more than that.

ORESTES. And what of me? I have no dreams to relate, but I am your son.

AGAMEMNON (*walking to* ORESTES). There is no doubt of that. Prince Orestes, my son, so anxious to show himself a man that he wears the panoply of my soldiers.

ORESTES. One of your officers sold it to me for a little wine. It's rather large now, but perhaps I'll grow into it.

AGAMEMNON. Be patient and I'll see you fitted with armor suited to the rigor and form of youth.

ORESTES. You mean fitted to one who's underweight?

AGAMEMNON (*forcing a smile*). Humor at your own expense? That's a good sign.

ORESTES. I hoped you would find me amusing, Father. It's a sign of character to enjoy a good joke now and then. For instance, today one had to laugh when he saw trembling wives presenting their warring husbands, who had been away ten years, with children who had not yet lived five.

AGAMEMNON. Not every man will have a happy homecoming.

ORESTES. Certainly not as happy as yours, Agamemnon. You have Electra's fifteen-year-old love to welcome you.

ELECTRA. He has all of ours.

CLYTEMNESTRA. Electra is young. Things are easier and less complicated for her.

AGAMEMNON (*warily*). I am happy it is easy for her to love me. I would imagine it quite difficult.

ORESTES. You are more perceptive than I thought.

AGAMEMNON. And what does that mean, Orestes?

ELECTRA. It means nothing. He is always saying funny things without meaning.

AGAMEMNON. That is a strange occupation for the Prince of Argos.

ORESTES. There are a number of things in Argos you'll now find strange.

AGAMEMNON. That must be expected. But I will go slowly and find a way suited to different times. I will learn, and I've brought the Trojan prophetess to help me.

ORESTES (*becoming impatient with the pretense and hints*). If she is a prophetess, I wonder that you're now here playing the loving father who's missed his dear family. I should think she would have prophesied how ludicrous you'd seem.

ELECTRA. Orestes, stop it. There are enough here who will say cruel things to him.

ORESTES. Oh, I'm tired of the farce. Who is this man leaning on a staff and calling me his son? Agamemnon, my father? What does he want here? His place is on pedestals and at the head of inspired armies. No, King of Argos, it is rather late to clasp me by the arm and call me son. It is embarrassing. This affectionate scene can go on now without me.

(ORESTES *exits.*)

AGAMEMNON. Orestes, don't go. Wait, I . . .

CLYTEMNESTRA. Your son, Agamemnon.

AGAMEMNON. But why should he behave in such a way? What is happening here? Was I too eager to see things as I wished them to be?

ELECTRA. Father, don't listen to what she'll tell you. Orestes was play-acting. He loves you and is happy over your return, I know that he is.

CLYTEMNESTRA. Enough, Electra. Orestes is insolent, indifferent, and has no use for anyone; least of all you, my husband.

AGAMEMNON. But why, why should he feel this way? I didn't understand a word he said to me just now.

CLYTEMNESTRA. He simply is not anxious to endorse you either as father or king.

AGAMEMNON (*to* CASSANDRA). Well, my seer, how does your prophecy now stand?

CASSANDRA. Here and well. Did I not say your son would be to you as a god? And how well would you understand one of them?

AGAMEMNON. You have a comfortable habit of suiting all events with your forecasts. Yes, Cassandra, I did well in choosing you. (*Turning to* CLYTEMNESTRA.) That Orestes feels thus about me is more than disappointing. I had hoped, hoped that at last I could be both king and father to him, but I was mistaken if I thought such a thing would be easy. All would have been too well with me if there were not some flaw in this meeting.

ELECTRA. You have always been father and king to me; you shall be to Orestes.

PENELOPE. Argos has been cruel and sterile since you left. It was not a land to nourish love.

CLYTEMNESTRA. That is not true. Love has grown in Argos, Agamemnon.

ELECTRA. No, not love!

CLYTEMNESTRA (*finally losing some of the control she has maintained during the scene*). Will you not listen to anyone but your childish daughter?

AGAMEMNON. She has not yet said anything to displease me. But perhaps I've not understood her meanings. I'm not certain I want to know them either.

ELECTRA. Father, I would never say anything to cause you pain; but if I do not speak, the truth will come from crueler lips.

CLYTEMNESTRA. Electra, leave us. As your mother and queen I order you to leave us.

ELECTRA. I will not do that. I know what you want to tell him and I'm going to stay.

AGAMEMNON (*his eyes on* CLYTEMNESTRA). No, Electra, you should go. Your mother wishes a private audience with the king, and she shall have it.

ELECTRA. If I do, will you remember my dream the way I told it to you? That is the way things will be in Argos. Remember that through all she says.

AGAMEMNON (*leading* ELECTRA *offstage*). I will remember, Electra. I will remember. (*He kisses her and she and* PENELOPE *exit.*) And now, Clytemnestra, there is no child to disturb your speaking.

CLYTEMNESTRA (*stiffening and summoning all her courage*). Must my feelings be articulated in words? (*Pointing to her face.*) Can you not read them here? I am not young like Electra and my face is not smooth with simplicity. It speaks with more eloquence than a child's tongue, Agamemnon.

AGAMEMNON. You know me a poor reader of such things, Clytemnestra.

CLYTEMNESTRA. Then let me direct your eyes, my husband. I hoped I would not have to, but your blindness leaves me no choice. (*She moves toward* AGAMEMNON.) Look closely at Clytemnestra. See how her mouth is drawn and bloodless and how her eyes refuse to reflect your image. Watch as I trace my fingers across her brow and point to the deep marks of fear your return has caused. Come, look at the curious crevices your return has put there. And now, closer, and put your arms about her and whisper of your decade-old love.

(AGAMEMNON *puts his hands on* CLYTEMNESTRA'*s shoulders. She remains unmoved, rigid, and turns from him.*)

Do you feel the resistance? Do you understand now the movements of a woman?

AGAMEMNON (*allowing his arms to drop to his sides*). I won't believe this, Clytemnestra.

CLYTEMNESTRA. What must I then say? That you are a ghost? Something I thought myself rid of and happy for it? How plain must I be with you?

AGAMEMNON. You can tell me why you have changed.

CLYTEMNESTRA. Why? Why is the beach of Argos bone white? The million grains of sand that make it so are without importance by themselves. And my reasons, infinite in number and tiny as sand, are the same.

AGAMEMNON. So my glorious victory brings me this. I must have seemed comical to you speaking of my fortune the way I did. I am glad I could entertain you.

CLYTEMNESTRA. You entertained me no more than the news of Iphigenia's death did.

AGAMEMNON (*angrily*). I will not be reproached with that by you. I could understand your anger if it were sincere, but don't use our daughter's sacrifice to excuse your weak behavior.

CLYTEMNESTRA. Weak? Yes, I am that. I was never strong enough to stand beside you on mountain peaks and gaze with an impersonal eye at the world which you molded to suit your great ideas. The clear air at such heights dizzies me. I belong on lower ground, where seasons change and where small desires and faults are shared and understood. I belong with one who knows the love of this earth.

AGAMEMNON. And so Clytemnestra took a lover.

CLYTEMNESTRA. Yes, and she is not ashamed of it. I have never claimed nor wanted the strength you admire so much.

AGAMEMNON. Such stories are so common in a soldier's camp; but I would never have thought it of you, Clytemnestra.

CLYTEMNESTRA. Thought? When did you ever think of me? When, even when you made love and breathed your affection upon me, did you ever think of my wants? You had a world to create, and perhaps there was a place in it for a queen, but certainly none for a wife.

AGAMEMNON. And so you crept out at night seeking attention in the shadow of walls.

CLYTEMNESTRA. It suits you to see such things on that level, Agamemnon. But no, I did not creep. I was not ashamed to love.

AGAMEMNON. I'm glad you have something to be proud of, Clytemnestra. So all of Argos knows of the new wound you've found to dote over.

CLYTEMNESTRA. They do. I have said it was not hidden.

AGAMEMNON. Well, should I be an exception? Can I not meet this one who proved himself the better man to Agamemnon's wife?

CLYTEMNESTRA. He is not frightened of you, but I pray you try to understand and not turn Argos into another battleground.

AGAMEMNON. I will do as I wish with him. But I'll tell you, Clytemnestra, that I have no desire to punish or shed blood. I see your face more clearly now, and I know I could gain nothing by it.

CLYTEMNESTRA. Thank you for that.

AGAMEMNON. Please, don't give me gratitude as a substitute for what I expected and thought of for ten years.

CLYTEMNESTRA. I still do not believe that, Agamemnon. Ten years of thought devoted to your wife? No, that was not the man whose marriage gift was the throne of Argos.

AGAMEMNON. Enough. I want to have done with this business. Send me your lover and let me judge if he is a worthy successor or not.

CLYTEMNESTRA. You will find him more than a lover, Agamemnon.

(*She exits.*)

AGAMEMNON (*to* CASSANDRA). Well, can you explain that miscalculation?

CASSANDRA. You refuse to pay attention to my words. Did I not say you'd find Clytemnestra a greater woman than you left her? You took leave of a faithful wife — that you have lost; but in her place you now have a queen who can stand against you.

AGAMEMNON. My wife pleased me better. Is this real? Is this actually happening? My son greets me as though he were mad and cares nothing for what I have done. My wife tells me that our love has been an illusion and is happy to display her new lover before me and all of Argos. Oh, it is amusing, is it not? Agamemnon can have all but the pleasures which are the right of the meanest criminal.

CASSANDRA. You forget Electra.

AGAMEMNON. Electra? Yes, only little Electra. Only a daughter who does not know me cared at all. It is a fine welcome Argos has given me. It seems now I can be nothing but a king.

CASSANDRA. It is not such a terrible fate. Many would sell their entire family into slavery for such a chance.

AGAMEMNON. And if I can do it well, Orestes at least might come to me. Yes, I shall rule Argos, and rule her well. I will work, go on with my plans, and build a new . . .

(AEGISTHUS *re-enters with two of* AGAMEMNON's *soldiers.*)

AEGISTHUS. Clytemnestra said you wished to see me.

AGAMEMNON. You, Aegisthus? You?

AEGISTHUS. I hope she was explicit, Agamemnon.

AGAMEMNON. She was. My home-coming party is over. You did well to leave when you did. You saved yourself from witnessing rather awkward scenes. It seems of all my family only Electra finds me tolerable.

AEGISTHUS. Yes, you have the untempered love of a child. Her affection is a little inordinate on such short acquaintance, but I'll not doubt its sincerity.

AGAMEMNON. This is, perhaps, more than I deserve. My life has not been suited to family affection and if I am denied it now it is only just. For this reason I can tolerate you, Aegisthus, as my wife's lover. I will not protest this, for there are many things left to me, and perhaps, through doing them well, I will win my wife and son back to me.

AEGISTHUS. Forgive me, Agamemnon, but your fever and journey have, I fear, blurred the true cause of things. It was I who arranged this greeting for you, but it was not to claim Clytemnestra's bed that I did so.

AGAMEMNON. Haven't you accomplished all you wished?

AEGISTHUS. No, only the first and least important part of it. Whether or not you were in accord with wife and child interested me only accidentally and only as an individual. It is as a ruler that I now wish to speak.

AGAMEMNON. As a ruler? As a ruler of what?

AEGISTHUS. Why, of this land, of Argos.

AGAMEMNON (*pauses and lets* AEGISTHUS' *words sink in*). I left you
here as my regent because I thought you to be an industrious and
humble cousin, and now I find you consider yourself as king.

AEGISTHUS. I'm not seeking an exchange of titles. I can easily rule
Argos as a cousin. Also, it will perhaps ease the shock somewhat
if I tell you that this desire to govern is inextricable from the humility you've always noticed in me.

AGAMEMNON. A humble wish to govern!

AEGISTHUS. It is when you consider yourself no better than the people you wish to rule. What could be more humiliating than the
realization that your only quality as a leader is in your equality
with those you lead?

AGAMEMNON. Enough! I'm not interested in your social logic. (*To*
SOLDIERS.) But why have you let him speak thus to your king? I
know your faces. I saw you on the day Troy fell. Why do you
stand behind Aegisthus?

AEGISTHUS. And I thought you had a sense of theatre, Agamemnon.
Can't you tell the only reason these men are here is to put a final
touch to my arguments?

AGAMEMNON. Not my soldiers . . .

AEGISTHUS. Exactly. I chose these men at random from among your
returning army, but any of the others I spoke with today would
have done as well.

AGAMEMNON. But I know these men. (*To* SOLDIERS.) We fought beside each other for ten years. There was never any question of
your loyalty then. You honored me as your leader and I respected
you as soldiers who would battle for . . .

AEGISTHUS. Oh, come now, Agamemnon! Even with your own family you couldn't use past sentiment.

AGAMEMNON. With my family I could understand my limitations,
but with my soldiers, whom I led home victorious, I cannot.

FIRST SOLDIER. Aye, you led us well, Agamemnon, there's no doubt
of that. But we know you. We know you can never rest for long.
Soon you'd be calling on us again to set off after you and telling
us we're being men when we threw ourselves into another fight.
No, Agamemnon, we're tired of that life.

SECOND SOLDIER. We're tired of being strangers to our own homes,
of having to struggle to recognize our children. I've spent twenty
good years in your army, and all I'm left with now is the fear that
it's meant nothing.

AGAMEMNON. Meant nothing? How, after all we have accomplished,
can you say it has been worthless?

SECOND SOLDIER (*shrugs*). It's something I feel. I know no more than
that.

AGAMEMNON. Something you feel? But what of the things you know? You have seen with your own eyes the improvements I've made wherever we've gone. You've listened to and understood the proofs that the right reasons for human action were with us. What is there left over to feel?

FIRST SOLDIER. What it is, I don't know. But I'm sure I felt it the day we stormed Troy. Just as I broke through the walls and saw the burning and the dead I asked myself what in the gloriful gods' names was I, a none-too-bright farmer, doing there? I had no answer, but there was a feeling. A feeling as if I'd been thrown from the earth and was hanging somewhere above it.

AGAMEMNON. And because of this indefinable notion of yours you would turn against me?

FIRST SOLDIER. Not against you, to Aegisthus.

AGAMEMNON (*for the first time showing signs of anger and frustration*). For what reason then? What did he promise you?

AEGISTHUS. Nothing. I merely assured them that the feeling you find so hard to grasp is a common one.

AGAMEMNON (*to* CASSANDRA). Come, you are a seer. Can you divine any meaning out of this?

CASSANDRA. To know the future means knowing what men will do. What they feel while doing it is quite another matter.

AEGISTHUS. If you give me a chance I will try at an explanation.

AGAMEMNON. By all means. But first I want these two traitors out of my sight. That is if you're not afraid of being without them.

FIRST SOLDIER. Traitor is a harsh word.

AGAMEMNON (*meeting the challenge*). I meant no compliment by it.

AEGISTHUS. Now, now, in ten years you should have had enough fighting. (*To* SOLDIERS.) Go wait outside for me, but not too far from the entrance. Agamemnon, I fear, has a temper, and he may dislike what I say to him.

(SOLDIERS *exit.*)

Now, will you listen without anger?

AGAMEMNON. You expect too much, but I am interested.

AEGISTHUS. I am glad, for a great deal depends upon your interest and understanding.

AGAMEMNON. Well, go on then. You make me feel as if I am about to hear a divine oracle.

AEGISTHUS. You are not far wrong. What I am going to tell you will have the consequences if not the ambiguities of divine sayings. It is simply this: you have failed, Agamemnon.

AGAMEMNON. That is an opinion, Aegisthus. I could have guessed you would hold it.

AEGISTHUS. Of course; but why I hold it is another matter.

AGAMEMNON. Then you have a reason greater than your desire for my position?

AEGISTHUS. Indeed I have, Agamemnon. Overlooking the insult in your question, I will tell you that you have failed because of an indifference to the characteristics of your own species; that is, if you'll forgive a much-misused word — man.

AGAMEMNON. My indifference? Oh, you must do better than that, cousin. My entire life has been involved in his problems. I've been halfway around the world correcting the injustices done to him. I've gathered the best philosophers together to decide on the government which would give him the greatest individual potential. I've set up courses of improvement that he might follow to a greater life. I've shown him the goals he thought unattainable, might be, with a little effort, reached. And by my own life I've proved them worth the greatest battles. Is this, then, indifference? I am a soldier, and the word comes heavy to my tongue, but it all seems closer to love.

AEGISTHUS. Exactly! I don't doubt your love, Agamemnon. I am a poet and not ashamed to use the word, for I share the feeling. But there is a great difference between us. You love man for what he might be; I for what he is. You glory in his potential, to use your own phrase; I sympathize with his existence as it is now and always will be. You cry for the heoric; I have tears of verse for the weak. You give him marble principles to live by; I give him imagined reasons to live. You want him to create justice and control life; I teach him to accept the fortuitous and relish obedience. In short, you have seen man as a cause — a noble sight, no doubt of it — but it is now time to look at him unadorned and naked.

AGAMEMNON. Do you think one can fight beside another, see his wounds, hear his hopes and screams, and still think of him as a cause? No, Aegisthus, I am not that blind.

AEGISTHUS. And yet you did not understand your soldiers' feelings. Your cool reasons had triumphed and all should be well with the world. The inertia of such logic may carry one along for a time, but soon it weakens and he is dropped back into the lonely desert of himself. What do you say to him then, Agamemnon?

AGAMEMNON. I would tell him to look with pride at what he had created.

AEGISTHUS. And I would ask him to watch a little longer until he saw his great edifice pass into dust.

AGAMEMNON. I would praise his acting as a man.

AEGISTHUS. I would say he had been playing a role far above his capacity, and that now, choked, blinking, and stunned mute by his past and future, he has finally joined the proper and true class of men.

AGAMEMNON. You think so little then of this class?

AEGISTHUS. Remember, I include myself in it.

AGAMEMNON. I don't think that alters my question.

AEGISTHUS. I think the moment our soldier spoke of — the moment he stood in the flamed confirmation of your strength and weakened; the moment he saw himself matched alone against an iced heaven; the moment he heard the great voice crack into dried laughter — this moment I consider the most important for all future politics which will show man a modicum of consideration.

AGAMEMNON. And I consider the moment when he drew his sword because he believed there was something greater than his life to defend refutes all you have said.

AEGISTHUS. Then we are still left with our difference of opinion?

AGAMEMNON. We are, and it will remain so.

AEGISTHUS. Unfortunately, it cannot. Such debates are enjoyable, but when so much is at stake they are the first expendable pleasure.

AGAMEMNON. You have a solution in mind?

AEGISTHUS. Unfortunately no. An order is the better word. Today there is to be a sacrifice. The armor of your soldiers will be burned as an offering to our gods. This will be, I hope, an obvious symbol for all that the strength and belief in the men who wore these odd-fitting suits are finished, and that greater powers will now control and order the world's course. I have planned that each man should voluntarily place his mail into the fire, and I had hoped that you would lead them in doing so.

AGAMEMNON. That you will never see, Aegisthus. It was the arms of men that conquered Troy and corrected the insolence and arrogance of the Trojans.

AEGISTHUS. Yes, yes, we have been through all that. I now no longer expect you to participate, but I do command you to abstain from any interference, either today or in the future.

AGAMEMNON. Such a pledge you will never have. If war has weakened my soldiers, there will be others who will follow me.

AEGISTHUS. I will let certain remarks pass and attribute them to unthinking anger. But I warn you, Agamemnon, I am as ready as you to defend my . . .

AGAMEMNON. Cause? Why don't you use the word, Aegisthus?

AEGISTHUS. Again the word is not important. You know the difference between us and the following each of us has. I beg you to act accordingly.

AGAMEMNON. Go attend your rituals, Aegisthus; you shall soon hear of my actions.

AEGISTHUS. I wish we could have agreed. It is a pity that at the same time and in the same city two men should want so much.

(*Exit* AEGISTHUS.)

AGAMEMNON (*turning to* CASSANDRA). How could you sit there and be silent during all that?

(CASSANDRA *shrugs.*)

Didn't you consider me right?

CASSANDRA. I may know all that will happen in the future and most of what has gone on in the past, but right and wrong . . . ? (*She shrugs.*)

AGAMEMNON. If you're trying to embarrass me into saying I'm not sure, either, it won't work. I'll not let my life be canceled in a morning's time. But tell me, and for once so there is only one possible meaning, what will happen if I oppose Aegisthus?

CASSANDRA. He will kill you.

AGAMEMNON. Hmmm! I've changed my mind. I'd rather have an ambiguous encouragement.

CASSANDRA. I can only tell you to look about and not be foolish.

AGAMEMNON. Look about me? Yes, there is little in my favor, and yet you know what I will do. (*Noticing sleeping guard.*) And Aegisthus considers that oblivious wretch there my cause!

CASSANDRA. Yes, while you and Aegisthus settled matters of heaven and earth, he enjoyed his own undisturbed illusions.

AGAMEMNON. From the idiot's grin on his face he must be cavorting with half the virgins of Greece.

CASSANDRA. You disapprove?

AGAMEMNON. I have no time to judge his fancies. (*Starting toward corridor.*) There is much to do.

CASSANDRA. Wait for a moment, Agamemnon, and I'll give you an unsolicited prophecy.

AGAMEMNON. Well?

CASSANDRA. It is that after many centuries no one will be able to prove which had more importance — your war of great truth with Aegisthus or this poor fool's lascivious dream.

(*Both look at* SOLDIER *who grunts and changes position as curtain falls.*)

CURTAIN

ACT II • SCENE 1

The same setting as in the previous scene. As curtain is raised, CAS-
SANDRA, *on stage, is engrossed in weaving a small wicker basket when*
PYLADES *enters.*

PYLADES. Good morning, old woman. Have you, by chance, seen
Prince Orestes about?

(CASSANDRA *goes on with weaving.*)

I say, have you seen the prince?

(*No reply.*)

Poor thing must be deaf.

CASSANDRA (*without looking up from work*). Do you expect a reply
when you address a woman enjoying the noonday brightness of
middle age as "old"?

PYLADES. Pardon, but if I knew your name I could salute you in a
less personal manner.

CASSANDRA. As you are young, you should be forced to undergo for-
mality. However, you may call me Cassandra.

PYLADES (*somewhat taken aback*). Cassandra? The Trojan prophetess?

CASSANDRA (*nodding and putting her work aside*). There, enough of
that. What one won't do to keep the mind busy.

PYLADES. If what I've heard of you is true, Cassandra, then I should
imagine you would have little trouble keeping yourself amused.

CASSANDRA. I judge you think the future is amusing.

PYLADES. No, interesting is probably the better word.

CASSANDRA. In any case you overestimate it. What is your name?

PYLADES. Pylades.

CASSANDRA. Well, Pylades, the future, unfortunately for those with
my gifts, is an unimaginable bore.

PYLADES (*laughing*). That might be true in general, but I'm sure each
man believes his own endowed with epic events.

CASSANDRA. Yes, I suppose, but when he stops believing and begins to
know it's quite another matter.

PYLADES. Don't suspect me of seeking a free consultation, but I wish
at times I knew mine.

CASSANDRA. Would you really, Pylades? Would you really wish to
know that in five years an indiscretion with the daughter of a
dangerously influential man will leave you an unwilling husband
and the father of red-haired twins? Would you care to discover

that the eight years following this unforseen slip will be crowned with two furtive adulteries, one summer cruise with your wife, and a physician's recommendation that you reduce your wine consumption? Would it please you to be told that the year following your wife's long-postponed death you will consider your life had enough unorthodox importance to embarrass the few friends left you with rather intimate memoirs? Shall I go on?

PYLADES. Is that really my life?

CASSANDRA. Perhaps. It is somebody's; I see the events clearly enough, but whose life they are a part of is still somewhat blurred. Still, Pylades, such is what one usually finds when he peeks over the present.

PYLADES (happily relieved). Cassandra, you are an old fraud — excuse me, I meant a middle-aged one.

CASSANDRA. In my profession, fradulence is a necessary defense.

PYLADES. Still, you did give me a fright. Red-headed twins! Brr! Such a thought could spoil some very pleasant moments.

(Enter ORESTES.)

Ah, just in time, Orestes, to find out your dismal future. (To CASSANDRA, under his breath.) Tell him about the memoirs. He'll explode.

ORESTES. I know enough already, Pylades. That's why I asked you to meet me here. (To CASSANDRA.) Good morning, Cassandra. I hope you forgive me for my quick and rather awkward departure yesterday?

CASSANDRA. Knowing the life you will have, Orestes, it is easy to forgive you.

PYLADES (egging her on). You know what's in store for our prince?

CASSANDRA. Not the slightest idea. That's why I'm sure he will have a hard time of it. A comfortable life spiced with ordinary happiness is easily predictable.

ORESTES. Happy or no, I can tell you what mine will be for the next few years.

PYLADES. What, then?

ORESTES. Pylades, my friend, Aegisthus has informed me that, due to my poor and flippant behavior at yesterday's sacrifice, I am to be sent on a long, long voyage so I may deepen my mind, broaden my point of view, understand world problems, and . . . What else did he say? Ah, yes, assume the serious attitude necessary for a prince of Argos. In a word, he has completely lost patience with me and has ordered this trip.

PYLADES. You lucky dog! Do you mean that your punishment for having dozed during the ritual Aegisthus prepared with such care is to be an indefinite voyage?

ORESTES. That it is, Pylades, and you are to come with me.

PYLADES (*elated*). I, too?

ORESTES. Aegisthus almost choked with delight when I demanded you accompany me.

PYLADES. Oh, the advantages of unpopularity. But this is really beyond belief. When do we leave? When can I say good-by to this silly city?

ORESTES. Tomorrow.

PYLADES. Tomorrow! Is Aegisthus really so anxious?

ORESTES. He is. That's why I wanted to meet you as soon as possible. You must be ready by tomorrow noon at the latest. Can you do it?

PYLADES. With a day to spare. I'm off right now to tie ends together and bring this happy news to my family. Now, when asked, they can say their son is traveling. Why, I'll have an occupation. (*Starts offstage.*) You see, Cassandra, your prophecy was not for me at all.

CASSANDRA. Perhaps, Pylades; but at any event I wish you a happy trip.

(PYLADES *exits.*)

(*To* ORESTES.) And are you as overjoyed about leaving Argos?

ORESTES. Of course! Why shouldn't I be?

CASSANDRA (*shrugging*). Some might consider it an insult to be told to leave their home and go broaden their point of view.

ORESTES. Some might were they prone to look for insults. I see only the pleasure of a well-financed, leisurely voyage, and this is enough to keep my small amount of pride standing erect.

CASSANDRA. Even when you know why Aegisthus is sending you?

ORESTES (*evently*). Yes, Cassandra. Even when I know that. I'm aware of the grand issues I leave behind me, but that's exactly where I want them to be.

CASSANDRA. You're wiser then than I was. I knew what would happen at Troy and had a hundred opportunities to leave also, but I had to feel I might be able to convince others of the idiocy which was to occur and perhaps help avert it. My reward? My countrymen thought me insane. I saw Troy burn to the ground, and just when all finally hailed me as the wisest of prophets, I was captured, turned into a slave, and my morals called into question.

ORESTES. And what do you think of the man who caused all this?

CASSANDRA. You think one man should be blamed?

ORESTES. I think one man contributed more than the ordinary share of responsibility to such things.

CASSANDRA. Your father?

(ORESTES *nods*.)

Perhaps; perhaps he was a great fool in many ways, but then there are so many fools who are small.

ORESTES. And harmless.

CASSANDRA. Not always. Paris, for example, was a small fool who placed overactive glands and twitching nerves above all else when he ran off with Helen. That was rather costly nonsense, wasn't it?

ORESTES. No one forced the Greeks to become the champions of virtue.

CASSANDRA. Nonsense! Do you think that is what sustained the Greek army for ten years in the field? Do you think the soldiers cared who crawled into Helen's bed? No, Orestes, Troy was a rich city, and if anyone had any ideals . . .

ORESTES. It was my father. My father, Cassandra, who led the whole affair. Paris might have slipped into the bushes with Helen and a hundred kings want Troy's gold, but it took someone with a keen moral sense to start and justify that war.

CASSANDRA. From what you're saying I can't understand why Aegisthus wants you to leave.

ORESTES. Don't be misled, Cassandra. Aegisthus may be less pretentious and a better psychologist than my father, but that's all that really separates them. He knows my feelings about his inverted philanthropy.

CASSANDRA. And if you had to choose between them?

ORESTES. But I don't have to. Between Aegisthus' creeping, crawling, microscopic figure who's buffeted by the gods and happy to be so, and my father's fumbling giant of the future who steps in everybody's garden and on everybody's toes with good intentions, the only choice is anger or laughter. I've taken the second.

CASSANDRA (*as if a suspicion has been confirmed*). Orestes, you're going to be a hero, but it will cost you a great deal.

ORESTES (*in amused amazement*). That's not only improbable but insulting.

CASSANDRA. Heroes may change, Orestes. You might find it suits you.

ORESTES. Oh, no, Cassandra, take a good look at me. I'm about to leave Argos and my father to be disposed of by my mother's lover. I have chosen as my sole friend and traveling companion a person whose only worth is his charming uselessness. I am sickened by state ethics, find religion, at its best, high comedy, and while having been tutored in wrestling since a boy, I can't remember having ever won a fight. How, Cassandra, can you fit those qualifications into a heroic pattern?

CASSANDRA. Hmm. I'll admit it wouldn't be easy, but I still feel you are marked for something. Perhaps standards will change.

ORESTES. Let's pray they won't. A world in which my attitudes would set a fashion!

CASSANDRA. In that case, Orestes, it will be up to you to change. Oh, don't scowl, I'm only trying to fit you into my premonitions.

ORESTES. Perhaps, then, they should be changed.

CASSANDRA. What, change the future?

ORESTES. Is it so eternally fixed?

CASSANDRA. It would seem so. Remember what I told you about Troy. It appears no matter how we squirm and invent happy alternatives there is only one future for us.

ORESTES. And you still think that in this I am to be a hero?

CASSANDRA. Give me time, Orestes. It's not easy to gather confirming details together. Let's just say it's a possibility.

ORESTES. Why do you bother me with possibilities? Their very infinity renders them meaningless.

CASSANDRA. Now don't be angry with me. I am trying to help you prepare in case you do find yourself acting a new part. I don't want you to be unnecessarily shocked by it, that's all.

ORESTES. There is nothing which could make me give up the role I have now.

CASSANDRA. Don't be certain, Orestes. It only takes one crashing moment to destroy the mind's labored perspective. The philosopher weeps at the pain of a dog even after he's decided that man and physics no longer deserve pity. The enemy of war, who describes brutality and death with such horrifying elegance, reaches for his sword and cries blood and vengeance when he discovers he's been made cuckold. The confirmed skeptic, who has never lost a logical argument, lets the death of a friend or a severe case of measles turn him into a fanatic worshiper of health foods and herbs. One time when the mind loses control, and who knows what acts you will commit, Orestes.

ORESTES. It will take then a moment greater than those you have just described.

CASSANDRA. Of course; but believe me, such exist.

(AGAMEMNON *enters dressed in his armor.*)

AGAMEMNON. Where is my sword belt, Cassandra? Why is it that since you started putting things in order for me everything has disappeared? (*To* ORESTES.) Well, has this afternoon's embarrassment worn off?

CASSANDRA. What are you doing dressed so ferociously?

AGAMEMNON. It's to suit the occasion, Cassandra. Yesterday Aegisthus dealt with a weary man supported by a staff. Now we shall see how he speaks to Agamemnon.

CASSANDRA. I wouldn't guess from your appearance that you were seeking conversation.

AGAMEMNON. We will let Aegisthus decide on the manner of communication. But I repeat, my sword belt, Cassandra, what have you done with it?

CASSANDRA. It was with the rest of your absurd utensils. If you'd take the trouble to look . . .

AGAMEMNON. Never mind the reproach. Go find it and bring it here.

CASSANDRA. As you wish, but I think you should listen to me first.

AGAMEMNON. Just the belt, Cassandra. And take your time about it. I want to speak to my son without being interrupted.

CASSANDRA. Well, you're sociable today. Let me know when you cease talking and want your sword.

(CASSANDRA *exits*.)

AGAMEMNON. A wonderful woman, but she has a fierce desire to mother someone, and, unfortunately, I've already had the experience.

ORESTES (*in feigned astonishment*). Really?

AGAMEMNON (*to* ORESTES). I hoped you would come back this afternoon.

ORESTES. It seemed the wrong time and setting.

AGAMEMNON. After ten years such social sensitivity seems inappropriate. (*Pause.*) Do you know I'm being kept prisoner here? In my own home and by my own soldiers? Today, however, this will be changed.

ORESTES. Today you show them king and general!

AGAMEMNON. And I hope something more inspiring.

ORESTES. You will have to perform a few miracles to inspire them back to your side. Weren't you present at the sacrifice?

AGAMEMNON. I told you I've been kept prisoner here. The guard you saw on your way in has orders to keep me from joining in the amusements of Argos.

ORESTES. Well, the gods and Aegisthus' poetry were too much for the soldiers to resist. They ended by cheering their new-found weakness and are so proud of it that they would tear anyone apart who dared doubt its existence.

AGAMEMNON. That I know. Aegisthus made all this clear to me.

ORESTES. Well, then, why all this? (*Indicating* AGAMEMNON'S *dress*.)

You don't think you can subdue them alone, do you? Even your legend never vouched you such power as that.

AGAMEMNON. No, not alone. I haven't spent ten years in war not to know something about numerical tactics.

ORESTES. There are a few old men and women about the island you might gather together, but I'm sure that would be all.

AGAMEMNON. I respect age, but at this time I cannot use it. No, Orestes, since Aegisthus' challenge I've put aside active anger and thought calmly about the situation. And, I must admit, there is some truth in what he said. Perhaps my campaigns have tried everyone's patience, perhaps I no longer strike the inspirational figure of the young, clear-eyed king out to better the world; or perhaps I still resemble him too closely, I can't be sure. I am certain, however, that alone I cannot match Aegisthus and the fatigued fear the war has carried into Argos.

ORESTES. Are you going to give Cassandra a sword, too?

AGAMEMNON (*laughs*). I think I'll have to settle on a weapon a little less original. You, Orestes!

ORESTES. I'm sorry but I believe I misunderstand you.

AGAMEMNON. I said you are the weapon I need.

ORESTES. You must be desperate! Haven't you heard how worthless I am?

AGAMEMNON. I took Aegisthus and your mother at their word on everything else, but about you they might have been mistaken.

ORESTES. Well, if it wasn't specific enough before, let me be quite plain now. First, I have no interest in your differences with Aegisthus; second, if I did, it would be to form a third party to hang you both; and third, I consider you, my father, nothing other than an interesting but dangerous antique which still thinks it is, in some way, functional. You are a curio of folly that should be placed under glass and studied to be avoided. Is that definite enough for you?

AGAMEMNON. You really despise me that much?

ORESTES. I won't allow myself to be interested to such a degree.

AGAMEMNON. Where do we separate, then? I don't want to embarrass you again, Orestes, but I might be able to defend myself if you attacked specifically.

ORESTES. But I don't want to attack. For what purpose? It has taken you a lifetime to become your son's aversion and I have no desire to rummage in your past.

AGAMEMNON. And then if I say to you that I regret nothing, that all I have done deserves only praise and imitation, you could only mumble that it is not your way and nothing more? Come, Orestes, as your father I deserve better than that.

ORESTES. What do you want to hear? What am I supposed to tell you? If it's one solid fact you want, I give you the name "Iphigenia."

AGAMEMNON. That is a name causing us both pain. The reasons are different, though, and that's what I wish to hear.

ORIESTES. Reasons? Beyond the fact you allowed your daughter, my sister, to die, or worse, ordered it? What reason has more effect than that?

AGAMEMNON. Do I have to tell you why I did that?

ORESTES. No, spare me that much, at least. I know how you suffer for things greater than the life of a daughter.

AGAMEMNON. Is that, then, our difference?

ORESTES. Stop prompting me into a logical outline of my attitude. Differences A, B, and C, met by counterobjections 1, 2, and 3. It is nothing so finely ordered, I assure you. Perhaps I merely envy you. Perhaps I'm jealous of your certainty. It could be that I, who believe nothing I would ask a dog to miss a meal for, envy you, who are certain to the point of a thousand deaths.

AGAMEMNON. How otherwise? The world is no given paradise, and if one is not at least certain of that, we drop to our knees with Aegisthus, weep away centuries, and roll our senses in the dust.

ORESTES. That might be better than rolling heads.

AGAMEMNON. Forgive me, but you speak from the advantage of an age I have helped create. It is easy when all is forged and polished to be contemptuous of the methods that struck at the crude, un-formed matter of the past.

ORESTES. If you could give me something completed and finished I might find an excuse to change my judgment. But what you offer is an unending chaos which makes improvement and justice sound suspiciously like destruction and rape. No, Father, I'm not going to be swept away by those currents. Orestes is going to walk peacefully along the shore.

AGAMEMNON. You will not stand with me and allow Argos to see that a new generation is willing to continue in my name?

ORESTES. Aegisthus has ordered me to take a maturation voyage. Tomorrow I leave Argos for, I hope, several years.

AGAMEMNON. You don't care that Aegisthus and his priests will turn your home into a primitive rock of superstitious reaction? You don't mind seeing the foundations of your father's life pulled apart by a puerile poet?

ORESTES. Come, are you going to make a speech? Perhaps man should stoop a little and cease thinking he has any power over the

few years we pick up and leave behind us. It sounds a good deal
less harmful.

AGAMEMNON. There I know you're in error, Orestes. Aegisthus,
with all his talk of acceptance, is not walking with you along the
banks, but rowing furiously in the middle of the river.

ORESTES. That may be, but I'm not seeking his company.

AGAMEMNON. No, it is you who are being sought. (*He pauses.*)
Orestes, I have never said this to another man, but I need you. Together we form a symbol of permanence showing others that all
does not begin and end with the oddities of a single personality.
We will make them conscious of a future where our and their
effects will be felt and praised. It will be said Agamemnon has a
son who will continue on in his spirit, and our blood will be
matched against Aegisthus' pity.

ORESTES. Can't I make you understand that I'm uninterested? Blood
and ideals, tears and gods, these offer me nothing. They go on
with their generalities well enough without me. All I could bring
to them would be annoying qualifications which no party would
care to hear.

AGAMEMNON (*desperately*). Orestes, you are my son! We must be the
same.

ORESTES. Shall I even answer that? Ten years and a legend separate
us and always will. I've grown accustomed to being alone and so
shall you.

AGAMEMNON (*somewhat calmer*). I can bear loneliness, Orestes,
better than most. I can move about with Clytemnestra's fear and
your contempt as well as with her love and your admiration.

ORESTES. I've known that for some time.

AGAMEMNON. But there are things I will not have taken from me.

ORESTES. Those, too, I can guess.

AGAMEMNON. Yes, now you do well without them, but for how long?

ORESTES. How many living years?

AGAMEMNON. They will not be living ones unless you decide.

ORESTES. As long as they leave no ugly traces I will judge them successful.

AGAMEMNON. Will you not judge the issues here?

ORESTES. I have, and you have had my opinion.

AGAMEMNON. Good, then, I will stop demanding and begin.

ORESTES. Begin? Surely you're not going on with this alone?

AGAMEMNON. For now, yes, but soon you will be, if not with me,
against Aegisthus.

ORESTES. You are mad if you believe that.

AGAMEMNON. No, Orestes, there is one thing that will force you from
your sunny shore and that will soon be accomplished.

ORESTES. No matter how you succeed, your life will never move me.

AGAMEMNON. But my death will.

ORESTES. Your death? What power will it have over me?

AGAMEMNON. My death, Orestes, will involve you. It will suck you into my current, for Aegisthus will be my murderer and, perhaps, your mother his accomplice. It will settle quickly over your life, and where before you were untouched it will carve indelible scars. You will no longer be the prince who laughs and stands aside, but the son who has not avenged his father's death. Wherever you go, you will be noticed and the world will argue and await your decision. You will be drawn into the current, and if you struggle back toward your peaceful shore shadows will be there to strike at your hands and force you out again into the center flow. You will amuse no one, for a man who bears the guilt of his father's death can make few people laugh. The world will begin to ask questions of you, Orestes, and will demand answers. And soon you will ask them yourself, and like the world you will be dissatisfied with tolerant, reasonable excuses. My death will be a fact — there in front of you, and you will step neither around nor over it.

ORESTES. Can you be that certain?

AGAMEMNON. I can, Orestes. My life and your contentment are minor things. I have begun the building of the best possible temple for man to live in, and Aegisthus could destroy and replace it with a lightless cave. You, now better than I, can prevent him. If I kill, it is the last spiteful vengeance of the past; but if you strike, it is the fresh blow of the future.

ORESTES. I kill Aegisthus for the coming world?

AGAMEMNON. No, you will kill him because he has slain your father and king. It will be that simple. But the reasons you give yourself and the world I leave to your imagination.

ORESTES. Your death will never force me so far past myself. Let the world drag me through its self-made judicial mud — I will let you die and do nothing.

AGAMEMNON. No, Orestes, you will strike, and when you stand with Aegisthus' blood spattered on you, you will say you did it for my beliefs and my principles. You will even live by them and force others to do the same. Soon, if you are not too stubborn, you will come to believe in them yourself. But all the while it will be my death speaking and moving behind you.

ORESTES. Your legend really never did you justice. You think your death will have such power? Here in Argos no one will care, I assure you, not even I.

AGAMEMNON. There is one: Electra, and she will turn to you.

ORESTES. She is a simple child.

AGAMEMNON. All the better, for she will demand a simple act from you — and will never cease demanding it. There will be no visitor to Argos who does not smell the stench of Aegisthus' religion and hear Electra's cry. Both will be spread through our world and both will find you no matter what corner you hide in.

ORESTES. You forget one thing. I leave Argos tomorrow, and will be miles away when, and if, you force Aegisthus.

AGAMEMNON. That would make no difference even if it held true. You would know the moment; you would hear Electra's voice. But as it is, Orestes, I believe you will be on hand as a close witness.

ORESTES. How then? Aegisthus has all he should want. You can do nothing to him, why should he risk the effects of violence?

AGAMEMNON. He will risk it because he is afraid. Fear always comes with the discovery that you have the power and responsibility of your ideas. Aegisthus is no different. Were it otherwise, he would not have been so anxious to explain all to me and find out my reaction. When he discovers that I decided to stand against him he will panic and strike. You can be sure of it.

ORESTES. It will take him some time to realize this.

AGAMEMNON. Just as long as it takes the guard who has been eavesdropping to report to him — a matter of minutes.

ORESTES (*runs to entrance at right of stage and discovers that the* GUARD *is no longer there*). And I thought you a fuddled dreamer who slaughtered, so to speak, by accident.

AGAMEMNON. One can be conscious of all and still dream, Orestes.

ORESTES. Then you knew the balance of pain in every measurement you took of the world.

AGAMEMNON. I made the choice.

ORESTES. Then, dear Father, I shall remember your death with peaceful satisfaction.

AGAMEMNON. We shall see when you are placed within it. But there is not much time. Our guard should have told his tale by now and I must be ready to receive the results with a certain amount of ceremony. (*Calling.*) Cassandra, Cassandra, I am ready now.

ORESTES. You have given me my first true feeling.

AGAMEMNON. Then I have already made progress with you, Orestes.

CASSANDRA (*enters, carrying sword belt*). Here, this should make your costume complete.

AGAMEMNON. Thank you, Cassandra. Above all I shall miss your company.

CASSANDRA. Why your sudden sentimental gloom?

AGAMEMNON. Have you forgotten your own prophecy?

CASSANDRA. So you are then determined.

ORESTES. When was he ever anything else?

CASSANDRA. If only I'd been taken by the lowest soldier in the Greek army. I no sooner grow accustomed to a life than it's destroyed.

AGAMEMNON. Had we both been somewhat younger, Cassandra, I might have sailed with you from Troy to some peaceful island. You are a woman one could learn much from.

CASSANDRA. You pick a poor time to make proposals. Oh, will you be the great fool to the end? Must you be more than mortal?

ORESTES. Tell him, Cassandra. Tell this martyr his death will harm no one.

AGAMEMNON. I do not need her prophecy. I have my own and the living pleasure of seeing it, in part, fulfilled. When Aegisthus arrives, say I'm in my chamber waiting for him. And, Orestes, through all that follows remember my advice. You will need it when it is your turn to act. Now, good-by to you both.

(AGAMEMNON *exits.*)

ORESTES. Cassandra, will he not listen to you?

CASSANDRA. You have heard him. He needs me no longer, for he knows what will come.

ORESTES. He is wrong. His death holds nothing miraculous in it. It is his natural end, a law of nature to be observed, marked down and never forgotten.

CASSANDRA. And yet he has moved you?

ORESTES. Less than a slave condemned to be hanged would. Death, even my father's, upsets me because it confirms my worst suspicions about this world. But that is all I feel, Cassandra.

CASSANDRA. We shall see, Orestes.

(AEGISTHUS *enters accompanied by* SOLDIERS *not dressed in armor. However, they all carry swords.*)

AEGISTHUS (*to one of the* SOLDIERS). Stay here by the entrance. No one enters or leaves until I return.

ORESTES. You are becoming more and more the soldier, Aegisthus.

AEGISTHUS. You, too, I understand, have changed. But where's Agamemnon? Where's our king who's dressed for war?

ORESTES. Listen to me first before you decide on any action.

AEGISTHUS. I have already made my decision. And as for you, Orestes, silence will be best.

ORESTES. Don't be a fool, Aegisthus. I don't know what gossip your guard has spread, but it is of little consequence.

AEGISTHUS. I know Agamemnon has bellowed threats, dressed in a fashion I forbid, and tried to enlist your aid.

ORESTES. That's true. He tried, but he will fail if you ignore him. Believe me, Aegisthus, he is harmless.

SOLDIER. Agamemnon harmless? You would not say that had you seen him at Troy.

AEGISTHUS. You hear, Orestes? It will do no good to try to protect your father. I must have seriously underestimated him. To have convinced you . . .

ORESTES. Aegisthus, I'm telling you he has convinced me of nothing but the necessity of letting him fade away unnoticed.

AEGISTHUS. He has already been offered that chance.

ORESTES. Don't offer it. Force him to take it.

AEGISTHUS. I plan to.

ORESTES. Not this way. Look calmly at what he is.

AEGISTHUS. Enough! I want to hear no more of this.

ORESTES. Then Agamemnon was right. You have panicked. You are frightened.

AEGISTHUS. Frightened? Yes, you could say that. I have just seen a hundred faces silently tell me what Agamemnon's resistance could mean.

SOLDIER. And I can tell you in words. No one could stop him from making us bow down to him again and set off once more. Yesterday there was no spirit in him, but if he's put on his armor he could make us yield without a blow.

AEGISTHUS. There, Orestes, the reason for my fright.

ORESTES. The armor is only a hollow symbol.

AEGISTHUS. But an effective one. You have already commented on my fear.

ORESTES. It is of what you shall do, not of Agamemnon.

AEGISTHUS. Perhaps, but it shall die with his death or rest unnoticed amid the gratitude of thousands.

ORESTES. It is useless.

CASSANDRA. It was the same at Troy. You can't halt the perpetual motion of such self-assurance.

SOLDIER. Come, let's get this over with. Each second we waste means the rest of the army'll have time to do more thinking. Now they'll accept Agamemnon's body with cheers, but in ten minutes . . . who knows? They've followed him a long time and I don't want to meet a hundred swords when we leave here.

(CLYTEMNESTRA *enters.*)

AEGISTHUS. Ah, here is the party we've been waiting for.

CLYTEMNESTRA. What I've heard is true, then? A sword is in your hand?

AEGISTHUS. Yes, my queen. I have come to give Agamemnon his moment. His short moment.

CLYTEMNESTRA. You can't do this, Aegisthus. You can't.

AEGISTHUS. What? Are you defending him, too, Clytemnestra?

CLYTEMNESTRA. You will mark me forever if you strike, Aegisthus. My name will be used in the whispered wit of slaves. My love for you will be forgotten and only my faithlessness to Agamemnon remembered.

AEGISTHUS. Your life with me will be your defense, Clytemnestra.

ORESTES. How is it we all feel ourselves before a court?

CLYTEMNESTRA. We shall all be judged, Orestes. For this day we will be tried, I know it.

AEGISTHUS. What are you speaking of?

CASSANDRA. For the moment she has forgotten her role as queen and is worrying about her reputation as a wife.

AEGISTHUS. And I was to let Agamemnon make boring speeches to himself. He has penetrated this far merely by changing clothes.

SOLDIER. Come, man, if we are going to kill, let's do it now. If not, let me beg Agamemnon's forgiveness for what I said yesterday.

AEGISTHUS. Oh, we shall kill him, friend. Agamemnon's armor will be lowered with him into a deep and dignified grave.

CLYTEMNESTRA. Aegisthus, I beg you to think of me. Do anything but kill Agamemnon.

AEGISTHUS. I am disappointed in you, Clytemnestra. We should be closer together in such matters. Perhaps if you take part too . . . (*He grasps* CLYTEMNESTRA's *arm.*)

CLYTEMNESTRA. No, I cannot.

ORESTES. Aegisthus, you are risking all for an empty reward. You will turn Argos into a stage for heroics and guilt. How well will that serve the small lives you claim to pity so much?

AEGISTHUS. It will serve them well. For it will be my sacrifice and my fear which will give their prayers content.

ORESTES. It's true. You're no different, Aegisthus. You and Agamemnon are both ready to set a style in suffering.

SOLDIER. All this talk. Do we go through with this or not?

AEGISTHUS. There is no reason for further postponements. Come, let us meet Agamemnon in all his splendor. (*Still holding* CLYTEMNESTRA, *he starts to exit with* SOLDIERS.)

CLYTEMNESTRA. Don't make me watch what you shall do. Don't make me see such things.

AEGISTHUS. Death will be a bond between us, Queen. (*To* ORESTES.) And Orestes, remain where you are. From now until you are safely placed in your boat I want to be aware of your presence.

CLYTEMNESTRA. You will make me a whore with this murder, Aegisthus.

AEGISTHUS. No, Clytemnestra, simply a widow.

(*They exit.*)

CASSANDRA. It seems you're taking a greater interest in family affairs, Orestes.

ORESTES. Does it, Cassandra? You can guess why, can't you?

CASSANDRA. Worried that what you consider trivial may drown you?

ORESTES. You put it well, but a little too calmly. I, more than Agamemnon, am threatened by our poet's sword.

CASSANDRA. Aegisthus has not struck yet. There is still time.

ORESTES (*bitterly*). It will not be stopped, Cassandra. You have known that from the beginning.

CASSANDRA. Ah, now you, too, are angry with me. But did I not warn you, Orestes? You should have run from Agamemnon as soon as he cried for his sword belt. But you were too curious.

ORESTES. It is well I didn't. I want it to be over with quickly. I want to see if I pass or fail his test.

CASSANDRA. His test? Oh, Orestes, I'm beginning to worry about you.

(ELECTRA *enters running past* GUARD. PENELOPE *tries to follow, but is restrained by the* GUARD.)

GUARD. Here, no one is allowed to enter.

ELECTRA. Orestes, I am so frightened. My father, what is happening to him?

PENELOPE (*to* GUARD). Let me by. I must be with the princess.

ORESTES. Neither of you should be here.

ELECTRA. I will not go. My father. Oh, Orestes, I am trembling so. Hold me.

CASSANDRA. She should stay, Orestes, if you really want a valid proof.

ORESTES (*looks at* CASSANDRA *and then down at* ELECTRA). Will you hear me, Electra? Will you understand my complexities before your father's simple truth?

PENELOPE. Don't listen to him, Electra. He will not help me. Realize what he is!

ELECTRA (*to* ORESTES). Tell me where our father is; tell me no one will harm him.

PENELOPE (*pushing against* GUARD). Let me pass, you fool. Let me pass before there is more than one death in Argos today. (*She draws a dagger.*)

GUARD (*disarming* PENELOPE). You witch! We'll take that. Now away with you. (*He drags* PENELOPE *out of sight.*)

CASSANDRA. You must speak quickly, Orestes. Any second now it may be too late.

ELECTRA. Too late? Oh, Orestes.

ORESTES. What is there now to say?

CASSANDRA. She is a child; plead with her.

ELECTRA (*less hysterical and more demanding*). I don't know what either of you mean. I want to see my father. I want to know he's unharmed.

ORESTES. Electra, listen to me. Your father never existed. You have put him together yourself.

CASSANDRA. Oh, much too abstract, Orestes. You will never succeed this way.

ORESTES. Do you know, Cassandra? Do you know what the simple answer is? Tell it quickly then.

(AGAMEMNON'*s cries are heard offstage followed by* CLYTEM- NESTRA'*s screams.*)

CASSANDRA. It is now too late.

ELECTRA (*screaming*). That was my father! He is being killed. Murdered! I know it.

ORESTES (*weakly*). Death is an ending, Electra.

ELECTRA. Help him, Orestes! Please help him.

(CLYTEMNESTRA *runs onstage.*)

CLYTEMNESTRA. Neither would stop. I tried, but Aegisthus' sword cut past me.

ELECTRA (*looking at her mother in horror*). My father — you have killed him.

(*There is another cry.* AGAMEMNON *screams* ORESTES' *name.*)

Orestes, go to him. Oh, some god help him!

ORESTES. I am no god, Electra.

CLYTEMNESTRA. Oh, I tried, but they both laughed. Agamemnon kissed me as he would a child. I knew this would come. I knew Agamemnon would have this moment. Aegisthus, oh, Aegisthus, why did you force me to use the sword, too? Oh, gods, I have murdered.

ELECTRA. Listen to her, Orestes.

(*There is another weaker cry.*)

ORESTES. Is it possible that a legend can bleed?

(AEGISTHUS *enters. He acts dazed and his sword hangs limply in his hand. He sees* CLYTEMNESTRA *and walks to her.*)

AEGISTHUS. No tears, Queen. Sores have been cut from us. Nothing but useless growths have been cut away.

CLYTEMNESTRA. I have murdered. There is blood on me.

AEGISTHUS. The gods will take our fear. It is over. Argos will know no more violence. (*He throws the sword in the center of the stage.*)

ELECTRA. Pick it up, Orestes. Take it and kill them both.

AEGISTHUS. The child is upset. (*To one of the* SOLDIERS.) Take her to her room.

ELECTRA. My brother, don't stand there. Strike now. They are all dazed.

(SOLDIER *takes hold of* ELECTRA.)

AEGISTHUS. And let us escort the prince to his boat. I want him to leave today.

ELECTRA. You cannot leave. Agamemnon is dead. Pick up the sword, Orestes. Take it, take it.

ORESTES. No! Let it rest. Let it rot and crumble where it is.

ELECTRA (*now offstage*). You will come back to pick it up, Orestes. You will come back.

CASSANDRA. How loudly the child screams!

CURTAIN

SCENE 2

The scene is on a hillside near Athens six months after AGAMEMNON'S *murder.* ORESTES, *pensive and weary-looking, is seated on the ground.* PYLADES, *wearing an expression of anger and impatience, speaks now with more bitterness than before.*

PYLADES. What a foul day! But, I must say, one perfectly suited to the occasion. (*Looks at* ORESTES, *who still sits dejectedly*.) And you don't look any too joyous either. Come, a bridegroom is supposed to tremble with excitement, pant with lust, and have a cretin's smile spread across his face.

ORESTES. I'm content, Pylades, and will remain so in spite of your mockery.

PYLADES. Mockery? Would I have the poor taste to mock an event as sacred as your marriage? Would I make sport of an alliance which, by coupling a fisherman's daughter with a prince, is a model of such true love that thirty eulogies praising your democratic glands have been read in the streets of Athens already? And, above all, would I say anything which might spoil such a moment for my oldest and best friend?

ORESTES. Please, Pylades, I'm not amused.

PYLADES. I no longer wish to amuse you. I want you to think of what you're doing!

ORESTES. I have thought of it, Pylades. My future wife is kind, cooks

well, keeps an immaculate house, and comes close to worshiping
me. Why should I wish anything more?

PYLADES. The honored head of the household!

ORESTES. Besides, Pylades, we are both tired of wandering from boat
to boat, city to city, island to island.

PYLADES. I agree there. But we had to keep moving on.

ORESTES. You know why that was! I kept hoping to find a town,
a village — any place where I'm not known as Orestes of the Unavenged Father.

PYLADES. And how will marriage affect this attitude toward you?

ORESTES. Perhaps when others see me as Orestes the simple husband
and doting father, sleeping in his orchard, playing with his fat,
plain-looking children — perhaps they'll stop thinking of me as one
meant for thundering deeds. Perhaps they'll see me as a man like
any other, a man with all the fears and burdens that are common
to them.

PYLADES. But you're not that type at all. An idiot could see through
your sham.

ORESTES. I will make myself this man, Pylades. I have to if I want to
know any peace at all.

PYLADES. And what of my peace?

ORESTES. You still have your travels and your pleasures.

PYLADES. And my reputation!

ORESTES (*completely stunned*). Pylades, are you serious?

PYLADES. Oh, I know you never think me so. I am the clown, the
entertainer of princes.

ORESTES. I don't understand you.

PYLADES. What I am saying is that I have no wish to be left out in
this world with your mark upon me. Pylades and Orestes, Orestes
and Pylades — these names hang together, bound by your crime.

ORESTES. My crime? And what is that, Pylades?

PYLADES. You know very well what that is. I am no moral person,
but would I stand by and see my father murdered?

ORESTES. So you judge me, too?

PYLADES. In the last months I have grown up, Orestes. I see things
as they are. The very day we left Argos I sensed we were wrong,
but I felt I had no right, being the sort of person I was, to preach
ethics to you. I thought once you were through with your fling
at nightly debauch you would come to your senses and realize
yourself what you had to do.

ORESTES. Don't you know I'm not ashamed of what I did?

PYLADES. Oh, come, let's not play with each other any more. The
fun is over, the trip has come to an end. Your father was mur-

dered and you accepted drinking money from his assassin. It's as simple as that.

ORESTES. As simple as that! How poorly you have understood things, Pylades. You have grown into a fine and proper man of affairs.

PYLADES. I can understand a coward, for I've been one myself.

ORESTES. Be silent! You are speaking to your prince, Pylades.

PYLADES. It's a bit late to claim such privileges.

ORESTES. Enough of this. I don't care what you think of me. I am to be married today — married and forgotten at the same time.

PYLADES. But I am not. I remain nothing but the friend of Orestes.

ORESTES. And that is now a punishment?

PYLADES. It is worse. A punishment is a private thing, begotten by one's own acts. I have mine because of yours.

ORESTES. If you feel that way, Pylades, we have nothing further to say.

PYLADES. No, I suppose we don't. I shall leave, go to a tavern and drink a private toast to your future. Then Pylades, friend of Orestes, shall sail away to spend the rest of his days in undeserved exile. Sleep well in your bed tonight, Prince. Don't let bad dreams disturb your nuptial amusements.

(PYLADES *exits.*)

ORESTES (*stands silent for several seconds*). And so Pylades is now a moral man. (*He wraps his cloak tighter around him.*) The wind moves through my body as though it were fleshless. (*It grows darker and he walks to front of stage.*) Look at the water. The waves are dancing like a thousand drunken Corybants. Oh, why this natural melodrama on my wedding day? Why couldn't we have an insipid drizzle or an unobtrusive flurry of snow? But no, for Orestes there must be the beginnings of a tempest.

(*Enter* PRAXITHIA.)

PRAXITHIA. Orestes?

ORESTES. What? Praxithia? You startled me. You must think I'm mad talking to myself this way.

PRAXITHIA. My father says he does the same when fishing alone in his boat.

ORESTES. But what are you doing here? Shouldn't the bride be at home, fussing with her family over the final wedding preparations?

PRAXITHIA. The bride? Oh, Orestes, I wanted to be that to you. From the moment I saw you land on our beach, a stranger who walked a distance away from those with him, I wanted to be your bride.

ORESTES. And so you shall, Praxithia, unless something's changed you.

PRAXITHIA. Why could we not be left alone? Why must others interfere in something so simple as our love for each other?

ORESTES. What has happened? What have you been told?

PRAXITHIA. That I am forbidden to marry you.

ORESTES. And who said this? Your father?

PRAXITHIA (*nods*). But it was not his fault. He wanted the marriage almost as much as I. He was proud to give me to you.

ORESTES. Well, then?

PRAXITHIA. We went this morning to the temple to ask the priests' blessings of the marriage. It is the custom in Athens, and my father is a good citizen who always follows the laws and traditions of the city.

ORESTES. And the priests refused to give this blessing?

PRAXITHIA. Worse than that, Orestes. They forbade the marriage entirely. They said your father's murder was unavenged and that you, as his son, shared the murderer's guilt.

ORESTES. And you believed this?

PRAXITHIA. But what do I know of such things? I pleaded with them; told them of your kindness to me and how gentle you are. But they were unmoved.

ORESTES. And your father, did he argue for me, too?

PRAXITHIA. I have never seen him in such a rage. Usually he is so humble when in the presence of priests.

ORESTES. And it all was to no purpose?

PRAXITHIA. He made the priests consult the oracle, and when they did, the pronouncement was: "The Orestes known to the gods is not yet born." The priests took this as approval of their opinion, and my father could only accept these words.

ORESTES. A divine oracle! The priests of Argos and Athens should meet to iron out theological differences.

PRAXITHIA. Orestes, what shall we do? We must think of something quickly before my father finds me.

ORESTES. Finds you? Then you ran away?

PRAXITHIA. When I realized he wasn't strong enough to stand against the priests I ran to look for you. But he will follow because he's frightened — frightened for me.

ORESTES. Oh, Praxithia, I loved you so much.

PRAXITHIA. Let us hurry away. We can take your boat and be far out to sea before they realize we have left together.

ORESTES. You would go away with me? Knowing the judgment of your priests and the wishes of your good father, you would go with me?

PRAXITHIA. I've spent my life in a small world, Orestes. The vastness of the sea frightens me and the strangeness of foreign cities makes me tremble. But I would sail with you, for your love wipes away the curse that Athens will put upon me. I will fear nothing if it is Orestes I follow.

ORESTES. Praxithia . . . But, no, it cannot be. I will not spoil your life.

PRAXITHIA. It is for my life that I'm asking you to take me with you away from this unfeeling city.

ORESTES. No, Praxithia. You don't understand how it would be. We could never rest, there would always be some remark, some disaster that would tear apart the life we tried to build for each other. You would suffer, I know that, and seeing you so would be yet one more pain for me.

PRAXITHIA. But you love me, do you not, Orestes?

ORESTES. Yes, but our love is so fragile and the gross hammers of the world would shatter it. You would have nothing but its bitter pieces to console you after all you renounced for it.

PRAXITHIA. You will not take me? You will leave, go away, and not take me?

ORESTES. There is no place left to take you, Praxithia. It was you who were to lead me, and now there is no place to be led to.

PRAXITHIA. I will not leave you, Orestes. No, I will not.

ORESTES. You must. Perhaps the oracle spoke correctly. Perhaps the true Orestes, the divine Orestes, is not yet born. And when he is, I doubt you'd love him.

PRAXITHIA. I would. I . . .

ORESTES. No, go back to your home and wait for someone who is not mixed in Olympian battles. Let him be the father of your sons — I cannot be.

PRAXITHIA. I don't know how to answer you, for I understand so little of this. But I will wait. I will always wait.

ORESTES. That is a lovely robe you wear, Praxithia.

PRAXITHIA. It was to be my marriage robe. I thought you might find it too plain. It has not gold or silk in it.

ORESTES. It is beautiful, Praxithia. It is very beautiful.

(*Exit* PRAXITHIA. ORESTES *sits and covers his eyes with his hands. After a short pause* CASSANDRA *enters.*)

CASSANDRA. Orestes? Orestes, is that you?

ORESTES (*at first not recognizing her*). Yes, what is it? I . . . Cassandra?

CASSANDRA. I met Pylades by the harbor. He told me where you were but refused to take me here. Have you two had an argument?

ORESTES. Pylades has aged faster than I it seems. We no longer feel comfortable in each other's presence. But you, Cassandra, what are you doing here in Athens?

CASSANDRA. Aegisthus gave me a choice between hanging and exile. I am an old woman, but I will enoy some aspects of living, so I took the latter. (*Extracting a purse.*) He also asked me to give this to you. It's to cover your expenses for another six months.

ORESTES. Aegisthus knew I was in Athens?

CASSANDRA. Oh, he watches your movements very carefully. I might say you're his favorite subject.

ORESTES. You can keep the purse. I no longer need his money.

CASSANDRA. Are you sure? Pylades told me you were about to take on the responsibilities of a husband and future father.

ORESTES. I was.

CASSANDRA. Past tense?

ORESTES. My wedding plans have just been canceled.

CASSANDRA. Did you think better of the idea?

ORESTES. No, her father did. Apparently the priests he consulted didn't find me a suitable Athenian husband.

CASSANDRA. I'm very sorry. Did you love this girl, Orestes?

ORESTES. Yes, I loved her — both for herself and what she offered me. I was to have children, I was to tell them stories with happy endings, and to make love with gentleness. I wanted to stay within our small garden and watch conception, birth, decay, and death, and to give myself to the same process.

CASSANDRA. You have changed, Orestes.

ORESTES. Perhaps I now wear the birthmarks of a hero. But enough of me and my troubles. Tell me about Argos, Cassandra.

CASSANDRA. There is little to tell. Aegisthus has set about hanging those whom he calls heretics. The people are discontent as all people are. Your father's name is scribbled on walls, sometimes with yours beneath it, as a sign of protest.

ORESTES. Then Aegisthus and his gods have not brought anything better to the city? My father's murder did not even serve that purpose?

CASSANDRA. Did you think it would?

ORESTES. But what of Electra? How is she?

CASSANDRA. As you said, Orestes, you have troubles enough.

ORESTES. Cassandra, I asked you to tell me of my sister. Has she been . . . ?

CASSANDRA. No, Aegisthus has not been her executioner, he has been her matchmaker.

ORESTES. What does that mean?

CASSANDRA. Your sister is to be married. To a priest, I believe.

ORESTES. To a priest? To one of those ancient disciples of my uncle? How easy it will be to dispose of her in that role. The wife of a priest makes an easier victim than a princess and daughter of Agamemnon. Aegisthus has learned his politics well.

CASSANDRA. Electra wanted this marriage, Orestes.

ORESTES (*a wild laugh*). Ha! What choice did she have? I'm quite sure no one else would have her. Agamemnon's children aren't excellent matrimonial bargains.

CASSANDRA. She has done this to punish herself in her father's name. She feels she is serving him by this act.

ORESTES. Yes, but she also thinks it won't last long. She waits for me to swoop down upon Argos and rescue her.

CASSANDRA. You have always known that, Orestes.

ORESTES. Everywhere I run, I am blocked, and, bit by bit, I come closer to Argos. Is there nothing else for Prince Orestes to wear but the ragged dress of yet another hero?

CASSANDRA. You see yourself as the liberator of Argos?

ORESTES. Why not? The world sees me thus. Find me one man who'll say I acted wrongly should I return to Argos and, in the name of my father's humanity, put an end to Aegisthus. Find me one voice who'll object to my killing my father's murderer and sister's pander. Find me one breast that'll be shocked by my slaughtering on principle.

CASSANDRA. If I could, I would find one as miserable as yourself.

ORESTES. The world demands that we inherit the pretensions of our fathers, that we go on killing in the name of ancient illusions about ourselves, that we assume the right to punish, order, and invent philosophies to make our worst moments seem inspired. Who am I to contradict all this any longer? I will return to Argos. I belong no other place.

CASSANDRA. So your moment has come at last, Orestes.

ORESTES. Is there another solution, Cassandra? Is there a way to deny Aegisthus' gods and my father's dangerous love of man? Is there a way to let a foolish sister suffer her mistake, without feeling the world is right in branding you a leper?

CASSANDRA (*wearily*). I don't know. I have never found it.

ORESTES. Nor have I, and we have both looked harder than most. You know I have no choice, don't you, Cassandra?

CASSANDRA. I am not the one to answer that.

ORESTES. You are a prophet. Tell me that if I don't return I merely postpone by refusal what I must become.

CASSANDRA. I am no longer a prophet but a soothsayer. I now tell people what they want to hear, what is best for them to know.

Doing otherwise has made me an exiled woman in my middle age.

ORESTES. Once more, Cassandra. Once more for Agamemnon's son.

CASSANDRA. I will not prophesy, but if you must have drama, I will play the poet for you.

ORESTES. I am your audience, Cassandra.

CASSANDRA. No, you are to be my player. You must imagine that this familiar place has the excitement of a stage you have never seen.

ORESTES. That is easy enough, but if I am your player, for whom do I perform?

CASSANDRA. Let us suppose that the sea is our audience, Orestes. Let us change each wave, each cap of white into a face — a spectator who we hope has some interest in the problems we act before him. And as the poet, I must understand those faces and see that they are masks for desires which, if I am to be successful, I must fulfill.

ORESTES. Cassandra, a popular poet?

CASSANDRA. In this instance, yes. Their wishes will mould my answer to your question. I will not be responsible.

ORESTES. Is it so clear then what they want?

CASSANDRA. Not at all. The business of a poet is a difficult one. We must look more carefully and try to judge. Hmm. Some, I believe, have very moral crests. They consider poor Clytemnestra's conduct inexcusable and would have Orestes return, if for no other reason than to curse in public the backstairs activities of his mother.

ORESTES. Cassandra, not . . .

CASSANDRA. Don't interrupt, Orestes. There's only a handful in this group, anyway. A somewhat larger collection, along the horizon there, in the cheaper seats, think that progress must go on, even at the expense of individual misgivings. They're quite scientific and see themselves as Agamemnon's followers.

ORESTES. I am glad I can't see that far.

CASSANDRA. And now, alas, we come to the majority. They are the ones who have been struck by the fact of murder and are this very minute preparing precepts that justify their wish to see you balance this fact with another. For them, dramatic justice is a non-too-complex equation which can be simply solved by death. They speak with Electra's voice.

ORESTES. And now as the poet you must choose, Cassandra.

CASSANDRA. But since we are engaged in popular drama, the majority dictates the plot. To please all, I must write of your return, your use of the sword upon Aegisthus, and, since the public never objects to a bonus slaughter, I'll add Clytemnestra as one of your victims.

ORESTES. So I am to play this role and no other. Congratulations, King Agamemnon! We have heard the future's judgment.

CASSANDRA. No, Orestes, we have obeyed the inclinations of the present. And look, see how the waves vanish and are replaced by others. It will be the same with the faces watching us, and, perhaps someday, through a chance collocation of atoms, we will have an audience other than the one we play for now. It might be that this new gathering will demand something better for your consent than edgeworn ideals and dramatic necessity. Even better, perhaps there will be a majority who would see you return to Argos with feelings other than tragic, but this, of course, would be unfortunate for the poet since such sentiment makes for bad drama.

ORESTES. You dream, Cassandra. There will never be such an audience in this world. Not as long as one person suffers in it. The sea will never change. The waves give birth to their own kind and are rooted in one order. The sea will always roar with Electra's cry; the waters will always rush toward Agamemnon's vengeance. It will cleanse or wash away the earth entirely, but it will never change.

CASSANDRA. Then you'll return?

ORESTES. I can resist these forces no longer. I will go back, murder, and say it's for a better world, for this must be said to prevent insanity. And when I'm standing, addressing the crowds of Argos, telling them what great things are to come because of my act, I will know it is nothing but weakness that brought me there in front of them. I will speak of the golden days to come and boast of my killing to achieve them; but, King Agamemnon, I will do so under protest. I will do so knowing I was not great enough to create something better.

CASSANDRA. Shall I wish you well, Orestes?

ORESTES. Wish? We both know how little wishes matter, Cassandra. You hoped for quiet years, and I for no more than a gentle wife. And what we have are our separate exiles. Good-by, Cassandra. Orestes has no more wishes and needs no more prophecies.

(ORESTES *exits.*)

CASSANDRA. Farewell, Orestes. Prince . . . of . . . Argos. (*Turning toward audience.*) The waters are agitating for grand tragedy, and I, too old for such things now, had best oblige them by leaving our stage emptied, and ready for the popular and typical hero to come.

CURTAIN

❖ ❖ ❖

STUDY AIDS

Act 1, Scene 1

1. What traditional function does the governess, Penelope, serve in this scene? Does she possess a distinctive personality?

2. What impression do you have of Electra in the opening scene?

3. What does Penelope imply about conditions in Argos during Agamemnon's absence?

4. What charges does Penelope make against Orestes? How does Orestes answer them? What sort of an Orestes appears to be taking shape in *The Prodigal*, even at this early point in the play? What sort of an Electra?

5. Aegisthus' manner, we are told, is "a mixture of effeminacy and strength." The priests who attend him are effeminate. What do you think is Richardson's purpose in so describing them?

6. What does the discussion concerning prayer disclose concerning the priests? What seems to be Aegisthus' attitude toward worship?

7. "I ask nothing of the gods, if there are such things, but to be left alone," declares Orestes. In addition to revealing his skepticism concerning the existence of gods, what else does the statement imply about Orestes?

8. With a show of scorn, Aegisthus says that one should expect nothing better from Orestes than "a very shallow performance." "If only no one would," replies the youth. What is the significance of the remark as it helps us to understand this Orestes? And this assertion: "I wish my freedom to be indolent, unobtrusive, and uninvolved"?

9. What was Aegisthus' method of achieving reform in Argos? How would you evaluate it?

10. Orestes clearly wishes to avoid any involvement in a battle between Aegisthus and Agamemnon over Argos, which he dismisses as "a worthless city." What are your feelings toward him at this point?

11. What is the nature of the relationship between Orestes and his mother?

12. What impression do you have of Clytemnestra after reading her scene with Aegisthus?

13. Describe the feelings of Aegisthus, Clytemnestra, Electra, and Orestes as they await the return of Agamemnon.

Act I, Scene 2

1. In describing Agamemnon, Richardson says he is not at all "the idealistic buffoon" Orestes has described. How might you account for the discrepancy? What do you make of the man as you study his dialogue with Cassandra? What kind of a person is she?

2. Why does Orestes find the "affectionate scene" of reunion with Agamemnon distasteful?

3. How does the scene between Agamemnon and Clytemnestra contribute to our understanding of these two? What feelings are engendered toward them? Do you feel any degree of pity or sympathy for Clytemnestra? For Agamemnon? Orestes declared in the closing line of the first scene that we must now undergo the painful experience of seeing a legend turn into a man. How has this experience been realized in the scene between Agamemnon and the members of his family?

4. How would you comment upon the speeches of the first and the second soldiers? How do their sentiments concerning the soldier's life fit into the context of this play? Do you think their sentiments are characteristic of men who renounce war?

5. Summarize what Aegisthus terms the "difference of opinion" between himself and Agamemnon concerning war and the nature of man. Why does Aegisthus feel Agamemnon has failed? What is Agamemnon's defense? The scene between Aegisthus and Agamemnon amounts to a kind of debate; is there a winner? With whom do your sympathies lie? Explain.

6. What is the significance of Cassandra's closing statements?

Act II, Scene 1

1. What is the tone of the dialogue between Pylades and Cassandra? Certainly it is quite in contrast to anything you would discover in the classic drama; how do you explain such an exchange in this play?

2. How does Orestes justify his attitude toward his father and Aegisthus?

3. What characteristics does Orestes possess which mark him as an anti-hero?

4. Does Cassandra appear to have a rather good understanding of human nature? Do you agree with her assertion that there is often a wide discrepancy between what a man says and what he does?

5. What purpose is served by the confrontation between Orestes and Agamemnon? Does the scene heighten your awareness of the essential differences between the two men?

6. Why does Clytemnestra oppose the murder of Agamemnon?

7. Referring to the sword Aegisthus has cast aside, Electra cries

to her brother, "You will come back to pick it up, Orestes. You will come back." Do you think she is right? Explain.

Act II, Scene 2

1. Why does Pylades turn against Orestes? What charge does he make?

2. Why does Orestes declare that he and Praxithia could never know happiness together?

3. Cassandra tells Orestes he has changed. Has he? In what way?

4. What does Cassandra tell Orestes about Aegisthus' rule in Argos? Is there a moral implied concerning despots and martyrs?

5. What does Orestes say about the demands the world makes of those who have inherited "the pretensions of our fathers"? Why does Orestes decide to return to Argos?

6. Summarize the sardonic conclusions at which Cassandra and Orestes arrive. What are the larger implications of these concerning human nature, the creed of vengeance, the concept of justice, and the role of those who would resist conforming to outworn ideals?

7. Why is the play called *The Prodigal*?

TOPICS FOR DISCUSSION

1. Orestes as an embodiment of the anti-hero. The nature of his appeal to modern audiences and the degree to which they might achieve empathy with him.

2. The dilemma of Orestes: the choice between loyalty to father and freedom for self. The moral issue involved in resolving the problem.

3. The implications of the denouement. An examination of the pressures leading to conformity and the degree to which public opinion dictates private conduct.

4. *The Prodigal* as a study in conflict. An analysis of the differences that separate Aegisthus and Agamemnon and Orestes from both.

5. *The Prodigal* as an exercise in the use of myth to convey a modern view. The playwright's success in infusing an old myth with a new view.

6. The element of characterization in the play: Richardson's concept of Clytemnestra, Cassandra, Electra, and Pylades.

7. The quality of writing in *The Prodigal*: fluency, wit, and style. It has been suggested that Richardson's writing is occasionally reminiscent of Giraudoux; do you agree?

PART THREE

Comment

The *Oresteia* of Aeschylus

Harry L. Levy

THE UNENDING FASCINATION of Greek drama, both in its original form and in modern adaptations, is constantly confirmed here in the United States and abroad by stage presentations. As countless lectures, symposia, and articles attest, the ancient Greek drama off-stage serves as a plentiful source of serious discourse for scholars and thinkers of our own time. The reason is obvious: the great Greek dramaturgists discerned and presented in striking form some of the most crucial problems with which thoughtful human beings of all ages and all cultures must perforce concern themselves. And so it is with the *Oresteia*, the great trilogy of Aeschylus: the *Agamemnon*, the *Libation-Bearers*, and the *Eumenides*.

The *Oresteia* commences with the return of Agamemnon from Troy and his slaughter by his queen and her paramour, tells us in the *Libation-Bearers* of the vengeance taken by Agamemnon's son Orestes, now grown to manhood, and ends with Orestes' persecution by the Furies of his mother, and his final release from the hounding of these monsters, who, changed to Eumenides, "The Kindly Ones," become a pillar of the Athenian polity. That, in brief, is the story: but what is the meaning of it as Aeschylus presents it? Richmond Lattimore, a superb translator and interpreter of Greek drama, thinks that he finds the answer, at least so far as the first two plays are concerned, in the dynamic contradiction between hate and love — he speaks of hate-in-love in the *Agamemnon*, and love-in-hate in the *Libation-Bearers*. For a full explication of his provocative theory, I refer you to his own writings.

But I should like to suggest to you that the problem which is central to the *Oresteia* is, if not altogether different from love and hate, at least more general: the problem of good and evil. The Greek dramatists boldly confront the fact that evil exists: they hold that it springs, sometimes from the machinations of the gods, sometimes from the faults of men. When evil comes into being, and harms or

From *Drama Survey*, Vol. 4, No. 2, Summer 1965. Reprinted by permission of *Drama Survey* and the author.

threatens to harm the lives of men, how are they to meet it? Shall they return evil for evil? This is the ancient law of the Near East, an eye for an eye and a tooth for a tooth, the *lex talionis*, the law of retaliation. Our trilogy is a study of the actual operation of this law in the first two plays, and of its partial setting-aside in the third.

The first play, the *Agamemnon*, centers upon a double retaliation: a single act of violence intended by each of its two perpetrators to avenge a different wrong. Clytemnestra, Queen of Argos, and her lover Aegisthus, as we have seen, murder Agamemnon, returning victorious from the Trojan war. The murderer-in-chief is not the man Aegisthus, but the woman Clytemnestra. Aeschylus makes much of this point, and it bears upon the problem of the relative position of man and woman in the structure of the Greek family, a topic to which we shall return.

Let us dispose at once of the minor retaliator, Aegisthus. He was avenging the horrible murder of his own brothers by Agamemnon's father, Atreus: one explosion in what we may call in modern terms a chain-reaction of evil, into the details of which it would be beside our point to go.

But what of Clytemnestra? What does she avenge by the killing of Agamemnon? It is the ritual slaughter of her and Agamemnon's daughter Iphigenia, whom Agamemnon had killed at Aulis as a sacrifice to angered divinities. The sacrifice was performed in order that the Greek fleet might have safe passage to Troy. Now let us break into the chain at this point and consider this single link. Had Agamemnon not killed Iphigenia, he would not have been slain in turn by Clytemnestra. Then the specific chain-reaction of which we are speaking would not have occurred. Could Agamemnon have avoided the killing of his daughter, when the prophet had told him that this was the only way to secure the safe-conduct of the fleet to Troy? Yes, he could: but it would have meant renouncing the *lex talionis* at this point; he would have had to forego the revenge which he felt he and the other Greek princes were in duty bound to exact from Paris, the seducer of Helen.

Here, then, we have in this chain of events what seems to me the first clear instance of the decision of human will in the face of evil. That Paris' act had been evil, a breaking of the laws of gods and men, those primary laws governing the sanctity of the family and of the host-guest relationship, none could deny. That Paris' crime deserved punishment none could gainsay. But who was to punish him? The wronged one, says old Near-East tradition, the wronged one, if he is still alive; the wronged one, supported if he is alive, and replaced if he is not, by his kinsmen. Had it been simply a matter of exacting penalty for an abominable crime, who, according to the morality of that early time, would have raised an objection? But here the gods intervene: to accomplish his mission of retaliation, Agamemnon must sacrifice one of his own blood, his beloved daughter, who had often joined with her clear maiden voice in his sacrifices to the gods. Agamemnon's anguish at the need for the choice is narrated by the Chorus. But anguished or not, he made his choice between his duty as a father and his duty as a ruler and warrior; he killed his daughter.

The girl is killed; the fleet sails; Agamemnon's host is victorious over the Trojans, and our heroic general returns in glory, to boast to the people of Mycenae that he has avenged the wrong done to Menelaus. In the vainglorious speech, there is no word of pity for the death of his innocent daughter; this is forgotten. So far is he from feeling any pity for one who must die so that his grand plans may advance, that he speaks with self-righteous assurance of using surgery to amputate any offending element in the state, all unconscious — a nice instance of dramatic irony — that the first victim of the knife is to be himself.

Well then, evil for evil: Paris has done wrong, Troy has been destroyed, Iphigenia has been cut down, to use Catullus' phrase, like a flower at the edge of the meadow, when it has been touched by the passing plowshare. Evil for evil, and there an end. But no: there is the seed of new evil here, for Clytemnestra, a woman with a man's will, does not accept Agamemnon's choice. He has killed her daughter; he must die in his turn. He dies, and Clytemnestra exults: "This is Agamemnon, my husband: he is dead; his death is the work of my own right hand, the work of a righteous craftsman. And that is that!" To the avenger, that is always that; the wrong is requited, the game is over. Nowhere does Clytemnestra show any wavering, any sense of a need for choice between slaying her king and husband, or leaving unavenged the evil of her daughter's death. Her womanliness comes out only in the fervor of her desire — vain hope — to have peace, now at last, to have an end of bloodshed. So ends the *Agamemnon,* the first great act of the trilogy: but just before the close, the Chorus foreshadow the next act. They speak of their longing for the return of Orestes, Agamemnon's young son, who has been sent away to stay with a prince in mainland Greece. Let him come back, they pray, to avenge his father's death. Upon whom? Upon the pair of murderers, they say. What of the fact that one of them is his mother? They take no note of that directly.

The middle play of the trilogy, the *Libation-Bearers,* is so called because its first half takes place at the tomb of Agamemnon, this at a time when, alarmed by a dream, Clytemnestra has sent her daughter Electra to pour libations on the tomb. These are drink-offerings intended to propitiate the spirit of Clytemnestra's slain husband, who is of course Electra's beloved father. But Orestes, grown now and returning to his native land in disguise, has already left an offering on the tomb. Now Orestes has come back to seek revenge: but there is this difference, that he comes at the behest of Zeus' radiant son, the god of light and healing, Apollo. Apollo has done more than urge Orestes to avenge his father's death; he has threatened him with the unseen but dreadful wrath of the father, which if unappeased by exacted vengeance will end by estranging the son from gods and men. This is the difference in the motivation: and there is a corresponding difference in the attitude displayed, not only by Orestes but by his sister Electra. Near the beginning of the play, Electra, for all her grief and hatred, has misgivings about calling down immediate and unqualified retributory death upon the head of her mother and Aegisthus. Should she pray that they be judged, or that they be punished out of hand? And when the Chorus of attendant women, representing her elders and public opinion generally, tells her simply to pray that someone come to kill them for the life they took, she asks whether she may pray thus without transgressing the reverence due the gods. Yes, says the Chorus, invoking the law of retaliation; and she accepts their judgment; but the important thing is, I suggest, not that she accepts the *lex talionis* in the end, but that she questions it in the beginning — a questioning that brings a new element into the story of the accursed house of Pelops. Agamemnon, to be sure, had hesitated before killing Iphigenia, but his was no ambivalence about inflicting vengeance on the guilty; it was rather reluctance to make a victim of the innocent.

In the *Agamemnon*, we are with Clytemnestra before, during, and after her awful homicide; yet, as we have said, never do we hear of a word of doubt, or of the slightest countervailing impulse. Now, in this new generation, we find Electra pausing to reflect, to wonder if the gods are on the side of blood vengeance. And for all his brave words about Apollo's command and Apollo's support, Orestes too, a member of Electra's generation, pauses to reflect before he brushes aside his mother's piteous plea to be spared. Again, the voice of public morals, here uttered by his comrade Pylades, is needed to harden Orestes' heart.

But does the son rejoice, as Agamemnon had rejoiced at Troy's downfall, and Clytemnestra at Agamemnon's? No — for all that he feels certain that her punishment was just, he sorrows for it. "I grieve for what I have done, and for the suffering, and for our entire race, I who bear the unenviable stains of this victory!"

So now—a victory in a vendetta can stain the victor, we learn! And both Chorus and Orestes feel that this is not the end; that there is trouble yet to come. Nor is it slow in coming. In a clear portrayal of the mind-shattering onset of unbearable feelings of guilt, Orestes speaks of defending himself before his friends while yet—and here I translate literally—"I am in possession of my senses," for he feels his senses slipping even before the dread phantasms of his mother's Furies, visible to him and to no one else on the stage, appear in their gory horror.

I referred before to the question of the new generation represented by Electra and Orestes: let me revert to the matter of generations for a moment, for, like the question of sex-roles in society, it is to have an important place in the last play of the trilogy. There are two lines in the *Libation-Bearers,* almost inconsequential in themselves, which none the less typify the relationship in Greece between the older generation and the younger: in ancient Greece, and, we may add on the basis of my wife's study of a village in present-day Boeotia, in contemporary Greece as well. It is on the whole a non-competing relationship, a relationship as if of heavenly bodies moving within sight of each other, but with different orbital radii; to abandon the metaphor, there is communication, mutual awareness, some conflict but little or no rivalry, and usually a reciprocal respect, each party remaining conscious of the rights and values of the other, whether or not he approves of them. So, at one point, Electra says to the Chorus of older women: "Teach me, the inexperienced one, leading me out of my ignorance!", and not fifty lines later, the same Chorus says to Electra: "Let me, old though I am, learn from a younger woman." Now when one realizes the importance that the giving and receipt of knowledge—teaching and learning—have always had among the Greeks, the significance of this interchange becomes more weighty.

The last play opens with a scene before the temple of Apollo in Delphi, to which temple Orestes, hounded by the Furies, has come for refuge. Here the symbolism of the conflict between Apollo, who is Orestes' protector, and the Furies, who are his would-be destroyers, requires some comment. Apollo, son of the sky-god Zeus, represents light, the light of the sun, of the upper air where his father reigns; here at Delphi above all is the center of Apollo's worship as the destroyer of the symbol of darkness, of the mighty snake Python.

Apollo is truly his father's son, the spokesman of the new regime,

which, having defeated Kronos and the earth-born Titans, wishes now
to rule with reason and with justice, with the proviso that justice
would be defined by the victor. Apollo speaks for those who admire
and are admired by the builders of roads, those who tame the wilder-
ness. And scarcely has the play begun when Apollo foreshadows the
end by speaking of judges and of words that soothe.

On the other side, the Furies, as they never tire of telling us, are
the daughters of Night; they represent the dark powers below the
earth, and the older generation of gods (please mark this) which has
been overthrown by Zeus and his fellow Olympians. They are
bitterly hostile to the new, bright gods. All their resentment is, as
the play opens, directed against the God of Light, who would protect
against their dark punishments a slayer of his own mother. Matricide,
matricide, they call Orestes again and again: for they are the
champions of what Bachofen was to call the *Mutterrecht*, the right of
the mother in the family; the supremacy of Her from the darkness of
whose womb, as if from the bowels of Mother Earth, the child has
emerged.

To the obligation of the child toward his father they give mere
lip-service; but the concept of obeisance to the mother, the queen of
her offspring, arouses all their emotions. They are primitive, they
belong to the early days of the world. Apollo calls them old, old
women who are at the same time children. They stand for direct
vengeance, with no intermediator between the wrong-doer and his
punisher — to a stage of development, if one thinks in evolutionary
terms, before society has organized to protect its members by group
action.

Here, then, we have the elements of a dualistic conflict: light against
darkness, the sky-father against the earth-mother, or, in terms of other
cultures, of *yang* against *yin*, of Ahura-Mazda against Ahriman. Yet
we know that Greek religion was not dualistic. How, then, is the
conflict to be resolved? This is the cosmic question which looms over
and magnifies, though it is never permitted, please note, to obscure,
the human travail of Orestes.

I told you a moment ago that Apollo foreshadowed the solution
by a reference to judges and to soothing words. I have waited until
now to tell you that he also referred to another divinity; to Pallas
Athena, the goddess of war and of wisdom. It was to her shrine that
Orestes was to travel, to Athens, the city which bears Athena's name.
The solution, then, is to come through the active intervention of a
divinity. Let us look at Athena's qualifications as a solver of the
conflict that we sketched above. How does she fit into a situation in
which a dominant motif is the conflict of mother-right and father-

right? She is peculiarly fitted for this role: for, though female, she is not born of a female: she sprang, the myth tells us, mature and fully armed from the brow of her father Zeus, the dazzling god of the skies. Not for her is the emergence from the darkness of the womb. Yet she is a woman, and the patroness of woman's crafts. Those who know the statue of the Lemnian Athena as Furtwaengler reconstructed it will have a perfect picture of Athena as the serene yet powerful embodiment of the beauty of the Greek intellect in feminine guise. What we have then is the nearest approach to an impartial arbiter in the cosmic dispute: a female divinity sprung solely from a male parent, an exponent of the masculine art of war who is also the patroness of the feminine arts of the household; Our Lady of Battles who is also Our Lady of Wisdom.

Yet it is deeply significant of the relationship between gods and men in the grand Greek tradition that Athena does not attempt to judge the case unaided. She summons a court of human beings, Athenians; they are to sit as judges on the hill of Ares, the *Areopagus*. It is the first supreme court in Western Europe, and Athena's charge to it could stand as a clarion call to every tribunal in the world (I use Lattimore's translation):

> No anarchy, no rule of a single master. Thus
> I advise my citizens to govern and to grace,
> and not to cast fear utterly from your city. What
> man who fears nothing at all is ever righteous? Such
> be your just terrors, and you may deserve and have
> salvation for your citadel, your land's defence,
> such as is nowhere else found among men. . . .
> I establish this tribunal. It shall be untouched
> by money-making, grave but quick to wrath, watchful
> to protect those who sleep, a sentry on the land.
>
> These words I have unreeled are for my citizens,
> advice into the future. All must stand upright
> now, take each man his ballot in his hand, think on
> his oath, and make his judgment.

This charge comes after argument and counter-argument, rebuttal and sur-rebuttal, with the Furies as plaintiffs, and Orestes as defendant, having Apollo as his mighty witness and attorney. The argument is sophistic: Orestes admits the killing of his mother, but pleads Apollo's command, and his obligation to his father. The Furies insist he will be condemned by the Court. "Why," says Orestes, "did you not hound my mother for having killed my father?" The Furies: "The man she killed was not of kindred blood." Orestes: "Am I the blood-relative of my mother?" "Yes," say the Furies, "She nourished you within her body." "No!" interposes Apollo; "The mother is no parent; it is the father who is the parent, while the mother is merely the fosterer of an implanted seed, an alien preserver of an alien spore. And here is proof that there can be a father without a mother: my mighty evidence is the daughter of Olympian Zeus, never nourished in the darkness of the womb!"

The arguments are over. Athena speaks to render her judgment. She presumes, or perhaps divinely foreknows, that the vote of the human judges will be a tie: in other words, that the claims of father-right and of mother-right are so evenly matched that the mind of man, unaided by divinity, could not reach a decision. And thus, before the ballots are counted, she casts the President Justice's deciding votes for Orestes, saying frankly that, save for marriage, she is always for the male, and strongly on her father's side. And now she orders the ballots counted: Orestes calls out to the shining Apollo; the Furies summon the Darkness of Night, their Mother, to be there to watch. The ballots are counted; they are equal for each side; the vote of Athena serves to acquit Orestes. For Orestes and his protector Apollo, the action is over; they have won; they depart. But what is in many ways the most dramatic part of the play is yet to come: the colloquy between the defeated, bitter Furies and the gleaming Athena who has encompassed their fall.

For Athena does not regard a decision imposed from above as a complete solution; she embarks with deep earnestness on what one of our social scientists has recently called the "engineering of consent," and what Athena later speaks of with affection as the "eyes of Persuasion, which guided my tongue and my mouth, when I addressed these wildly angry ones." I can do no better in an attempt to communicate to you the quality of her persuasion than to quote you Lattimore's translation of one portion of the collquy: Orestes and Apllo have departed in triumph; the Furies speak:

> Gods of the younger generation, you have ridden down
> the laws of the elder time, torn them out of my hands.
> I disinherited, suffering, heavy with anger
> shall let loose on the land
> the vindictive poison
> dripping deadly out of my heart upon the ground;
> this from itself shall breed
> cancer, the leafless, the barren
> to strike, for the right, their low lands
> and drag its smear of mortal infection on the ground.
> What shall I do? Afflicted
> I am mocked by these people.
> I have borne what can not

be borne. Great the sorrows and the dishonor upon
the sad daughters of night.

Athena answers:

Listen to me. I would not have you be so grieved.
For you have not been beaten. This was the result
of a fair ballot which was even. You were not
dishonored, but the luminous evidence of Zeus
was there, and he who spoke the oracle was he
who ordered Orestes so to act and not be hurt.
Do not be angry any longer with this land
nor bring the bulk of your hatred down on it, do not
render it barren of fruit, nor spill the dripping rain
of death in fierce and jagged lines to eat the seeds.
In complete honesty I promise you a place
of your own, deep hidden under ground that is yours by right
where you shall sit on shining chairs beside the hearth
to accept devotions offered by your citizens.

In the speech immediately following, Aeschylus has the Furies
repeat their long tirade verbatim, stubbornly, just as if Athena had
not spoken at all. But Athena takes their intransigence calmly: she
says that she will bear their anger, for they are older than she, and
thereby much wiser; yet, says she, "Zeus has given me too the ability
to make no mean use of my brain." And so, in different language,
she repeats the substance of what we just heard her say. And this
time the Furies reply with a shorter outburst, still bitter, but shorter.
They are becoming convinced, albeit against their will. A reprise by
Athena; they reply *da capo* with their shorter blast, again verbatim.
Athena paraphrases her rebuttal. And then: the unmistakable sign
of the once-rigid who will now yield. They cease to rant, and ask a
question. "Lady Athena, just what post do you promise me?" She
patiently explains that they will be the guardians of Athenian marriage, in which, we may observe, the mother-right and the father-
right are conceived of as blended, not separate and opposed. "Without you no house will flourish." They say openly that they feel
themselves yielding; she encourages them further; they capitulate.
Henceforth they will be the Eumenides, the kindly-minded ones,
protectors of the sanctity of the family hearth, protectors of the City
against internal strife. And as such they utter a prayer of deep significance:

This my prayer: Civil War
fattening on men's ruin shall
not thunder in our city. Let
not the dry dust that drinks

> the black blood of citizens
> through passion for revenge
> and bloodshed for bloodshed
> be given our state to prey upon.
> Let them render grace for grace.
> Let love be their common will;
> let them hate with single heart.
> Much wrong in the world thereby is healed.

The play closes with a recessional in which the women of Athens escort their newly-inaugurated goddesses to their new abodes, welcoming them as the great, honored, aged children of Night, who will abide in state in the dark recesses of the earth, venerated by the Athenians with sacrificial rites. Chanting, all depart and clear the stage.

Let us reflect for one last moment on what has happened. Within the polity, the chain has at last been broken: the chain of evil inflicted and evil repaid, only to lead to further infliction and further repayment, has been brought to a close in an atmosphere of deep reconciliation. But only within the polity: it is only the blood-feud between clans within the state, it is only civil war that has been abrogated. Hatred between states is still envisaged as inevitable: all that is asked of citizens is that they have the same friends and the same enemies. In other words, if we make allowance — a great allowance, to be sure — for the growth of the city-state into a nation-state, then Aeschylus has taken us as far as modern civilization has gone: to a situation in which the society uses collective sanctions to protect citizen against citizen. But what of protecting state against state? There I fear we remain where Aeschylus' *Eumenides* left us. We have tried feebly and failed wretchedly to establish a world tribunal in which weak nation and strong nation may be equal before the law. Where is mankind's Areopagus, the world's defense, untouched by money-making, grave but quick to wrath, watchful to protect those who sleep, a sentry on the Earth?

❖ ❖ ❖ The Electra of Sophocles

Thomas Woodard

THE *Electra* turns around Electra, but in order to appreciate her we must appreciate her play. Therefore let us take the *Electra* as a whole for our point of departure. What place does Electra occupy in it? What is her role in the history and action that absorbs us from beginning to end?

We may approach an answer by realizing that Electra is curiously alienated from one level of action through most of the drama. For at the outset Orestes and his men set in motion a plot to overthrow Clytemnestra and Aegisthus which continues, unabated, more or less behind the scenes, until it reaches complete fruition; reminders of it occur indirectly in every episode, and quite overtly when the Paedagogus enters to tell his false tale. The myth of the *Electra*, indeed, virtually passes over the heroine; as Aeschylus did in his *Oresteia*. History is made, in other words, even when Electra is oblivious of it. She initiates little of this larger action, and participates in it enthusiastically only after rebuke, and only in the closing minutes. And we must admit that this myth of vengeance could have provided a thrilling play by itself, without the presence of Electra; that in fact it does create suspense throughout the play as it stands, and dominates the finale. Electra's predicament is resolved, if at all, only in the resolution of the history of Orestes' return and revenge.

The structure of the *Electra* makes the heroine stand on stage in the midst of an initially alien world, that of the men's plot, and play out her drama in relation to this, merging with it toward the end. More exactly, she lives out her own history while the men are making history in another sense; the *Electra* develops two kinds of

Reprinted by permission of the publishers from Thomas M. Woodard, *Harvard Studies in Classical Philology*, Vol. 68. Cambridge, Mass.: Harvard University Press, copyright 1964 by the President and Fellows of Harvard College; and from Thomas Woodard, "The Electra of Sophocles" in *Sophocles: A Collection of Critical Essays,* © 1966, by permission of Prentice-Hall, Inc., Englewood Cliffs, N.J.

action simultaneously, one in counterpoint with the other. We may describe these two kinds of action, these two dramatic *genres*, in terms of the theater of the fifth century B.C. The men act in high melodrama, serious, suspenseful, noble, and successful; Electra lives in the *agones*, or conflicts and suffering, of the older tragedy.

If this duality informs the *Electra*, Electra's experience cannot be simple. She must find her place in a larger order, the play as a whole; she must come into relation with a contrasting order, the world of the men. And so she does, superbly. Unlike Aeschylus, Sophocles makes Electra the focal point; and she overpowers the men's plot with her own strength and passion. We almost cease to feel suspense about revenge in our concern for her. Her figure dwarfs all others. In short, her tragedy bursts out of the framework of the double plot, just as her form of heroic action seems incommensurable with the men's activities.

For Electra dominates the *Electra* excessively: her speaking part is one of the longest in Greek tragedy; she remains in full view nine-tenths of the time; she includes the heights and depths of emotion in her range; she chants more lyrics than any other Sophoclean protagonist. We must suspect that these excesses of speech, stamina, passion, and lyric express something essential to Sophocles' conception of his heroine. At the same time, we are struck by what would ordinarily be outright defects: her ignorance of Orestes' return and strategy; her physical inactivity; her wrangling and iteration; her mistaken opinions; her hate. Yet these too seem to contribute to her power in the theater; these too must be essential to her heroic character.

We begin to appreciate Electra's world when we realize how in all her traits she defines herself by antithesis to the men. They are laconic; move on and off the stage with facility; display little feeling; have no lyrics. They know what's afoot; and behave with restraint, prudence, reasonableness. In fact, the men's dramatic personalities oppose Electra's at every point. As in action and *genre*, the *Electra* combines two distinct kinds of character.

In the course of her history Electra changes. At the beginning she is poles apart from the men. But by the time Orestes rejoins her, she has developed toward him in certain respects, so that they can work as partners in the finale. The present interpretation sees a dialectical pattern in the initial separation and subsequent reunion of brother and sister, and sees dialectic throughout in Electra's struggles and debates, internal and external. But when all is said and done, Electra triumphs. Though paired with Orestes, she is incomparable; and all the antitheses in the play are similarly imbalanced.

The Prologue scene initiates the design of dialectic and imbalanced antithesis. It has one feature unique in the extant work of Sophocles: it is divided between characters who neither address one another nor occupy the stage together. The separation of brother and sister, and the astonishing differences between the feelings and thoughts expressed by each, present to our eyes and minds a number of fundamental contrasts, built into the divided scene. And while the men's half of the Prologue prepares for the entrance of Electra, the intensity of our response to her presupposes a response to them, since she startles us out of a world that we have taken for granted. We enter Electra's world, then, through a door provided by the play, the men's world.

In the theater what we see and hear coalesce, or rather exist as one. The contrasts in the Prologue are all self-evident in the sense that they are present in what the characters do, say, evoke, and imply. The halving of the Prologue corresponds to a number of dualities, but most obvious, perhaps, is that of the sexes. First three men occupy the stage, then Electra, who is soon joined by the chorus of women. Sophocles found this dramatic contrast close at hand, in the rigorous social differentiation of men and women in fifth-century Athens. Women tended the home while able-bodied men controlled all public affairs as well as trades.

We see the Paedagogus and Orestes confidently, rationally, briskly planning a course of action. And both conclude their opening speeches with references to *erga,* acts, deeds, exhorting one another to set to work. *Ergon* implies not only many specifically male livelihoods and their products, but "job" or "industry," "possessions" in general, and "interest" in the economic sense. So also both men stress the *kairos,* which means "profit" as well as "the right time." Their avowed goal in fact is *kerdos,* gain, profit, and wealth; they are even willing to get it by theft if necessary. Orestes announces his readiness to use *dolos,* cunning, deception, specifically by means of speech, to gain his ends. He has no hesitation about lying for profit. The oracle of Apollo itself had urged *dolos:* deceitful means to a just end. Orestes proves himself full of craft by outlining a lie, a *mythos,* for the Paedagogus to tell.

Orestes' language weaves a network of other allusions to the public life of an Athenian man. He sees himself engaged in the masculine occupation of warfare and pictures himself in competition at the games. He is an adventurer, an exile seeking to recover his patrimony, and virtually a wandering merchant or soldier of fortune; but he is also a vigorous young worker, bread-winner, and man of affairs. His venture is just, we cannot doubt it as he speaks: it is as just as com-

merce, as just as a prayer for success heeded by gods, as just as battling to win back a homeland. Our favorable impressions of him
make us acquiesce in his ethic: a good, gainful end justifies any necessary, sanctioned means.

Orestes' mentality has usually perplexed critics, since he seems without any sensibility at all. He seeks his goal with complete assurance
and no scruples, doubts, or passion. We see him lucidly and coolly
plotting a venture of life and death. The reason for these peculiari-
ties of "personality" is now clear. Orestes symbolizes a mind that
exists only in external action, only for external action, rational and
realistic.

The speeches of Orestes and the Paedagogus define more precisely
this mentality and the dramatic world inhabited by the men. It is a
world of *ergon* — bodily activity, externality, work — in which *logos*
— utterance, thought, language — depends on *ergon* — the product, action, fact—for its validity. In these terms Orestes' set-speech contrasts two kinds of *logos:* valid, correlated with *ergon;* and spurious,
opposed to it or separated from it. For him and the Paedagogus,
meaningful *logoi,* words, statements, further the deed or spring from
actualities. *Logoi* of this sort are a prerequisite for effective action
because they lead to clarity about the best plan: we see the men using
speech in this way in their discussion. In this sense also *logoi* correspond to *erga* as a true proposition or conception corresponds to
the way things really are. Such *logoi* can be an instrument of action
as well: the essential feature of Orestes' plan is a *mythos* or story for
the Paedagogus to tell. Thus *logos* can connote pretense, since it can
conceal the true state of affairs though grounded in it. In this vein
Orestes draws on the common Greek antithesis of false *logoi* and the
erga of truth:

> Why should it grieve me, if I die in pretense (*logos*)
> But in reality (*erga*) stay safe . . .

In this way too, Orestes affirms *erga,* since they cannot possibly be
inauthentic and since they define the truth and falsehood of *logoi.*

Orestes' language is discursive, orderly, logical; and *logos* for him
means prose. He speaks well, but his rhetoric is conventional, that
of the public assembly, military strategy, or princely directive.

Orestes' speech as a whole is itself a *logos* corresponding to an
ergon outside it, the physical action of the drama. For both the
speech and the play begin with the Paedagogus; both continue with
planning. The phrase, "Let that be the story," stands at the exact
center of the speech; the Paedagogus' story appears at the exact
center of the play. Then Orestes alludes to his reappearance with

the urn, then to his "rebirth" to confound his enemies. And, finally, the speech ends, as the play, with the *ergon* of slaying and vengeance.

At the end of the speech the three men prepare to leave the stage. They exit in different directions: the Paedagogus will act by *logoi*, befitting his age or his profession; the younger men, physically. Discussion has served its purpose. The end of their colloquy is the beginning of vengeance.

Through its atmosphere of intrigue and adventure, and by the sheer logic of its development, Orestes' exposition brings us to a full sense of impending action. The exchange between him and his Tutor, then, after a voice moans off-stage, springs from the opposition of *logos* to *ergon* that comes into being when preparations are finished. "Should we wait and listen to the lament?" asks Orestes. "By no means," answers his instructor, "nothing should be set before the necessary actions that will lead us to victory in our task." The rejection here of *logoi* (in the form of *gooi*, cries), for the sake of *erga*, sums up their dramatic world.

When Electra steps from the palace and begins her dirge, we are struck immediately by two things. First, the shift to lyrics, to the free anapests of chanted lamentation, breaks abruptly with the iambics of the preceding dialogue. Second, at the center of the stage we see a lone young woman in place of three men of varying ages. We may now appreciate that these contrasts re-enforce a distinction between a masculine world of *erga*, in which *logoi* are mere servants, and a feminine world of *logoi*, here laments, which preclude physical effectiveness but have another power all their own.

If Orestes is free-ranging, conscienceless, professional, athletic, and businesslike, Electra is tied to the home, unambitious, poverty-stricken, despairing, and frenzied. She stayed behind when Orestes was taken abroad. She is miserable at home because she is treated like a slave. This is her economic condition by contrast to Orestes'. She refuses to seek to better her standard of living. She does not see herself engaged in any public life at all. The palace walls bound her world.

We first hear Electra's voice ringing inside the palace. The Paedagogus stresses its location. When she comes forth through the doors we soon realize that she embodies the interior of that terrible dwelling, her backdrop throughout the play.

Electra's woman's life indoors symbolizes her essential sphere: the internal world of idea, image, and emotion. She grieves in her own bed at night; she locates the source of the family's ills in lust. She is a sensibility laid bare: there is her pity, her hate, and her depression. Orestes plans and acts; Electra suffers and endures. The men confer with one another, within an explicit context of communication.

Electra soliloquizes, or rather addresses herself to the elements. She
laments: reiterates the memories that haunt her, and dwells on her
sufferings. The explicit context of her lament is lamentation itself.
A typical one is in progress, and she asserts her intention to repeat
the liturgy as long as she lives. Threnody is Electra's occupation,
her only mode of action in the sense that Orestes recognized speech
as a mode of action. But lamentation is not effectively instrumental,
nor does Electra make that claim for it. Viewed as to results, it at
best exhorts the spirits of the dead and the nether gods to send
Orestes. Her threnody reaches its climax in a cry for her brother.
He is to her as he is to himself and the Paedagogus: the requisite
avenger of Agamemnon's murder.

Electra's language moves beyond prose. Her threnody is not organized schematically; its imagery evokes unreflecting response. It
replaces logic with imaginative *logos* in organic rhythms. Electra's
inward universe obliterates distinctions of time and place, and trans-
forms everything tangible into a creature of her own experience.

Whether mourning becomes Electra or not, it has become her life.
The thrust toward the future and the suspense built up in us by
the schemes of the men recede and vanish. Harmonious exchange
of advice has been supplanted by the echo of Electra's voice crying
in public solitude, as she vows

> With continual wailing, before paternal doors,
> To utter a resounding cry for all to hear.

Electra's grieving is, in a sense, self-perpetuated; yet it flows from
a perception of real horror and torment. Through her eyes we see
the murder of Agamemnon, as well as the wretched life that she has
led since. She draws us into the domestic torment and tension as we
respond to her inwardness, and into her inner torment and tension
as we respond to the domestic.

In forcing us to enter her private world, Electra lodges us in an
atmosphere that will dominate the play. *Logos* and *ergon* have reversed their relationship, for Electra suffers under *erga*, rather than
produces them. Her *logoi* express emotion, rather than plot deeds.
Her power lies all in *logos;* physically she is impotent. We are already aware of the tension within *logos* between truth and falsehood.
Now we begin to realize that *logos* is an absolute, and in part beyond
this distinction.

The Parodos, significantly in the form of a lengthy *kommos* or
liturgical lament, turns not on any doubts about the condemnation of
the vicious Clytemnestra but on the Chorus' friendly criticism of

Electra's excessive talk and mourning. "Why do you continually lament?" the Chorus ask. "Why do you desire to suffer?" The questions and objections of the Chorus concerning Electra's verbal activity evoke the greater part of what she chants. From the outset she accepts the character ascribed to her. She links herself with the fabled singer, the nightingale, and with the perpetually weeping Niobe. She too will persist in rage, frenzy, and "countless threnodies."

The Parodos achieves a remarkable dramatic result. Electra wins our closest sympathy and touchingly defends her stance; at the same time, she exhibits and avows shameful behavior, irrationality, and sheer, self-defeating stubbornness. She defends lament for its own sake, though she grants that it is self-lacerating and self-degrading. She is, by a kind of necessary, heroic obstinacy, at war with herself as well as with her environment. Lamentation and rebuke make up her *ethos*, and this is a habit-and-trait that she feels futile and, in one sense, immoral. She can fully affirm only the righting of a now doubly violated moral order; and this would require an act of vengeance. But, alone, she is able only to mourn and censure the moral disorder, thus further separating herself from the wholly valid. Electra acts under a necessity more profound than moral "principles"; enduring her own conflict while facing her environment manifests her peculiar moral intuition. Her heroism, in other words, as it claims our sympathy in the theater, must express itself in contradiction. We must identify *logos* with this paradoxical intuition.

In part, Electra endures the inherent duality of *logos*: a meaningful activity and a mere substitute for action. Her *logoi* spring from *erga* that have impinged on her, that oppress her now, over which she has no control, and against which her only weapon is speech. On the other hand, her *logoi* possess the autonomy and literally incalculable power of lyric and liturgy.

> I am ashamed, ladies, if I seem to you
> To grieve too much with many threnodies.
> But violence forces me to do them.

Beginning her first set-speech in this vein, Electra assents to the whole drift of the Chorus in the Parodos. She is trapped in a woman's world of polemic and lament. In entering her world of *logoi*, we enter on a series of scenes made up precisely of oratory, polemic, and lament. The issues intrinsic to the distinction of *logos* and *ergon* are debated, implicitly and explicitly, in scenes that advance the physical action, the external plot, hardly at all. These scenes are equally portraits, trials, and punishments. But, passing through these scenes, Electra advances, still within the dilemmas of isolated *logos*, to a recognition of the necessity for external *ergon*. Then the final episodes in the drama present effective action more than they debate issues; Electra becomes Orestes' colleague and subordinates herself to the necessities of vengeance. Yet the heart of the *Electra* remains Electra in isolation and *logos* divorced from *ergon*, not only because of quantitative proportions but because this tragic Electra moves us as the melodramatic Electra cannot. And we recognize that, in the central scenes, *logos* justifies itself in a way that survives the apparent triumph of *ergon* in the finale. In spite of all our preconceptions about the sanctity of literal truth and the urgency of efficient action, in spite of Electra's own acceptance of the correlation of *logos* and *ergon* as Orestes expressed it in the Prologue, the *Electra* shows *logos* omnipotent in its character of faith, ideal, and imaginative language.

The ostensible issue in the first encounter of the two sisters is how one should live, and what one should do, in evil circumstances. But these questions of action are turned into questions about what one should say, believe, and rely on, and the point of the scene virtually becomes Electra's oral forcefulness. The persuasive force of her arguments contains her moral supremacy, as it comes across to us in the theater; her directives as to what Chrysothemis should do (and not do) finally prevail. Though Electra boasts of active resistance, we discover that her accomplishment remains wholly verbal. The ironical result of the scene is that only poor Chrysothemis must actually run a risk, in disobeying her mother and offering a substitute sacrifice to her father.

In the first part of the scene, both sisters show much contempt for mere *logoi*, and both attempt to prove that the other lives by *logos* rather than by *ergon*. Chrysothemis' opening words challenge Electra's futile talk and futile passion. Chrysothemis then charges that Electra only *seems* to be doing something, while really she harms no one, effects no result. Electra then claims that *she* has been the one engaged in *erga*. Chrysothemis has hated their common enemies merely in speech, or "in pretence," while "in reality," "in truth," living comfortably with them (*men logo/ergo de*).

To Electra's brilliant dialectical defense of her mode of life by contrast to her sister's, Chrysothemis makes no reply whatsoever, but brushes the whole speech and all its arguments aside by saying to the Chorus: "I am quite used to her talk (*muthon*)." And she simply turns to another topic, which proves to be the plan of Clytemnestra and Aegisthus for silencing Electra's "great groans," *ton makron goon*, a phrase suggesting *hoi makroi logoi*, "long or over-long speeches," which we shall hear more than once in connection with

Electra later in the play. The antithesis of this latter phrase, in fact, occurs a few moments later, when Electra asks for a report of Clytemnestra's dream.

> CHRYSOTHEMIS. Do these night terrors make you hopeful?
> ELECTRA. If you told me the vision, then I might say.
> CHRYSOTHEMIS. But I know only very little to tell.
> ELECTRA. Then say *that*. A few words (*logoi*) have often
>   Overthrown or re-established men.
> CHRYSOTHEMIS. The story is. . . . (The *logos* is. . . .)

These lines might be said to speak for themselves. Electra's gnomic pronouncement about the power of "a few words," *smikroi logoi*, deserves amplification, however. These *logoi* are at once instrumental, instructive, and potent in themselves. Her defense of *logoi* as autonomous forces in human life coheres with her own reliance on the ritual *logoi* of lament, the competitive *logoi* of persuasion and self-defense, and the battling *logoi* of reproach and insult.

The debate ends with Chrysothemis persuaded to do as Electra bids.

> CHRYSOTHEMIS. I will do it. It is not reasonable for two people
>   To dispute what is just, but rather to hasten to do it.

She contrasts the fruitless *logoi* of dispute with daring action (*to dran* and *ton ergon*). Then she begs for silence, the necessary companion of a successful venture. We shall meet this corollary of the basic duality again later. We may notice here that the colloquy between the sisters ends with the commencement of a deed, as at the exit of the three partners in the Prologue. The silence of the interlocutors thus has positive dramatic effect.

Clytemnestra enters with attendants bearing ritual offerings such as Chrysothemis had carried in the previous Episode. In their first words both mother and sister rebuke Electra for again being outside the palace talking. In both scenes Electra proves stronger; here she convicts her mother of criminal guilt. For it is a case of murder; or, rather, there are two murders, Iphigeneia's and Agamemnon's. Electra acts as prosecutor against her mother, and as lawyer for the defense of her father. The language of the interchange seats us in the lawcourts. And the whole scene ultimately turns not so much on questions of substantive justice as on an examination of the debating process and of the use of speech as a mode of action.

Were we not attuned to the issue of *logos* and *ergon*, it would be hard to understand why the most violent exchange in this most violent scene uses such abstruse language.

ELECTRA. Shameful deeds are taught by shameful deeds.
CLYTEMNESTRA. O shameless creature, I and my words
    And my deeds make you say much too much.
ELECTRA. *You* say it, not I. For you do
    The deed; and deeds find words for themselves.
CLYTEMNESTRA. By Lady Artemis, you'll pay for this impudence . . .

Clytemnestra's pairing of words and deeds, implying the sum total of behavior, contrasts to Electra's sole activity, talk. The phrase, "make you say too much," *agan legein poei*, presents the central duality in miniature. Electra's paradoxical reply, "*You* say it," attempts to justify her talk by pleading the compulsion of deeds. "You do the deed," she says, *su gar poeis/tourgon*, implying not only that Clytemnestra is her antithesis (as *ergon versus* her *logos*), but that deeds or circumstances produce speech.

"Deeds find words for themselves": *ta d'erga tous logous heurisketai*. Electra's ultimate line of self-defense implies that words are subservient to deeds, as passive to active, or as effect to cause. Thus she expresses the ambiguous autonomy of *logos* and of her own character in the face of *erga*. The debate between mother and daughter quite literally consists of words sprung inevitably from foul deeds. The next scene presents words necessitated by a just enterprise. In a sense not intended by Electra, "deeds find words for themselves" implies that deeds require *logoi* as means, and hence that the deed afoot, Orestes', will call forth the *mythos* of the Paedagogus. Thus the proposition serves as a transition in the theater.

The Paedagogus' false account of Orestes' death (the longest set-speech in the extant work of Sophocles) complements Clytemnestra's self-convicting prayer, and, by eye-for-eye justice, gives her what she deserves. But the *mythos*, which we have been expecting since Orestes outlined its plot in the Prologue, also complements Electra's verbal virtuosity. Her character, with its essentially monochromatic reliance on verbal action, and its duality of pathos and power, leaps to accept the Paedagogus' story in its shattering ramifications. Her suffering is real, and affects us. But we realize at the same time that it is consonant with her character to be taken in by a verbal stratagem, by verbal seeming. Clytemnestra says that *she* will wait for the ashes, as proof of the story. But Electra interrupts and pushes away the Chorus' suggestions about hope for Orestes' life. The succeeding scene will show Electra rejecting even concrete evidence on the question of the alleged death, and able in her turn to give a plausible explanation (*logos*) for Chrysothemis' discoveries. Electra shows a stubborn refusal to doubt the worst; an immense capacity to endow thought with reality.

The Paedagogus' speech stands dead-center in the play. It is not without significance that both the plan of Orestes and the total action of the drama pivot on this unrivaled exhibition of verbal verisimilitude. For us as audience, the speech flows naturally as part of the original scheme. But now the story has another level of impact on us. It completes the pathos of Electra; the compulsion behind her suffering as she listens proves its noble strength. The *mythos* becomes an *ergon* tormenting her.

The Paedagogus' speech deploys the power in *logoi*, just as Electra had in persuasive colloquy with Chrysothemis or in her admirable prosecution of Clytemnestra. And, in the Paedagogus' speech shines again and double nature of *logos*. The speech is instrumental, valid, justified, and effective, in the strategy of revenge; it is deceiving, spurious, and grievous in its immediate effects. We marvel at the persuasiveness of a story which we know is false. We suffer with Electra though we know that she will eventually rejoice.

Because the lie completes Electra's pathos, her transformation begins. In despair she finds new determination. For the first time in the play she makes a decision to act physically. The second confrontation between the sisters contrasts at many points with the first, emphasizing Electra's new attitude. Before, she had succeeded in persuading Chrysothemis to do something, however minimal, by way of rebellion; here, she fails to persuade, but vows she stands ready to act alone. She abandons the effort at persuasion. But, at the end of the scene, Electra does not depart. Chrysothemis she sends away, remaining on stage during the second Stasimon. For after all, we reflect, Orestes will come, has come; and Electra will never do the deed.

There is, in fact, similar irony throughout the second meeting of the sisters. Electra defends the deed that she proposes by stressing the good repute, *logon eukleia*, that will accrue. Again and again she argues from what others will say, quoting finally an imaginary eulogy at length. These rather suspect forms of reputation, spun out into a fable with a happy ending, contrast with the honor, accompanied by lands and rule, which Orestes seeks. The scene as a whole impresses us once again with the schism in Electra's stance. She would venture on deeds in pursuit of kind words.

The same schism lies behind the dispute over the tokens. Electra presents herself to Chrysothemis as tough-minded, and claims to judge by the way things are rather than by private opinions. She accuses her sister of being deceived by words.

> ELECTRA. Alas! Who told you this story (*logos*)
> That you believe in all too fully?

Chrysothemis argues that her "hypothesis" is warranted by clear evidence.

> CHRYSOTHEMIS. I saw clear signs for myself,
> And do not believe another's story.

The irony of Electra's position in this interchange is patent. So it is also in her last exhibition of persuasive force, when she counters Chrysothemis' self-conscious deduction from the tokens to Orestes' presence with her own evidence, mere hearsay.

> CHRYSOTHEMIS. Alas! Who told you these things?
> ELECTRA. The man nearest when he died.

For us, the plausibility of her explanation of the tokens hardly belies its pathetic spuriousness. However, while Chrysothemis had shown a merely logical skill, Electra's moral and emotional force carries the day. This dispute, then, exposes the deceitfulness of *logoi* (words, arguments, reasons) when divorced from *erga* (acts, facts, things), but simultaneously exhibits the potency of autonomous *logos* (conviction, imagination, inwardness). If Electra reaches her largest heroic stature in this scene, it can only be because her force and her folly unite in her essential commitment to pure *logos*, and only because *logos* itself possesses an authenticity beyond the judgment of reason and the world. Here *logos* completely triumphs over logic.

Since Orestes and Electra are living emblems of the play's basic conceptual duality, in the "recognition" scene visible dramatic effects stand out, corresponding to their physical reunion. Orestes enters carrying an urn. This urn, like a third actor, dominates the stage until the final minute of the dialogue. It is the reason given for the stranger's presence; Electra cries out at the sight of it, and, holding it in her arms, addresses it in a long and moving lament; finally, Orestes tries to recover it from her, and his explanation of who he is revolves around explaining what the urn is not.

> ORESTES. Give up this urn then, so you may learn all.

For the urn is a surrogate Orestes, an Orestes by sham, a fiction posing as fact. What Electra and we alike "recognize" in the scene is a distinction between reality and supposition, between expectation and event, between true and false evidence.

In fact, something similar happens to Orestes as well. He suffers in seeing (and hearing) Electra's suffering, and alters his course of action. As he replaces concealment through silence with revelatory speech, Electra replaces her compelling though misdirected lamentation with joy. From this mutual shift results the sweetness of the climactic moments: Electra releases the urn, soon to take Orestes himself in her arms. Orestes with one hand shows Electra the ring that proves what the urn that he holds in the other had only shammed. At the end of the dialogue, the urn recedes from the level of personage to that of mere object, and all our attention rests on the living pair.

But speech plays a major role in this scene alongside the urn. Electra's lament overpowers us; and it overpowers Orestes. At its conclusion he finds himself at a loss for words:

> Woe, woe, what shall I say? So perplexed,
> Where can I go in speech? I no longer have the strength
> to control my tongue.

For the first time in the play, Orestes suffers under the force of evils from without. Thus he shares, at least momentarily, his sister's trait of compulsive speech and also her relationship to *erga kaka*. At their moment of reunion Orestes enters the world of Electra, just as she had already gone far toward entering his in the preceding scene. For this reason, contrary to plan, Orestes admits his former lie, saying that the urn is "not Orestes, except tricked out in speech (logo)."

The mutual recognition of brother and sister, and their experience of self-recognition, achieve a fragile resolution of conflict in this scene. But it lasts only a moment. We then plunge back into tension between talk and the deed at hand which pulls apart the newly joined couple.

The seeming duet between Electra and Orestes actually shows no harmonizing at all. For Orestes does not join in; he has no lyric lines, only the rational iambics of discourse. We see dramatized again, in fact, the contrast so striking in the Prologue, between Electra's threnody, here reversed to exaltation, and Orestes' controlled deliberations. Orestes' constant effort is to terminate this "duet." We have forced on us again an awareness that a violent endeavor, demanding secrecy, is in progress, and that talk may give everything away and bring disaster.

The scene between the song and the short third Stasimon serves as a vital transition to the so-called Exodos, which is the climax of the action. The transition involves a gradual alteration in the attitude of Electra; and a few more, final touches in the education of Orestes, supplied by the Paedagogus. The scene takes us closer to the means and the end represented by the Paedagogus, and more fully into his world of *ergon*.

At the beginning of the dialogue Orestes puts his attitude toward

Electra's melic interlude as vigorously and as bluntly as possible: "Cease all superfluous speech." In a coherent, concise statement, built around a rhetorical opposition of *logos* to *ergon*, he requests Electra not to waste precious time with a recapitulation of the past. "For," he says, "talk (*logos*) would hinder the moment of opportunity (*kairos*)." In a gracious though roundabout reply, Electra agrees to cooperate, and gives him the facts that he needs to know. She thus explicitly recognizes the urgent requirements of the situation.

The Paedagogus' outburst, as he reenters, puts more strongly what we ourselves feel increasingly: the crucial act can wait no longer. He denounces both brother and sister because they could have been overheard inside if he had not been on guard. The conclusion of his speech sums up the dramatic moment as we experience it in terms of the necessity to put talk aside.

> Now cease your long speeches
> And your insatiate cries of joy.
> Go in: in these circumstances, delay
> Means ruin, but the time is right for success.

But there is more delay, as Electra recognizes the old man and realizes that he had "killed her with lies (*logois*), while knowing the sweetest truths (*erga*)." Then, with his last words in the play, the Paedagogus calls on the concepts crucial to his first speech in the Prologue, *kairos* and *ergon*. From now to the end of the drama, he remains silent, because the action moves ahead on schedule. After Orestes transmits a final directive to his partner,

> We have no more need of long speeches,
> But only of getting inside as quickly as possible,

the men perform the ritual reverences preparatory to the sanctified slaying, and leave the stage in silence. As her part in the venture, Electra offers a prayer to Apollo. It contains suggestions that this verbal ritual is her best aid.

In this transitional scene, therefore, Electra begins to share the men's view of speech as an accompaniment to silent endeavor. In the concluding minutes of the play, she will turn her formidable verbal powers into instruments of vengeance: by reporting what happens; by deceiving Aegisthus; and by crucial exhortations to action.

At the outset, the final scene gives us two surprises: Electra leaves the stage for the first time since she entered in the Prologue; and, in the *kommos*, she has no lyrics, but leaves them all to the Chorus. Her first words convey the change that has occurred:

> Dear ladies, now in a moment the men
> Will finish their work. Wait in silence.

This directive to the Chorus repeats almost word for word Orestes' first objection to her joyous song. Her alliance is now with *tourgon* and she realizes that it requires silence. She re-enters, she tells the Chorus, to serve as lookout: she is on stage to *do* something. Then Clytemnestra's death-cries bespeak the effectiveness of Orestes. Electra encourages him to strike again. Indeed, what we see and what we hear at the moment of matricide make Electra the dramatic agent of vengeance. It is as though her shouts were swords.

Next, Electra deals with Aegisthus, in a masterpiece of *double entendre*, telling the truth and deceiving at the same time. Previously we have seen Electra in the reverse position, the victim of a lie. At other times she was unable to distinguish between literal truth and literal falsity. Now that she knows how things stand, she employs her wit to keep us constantly aware that she knows, while lulling Aegisthus to ignorance of his danger.

> AEGISTHUS. Where might the strangers be? Tell me that.
> ELECTRA. Inside. They have reached a kind hostess.

Here Electra's verb, *katenusan*, means not only "they have reached the house," but "they have accomplished the murder" of their "hostess." In this way, Electra proves her talent for *dolos* of a sort even more highly refined than the men's. Similarly, in the next exchange,

> AEGISTHUS. And did they genuinely report his death?
> ELECTRA. No, they have brought himself, not news alone.

Evidence and hearsay, truth and falsity, Electra plays on these ground-themes while sustaining ambiguity perfectly.

Clytemnestra's body under the sheet plays the same part as Orestes' urn: both serve as pivots for a reversal from delusion to truth. "Alas, I understand your word. It is Orestes speaking to me"; Aegisthus recognizes Orestes by what he says. This transition from the dead mother to the living son, and from sight back to speech, shifts our attention to the dialogue itself and prepares us for the climax of the role of Electra, as she interrupts the desperate attempt of Aegisthus to stall for time:

> AEGISTHUS. Just let me say a little bit.
> ELECTRA. Don't let him say any more!
> By the gods, brother, do not prolong speeches.
> What profit can delay bring, when a man
> In the midst of trouble is about to die?

Her rejection of talk, of "long speeches," here, in favor of pressing speedily toward the deed and the profit, completes her evolution into an effective ally for Orestes in the vengeance.

Just as Electra alters in her relation to *logoi*, so she will no longer remain crushed by *erga*. Aegisthus' instant death will relieve her. Her final words in the play encourage her brother in the style of the Paedagogus (though Orestes needs little chiding), adding a bitter sense of intolerable *kaka* all her own. Only by full requital of the extreme *kaka* under which she has suffered can she find release; thus she demands the harshest treatment for Aegisthus' body.

Orestes pushes Aegisthus inside, the concluding exit-for-action of the drama, leaving us with a statement of his attitude toward requital. Illegal or foul deeds beget just deeds as punishment, even if these just deeds mean murder. He is still firm in his belief that by the appropriate *ergon* we can diminish to *panourgon*, evil-doing. To this end, in silence Orestes and Aegisthus enter the palace; Electra watches in silence.

Thus the *Electra* plays out the dialectic of *logos* and *ergon* and presents Electra first and foremost in her relationship to these two principles. Throughout the play her temper remains constant, as does her reliance on *logoi;* yet her final attitude, for all practical purposes, is equivalent to that of Orestes in the Prologue. But what is our final attitude toward her? The last utterances of Orestes and Electra each show fully their characteristic mentalities: his legalistic, simplisitic efficiency; her passionate, urgent absolutism. "Kill all wrongdoers"; "Thow him to the fitting buriers." And so, despite her evolving determination to act, Electra remains essentially the same from beginning to end. And so also our response to her in the Exodos or finale remains as it has been throughout, divided between admiration and disquiet. Yet, like *logos* and *ergon* and the other antitheses of the play, admiration and disquiet are incommensurable in the theater: Electra carries us away beyond criticism. In the lament over the urn, in the *kommoi* and the songs of joy, she retains the power that encounters us in her opening *threnos*. This is the power of *logos*. It draws us to the end.

Since the essential autonomy of his protagonist lasts as long as the play, Sophocles affirms a necessity beyond the practical and "realistic" necessity for the coordination of *logos* and *ergon* that we see in the Exodos. This other, higher necessity is that implied by spiritual *logos* in isolation from worldliness. The schism we notice within Electra and within her world dramatizes the contrast between a *logos* more profound than logic and a *logos* defined wholly in terms of external *ergon*. It is this latter *logos* alone that Orestes uses. By the end of the play Electra has shown some capacity to include the calculating, "rational" *logos* within her primarily emotional, intuitive, and imaginative *logos*. Thus again we find her bursting beyond the balance of opposites into a more capacious wholeness.

Electra dominates the other characters and the drama as a whole because she commands a language moving beyond logic. We recognize her nobility and strength most fully during the very moments in which she fails most pathetically to grasp *ergon* (facts, evidence, material reality). When she is in error about the tokens, deceived by the Paedagogus' lie, or deluded about the urn, she surges forth, deciding to act alone, enduring the torments of despair, lyrically overwhelming us with noble grief. In this way, each scene from her threnody on shows Electra's spiritual *logos* in tension with the demands of fact and deed. But this state of tension too is imbalanced. Its constant ironical undertone cannot counteract our attachment to Electra's truth. The tension only serves to bring into the light the essence of her truth: paradox. The paradox of Electra informs each scene; she so transcends ordinary logic that she draws our sympathies most when least reasonable.

The opening and closing of our play both show the world of *ergon* ostensibly dominant; both present the men in control, and support their world conceptually as well as dramatically. The large center of the play criticizes the world of *logos;* its keystone is the great speech of the Paedagogus, at the exact middle. With this structure, the *Electra* asserts the practical and literal truth of *ergon,* but also, shattering this frame, the uncanny force of *logos.* In the center, speeches, lyrics, and faith prove more authoritative than deeds, and Electra holds sway in a rhythmic world of meaningful pathos, ritual, and chant.

Because the center shatters its frame, the finale does not simply balance the beginning in abstract symmetry. It is not the same unambiguous melodrama, but sardonic and tense. And, while validating the men's purpose, it vindicates an Electra who remains self-contradictory. Her vindication, even her redemption, leaves us with unresolved issues, permanent paradoxes: the role of her thrust toward infinity in a finite world, the fate of her ideals in the midst of actuality. Forever intersecting and separating, these incommensurables are somehow, beyond our understanding, related. The limits of our understanding, after all, are those of logic in the face of *logos.* That the incommensurables are truly related, however, the play proves in its own perfect union of deed and word, real and ideal.

Silence, as we have noticed, has a positive dramatic function in the *Electra.* From her entrance on, Electra stands silent during only three periods of any length: the first two Stasima and the *mythos* of the

Paedagogus. We appreciate well the force of the Paedagogus' speech and its relevance to Electra's symbolic character. The two choral odes, in a similar way, also derive an important part of their force and significance from Electra. The Chorus not only speaks in her favor but hardly exists at all in this drama except as an adjunct to her; always subordinate, always a helpful backdrop for her attitudes, merits, emotions, pathos. In the only two developed choral odes, then, I suggest that the Chorus remains an extension of Electra's character and continues to bring it out and augment it: the Chorus represents her participation in the communal *logoi* of ritual. Electra can willingly stand silent on stage during these odes because the Chorus acts out, in lyric and dance, her own dedication to the liturgical truths of tradition, inwardness, and faith. As at the very end of the drama, Electra's silence displays assent, communion, and assurance; justice will prevail, it implies; divinities are working invisible like words.

This essay can only suggest in conclusion that the *Electra*, like its heroine, takes on its most profound dimension by uniting *logos* and *mythos* (terms used interchangeably throughout). For the men the prime example of *mythos* or *logos* is no doubt the well-wrought scheme or lie. For Electra, however, the *logoi* or *mythoi* imitate and exemplify the ebb and flow of nature itself. The cycles of nature — nature's rituals — like the seasons, life and death, or night and day, form *logoi* or *mythoi* (meaningful patterns), just as they form the basis of human ritual and of the traditional myths. Electra symbolizes *physis*, nature, in her endurance, her attachment to blood, her repetitions, and her refusal to compromise. Electra's truth (and her meaning), like that of nature, is beyond appearances, the surface truths or *erga* apprehended by the senses or sensible intelligence. The appearances are indeed against her; but only the appearances.

Ergon vs. logos, appearance *vs. physis*, fact *vs.* faith: Sophocles captures these great *agones* or conflicts by dramatizing them in perpetual motion, by imitating them for all time in a ritual drama in which the *agonistoi* or competitors play out their war over and over, the struggle without end, the whole ordered and stable. He triumphs by integrating dramatic *erga* and *logoi*, realism, fiction, and rite. But *logoi* and *mythoi* themselves triumph, by expressing the essence of the drama. And our access, such as it is, to this drama is also through *logos* and *mythos*: imagination allowing us to participate in another world.

Electra

G. M. A. Grube

THE AUDIENCE which gathered to witness the first performance of *Electra* must have been surprised to see none of the usual heroic paraphernalia on the stage set for the performance; no palace, no great altar tomb or the like; only a peasant's cottage, surely an undignified setting for tragedy. The time is about dawn and the play begins as a poor man comes out—he might be a slave except that this is improbable in so poor a dwelling; he must be the peasant owner of the house. Thus our first impression is of poverty, and it will be something of a shock to be told that this poor countryman is the husband of Electra.

The first part of the monologue is on quite conventional lines. He tells us very briefly of the Trojan War and the death of Agamemnon "by the guile of Clytemnestra and the hand of Aegisthus." He then explains that Aegisthus now reigns in Argos with Clytemnestra as his wife, that the infant Orestes was smuggled out of the country, while Electra remained but was forbidden to marry any of the Greek noblemen that came to seek her hand for fear she might give birth to an avenger. The peasant then passes to a description of the present situation and the factors involved:

> Since of this also Aegisthus was much afraid, that she should bear in secret the child of a noble father, he decided to kill her. But her mother, cruel though she be, saved her from Aegisthus' hand. She had a pretext for the murder of her husband (Iphigenia) but was afraid to offend by the murder of her children.
>
> Aegisthus then devised as follows: he put a price on the head of Agamemnon's son who had escaped this land into exile, and gave Electra to me as wife — I too am of Mycenaean blood and I can prove it, noble by race but poor in wealth, and poverty is death to nobility — that by giving her to a weak man he might find his fear the weaker. For if some man of reputation had her, he would arouse from slumber the murder of Agamemnon and justice would overtake Aegisthus.

Reprinted from *The Drama of Euripides* by G. M. A. Grube by permission of Methuen & Co., Ltd., Publishers.

And I who stand here (ἀνὴρ ὅδε) — the Cyprian be my witness —
have never put her to shame upon the bridal bed. She is a virgin still.
I should be ashamed to ill-treat the children of the great, being myself
unworthy. I weep for Orestes, if he should ever come to Argos and
see his sister's unfortunate marriage.

If any man call me a fool to take a young maiden into my house
and then not touch her, he but betrays his own nature by judging
modesty after an evil measure.

These words show the peasant's homely character, his respect for
the great house of Agamemnon, his humility, quaintly contrasted with
his pride of ancestry, his essential kindliness and his shrewd common
sense, for, if he is sorry for Orestes, he might also well be a little afraid
of the consequences, should he assert his marital rights. His part is
small but he is generally recognized as one of our dramatist's most
successful minor characters.

There is a good deal more to learn from this monologue, and especially from the passage quoted, for Euripides is giving the legend
several curious twists of his own. We note that Aegisthus is very
much the dominating partner, at least since the murder, indeed that
he has taken an active part in the murder itself. Electra's continued
virginity is an essential part of the legend, but her marriage to this
humble peasant, and the poverty that goes with it, are entirely new.
We shall see how subtly they are used in the delineation of her character. Above all, we should note that Clytemnestra saved her daughter's life; this, and her relation to Aegisthus, lead us to expect a very
different woman from the magnificently evil character we know in
Aeschylus.

The peasant retires for a few moments[1] as Electra comes out of
the cottage. She is on her way to fetch water from the spring and extremely conscious of the indignity of her task:

Not that I have come to poverty so extreme, but that I may show
up before the gods Aegisthus' insolent pride (ὕβρς). The accursed
daughter of Tyndareus, my mother, cast me out of the house as a
favour to her husband. . . .

There is here no suggestion that Clytemnestra saved her daughter's
life, for to Electra all that her mother does is evil and accursed.
Though there is no contradiction of fact with the peasant's account,
the tone is very different.

The peasant now returns:

[1] It seems that he should not hear her first short speech as there is then
more point to his anxiety that she should not do too much to help him. He
can easily walk round to the back of the house to fetch some farm imple-
ment or the like. [Author's notes.]

Poor woman! Why do you work so hard for my sake, you who were so gently nurtured. Even though I tell you to desist, you will not.

We get the feeling that this little scene is a daily occurrence: he begging her not to work so hard, she insisting that she must. She fully appreciates the delicacy of her husband's conduct, and in this we get a glimpse of the Electra she might have been:

> You are to me a friend like to a god, for you have not ill-treated me in my misfortune. Great good fortune it is for men to find some one to heal their misery, as I have you. So surely I must lighten your burden so far as my strength allows, even though you bid me not. You have enough to do outside. It is my part to keep things nice inside the house. 'Tis pleasant for a man who comes home from work to find all well within.

The desire to share his labours was not the motive she gave when she was alone, for fetching water. Not that she is lying now. Of course she wants to help him, but her obsession of revenge and self-pity has reached such a pitch that she cannot do anything simple in a simple way, that she must bring Aegisthus and Clytemnestra into everything, even the everyday task of fetching water from the spring. The reply of her matter-of-fact husband is disarming in its robust good sense:

> Go then, if you think it best. The spring is not so far from this house after all.

And with a few homely words on the need to work for a living he departs, as she too goes on her errand. This little scene (28 verses from the entrance of Electra) is a masterly piece of theatre, with its effective contrast between the peasant's blunt good sense and the sickness of Electra's mind.

The stage is empty. Orestes enters, accompanied, as the legend required, by the faithful Pylades, who is a mute character throughout, and by a few attendants. As he addresses his companion by name his identity is clear at once:

> Pylades, . . . you alone have honoured me, Orestes, in my present plight, wronged as I am by Aegisthus who slew my father — as did my murderous mother.

Note that Clytemnestra's name follows a momentary hesitation.[2] Orestes will express himself in this way throughout. To Electra the murderer is Clytemnestra, with Aegisthus; to Orestes it is Aegisthus,

---

[2] The Greek makes this quite clear, for the relative ὅς is masculine, the verb κατέκτα singular, and the following nominatives χἠ πανώλεθρος μήτηρ have no construction.

with Clytemnestra. He speaks in this manner, not indeed because he
considers his mother less guilty, but because her guilt is horrible to
him, as is the knowledge that he must kill them both. The use of the
plurals "murderers," "rulers of this land," shows this to be his intention and the duty put upon him. Yet he avoids any direct reference
to Clytemnestra's punishment as long as he can. Unlike the embit-
tered Electra, he nowhere forgets that Clytemnestra is his mother.
Orestes' first speech has something of the conventionality of an intro-
ductory monologue, and indeed it has a similar function. Hence we
shall not be surprised to find him explaining, what Pylades must know
as well as he, that he has come secretly, that he has sacrificed at the
grave of his father, and is now intending to find Electra and see what
can be done.

In order not to be prematurely discovered, the men hide to await
some one they may question. They see a woman approaching, carrying water, and suppose her to be a slave. It is, of course, Electra,
lamenting as she goes:

> Hasten thy step. Time presses.
> March on, march on and weep.
> Alas, ah me!
> I was born the daughter of Agamemnon
> And the hateful Clytemnestra, daughter of Tyndareus, bore me.
> In the city they call me Electra the unfortunate.
> Alas for my terrible troubles,
> Alas for my hateful life.
> O Father, thou liest in the house of Hades,
> Murdered by thy wife and Aegisthus,
> Agamemnon.

It is not enough here to say that Electra names herself so that Orestes
shall know her. That is indeed necessary, but an artist is great in so
far as he can make dramatic use of dramatic necessity. After the
water-pitcher scene, the words which incidentally tell Orestes who
she is mean to us: There is no nobler blood than mine and look at
my poverty. She does *not* say "I am Electra," but "I was born the
daughter of Agamemnon . . . they call me Electra the unfortunate. . . ." She then, in the second stanza, calls upon Orestes to return from exile:

> Come and deliver me from my misery and misfortune.
> O God! O God! and come as an avenger of our father's murder. . . .

The order "My misery . . . my father's murder" seems wrong. It
will recur. She then puts down her pitcher and sings a short, moving
lamentation over the death of Agamemnon, but her sorrow soon turns

into hatred as in the last stanza she goes over the details of his terrible death at the hands of his wife, for Aegisthus' sake. As her song ends the chorus enter. They are Argive women who sympathize with Electra, are indeed wholly on her side, so that their continued presence offers little difficulty.

In the lyric interchange that follows we learn that they have come to bid Electra join them in the ritual procession of Argive women to Hera's temple. Her reply is characteristic: she will never join the dance again. Look at her shorn locks, her sordid clothes; are they suitable for a princess, the daughter of Agamemnon? The perverse pleasure she takes in enlarging upon her poverty continues what we may call the water-pitcher theme, until it becomes a major theme of the play — "I was born the daughter of Agamemnon." The women press their invitation with an ingenuous offer to lend her clothes and jewellery — as if that were the real trouble! — but she answers only with tears, and laments that the gods have not answered her prayer, Orestes is far away:

> While I in a poor dwelling am wearing out my soul, exiled from my father's house on the slopes of the mountains, my mother in a murderer's bed has found another husband.

Orestes and his companions come forward. Electra's terror when she sees the strangers — she tells the chorus to run for their lives — seems exaggerated and betrays her unbalanced state. The men, it is true, are armed, as was every traveller. There is no indication that the chorus share Electra's panic. Orestes protests he has no intention of doing her harm and manages to calm her. He then introduces himself as coming from Orestes, who, he tells her, is alive. Reassured on this point, Electra once more describes her own poverty, bewails her "deadly marriage," though she gives full credit to her peasant husband for his kindly treatment. Once more she blames Clytemnestra for having cast her out and her contemptuous words:

> Women hold their men, not their children, dear.

are infinitely pathetic and revealing from one who has been kept from a true marriage. She reassures Orestes that the chorus can be trusted and thus emboldens him to ask the question for which he came:

> What could Orestes do if he came to Argos?
> — You ask that? For shame. Is the time not ripe?
> — If he came, how could he slay his father's murderers?
> — By daring what his enemies dared against his father.
> — And would you dare to help him kill his mother?
> — Yes, with the same axe by which his father died.

> — I will tell him. Is your help quite certain?
> — My mother's blood to spill, then death were welcome.
> — Ah!
>   Would that Orestes were near by to hear you.

These lines are important. There is no specific mention of Aegisthus, because the youth has no scruples on this score. The question he asks is the one question that troubles him. How does Electra feel about Clytemnestra? On this point he at least is far from certain, and her appallingly bloodthirsty answer makes him pause: "Would that Orestes were here," and Electra tells him, what is by now obvious, that she would not know her brother. No one in Argos would know him except the old man who smuggled him away years ago . . . and Orestes changes the subject by asking about the tomb of Agamemnon. That this is merely to gain time is obvious, as he has already explicitly told us that he visited his father's grave that very night.

If we read the passage aright — the acting would make it obvious — it gives the answer to a puzzling problem. Why does Orestes delay so long before he makes himself known? Until this moment there is no great difficulty: he did not know Electra when he first saw her approach, and as soon as her lamentation was ended the chorus arrived. A public declaration of identity would clearly be injudicious and, though she has reassured him that the women are trustworthy, he takes advantage of his anonymity to find out what she really feels about the prospect of murdering her mother. Electra has expressed in no uncertain terms her willingness to help him. Now he should, now he surely must, reveal himself. Yet he does not do it. On the contrary, he tries to justify his very obvious agitation by saying that one cannot but be affected by the sorrows of a friend.[3]

The reason is to be found in Electra's violence, in the joy she feels at the thought of murdering her mother. It is her bloodthirsty wish that makes him pause. Such hesitation before the awful matricide is entirely to the young man's credit. He is not blinded with hysterical hatred as Electra is, and he now knows that the moment he does reveal himself to this unbalanced virago of a sister he will not be allowed further delay but plunged into possibly the most reckless course of action. So he changes the subject, and a few moments later asks, in a somewhat laboured manner, what he is to tell Orestes of the present state of affairs. The question leads to a set speech from Electra, as it was meant to do.

A most revealing speech it is:

[3] See S. M. Adams in *Classical Review*, 1935, p. 120. But I do not think that cowardice is the right explanation.

> I would tell you, if I must, and one must speak freely to a friend, of
> my grievous misfortune and that of my father. And since you wake
> my tale, stranger, I beg you to report to Orestes my ills and his. First,
> what kind of clothes I wear, and what I have to drink, under what
> roof I dwell after the palace of a king. Myself I weave clothes to
> protect my nakedness, myself I fetch the water from the spring. No
> part have I in festal rites, I am denied the dance. . . .

We remember that she need not fetch the water and that the chorus
came for the express purpose of asking her to the dance. The latter
Orestes himself has heard. Electra then goes on to contrast her own
poverty with the luxurious life of Clytemnestra amidst the spoils that
Agamemnon brought from Troy. Then, and only then, does she
mention the desecrations to which Agamemnon's grave had been sub-
jected by Aegisthus (there is probably at least as much exaggeration
here as before), and she adds how he jeers at Orestes, thus trying to
spur her absent brother to revenge.

How clearly she betrays herself in this speech as a woman whose
desire for revenge has through continuous brooding become a completely self-centered obsession! Her motive is now hatred for her
mother rather than love for her father and her soul, tortured by this
unnatural loathing which circumstances have forced upon her, as
well as by prolonged virginity and loneliness, has at last become a terrible, perverted and ugly thing. The order in which the different
items are mentioned is truly disgraceful. First her own misery and
degradation (far more profound than she realizes), then her mother's
luxurious life, and last of all Agamemnon in his grave. Whereas
surely it is the last, and that alone, which could spur Orestes, or any
other sane youth, to the bloody act which he knows to be his duty.
And after this she taunts Orestes, by proxy as it were, for his failure
to come. Can the son of the conqueror of Troy not kill one man?
What must Orestes be feeling at this moment? It is not the man
whom he hesitates to kill.

Once more he is enabled to put off the painful moment of self-
revelation, this time by the return of the peasant, who, in a short
but vivid scene, brings a momentary relief of tension. The good
man is somewhat shocked to find his wife talking to strangers, but
when she tells him that they have come with news from Orestes —
the while apologizing to the gentlemen for the poor fellow's rudeness
— he cordially welcomes them and puts his house, poor as it is, entirely at their disposal.

The moment now seems to have come when Orestes can no longer
avoid telling them who he is. Instead, he tries to cover his confusion and avoids facing the real need of the situation by elaborate,

and somewhat stilted, reflections on the relation of goodness to high birth, for here is a man of the people (ἐν τοῖς δὲ πολλοῖς ὤν) who has proved the nobility of his nature: where then are we to find a true criterion of goodness? This speech is generally condemned as an outstanding example of irrelevant philosophizing. Yet we should not forget that it fulfills a dramatic function: it underlines Orestes' hesitation and unwillingness to reveal himself; it brings out the essential contribution of the peasant to the play: that the humble can be noble, in contrast to the wickedness of the rulers of Argos; finally the question he here debates is a burning issue in Orestes' own mind. Is it indeed his duty to kill his mother? Is that the nobler part to follow? Where can one find a sure criterion of nobility? [4] There is none.

When Orestes has thus spoken, Electra somewhat snobbishly reminds the peasant that there is nothing in the house worthy of these high-born guests and she sends him to find an old and faithful retainer upon whom she knows she can rely to provide the wherewithal for their entertainment. The peasant goes out, grumbling that there is quite enough food in the house, that rich men cannot eat more than the poor. We shall not see him again.

The others go in, and the interval necessary for the old retainer to arrive — he will of course be the slave who smuggled the infant Orestes out of the country years ago — is filled by the first stasimon. The chorus sing of the Trojan War, of the Greek fleet on its way to Troy and of the bringing of the shield to Achilles; then a final reflection on the greatness of Agamemnon, evilly slain by Clytemnestra, and a prayer that they may see her die in expiation for her crime. This last stanza echoes the eager wish of Electra and foreshadows the vengeance to come. The rest of the ode has little direct relevance to the immediate context, but, as in *Andromache*, it provides the legendary background, that Trojan doom from which so many later tragedies derived. There seems no particular reason for the lengthy description of Achilles' shield, though the choice of images — the Gorgons, the stars that strike terror on Hector's eyes, the Sphinx — are in strong contrast to the Homeric description and seem deliberately chosen to enhance the horror of this tragedy which gives the reverse side of the heroic legend, the sorrows and the vengeance rather than the honour and the glory.[5]

---

[4] Note how the peasant and himself are joined in his thoughts: "For this man here is worthy, as is the son of Agamemnon who is not here, and for whose sake we came." The relevance of this speech is in no way invalidated by the usual anachronism, as when he says that it is such good and humble men who administer both house and city best, or the reference to "the brainless brawn" that is the pride of the Assembly.

[5] See S. M. Adams in *Classical Review*, 1935, p. 121.

The ancient retainer, bent with age, panting with haste and excitement, comes hurrying up the hill to the cottage, seeking the princess Electra. She comes out to meet him and he hands over the foodstuffs he has brought. Asked why there are tears in his eyes he explains that he stopped at the grave of Agamemnon to pour a libation and found that a sacrifice had recently been offered there. As no Argive would dare to do this, the thought came to him that perhaps Orestes has returned and that the lock of hair dedicated on the grave is his. He even suggests that Electra compare the colour of it with her own.

She dismisses all this as foolishness. Her brave brother would not come secretly! With the same contempt she brushes aside his next suggestion that she should see whether the footsteps at the grave correspond with her own, as well as the futile inquiry whether she would recognize as her own weaving anything that Orestes might be wearing. No one would deny all this to be a parody of the recognition scene in Aeschylus' *Libation Bearers*,[6] yet the old man's foolish suggestions contribute to the development of the drama: they make it very clear that, led by the unusual sacrifice at the tomb of Agamemnon to think Orestes is back — nor is this forced, in view of the fact that they have all been eagerly awaiting his return for years — the old man desperately wants to believe that he has come and casts about for any possible means of identification. Electra, on the other hand, feels it an insult even to suggest that Orestes would sneak into the country unobserved; her romantic imagination pictures him returning in full glory, and she will not easily accept the hesitating youth, who asked what Orestes could do if he came, as her brother. This in part accounts for her disbelief when the old man does recognize Orestes, and her hesitation is the more natural in view of the foolish suggestions he has made.

When Orestes comes out of the house, he is somewhat disconcerted to find himself face to face with the only man in Argos who may be expected to recognize him (ἔα), and gives him no help:

> Why does he look at me as if he were examining the mint-mark on a coin? Does he think I am like some one?

And again: "Why does he circle round me?" He then remains silent while the old man tries to convince Electra that this is indeed Orestes.

---

[6] The tokens of recognition in that play are exactly those rejected here. Euripides is obviously ridiculing the naïve nature of these tokens, and the audience is meant to enjoy this satire on the earlier play. This no doubt accounts for the length of the passage, but it should not blind us to its contribution to this drama also. Whether such a satire is appropriate in drama is a matter of taste, on which we may differ, as the Greeks probably did.

Yet he can hardly go so far as to deny his identity, and he finally joins his sister's joyful exclamations of recognition, while the chorus too greet him with words of triumph.

He then withdraws from Electra's embrace to inquire how they are to proceed to take vengeance on Aegisthus — and Clytemnestra.[7] The reference to Clytemnestra, though repeated by the old man, is not immediately followed up as they proceed to plan the murder of Aegisthus who is providentially in the country at this very moment with but few attendants, preparing a sacrifice to the Nymphs. The plot is worked out, as so often, in alternate lines of dialogue. Orestes seems to show some misgivings: he wants to be reassured that no one will recognize him, that Aegisthus' attendants will accept a *fait accompli*, and the like. We should remember, however, that elaboration of the obvious is a regular feature of stichomythia, and also perhaps that the youth is almost alone in the land of which he intends to murder the reigning king. We should not take his questions as signs of cowardice, but, at the most, of a nervous temperament. Even this should not be pressed.

So far Electra has taken no part in the conversation, but when they wonder how they can proceed against the queen she suddenly comes forward: "I will arrange the murder of my mother," and, after a remark that fortune will favour them there also, it is now Orestes who keeps silent while Electra explains her plot to the old man's wondering approval.[8] Her scheme is horrible. A message is to be sent to Clytemnestra that Electra has been delivered of a son ten days previously, so that the time of the birth-sacrifices has now come.

> OLD MAN. How will this help your mother's murder?
> ELECTRA. When she hears of my labour pains, she'll come.
> OLD MAN. Why? Do you think she cares for you, my child?
> ELECTRA. Yes, she will weep for my child's poverty.

---

[7] The order of words is almost the same as in his first speech noted above: "Tell me, what should I do to take vengeance upon my father's murderer, and my mother, his partner in unholy wedlock?" and there is the same awkwardness in the construction. The singular "murderer" (Aegisthus) and the unsatisfactory text of the second line lead Wilamowitz to delete the reference to Clytemnestra. This would strengthen the impression that Orestes avoids mentioning her, but, in order not to support a thesis by deletion, we may be satisfied to adopt Canter's emendation: adding τὴν after μητέρα τε.

[8] The change of speakers is significant at that moment, as are the words they speak; but we should avoid attaching too much importance to the silence of the third character in each case. A conversation between three persons is very rarely kept up in Greek tragedy, and the tendency always is to divide it into longer passages between two persons only. Nevertheless that Orestes does not refer to this plot when he does speak may be taken as significant.

There is a sneer in these last words, but it remains true that Electra is sure of Clytemnestra's affection and that she plays upon that affection to bring her to her death. And she is right, for Clytemnestra will come. Orestes expresses neither agreement nor disagreement. When he speaks again it is only to say that he is ready to go and kill Aegisthus if some one will show him the way to the king. Brother and sister then join in a prayer for his success, and Electra exclaims that she would not survive her brother's failure; she speeds him on his way, exhorting him "to be a man," words in which we may perhaps see a trace of her fear that this Orestes who came in secret is not the avenger she dreamed of.

The two men go on their way. Electra withdraws into the house and the chorus sing the second stasimon which, like the previous one, helps to make us realize these events as but the last link in a series, here as deriving from the curse of Thyestes, father of Aegisthus, and Atreus, father of Agamemnon. Though they do not specifically mention the banquet at which Thyestes was made to eat his own children (the legend was well known to the audience), they imply its horror by dwelling upon the tale that the stars changed their course,[9] and then link their song with the present situation by reflecting, at the end, that Clytemnestra did not think of these things when she murdered her husband.

A confused clamour is now heard in the distance. Anxiously the chorus call Electra out of the house, and once again she shows signs of hysteria: when they cannot distinguish what the shouting portends she gives up all hope and is with difficulty restrained from suicide. Even when the messenger comes with news of success she is afraid to believe him until she recognizes him as one of her brother's attendants, and then she plies him with eager questions.

It is typical of Euripides that he makes the murder of Aegisthus extremely unpleasant. The conspirators find him walking in his garden, are cordially welcomed and invited into the house to share in the sacrifice to the Nymphs. Orestes does indeed avoid technical impiety by refusing to wash his hands — i.e. to purify himself for worship. The whole scene is one of unsuspecting peace on the part of Aegisthus and his household: he prays for himself, for Clytemnestra and for the defeat of his enemies, "by which," the messenger somewhat naïvely adds, "he meant Orestes and you, and my master prayed the opposite, though he did not speak the words." It is Aegisthus himself who gives them their chance by suggesting that his guest,

[9] The previous chorus also has a mention of stars on Achilles' shield. In their disbelief of the story that the sun altered its course, we have the usual anachronism.

who claims to be a Thessalian, shall give them an exhibition of bull-flaying. This enables Orestes, who naturally chooses Pylades to help him, to make the attendants fall back. They had already put their arms down to devote themselves to sacrificial duties. The entrails are found to be unfavourable and Aegisthus expresses his concern, his fear of Orestes. "Why fear an exile?" chides the other as he calls for a chopper to cleave open the bull's chest. This is provided, and as the king bends over to examine the entrails more carefully, Orestes smites him in the back, breaking his spine and leaving him to die in agony. A declaration of his identity is then enough to bring the servants over to him.

The unpleasantness of this murder is not due to Aegisthus' being stabbed in the back. To regard the murder as "unsportsmanlike" on this account is to introduce modern, and probably false, values. Trickery was clearly essential. The unpleasantness to a Greek was due to being killed while offering sacrifice. Orestes, in fact, does what Hamlet failed to do, and the horror is then increased by the manner of the blow, for Aegisthus is hacked down like an animal.

Cries of joy follow this narrative, both from the chorus and Electra, a paean of victory, and when Orestes enters he is greeted as καλλίνι κος, victor triumphant, by Electra, who crowns him and Pylades with garlands. Orestes has now proved himself a man. He modestly gives the greater part of the credit to the gods whose bidding he has obeyed. Perhaps he is hoping that the gods will take the responsibility for the next murder too. He then surrenders the body of Aegisthus to Electra to do with as she pleases.

After a moment's hesitation lest it be invidious to insult a corpse, and "our city is quick to displeasure and prone to slander," she is reassured by Orestes, turns to the dead Aegisthus, and says all she would have liked to say to him while he still lived, had she ever had him in her power. This speech is no outburst of real passion; after a simple statement of facts which contrasts him with Agamemnon in that he enjoyed the spoils of the East yet never went to war, her words become stilted, full of generalities, artificial. The reason is not far to seek: to Electra Aegisthus was always incidental; she saw in him only the husband of the accursed Clytemnestra. It is against her mother that the passion of hatred which is eating out her heart is, and always was, directed. Aegisthus was only an accessory and now that he lies dead before her she still despises him as no more than "the husband of Clytemnestra" which, in view of all we have been told about him by others, is palpably false. Electra's statement that Clytemnestra was as bad a wife to him as to Agamemnon and that each partner found shame in this marriage follows her own idea rather than the truth, and the same might be said of her description of Aegisthus as a pretty, effeminate man, no warrior, the sort of man she despises. There is no evidence that Aegisthus was such, but it follows from Electra's belief that Clytemnestra was ever the moving spirit of all their misdeeds, and from the father-fixation (if the modern term be allowed) which leads her to belittle him as the opposite of Agamemnon in every respect. It is difficult to avoid the conclusion that the death of Aegisthus is not giving her as great a satisfaction as she had expected. How far more terribly this will be true of the death of Clytemnestra she will not learn until too late.

Orestes sees Clytemnestra approaching in the distance, and in the few minutes that remain before her arrival, now that he finds himself face to face with that matricide he has dreaded so much, he would fain draw back. He sees himself accursed, he doubts the wisdom of the oracle that commanded her death, and indeed wonders whether that command came from Apollo at all. Electra has no such doubts; for many years she has longed for this moment; she has no sympathy with Orestes' hesitation; on the contrary, she taunts him with cowardice until he withdraws into the house, strengthened but still distressed.

Greeted with lying flattery by the chorus, Clytemnestra enters, seated in a magnificent carriage, with Trojan women slaves in attendance, and we find the contrast with Electra's poverty here enacted before our eyes. Clytemnestra speaks:

> Get out of the chariot, Trojans. Take my hand that I may put my foot to the ground. The houses of the gods are decked with Phrygian spoils. I have these women, the flower of Troy, in my house as a glorious prize — small return though it is for the child he lost.[10]

With a remarkable economy of words the dramatist gives us an immediate insight into Clytemnestra's character. She too has brooded for years, but it is the sacrifice of Iphigenia that she cannot forget. There is biting irony in the repetition of the name of Troy: "Trojans . . . Phrygia . . . Troy; and she finds a consciously sardonic enjoyment in the luxury obtained at the price of Iphigenia's death, knowing well how Electra hates her for it. The latter now comes forward:

> Cannot I — a slave cast out of my father's house, living in this miserable dwelling — hold your prosperous hand?

But Clytemnestra (unlike Agamemnon in Aeschylus) is not to be tricked into accepting a slave's duty from her daughter. That is not Euripides' way of solving a moral dilemma.

---

[10] "He lost," ἀπώλεσε, is the reading of the MSS., though some editors have corrected it to ἀπώλεσα, "I lost," thus deleting the reference to Agamemnon.

These slaves are here. Do not you trouble.
—Why so? You cast me out of my home like a captive. My house
was captured and so was I, and left, just as these women are, an orphan
by my father's death.

For Electra is still dwelling on her poverty, and by her every word
tries to put herself on a level with the Trojan slaves; she takes a bitter
pleasure in exaggerating the contrast between her and her mother,
with a keen unspoken anticipation of the vengeance to come. Her
words sting Clytemnestra to defend herself in a speech which, though
full of special pleading, yet shows that all justice is not on the other
side, when she tries to justify her hatred of Agamemnon. She first
describes the trick by which Iphigenia was lured to Aulis:

And if he had killed one child to save many lives, to prevent his
country's downfall, to benefit his house or save his other children, he
might have found forgiveness. But as it is he slew my child because
Helen was a wanton and her husband knew not how to punish his
treacherous wife.

This implies that the murder of Agamemnon was in revenge for the
death of Iphigenia, but her next words belie this:

On that account, though wronged, I would not have indulged my
wildness, nor killed my husband. But he brought home a mad girl,
god-possessed, and took her to his bed, and kept two wives within
one house.

Here she betrays herself; for her plans were laid long before Agamemnon's return. She proceeds:

Women are wild things, I do not deny it. But when, in view of
this, a husband spurns her bed within the house, then the women will
act as he does and turn to another friend.

We know that she was living with Aegisthus long before Cassandra's
arrival.[11] She then makes a bold claim to equality which probably
found little sympathy with a fifth-century audience, yet is typical of
the thought of the time: how, she asks, would Agamemnon have
liked it if the parts had been reversed, if she had sacrificed Orestes in
order to keep Menelaus for her sister Helen? Why then should not
Agamemnon die?

[11] That is the well-established legend, and it would be a mistake to take
Clytemnestra's defence as literally true. Such a definite change in the legend
would have been noted in the prologos. Besides, that much at least of
Electra's accusation must be true, and the wavering between the two motives
(Iphigenia and Cassandra) in Clytemnestra's own defence points in the same
direction. Clytemnestra is in this also the sister of Helen.

> I killed him. I turned the way I had to go, to those that were his
> enemies. Who of his friends would have helped me in this deed?

She grants Electra permission to reply, and this reply is a very different performance from the jejune funeral speech over the body of Aegisthus. Here Electra stands before her real enemy and she rises to the occasion. With angry passion she declares that Helen and Clytemnestra, with their evil beauty, are a worthy pair, that no one will believe the claim that Agamemnon died because of Iphigenia's sacrifice (we saw that Clytemnestra did not really believe it herself). She jeers that no sooner had Agamemnon gone than Clytemnestra was adorning herself with care and looking for another man, the only Greek woman to rejoice at news of Trojan successes and to sorrow at their defeat, unworthy wife of a great husband. If the murder was simple vengeance, why then make Orestes and herself suffer? They had not done Aegisthus any harm.

This last is disingenuous, not because Aegisthus is lying dead within, but because both she and Orestes clearly would have killed Aegisthus long ago if they had had the opportunity. Then follows a curious passage in which, as so often in Euripides, Electra condemns herself out of her own mouth, puts herself, as it were, on the same level as Clytemnestra. She says:

> If one murder justifies another, then I shall kill you, and Orestes
> with me, to avenge our father, for if your action was right, then so
> is this.

which is the literal truth, but she does not realize that she is in effect saying that the one murder is no better than the other.[12]

To this violent denunciation Clytemnestra does not reply in kind. There is weariness and resignation in her answer:

> My child, you were born to love your father always, and it is true
> that some children belong to the man, while others love their mother
> better than their father. I shall forgive you. Indeed, I am not so very
> pleased with what I did.

[12] The last three lines of her speech, the customary general reflection, seems at first sight irrelevant: "Whoever, looking to wealth and high birth, marries a wicked woman, is a fool; a humble but modest partner is better than a powerful marriage." These words, however, have a double relevance. In the first place, Electra is thinking of Aegisthus, whom she has just mentioned; as before, she looks upon Clytemnestra as the dominant partner and upon Aegisthus not so much as a powerful enemy as a fool to have married her, a folly the price of which he has already paid. But there is more: Electra herself was far from pleased with her own marriage to one good but humble. She twice shows herself in the wrong, and the conviction grows upon the audience that she is herself acting evilly, thus preparing for her later reaction to the murder itself.

The debate is now over and Clytemnestra turns to the matter in hand:

> But you are fresh from birth-pangs, unwashed and thus poorly dressed? I counselled badly and drove my husband to too great an anger.

Electra, however, is not to be conciliated:

> Your regrets come too late. You have no remedy.
> My father is dead now. Why not recall your son
> Who wanders as an exile in foreign lands?
> — I am afraid, but for myself, not him. They say
> his father's death has roused his anger.
> — Why is your husband so furious against us?
> — It is his way. You too are obstinate.
> — Because I suffer. My anger shall cease.
> — He also then will surely cease from burdening you.
> — He has great pride. He dwells in my house.

Throughout this dialogue Clytemnestra tries to make peace with her daughter and she must think she is succeeding, while Electra is indulging in cruel irony. The last line is taken by Cassandra to mean that Aegisthus is a usurper in the palace, and she rebukes Electra for starting the quarrel all over again. Electra then exclaims that she sent for her mother to perform the birth-sacrifices, as she had no help with her confinement. Clytemnestra, quite without suspicion, accepts the request and is thus lured into the house where Orestes awaits her. As she goes, Electra speaks the most horrible words of all:

> Enter my humble dwelling, but beware lest the smoky roof should soil your robes with soot. You will now perform the sacrifice you must.

and before, following her mother in, she almost hisses her ugly triumph:

> The offering is ready. The dagger that killed the bull is sharpened, by whose side you shall be struck down. You shall be his wife in hell as you slept with him on earth. That is the great favour I shall grant you, the penalty for my father's death.

In two short stanzas, the chorus sing of Agamemnon's murder that is about to be expiated; they recall his cries as he was struck down, and we hear Clytemnestra's own cries for pity from within, a last cry of pain. She is dead.

The news of Aegisthus' death was followed by paeans of joy and the crowning of the hero; now there is only horror as the chorus see the two murderers stagger out through the open door, bespattered with their mother's blood. Not only Orestes, but Electra herself, is appalled by what they have done as they recall in broken lyrics the details of the deed and we learn that it was Electra, eager to the last, who guided Orestes' sword into his mother's bosom while he still drew back. She too now feels the burden of her responsibility[13] and he foresees the long wanderings that will be his.

Hysterical and half-crazed by the knowledge of what they have done, they cover the body of the murdered queen. Castor and Pollux, the divine brothers of Helen and Clytemnestra, appear above the house and foretell the future that awaits them all. Electra shall marry Pylades, and Orestes, who will be pursued by the Furies of blood-guilt, will find release at Athens before the tribunal of the Areopagus, where Apollo will accept the responsibility for the matricide. The aetiological element is strong in this speech which contains an account of the origin of, and divine sanction for, the Areopagitic council, and of the custom that equal votes mean acquittal. The Dioscuri themselves do not hesitate to blame Apollo. After a further declaration of divine responsibility we have a farewell scene between brother and sister which touches even the gods themselves. They then declare they are on their way to Sicily where they will protect at sea those who deserve it (a possible reference to the Athenian fleets at Syracuse, but at best doubtful). Orestes has already gone and the chorus bring the play to a close.

This last scene with the Dioscuri, though of unusual length, especially the lyrics, offers little difficulty. That Castor and Pollux blame Apollo will not surprise us; the epiphany fulfils its usual dual function: it foretells the future and has a strong aetiological interest. The farewells of brother and sister give the last note of pathos: they are now suffering so much in common that their love for, and their need of each other is the greater, and now they must separate, so shortly after they have found each other. The whole play ends on a note of gloom and despair which neither the promise of marriage of Electra nor the ultimate acquittal of Orestes can dispel.

Euripides' mastery as a painter of human character is universally recognized, and he has deservedly been called the first psychologist.[14] We have already studied several remarkable creations of his psychological insight but none, not even Medea or Hippolytus, is greater than the Electra whose distorted soul he has just so terrifyingly laid bare. Other plays are as great, but for different reasons — *The Bacchants* for example, or *The Trojan Women*, or *Hippolytus* — but as

---

[13] There seems no sufficient reason to transfer any of these lines to the chorus. Electra is addressing herself.

[14] Werner Jaeger, *Paideia*, p. 350.

a drama of character, *Electra* is supreme. Not only the heroine, but the secondary personae, Orestes and Clytemnestra, even the minor characters, the peasant in particular, are, as we have seen, depicted with care, precision and startling vividness. In its own genre, this is undoubtedly Euripides' masterpiece.

At War with Electra

John Gassner

I

I "discovered" Giraudoux in the late nineteen-twenties when his *Siegfried* impressed me as an intelligent contrivance. His comment on the evils of nationalism did not exactly startle me with originality or stir me with passion, but he had an engaging way of projecting a point of view. He was suave, aloof, and ironic while other European pacifist playwrights of the period usually sputtered with anguish and worked themselves up to expressionistic frenzies of protest. He was as articulate as they were inarticulate, and as urbane as they were hysterical. The Giraudoux of my first encounter was an exquisitely civilized writer. And in contriving a tale of amnesia and mistaken identities in consequence of which a French soldier became a German after World War I, Giraudoux was plainly a "fabulist." His favorite strategy, that of inventing or adapting a fable or myth, was also already in evidence, although *Siegfried* had originally been a novel by Giraudoux. Only one unavoidable reservation dogged my awareness of the new playwright introduced to New York by Eva Le Gallienne at her Civic Repertory Theatre. He seemed to be self-consciously ingenious and more taken with his complicated plot than with his meaning.

It would seem that the clever trickster, man-of-the-world, and littérature has always stood between me and my inclination to acknowledge Giraudoux as a major dramatist, and it is my ambivalence toward this immensely attractive author that concerns me here. It came to a climax when I got to know his *Electra* in the late nineteen-thirties and my ambivalence toward this notable work has never left me. I have had divided feelings about other plays by Giraudoux, but the discomfort of division has usually been less pronounced in my reaction to them. His *Judith* has troubled me more. But, then, I think

From the *Tulane Drama Review,* Vol. 3, No. 4, May 1959, copyright © 1959 by the *Tulane Drama Review.* Reprinted by permission of the author and the *Tulane Drama Review.*

I really dislike *Judith* (I shall have to reread this play to be sure that I do) whereas I have admired most of the Giraudoux canon. His *Electra*, in brief, epitomizes the positive and negative characteristics of playwriting which will keep Giraudoux in the honorable limbo of distinguished playwrights who have just missed giving greatness to the modern drama.

One aspect of Giraudoux' artistry, his comic leverage, has never given me pause. Whenever he was consistently light of heart or light of fancy, he was thoroughly enchanting. His success was then complete within the bounds of his favorite mixed genre of comedy and fancy. *Intermezzo*, unsuccessfully presented on Broadway in an awkward production under the title of *The Enchanted*, seems to me his best play; and I can level no more serious charge against his entertaining one-actor *The Apollo of Bellac* than that its farcical oversimplifications are somewhat too strenuous for my conservative taste. I have not found *The Apollo* as captivating as some reviewers have, but this little comedy is good literature of "fancy," if not of "imagination," and nobody has, to my knowledge, written anything as charming in English since Synge and Lady Gregory stopped writing one-act pieces for the Irish stage.

His *Amphitryon 38* is an entrancing comedy. It is equally satisfactory as a literary *tour de force* and as bedroom comedy, although it would be difficult to notice any marked distinction between the two in this instance. Nor is my high estimation of the author's poetic-comic vein a recent opinion conveniently formed for the purpose of withholding any other kind of approbation from the author. I have objective evidence that this is not so, since my enthusiasm for *Amphitryon 38* some twenty years ago resulted in the Theatre Guild's Alfred Lunt and Lynn Fontanne production that gave the author his first and probably greatest success on Broadway.

It is not my intention to acclaim Giraudoux as a minor writer in order to avoid considering him a major one. His claims to be considered for that status were fully evident to me, I believe, the moment I read *Electra* for the Theatre Guild in 1937 or 1938 and concluded that, although the chances of presenting it successfully on Broadway were slim, the play deserved our high regard. *Electra* continues to engage my interest even now as a remarkable work that could have arisen only out of a largesse of mind and spirit that has rarely graced the contemporary stage.

And *La Guerre de Troie n'aura pas lieu*, now known to us from the recent Christopher Fry translation as *Tiger at the Gates*, *Ondine*, *Judith*, and *The Madwoman of Chaillot* also advanced various claims to importance I should have been pleased to be able to endorse wholeheartedly. If I can cite only a few titles the reason is not that Giraudoux was infertile — he was a prolific author as well as a busy man of affairs — but because he did not bring his talent to the theatre until he was forty-six years old. Sooner or later, however, the spell of this master-stylist lifting, I found myself holding on to dramatic works that seemed to be running out between my fingers like quicksilver. No one in France except Claudel had more of a right to be regarded as a playwright of real importance, and no one left me with a more uneasy feeling that I had been deluded by literary witchcraft. I was distressed to discover that I could not add Giraudoux' name to the company of major modern dramatists which includes the names of Ibsen, Strindberg, Hauptmann, Chekhov, Shaw, O'Neill, O'Casey, Pirandello, and perhaps Brecht.

In view of the unquestioned talent of the writer — his intelligence, verve, and mastery of language — my conclusion seemed to me grossly unfair. Yet such was my reaction or, for that matter, my verdict, and such it remains. *Electra* has continued to fluctuate, in my impression of the play, between profundity and arty sophistication. It is alternately tragic and arch, now devastatingly ironic and now merely clever, now penetrating and now boulevardishly bedroomy, now dedicated to dramatic truth and now to dramatic legerdemain. I believe that *La Guerre de Troie n'aura pas lieu* is a brilliant conceit and a sardonically moving drama. But I have also found it somewhat artificial and skittish, as well as wordy in commentary without being wholly convincing in content. In pricking the vanity of warmongering individuals, the author draws blood only from the epidermis. Certainly when World War II broke out less than five years after the composition of the play, Giraudoux' commentary on the causes of war seemed to me generally superficial. To take the final measure of this play it is necessary only to turn to *The Trojan Women* of Euripides and *The Plough and the Stars* of O'Casey. The comparison would be individious, and perhaps it shouldn't be made at all if our object were merely to determine whether Giraudoux' play has merit, which it indubitably has. The play has many admirable qualities, including the qualities of a satiric essay, but when we add them up the total still does not amount to a great dramatic experience.

Ondine is a beautifully composed fairy-tale, rich in poetic pathos and despair, but the very character of the fable concerning the love of a watersprite and a knight attenuates tragic conflict and favors atmospheric rather than dramatic pressure. *Judith* seems to me too greatly entangled in motivation and counter-motivation, too much involved in analytical complexities, to deliver the dramatic power promised by the tone and substance of the play. I doubt that we are likely to derive more light than smoke from it; and regardless of the interest we can take in the twists and turns of Judith's attitude toward herself and Holofernes, we can hardly elevate that interest to any altitude from which the human condition can be comprehensively observed. Even though *Judith* offers itself to us as psychological drama, it is circumscribed, like *Ondine* and *La Guerre de Troie*, by a congenital essayist's fondness for playing with notions.

Nor is even *The Madwoman of Chaillot* exempt from the criticism that a notion, or *apperçu*, is an inadequate foundation for great drama. We can cherish the play as a delightful fugue of bizarre improvisations and poetic moods. *The Madwoman*, however, promises more with its theme of the annihilation of the predators of modern society than it delivers. It withholds wholly adult statement on the rapacious society that aroused Giraudoux' distaste; it offers, instead, a fairy-tale resolution when the lurid old Countess bottles up the entrepreneurs in the sewers of Paris. We should be grateful of course that Giraudoux spared us a dull anti-capitalistic disquisition. The result is a mad and rueful dramatic statement in the modes of comedy, satire, and poetry — a work that is as indefinable as it is ingratiating. My gratitude, however, does not extend so far that I can put *The Madwoman of Chaillot* on a par with, let us say, *Major Barbara*, *The Vultures*, or, to diverge a bit more, *John Gabriel Borkman*, *The Marquis of Keith*, and *Heartbreak House*. Giraudoux' play is only a brilliant display of fireworks by comparison with the heavy artillery trained on the spirit of *laissez-faire* by some other modern playwrights. The author runs head-on to confront an issue, then sprints away from it with equal brio. He raises a clamor and runs away from its consequences. He vacillates between poetry and vaudeville (though it is, fortunately, superb vaudeville), and between saturnine seriousness and frolicsome triviality.

II

The Madwoman of Chaillot brought Giraudoux closest to a wrangle with the contemporary world that ruffled his aplomb as a gentleman, diplomat, and man of letters. But it is his spirited *Electra* that carried him to the altitudes of tragic art, and so it is in this work that we may best observe the distractions, discrepancies, and divided aims of his artistry — the qualities, in brief, that made him so fascinating a playwright but also left him stranded midway in his dramatic ascent. *Electra* may be described as a perfect example of the dilemma of ultra-modern, ultra-civilized playwriting whenever the playwright wants to be tragic yet urbane, passionate yet detached, emotional yet intellectual, vigorous yet literary, all at the same time. The opposite example of an O'Neill who was as decidedly tragic as he was decidedly *not* urbane is familiar enough. But it cannot be said that adherents of the postwar literary generation have been eager to approve a playwright whose sense of tragedy lacks the finesse required by their literary training; and O'Neill was quite heedless of the refinements of irony that best reflect their anomalous situation as members of postwar futile intelligentsia. Giraudoux' success in writing urbane tragedy, or in writing tragedy urbanely, has been of greater moment to this generation, whose chosen predecessors composed the avant-garde of Paris prior to World War II. But actually how great was Giraudoux' success? I have fluctuated in my regard for his Electra drama and had mixed feelings about it ever since first reading it; and these have been shared by many of my graduate students, all of them dedicated to the theatre and to the search for new avenues of dramatic art. I can only conclude that Giraudoux won an ambiguous or inconclusive success with one of the plays that should have qualified him for the select company of great modern playwrights. Tragedy and urbanity did not mix well in his *Electra*, at least not well enough.

To say that Giraudoux did not write *Electra* with conviction would be to ignore his entire political career and to be insensitive to the pressure of his irony. He followed tradition in France, where the classics have been rewritten periodically ever since the Renaissance. But far from being a literary exercise, *Electra* expressed its author's continuous concern over the hatred that had poisoned relations between France and Germany ever since the Franco-Prussian War. Two ruinous wars had apparently not sated the chauvinistic lust for vengeance to the extinction of which Giraudoux, the German-educated French diplomat, dedicated both his diplomatic and literary career. Adopting the Euripidean rather than the Sophoclean view of the Oresteian legend, Giraudoux saw no liberating glory in the vengeance of Agamemnon's children, credited Clymnestra with remorse and Aegisthus with some nobility, and made his vengeance-bent Electra obsessively neurotic. Electra is an unlovely heroine, horror attends her steps, and at the end she has not only caused the death of her mother and Aegisthus, but has brought ruin to her country and death to many of its innocent inhabitants who might have lived out their lives in peace. The symbolic Furies, who were nasty little girls in the first scene of the play, are full-grown, having reached the size of Electra, at the end of the play. As the flames consume the city, Giraudoux' frantic heroine is left clinging only to her belief in the

rightness of her position and to the dubious comfort that her country
will be reestablished on new foundations of truth. A mordant power
informs Giraudoux' tragedy. His abhorrence of violence even in the
name of justice inspires an especially effective exchange of speeches
between his heroine and the Furies, one of whom, observing the conflagration in the city declares that this is the light Electra wanted
with her demand for the truth. To this, Electra replies with desperate
futility, "I have my conscience. . . . I have justice, I have everything."

The thrust of this dramatic warning is greatly strengthened by the
tensions between mother and daughter, mother and son (the avenger-
son Orestes), and Electra and Aegisthus, who comes to admire her
after undergoing an ironic transformation from lecherous poltroon to
a person capable of appreciating nobility. (And Electra is, alas, relentlessly noble.) A fierce quarrel between Clytemnestra and Electra
over the question of how it happened that the infant Orestes fell
out of his mother's arms twenty years ago (whether or not Electra
jealously pushed the child out of its mother's arms) is poignant in its
absurdity. Now and again brief bursts of irony brighten the sultry
atmosphere of the work, and the huge irony of Aegisthus' transformation into a hero capable of saving his country just before he is an-
nihilated by Electra's righteousness is immensely effective. It draws
Electra's bitter protest against the gods' "hypocrisy" and "malice."
They can't do this to her, she cries out; they simply can't change "a
parasite into a just man" and "a usurper into a king."

A symbolist imagination also courses through the play and deep-
ens its hues. Giraudoux' vision of a sanguinary reckoning in ancient
Greece, indeed, was about to find a close parallel in the Nazi pro-
gram for devastating the world in order to wipe out and avenge the
defeat of Germany in 1918. *Electra* was produced in 1937, about two
years before Hitler's troops started their march across Europe. The
effect of the horrible little Furies is as eerie as the sense of ripening
doom is oppressive. The nasty children who call themselves "the little
Eumenides" grow and "get fat" as one looks at them; one can even
watch their eyelashes growing. A vulture hovers over Aegisthus
when Orestes appears; and when Aegisthus behaves humanely, in-
judiciously releasing Orestes from his chains, the bird begins to
descend. Nor is the preternatural figure of Zeus in the role of the
Beggar less grim as he follows the folly of human action with super-
cilious indifference to human suffering.

What is it, then, that essentially limits Giraudoux' achievement in
Electra? It is, I would say, a work of over-insistent *wit*. Giraudoux
apparently could not resist delivering himself of a bright sally of

words or a clover turn of events. In *Electra*, this inclination carries
him so far from the swirl of the conflict engulfing Clytemnestra, her
lover, and her children that long discursive passages impede the action
or swerve it from its direction. This diversionary tendency becomes
a veritable technique indeed, and it crops up not merely when characters discuss the issue in view, but when their concerns are, at best,
only peripheral. One, by no means slender, portion of the play is
virtually indistinguishable from Parisian boulevard comedy or farce.
The President of the Council is being betrayed by a flighty wife.
He is personally connected with the Electra drama solely as the
cousin of a Gardener who has been selected by Aegisthus to marry
Electra and so prevent the rebellious girl from causing mischief.

The comedy of adultery lightens the work and constitutes a sub-
plot in the manner of Elizabethan drama; and it is actually woven
into the play so deftly that it does not block the traffic of the central
action. And yet it is obtrusive enough to call attention to itself as
superimposed by-play by a worldly writer. The author seems to
invite the audience to observe how adept he is at playing the boulevard modernizer of myth. And Giraudoux' attitude of sophisticated
detachment is even more pronounced in the airy way in which he
weaves his way in and out of stage illusion.

The playwright seems to flaunt both his ingenuity and his detachment from so simple a thing as belief in the reality of the work with
which he expects to engage the spectator's interest. In two instances,
he actually explodes the structure of his play in order to tell us that
he is entirely conscious of contriving a play and beguiling an audience. He goes out of his way to make it plain that both the author
and the spectator are in the theatre rather than in the midst of life,
and that there is an understanding between them. This is apparent
when the Gardener, relieved of the obligation to marry Electra, steps
to the front of the stage and harangues the audience, declaring "I'm
no longer in the running. That's why I'm free to come and tell you
what the play can't tell you."

Wit will out, and "The Gardener's Lament," as this interlude is
called, is a truly marvelous passage of verbal pyrotechnics. But it is
the very next thing to winking at the public to tell it that the author,
anxiously guarding his claim to urbanity, is not involved in his play —
which is not the case at all, of course, since he is deeply engaged in
his theme. The other deliberate violation of stage illusion occurs
somewhat earlier, in the curtain scene of the first act, when the Beggar, now recognizably Zeus, comments on Electra while she lies
asleep on the ground with her brother Orestes. That the Beggar's
long speech, a virtuoso's display of rhetoric, is directed at the audi-

ence is clearly affirmed when the fluent god departs with the admonition to the spectators: "But all you who remain here, be quiet now: This is Electra's first rest and the last rest of Orestes." Once more wit wins out, and once more the audience is reminded that the author is aware of its presence and by no means naive enough to lose himself in an illusion of reality or to expect that the playgoer will. Giraudoux contradicts himself, besides, since some of the scenes that follow, like some of the scenes that came before, have the dramatic power to produce as much "illusion of reality" as any realist could desire. By comparison with their intense immediacy, the monologues of the Gardener and the Beggar can seem pretentious, on the one hand, and academically labored, on the other. And the device of intrusion itself, while theatrically arresting, is dramatically questionable. Its obtrusive cleverness calls attention to the author's self-conscious and exhibitionistic virtuosity.

"Wit" has, in these instances, become ostentatious theatrically, and it has the effect of casting doubt alike on the truth of the play and the sincerity of the author. Theatricality has both enriched the play's external action and undercut the validity of its claims upon the audience as an engrossing experience. *Electra* thus becomes an amalgam of absorbing drama and a facile lecture-demonstration, and it advertises itself as a display-piece of ingenious fabrication. The play contains an episode toward the end where the Beggar describes the murder of Aegisthus *before* Orestes kills him, and it is a brilliant piece of imaginative theatricality. It is a "trick" in the best sense of a Cocteau *truc*. It is also a convenient condensation of action at that point in the play. But it is, of course, a transparent and fundamentally gratuitous contrivance that diverts attention from the dramatic substance of the climax to the dramatic method *as method*. It is not merely this detail, however, but the more conspicuous previously mentioned intrusions of the playwright into the illusion of the play that comprise the crux of Giraudoux' self-conscious and self-advertising playwriting. And I cannot but believe that the supererogatory display of the author's independence from his story, the superfluous assurance that he is contriving "theatre," makes his *Electra* rather labored and precious. A potential masterpiece was botched in this instance by the "modernism" of a writer in whose case wit, imagination, dramatic talent, and theatrical skill did not issue in indubitably great drama.

We shall continue to owe Giraudoux much admiration, I believe. But it will be decidedly risky to make a leader of him, to follow him as the prophet of a new dispensation in dramaturgy and dramatic style. He was distinctly Parisian in literary tradition and in the tradition of retheatricalized 'theatre-for-theatre's sake' French theatre started by Coceau and sustained by his disciple, Giraudoux' gifted friend and producer, Louis Jouvet. Giraudoux brought vivacity, grace, and keen intelligence to that tradition, of which he became the chief ornament and justification among playwrights. He did not, however, overcome its pitfalls of cultivated artifice when he succumbed to the cultivation of baroque rhetoric, at which he was supremely adept, and of arch and tricky dramaturgy, at which he was also skillful. Although the results were delightful so long as he confined himself to comic improvisation and genial fancy, they also fixed the bounds beyond which he could not move without peril. As may be seen in his *Electra*, artifice in dialogue and dramaturgy did not serve him unequivocally when he aspired to deep emotion or high passion. And in this respect, too, we find this moderate diplomat-dramatist and wit a man of his *milieu* and quite at ease in it rather than a pioneer to be followed into new pathways. Giraudoux came to the theatre as a middle-aged man with a number of well polished novels to his credit, and as a gentleman of settled taste formed by the political and cultural world of the early decades of our century. Nor did he undergo a transformation of personality or experience illumination on some new road to Damascus during the cataclysmic last decade of his life, from 1934 to 1944. (It is characteristic of the career-diplomat that he should have served as Chief of Information for the Daladier government briefly in power before France surrendered to Germany.) Compared with the unimaginative realists and near-analphatetes who still rule the commercial stage, Giraudoux can of course always qualify as a leader of the avant-garde. But we shall be more correct in honoring him as the dramatist who *closed*, rather than opened, an era in theatre with his characteristic merits and limitations.

❖ ❖ ❖   *Mourning Becomes Electra*
and *The Prodigal*

Philip Weissman

OFF BROADWAY, this season, a striking psychological portrait of a modern Orestes has been created by twenty-four year old Jack Richardson. His play, *The Prodigal,* based on the original House of Agamemnon legend, recreates the spirit of Athenian times.

In the fifth century B.C., a middle-aged Athenian could have seen during his lifetime the original productions of Aeschylus', Euripides', and Sophocles' plays based on this legend. Today a middle-aged New Yorker could have seen the original productions of two great modern psychological dramas based on the same legend, *Mourning Becomes Electra* and *The Prodigal.*

The Prodigal is as reflective of today's generation as O'Neill's play mirrored the mood of the preceding generation. For both O'Neill and Richardson are clairvoyant spokesmen of their respective eras. The late twenties and early thirties were imbued with the new discoveries of Freud. Man's fate and destiny were reshaped and reevaluated by artists as well as scientists in the context of this new knowledge. O'Neill's *Mourning Becomes Electra* succeeded in such an undertaking. In his working notes on this play, O'Neill commits himself to create a drama in which he can "give modern Electra figure (Lavinia) in the play a tragic ending worthy of character." He wanted to convey "a modern tragic interpretation of classic fate without benefit of gods — for it must, before everything, remain [a] modern psychological play — fate springing out of family life."

O'Neill's sense of tragedy, often referred to as his sixth sense, seems to stem from his tragic personal life. Biographical and pathographical studies of O'Neill show that he was unconsciously not allowed to en-

From *Modern Drama,* Vol. III, No. 3, December 1960, pp. 257–259. Reprinted by permission of *Modern Drama* and the author. Portions of this article appeared in Mr. Weissman's book, *Creativity in the Theater: A Psychoanalytic Study,* Basic Books, New York, 1965.

joy a happy fulfillment of family life and fatherhood. From this design of his own destiny, he was sensitive to an original artistic understanding that Electra was not fated to "peter out into undramatic
married banality." (O'Neill did not note that the Greek word "Electra" — "A-lektra" — means "the Unmated.") He recreated her as an
eternally haunted character, such as he himself was. So personal was
his empathy, that O'Neill, who was raised in New London, Con-
necticut, could only envision Electra's tragedy in terms of Lavinia
Mannon, a New England character of the latter half of the nineteenth century.

Although he has deprived us of the universality of the original
legendary images, his more personal and contemporaneous transformation of the characters has enriched them with more vitality than they
originally had. We can more readily feel a personal identity with
O'Neill's less dated alternates. His portrayal of the members of the
Mannon family finds confirmation in the most recent psychoanalytic
concepts on the process of mourning. *Mourning Becomes Electra*
ante-dates the fuller scientific formulations on the structure of mourning by some years. Nevertheless, his is not the mastered knowledge of
the scientist. In his attempts to understand himself, his insight is
mundane. Only in his created characters does he approximate ex-
quisite psychoanalytic elaboration of personality structure.

Today's young men are the children of O'Neill's generation. The
understanding minds of the thirties had tried to instill in this generation the right to be free — as they themselves were not — of unconscious blind ties to their parents. It seems to me that young Richardson is a hopeful spokesman of this effort. The misinformed parents of
the thirties, equally in pursuit of psychological liberation for their offspring, reared their children to be free to yell "no!" much beyond a
permissible age. The child's negativism was never modified into
justifiable dissent and meaningful cooperation because these parents
feared that such direction might be regarded as expressed hatred towards the child. To what extent such upbringing has given rise to a
flourishing new generation of nihilistic and angry artists and citizens,
is an important problem for psychological and sociological research.

Richardson's Orestes can be taken as a symbol of the more successful results of the experimental efforts of the thirties. We see a clear-
minded Orestes who wishes to disentangle himself from the pre-or-
dained, childhood phenomenon of either rigid loyalty to or violent
rebellion against his father. Richardson creates a dispassionate Orestes
who stands apart from his overdetermined duty to revenge himself
upon his mother, Clytemnestra, and her lover Aegisthus, the murderers
of his father, Agamemnon. In his Orestes one can find the symbolic

spokesman of the young man of today. Unlike Prince Hal, he disavows his father's ideals of the pursuit of power through endless wars. Unlike Hamlet, he looks down upon his mother's infidelity and her lover's usurpation as the misdirected deeds of immature elders who have misunderstood the purpose of life. Orestes is dedicated to self-fulfillment, unhampered by the unfinished business and blunders of his parents. He welcomes his enforced exile from his homeland as his expectant path to liberation. However, state and society will not permit him to marry and dwell in biological anonymity until he avenges his father's death. Thus, he too must bear the yoke of his imperfect heritage.

Unlike O'Neill, who transfigured the characters into a nineteenth century New England family, Richardson has rewritten the ancient tragedy in its original setting. *The Prodigal* retains the sense of the past. Mr. Richardson's personal relationship to the Greek tragedy is more successfully kept out of sight. For this he pays the price of a more cerebral and less emotional drama. O'Neill seems to have been personally and emotionally driven, whereas Richardson appears to be intellectually motivated and personally liberated. Yet, what both dramatists share is the use of the Agamemnon legend to express a modern point of view.

Our great legends are our legacies. They are the highest peaks that creative man has aspired to climb, over and over again. Freud, for example, found that man's universal and major unconscious conflict — the Oedipus complex — was thoroughly depicted in ancient Greek legend. The House of Agamemnon legend is of similar stature.

Man's basic drives are love and aggression. King Agamemnon's inner conflict lies between his drive for power and his love of woman and family. His wife, Clytemnestra, struggles with her needs to love and be loved, with her conflicted loyalty to a long-absent husband, and her murderous hatred of him for inflicting such deprivations upon her. Their children, Orestes and Electra, already damaged by their parents' problems, have still more complex conflicts. May a child kill the mother who bore him, no matter what her crime was? Can such a child live in any sort of peace after the avenging murder is consummated? Muddled by the passions of love and hate for the parents natural to childhood, their dilemma seems insoluble.

These are the problems that Aeschylus, Euripides and Sophocles attempted to resolve two thousand years ago. Shakespeare's Princes Hal and Hamlet bear the stamp of the same theme. One would venture the guess that literally hundreds of plays can be traced to the same source. O'Neill struggled to find a modern psychological solution for Electra. Can an Orestes or Electra finally stand apart and declare himself or herself nonpartisan to parents' lives and demand the right to live one's own life? This is the new solution offered by Mr. Richardson, a young man of today.

Writing Suggestions

The writing suggestions which follow do not comprise an exhaustive list. They are intended to serve merely as a starting point, one from which departure may be made in the direction interest leads. Papers might fall into two general classifications: those which examine the plays themselves, and those which extend beyond the plays into a study of period, playwright, or criticism. The search for a suitable essay topic might begin with reference to the three components of drama which are generally considered indispensable to the play form: plot, character, and theme.

1. *Plot*. The plot of a play is the sum of its parts as these have been selected, arranged, and articulated by the playwright. An understanding of the structural elements from which a plot is constructed increases one's awareness of the dramatist's methods at the same time that it heightens appreciation of his skill. Structurally a plot is composed of some or all of the following elements: exposition, point of attack, and foreshadowing; complication, crisis, and climax (these last two may occur simultaneously); and the final episode in the play to which the French assigned the name *denouement*. Aristotle asserted in the *Poetics* that a plot should include scenes of reversal and discovery, and we are all aware of the ways in which the qualities of suspense, surprise, and irony add dimension to drama. The inspiration for an essay might well be found in the opportunity to compare and contrast the use the playwrights have made of selected aspects and elements in their treatments of the story. Helpful comments concerning the structuring of plot may be found in Theodore W. Hatlen, *Orientation to the Theater* (New York, 1962); Albright, Halstead, and Mitchell, *Principles of Theatre Art* (Boston, 1955); and George R. Kernodle, *Invitation to the Theatre* (New York, 1967). Useful in seeking definitions is Barnet, Berman, and Burto, *Aspects of the Drama* (Boston, 1962).

2. *Character*. Useful and informative essays might derive from an intensive study of the treatment of character in the plays; a comparison of all the Electras, for example, might have merit, as might a similar study of the contrasting depictions of the Orestes, the Clytemnestras, or certain of the lesser characters.

3. *Theme*. Each of the plays in this book was written to make a point; some make several. A comparison of themes could prove quite

enlightening. Motivation for a paper in this area or one based on plot or character may be found among the study aids or topics for discussion which follow each play.

Those wishing to go beyond the plays themselves for material might find a challenging thought among the essays that are here included. Or they might be interested in examining the attitude of the current American theatre toward producing the classics, the hospitality the off-Broadway theatre offers new playwrights, or the use Hofmannsthal, O'Neill, or Sartre made of the Orestes-Electra myth. One might, in fact, want to go beyond the drama into the realm of poetry (Robinson Jeffers, "The Tower Beyond Tragedy") or the novel (Gladys Schmidt, *Electra*) for his topic. The problem is less that of selecting a subject than that of deciding which ones to reject. Perhaps the following suggestions will be useful in helping you to select a suitable essay topic:

1. The role of destiny in the life of man: the ancestral curse and the consequent suffering.

2. The destructive power of vengeance and its corruptive effect upon human personality.

3. Contrasting uses of selected elements and techniques in the Orestes-Electra plays of Aeschylus, Sophocles, and Euripides.

4. The Orestes-Electra plays of Aeschylus, Sophocles, and Euripides: an analysis of the contrasting employment of myth and character.

5. Euripides' Electra and O'Neill's Lavinia Mannon: a study of the classic and the modern depiction of the neurotic heroine.

6. Giraudoux' *Electra:* a political metaphor.

7. The *Electra* of Giraudoux and *The Flies* of Sartre: modern applications of an ancient myth.

8. Urbanity, wit, and symbol in the *Electra* of Giraudoux.

9. Hate as a destructive agent in the Electra plays of Sophocles and Hofmannsthal.

10. The forging of a hero—the liberation of a man: the Orestes of Sartre's *The Flies* as contrasted with the anti-heroic Orestes of *The Prodigal.*

11. The element of theatricality in the Electra plays of Giraudoux and Hofmannsthal.

12. Critical and popular response to recent productions of the Orestes-Electra plays.